AF600608

The Effects of Rhetoric and the Rhetoric of Effects

Studies in Rhetoric/Communication

Thomas W. Benson, Series Editor

The Effects of Rhetoric and the Rhetoric of Effects

Past, Present, Future

Edited by
Amos Kiewe and Davis W. Houck

The University of South Carolina Press

Published by the University of South Carolina Press
Columbia, South Carolina 29208

www.sc.edu/uscpress

Manufactured in the United States of America

24 23 22 21 20   10 9 8 7 6 5 4 3 2

Library of Congress Cataloging-in-Publication Data

The effects of rhetoric and the rhetoric of effects : past, present, future / edited by
Amos Kiewe and Davis W. Houck.
pages cm. — (Studies in rhetoric/communication)
Includes bibliographical references and index.
ISBN 978-1-61117-455-7 (hardbound : alk. paper) 1. Rhetoric. I.
Kiewe, Amos, editor.
II. Houck, Davis W., editor.
P301.E37 2015
808—dc23
2014032919

Contents

Series Editor's Preface

In "The Literary Criticism of Oratory," an essay that has long been canonical for rhetorical critics, Professor Herbert A. Wichelns of Cornell University wrote in 1925 that the point of view of "rhetorical criticism . . . is patently single. It is not concerned with permanence, nor yet with beauty. It is concerned with effect. It regards a speech as a communication to a specific audience, and holds its business to be the analysis and appreciation of the orator's method of imparting his ideas to his hearers." Wichelns was writing as the discipline of rhetoric was finding its place in newly founded departments of Speech and Drama. His formulation of the central purpose and point of view of rhetorical criticism was widely accepted, occasionally amended or supplemented, and put to use in practical criticism. Then in the 1960s a disciplinary narrative began to claim that the Wichelns admonition about effect had ossified in practice into mechanical and largely tautological claims about cause and effect in rhetorical practice. From time to time since Wichelns the issue of whether and how rhetoric might be said to have "effects" has arisen in new forms. In *The Effects of Rhetoric and the Rhetoric of Effects,* editors Amos Kiewe and Davis Houck bring together a group of rhetorical theorists and critics to re-examine the history and the current prospects of the notion of "effect" in rhetorical criticism. Kiewe, Houck, Carole Blair, Robert C. Rowland, Pat J. Gehrke, and David Frank take on "effect" as a question of theory. Their essays are followed by a section of critical studies, in which Stephen H. Browne, Sara A. Mehltretter Drury, Adam J. Gaffey, Amos Kiewe, and Erin J. Rand examine what it means to make claims about effect in public address. In a final section, Anne T. Demo, Aaron Hess, and Gregory Dorchak offer examples of how the notion of rhetorical effect may usefully be refreshed in studies of documentary, ethnography, and music. Davis Houck concludes the volume with an essay offering challenges to contemporary scholars who venture into the terrain of claims about effect.

The Effects of Rhetoric and the Rhetoric of Effects is a diverse and vigorous call to renew Herbert Wichelns's challenge to critics and historians to "examine more thoroughly than they have as yet done the interactions of the inventive genius, the popularizing talent, and the public mind."

Thomas W. Benson

Introduction

AMOS KIEWE AND DAVIS W. HOUCK

> Once he has classified the types of speech and of soul, and the ways in which the various types of soul are acted upon, he will go through all the causes, fitting each type of speech to each type of soul and explaining what it is about the nature of particular kinds of soul which makes them inevitably either persuaded or unpersuaded by speeches of a particular kind.
>
> *Plato,* Phaedrus, *271b*

> My, I felt this thrill going up my leg. I mean, I don't have that too often.
>
> *Chris Matthews,* Hardball

Rhetoric, as the art of persuasion, seeks to produce effects in others; thus, rhetoric's instrumental objective is audience oriented. We assume that there is no disagreement over this long-standing assumption. The disagreement scholars have had and continue to have is a critical one: how to address rhetoric's effects, if at all? Indeed, the history of rhetorical theory and criticism is replete with arguments and controversies over whether the parameters of rhetorical criticism should include rhetoric's effects. As we celebrate the first centennial of our discipline—one of the first departments of oratory appeared on the scene at Syracuse University in 1910—we are no closer to having a clear consensus on the subject of rhetoric's effects. But as the Platonic Socrates clearly indicates, the question of how rhetoric works on different "souls" has been with us from the very beginning.

Indeed, the story of rhetoric's effects has a tortured history in rhetorical studies. It was hailed as the key focus of rhetorical criticism but later dismissed, its scope narrowed then elevated, later impugned and then recently resurrected by several prominent scholars. After some eighty-five years of arguing its merits and pitfalls, it is easy to dismiss any new discussion on rhetoric's effects as a tired endeavor. This is not our belief. Rather, we come at this discussion with a serious concern—that we have relegated the study of effects largely to disciplinary oblivion, and yet the importance of rhetoric, we believe, cannot stand on firm scholarly grounds without acknowledging that the primary instrumental function of rhetoric is to influence others—whether by creating a thrill going up one's leg induced by a presidential candidate or by directing pedestrian traffic flows at the Civil Rights Memorial in Montgomery, Alabama. This is rhetoric's objective; to say otherwise is to move into different disciplinary terrain.

We begin our discussion on rhetoric's effects by resorting to one case study, anecdotal and not fully representative of the entire field of rhetoric but, we contend, quite representative of a more general assessment of rhetorical theory and criticism. A serious challenge to the relevance of rhetorical studies in general, and presidential rhetoric in particular, provided a rather urgent impetus for several scholars to contemplate the status of rhetoric's effects within the field. With the publication of *Beyond the Rhetorical Presidency,* the political scientist George C. Edwards III raised critical questions about the gap between the stated purpose of rhetoric to influence and the lack of such evidence in the work of some of the field's most distinguished scholars.[1] Absent such evidence, Edwards seriously questioned the "consequences of rhetoric" altogether.[2] Seeking to be constructive in his criticism, Edwards offered suggestions for evidence that could prove the merits of rhetoric. His list of potential evidences includes poll data, public opinion, journalistic coverage, elite opinion measurements, and overall media responses.[3] Yet, unsure whether rhetoricians would heed his call, Edwards pinpointed his criticism, stating that "*the issue for students of rhetoric is not lack of information, it is the unstated premise that these scholars have no need for it.*"[4]

Edwards's challenge needs to be understood in the correct context; his focus is on presidential rhetoric, and he targets primarily televised presidential speeches as ineffective in mobilizing public support for specified propositions. Yet Edwards is not just another uninformed political scientist dismissive of the interpretive methods often employed by scholars in rhetoric and public address but rather a prominent presidential scholar. His views on the evidence or lack thereof of rhetoric's effect as were addressed to scholars in rhetoric and public address, specifically those attending the inaugural presidential rhetoric conference at Texas A&M University in 1995, chastising several of them for employing causal language without evidence to support claims about presidential rhetoric and its effects on constituents. More recently, Edwards has expanded his criticism, arguing in *On Deaf Ears* that presidential communication is by and large irrelevant. And, although his survey of presidents is limited to very recent ones, Edwards points to the limitation of presidential communication altogether, concluding that rhetoric does not really matter. Yet Edwards equivocates on whether his conclusion is warranted, as he puts the issue in conditional form: "if we conclude that there is little potential for public leadership, we must ask whether we are looking in the right direction as we seek solutions to problems of governing."[5] Edwards is clearly of the opinion that presidential communication matters little, if at all, and he laments any scholarship that would "focus directly on the effect of presidential leadership or opinion."[6] The challenge posed by Edwards has resurfaced recently in an article in *The New Yorker* (2012), "The Unpersuaded," wherein the writer, Ezra Klein, retrospectively notes Edwards's surprise at rhetoric scholars who put forward claims about presidential persuasion with "no rigorous evidence." Edwards goes even further, arguing that these scholars discuss "presidential speeches as if they were doing literary criticism."[7]

Edwards's criticism is altogether unfair, but it stings nonetheless. He operates from the premise that "Presidents are rarely able to move the public to support their policies" and that neither "is the bully pulpit much help to chief executives in increasing their own approval ratings. Findings so contrary to the conventional wisdom and to presidents' core strategies for governing require an explanation."[8] Martin J. Medhurst, editor of *Beyond the Rhetorical Presidency,* accepts Edwards's call for more evidentiary proof for claims scholars make about effects but also takes issue with Edwards's narrowcasting of rhetoric "as nothing more than a causal factor in the chain of cause-and-effect reasoning." Edwards fails to appreciate, writes Medhurst, the differences between the "language arts" and "numerical arts" and the fact that language arts are not "amenable to study through the various methodologies of the social scientific enterprise."[9] The fault in Edwards's reasoning lies in misunderstanding the rhetorical process altogether and in treating it as a testable formula—as effects with observable causes. The fault also lies in the way he operationalizes his research, discounting the qualitative value of presidential communication and the abundance of sources, especially primary sources, that often shed more accurate light on an individual president and the effect of specific speeches. For example, Edwards goes to some length to dismiss Franklin D. Roosevelt's First Fireside Chat and its effects on solving the acute banking crisis of 1933 (more on this in Sara A. Mehltretter Drury's essay); yet he does not offer evidence that the First Fireside Chat had no effect on the American people but simply discounts the possibility.

In reacting to Edwards's general criticism regarding the lack of evidence for presidential rhetoric's effects, David Zarefsky artfully dissects his thesis, showing that the narrow application of the terms "presidential rhetoric" and "effect" lies at the root of the misunderstanding of presidential appeal. A social science methodology of framing presidential speech as data and its consequences as an independently measurable variable may, indeed, not find that such speeches lead to opinion or attitude change.[10] This is the case because "rhetorical transaction," Zarefsky opines, "emphasizes contingency and choice rather than predictability and control," and "those choices—about such matters as argument selection, framing, phrasing, evidence, organization, and style, as well as about staging, choreography, and other aspects of the presidential performance—are embodied in the text that the rhetor composes and the context in which it is delivered. An audience, also influenced by context, perceives this text, interprets it, participates thereby in determining what it means, and is affected by it."[11] The evidence for the impact of presidential rhetoric (or the ability to define, as Zarefsky suggests) "can be found in the texts of public statements, the audio and video records of presidential performance, comments by the president or his aides about his purpose, and the informed speculation of commentators."[12]

Both Medhurst and Zarefsky seek to show how rhetoric and its effects cannot follow the methods of the social sciences and that a different set of questions guides, as well it should, the rhetorical investigation. We acknowledge that presidential rhetoric rarely yields discernible effects and that rhetoric in general cannot be assessed from the effects criterion alone. Yet it also stands to reason that had rhetorical critics developed conclusions about rhetorical processes, specifically by providing some evidentiary grounds for their claims about rhetoric's work—presidential or not—with real audiences or for the potential for agency to reside in audiences, we would be on stronger grounds. This is the challenge we pose to rhetorical scholars.

In many respects, Edwards arrives at the end of a long discussion on rhetorical effects, and, finding the Achilles' heel, he kicks it to full effect (pun intended). Edwards's position notwithstanding, several recent attempts to sort out the status of the study of effects illustrate new directions in rhetorical criticism. They include, among others, work by Michael Leff, Leah Ceccarelli, Carole Blair and Neil Michel, Davis Houck and Mihaela Nocasian, and Amos Kiewe.[13] In a 2001 special issue of the *Western Journal of Communication*, Leff admits that the long-standing approach to rhetorical studies "was to avoid reducing rhetorical criticism to the study of effects and to distinguish the invitation to meaning constructed within the text from its actual reception."[14] In seeking to correct this earlier constraint, Leff looked again at Lincoln's Cooper Union address and found evidence of its reception in several newspaper editorials, such that his assessment of the address was now informed also by a sense of its effects. Leff notes that, in "reducing rhetorical criticism to the study of effects," critics began "to hunker down within the boundaries of the text," to the detriment of understanding a text's reception. With a better appreciation for the reception of rhetoric, Leff argues that "contexts themselves are, at least to some extent, rhetorical and interpretive constructs and thus the text/context relationship emerges as mobile and negotiable."[15] In the same special issue, Leah Ceccarelli makes an explicit call for "uncovering fragments of reception that indicate how audiences interpreted the primary text."[16] More recently, work by Erin Rand on the rhetorical agency that arises from polemics and its construction of audiences and publics has opened the door to conceptualizing effects not necessarily "through the humanistic understanding of agency of individuals, but through the force of institutions, where form appears as a particular manifestation of institutional power."[17]

Other scholars, such as Houck and Nocasian, examined the effects of Roosevelt's first inaugural address by paying close attention to the many letter writers who sent their responses to the new president. They suggest that they "begin [their study] with reception and work backwards" in order "to illustrate just how a reading that begins with a speech's listeners and their collective reactions can inform the formation of that speech and its historical contexts."[18] In so doing, they remind us that "the relatively recent 'renaissance' in public address scholarship has not been borne on the back of Herbert Wichelns and the concept of effects, but rather on the internal workings of the speech itself, and the relationship of those workings to the rhetorical situation."[19] In studying Franklin D. Roosevelt's First Fireside Chat, Kiewe examined the letters many citizens sent the president immediately following the radio address on the banking crisis. He argues that the effect of the address can be found both in economic indices that improved the nation's banks in a matter of days and in the sentiments of thousands of letter writers.

Though discussing not a speech but a rhetorical artifact, Blair and Michel, in their study of "The Rushmore Effect," argue for the need to "inquire [not only] into the history, form and meaning of the monuments as artifacts, but also into the history of their use and reuse."[20] They approach their study of Mount Rushmore by examining the ways in which the site has manifested itself in the construction of "communal identity, character and collective virtues," stating that "it is imperative to assess the image it offers its audience."[21]

Indeed, the area of visual rhetoric in particular has seen a recent surge in studies that have conceptualized rhetorical theory to account for the societal impacts of the visual. Robert Hariman and John L. Lucaites, in their important book, *No Caption Needed,* make several allusions to the effect of images. Their key argument about the function of visual icons is inherently about the effects of widely circulated and reproduced images that have grown into cultural staples with specific meanings and implications. That iconic images "provide a more or less idealized sense of who we are and what we ought to be" speaks to the acceptance of such images as possible cultural guidelines.[22]

Hariman and Lucaites believe that the influence of iconic images is not easily discernible because there exists "too narrow a conception of what is being considered influenced," and they argue that such influences can vary and include the reproduction of ideology, modeling citizenship, the communication of social knowledge, the shaping of collective memory, and the provision of the incentive for communicative action.[23] Such a varied sense of rhetorical effectivity is still consistent, Hariman and Lucaites argue, with traditional rhetorical theory that looks at successful persuasion that "taps into the tacit knowledge held by the audience as they are members of a society."[24] The circulation of iconic images can result in identification between its art form and specific audience, but the authors also allow for "how public culture is being extended and negotiated through image circulation."[25] To this we would add that the very cultural designation of an image such as a photograph as *iconic* is always already a measure of rhetoric's effects.

The work of rhetorical critics, then, is not done in a vacuum. On the contrary, such work relies heavily on historical context and is often replete with political, economic, and social implications. Given the spread of topics such as political rhetoric, the rhetoric of the public sphere, the rhetoric of public memory, and visual rhetoric, as well as public address, a distinct focus on close textual analysis—thus Leff's "hunkered down"—is rather circumscribed in scope. For those in other disciplines who may be interested in our scholarship, pointing to the fact that rhetoric yields results (effects) requires some proof or evidentiary quality to back up such claims. As Carole Blair has noted, "rhetorical practice still has material consequences," and "rhetoric still does things."[26] To this we add that we need to show this to be the case.

The argument we present here is that the critic needs to engage a text's interlocutors in order to understand how a message has resonated (or failed to resonate) with them, especially when such evidence is available. This objective is critical and significant if we wish to argue that rhetoric matters. Though recent scholarship in American public address has shown some renewed appreciation for the study of effect and its importance in comprehending the totality of the rhetorical act, the limitations posed by studying effects and the paradigmatic centrality given to close textual studies still overdetermines much of what rhetorical critics do—and don't do. In order to discern how we almost abandoned rhetoric's effects or put its consideration as a probability at best and impossibility at worse, we start at the beginning and seek to untangle some of the arguments and critical threads that shaped the approaches to the study of public address and rhetorical criticism.

First, though, a point of clarification: we are not interested in rehashing issues already discussed previously and over several decades. We highlight several important junctures in the discussion over rhetoric's effects in order to advance a new perspective—figuring out how to engage evidence of effects available to us today. The Internet in particular has presented us with myriad sources for effects ranging from "talk back" reaction websites to specific outlets for posting opinions, such as Facebook, YouTube, Twitter, chat rooms, and blogs. If we were to simplify the difference between past perspectives on effects and contemporary ones, it would go like this: in the past, we were told that we really could not study effects because we truly did not have access to them, while today we are so inundated with effects-related materials that we are constrained in accounting for their sheer volume. Our overriding concern is that if rhetorical studies ought to be viewed as having merit and significance, we need to show this and not limit our focus to interpretive conclusions that are based exclusively on the internal dynamics of a text.

Rhetoric's Effect: Early Stipulations

The discipline's founding essay, Herbert Wichelns's book chapter "The Literary Criticism of Oratory," has often been cited as the clarion call for a new discipline that focuses on the criticism of oratory and rhetoric. Yet, nine years earlier, the first volume of our leading academic journal, the *Quarterly Journal of Public Speaking* (the precursor to the *Quarterly Journal of Speech*), included a committee report that emphasized the need to research the effects of a speech, including empirical assessment thereof.[27] Before we explicate Wichelns's advocacy, we need to understand the context of his call. Wichelns sought to create a place for studies of oratory (specifically the criticism of oratory) that was distinct from literary criticism. He wrote his seminal chapter when many "speech" scholars pursued a very narrow focus—that of studying great orators.[28] It should come as no surprise, then, that Wichelns's focus remained within the tradition of his time, but, as we will also show, his notion of rhetoric's effects was not exclusively the domain of the orator. Wichelns was clearly concerned with the immediate audience and thus commended the few critics who remembered "that the orator has as his audience, not posterity, but certain classes of his own contemporaries."[29]

Wichelns stated famously that rhetorical criticism "is not concerned with permanence, nor yet with beauty. It is concerned with effect. It regards a speech as a communication to a specific audience, and holds its business to be the analysis and appreciation of the orator's method of imparting his ideas to his hearers."[30] He also opines that rhetorical criticism "lies at the boundary of politics (in the broader sense)" and that its concern "is with the ideas of the people as influenced by their leaders." With these principles in mind, Wichelns advises that "the critic speaks of the orator as a public man whose function it is to exert influence by speech."[31] The trajectory Wichelns espouses is that of oratory or public address (citing C. S. Baldwin) as moving people in the direction of assent and action.[32]

The principle idea Wichelns advocates is that rhetorical criticism should be audience centered, since oratory's instrumental concern is with producing desired effects. We assume that on this point alone some would argue that Wichelns did not advocate an audience-centered focus and that he remained within the speaker-oriented paradigm. Wichelns was not specific about how one is to interpret the notion of effects, as it is not clear if he equated the reporting of effects with the study of effects, for instance. We are left with the option of trying to glean a perspective from various statements made in the seminal chapter. For examples, when discussing Lecky's description of Edmund Burke's oratory, the account relies on contemporary witnesses to Burke's speaking.[33] Similarly, the account of Gladstone's oratory by Morley relies on contemporary reporting, including journalists' accounts.[34] And, in the most specific advice Wichelns imparts to rhetorical critics, he states that "the effect of the discourse on its immediate hearers is not to be ignored, either in the testimony of witnesses, nor in the record of events."[35]

But the notion of using effect as the defining element of rhetorical criticism was never easy, given the complexity of accounting for it—or even agreeing on what it was. Wichelns admitted as much, stating that "oratory is intimately associated with statecraft; it is bound up with the things of the moment; its occasion, its terms, its background, can often be understood only by the careful student of history." As such, "the difficulty of reconstructing the conditions under which the speech was delivered" makes the "historical study of speech making . . . far from easy."[36] It is important to note that Wichelns did not suggest the reduction of "the study of oratory to the single question of its effect on the immediate audience."[37] Having stated that, though, we point out that effect for Wichelns is a defining focus for the rhetorical critic. In highlighting what speech was doing using the vernacular of causes and effects, Wichelns continued a line of inquiry extending at least as far back as fourth-century-B.C. Athens: Plato's souls and types of speech and Aristotle's genres, artistic proofs, political constitutions and the audience's age share the scientizing impulse of determining what causes what.

Yet, some twenty years later, challenges to the study of effects were raised. Ernest Wrage situated the study of public address as part of a larger objective of historical understanding, noting that "the rhetoric of public address does not exist for its own sake, that its value is instrumental" and that "the basic ingredient of a speech is its content."[38] Recognizing the value of the "speaker centered" and the "idea centered" approaches to the study of public address, Wrage set as his primary concern with the study of speeches "against a backdrop of history."[39] Wrage placed the weight of a speech on its larger historical significance. The effects of rhetoric were not his focus; rather, he was concerned with the interplay between a speech and its historical forces whereby influence is present.

Several years later, Wayland Maxfield Parrish, weary of the enormity of the task of studying "all the factors in the historical situation," suggested that the critic be selective and focus primarily on the intrinsic elements of the speech. He cautioned critics not to be "diverted into an attempt to assess the *results* of the speech except as its effect may help us to judge the quality of the speech itself." In a direct challenge to Wichelns, Parrish contended that rhetoric, strictly speaking, "is not concerned with the *effect* of a speech, but with its *quality,* and its quality can be determined quite apart from its effect."[40] And, though Parrish contended that "a speech is an utterance meant to be heard and intended to exert influence of some kind on those who hear it" and that "the kind of influence intended may be described as persuasion,"[41] he clearly opposed the study of effects.

But why pursue such a position? Parrish rationalized his view, stating that "the effect of a speech may bear little relation to its intrinsic worth," which essentially means that speaking well does not necessarily create audience appreciation and that the failure of a speech may not be caused by ill speaking.[42] Citing the example of John Brown's moving speech in his own defense upon receiving the death sentence, Parrish argued that the speaker knew his case was hopeless and thus likely spoke to posterity. With this example Parrish believed that the study of effect would render irrelevant the entire exercise in rhetorical criticism. Similarly, he asked hypothetically, how could anyone "determine today the effect of Woodrow Wilson's pleas for the League of Nations? How can one determine the actual influence of Lincoln's plea for malice toward none and charity for all?"[43] Yet, common sense would dictate that a person condemned to die would not succeed in averting the final judgment no matter how great his speech and that such an example is too narrow a premise on which to generalize against studying rhetoric's effect. Similarly, we hold that dismissing as an impossibility any assessment of the effects of speeches by Wilson or Lincoln at a particular historical juncture is too narrow a perspective, if not altogether an erroneous one. If anything, Parrish seemed to consider effect only as the immediate results of a speech, discounting its long-range effects.

Parrish advised students of rhetorical criticism not to be too confident of their ability to study a speech's effects and thus preferred to leave this task to the historian. Rhetoricians, in turn, ought to limit their focus to an assessment of the causes of the speech's success or failure, evidence to be discovered in the speech itself. For Parrish, then, rhetoric's purpose is persuasion, which cannot be explained or evaluated "until we have learned a great deal about the occasion which called it forth, the speaker's relation to the occasion, the resources available to him, and the climate of opinion and current of events amidst which he operated."[44] If rhetoric's effect is to be studied, this task should be left to historians, who, upon reflection would have better tools of assessment for such a judgment. Of course, this begs the question of what tools the historian has that the rhetorical critic doesn't. Possibly, Parish saw a disciplinary divide that left rhetoricians to contemplate the inner workings of the text, relying on historians to do the legwork necessary for understanding situation, context, and effects.

In a 1947 essay in the *Quarterly Journal of Speech,* Wayne N. Thompson argued for scholarship in public address born out of a focus on contemporary speeches. Thompson called for the study of speeches that are "directly observed by the research worker and his colleagues and reported at once or shortly thereafter."[45] This call was made amid an assessment that such a focus would provide future scholars with valuable information and insight into the circumstances as well as the effects of a given speech and that those who would study a speech from a more historical perspective would also have in their possession an accurate assessment of contemporary reactions to a speech. Ideally, the merging of immediate and later reflections would provide the richness needed to the study of public address. After all, speeches in general, especially those of a controversial topic, are difficult to assess "in their own time";[46] yet records of their immediate reception would be of indispensible importance to the critic who would enjoy the advantage of having a historical perspective. For Thompson, the contemporary assessment of a speech should clearly include an account of its effect.[47] In short, the public-address scholar "must study language as it is heard, speech structure in relation to its effect at the time of delivery, the ethical power of the speaker as he stands before the audience."[48]

Thompson also raised the possibility that not only are effects the result of a rhetorical act but that social and political institutions have effects upon public address.[49] He did not elaborate on this last point, but its significance must be appreciated as it points to the contingent and interdependent nature of public address on other perceptions affecting its substance as much as public address affects audience and situations thereof. In other words, we need to expand our understanding of rhetoric's effect to include the influence of other discursive entities and paradigms on a given rhetorical act. This suggests that rhetoric's effects are not solely the making of the speech but are also the result of other influences on it.

A similar view was espoused by A. Craig Baird, who stated that "The speaker's impression is to be measured not simply by the intrinsic value of the speech itself, as well as we can estimate it from the printed page, but by its impression upon immediate and later audiences."[50] Baird acknowledged the difficulty of judging the effect of the speech by hidden as well as outward audience response. Acknowledging the constraints of assessing effects, such as by the use of audience polls, which can be misleading, Baird did not shy away from this objective, stating rather emphatically that "[o]ne important evaluation of the speech, nevertheless, must be through its immediate and later social results. Do the ideas work? Do they create more than a ripple? Do the wider currents point to historical vindication of the speaker's influence?"[51] Baird also posited that, "[a]s historians and logicians, we will pronounce with caution. At the bottom, our judgments depend upon our standards of value," suggesting that constructive speeches can be assessed for their value in effecting change while the demagogue-speechmaker's discourse would be pronounced a failure.[52] Rhetoric's effects, though constrained by the values or morals of the speaker or speechmaker, are nonetheless a critical imperative for Baird.

Along with the reprinting, in 1958, of Wichelns's landmark chapter in *The Rhetorical Idiom: Essays in Rhetoric, Oratory, Language, and Drama,* edited by Donald C. Bryant, the chapter in that volume by L. H. Mouat stands out in discerning the status of rhetoric's effects. Mouat summed up the work of rhetorical criticism as essentially the "examination of the effect of public address or of one or more causal determinants of this effect."[53] Acknowledging the "frequent disagreement among critics and the critics of critics, as to what, in a given case, the effect may be, and little or no agreement as to which of the one or more possible causes produces the effect or how it does it," Mouat offered a set of guidelines to rhetorical critics that includes an insightful statement about effects: "the ultimate function of the critic is not fulfilled until he evaluates the effect."[54] He also suggested that, in executing such an evaluation, the critic ought to establish a causal relation between an element in the speech and its outcome. Mouat cautioned that if the critic is concerned just with the cause, then that critic is merely describing and not evaluating.

For Mouat, "the area of effect can be reduced to relatively narrow limits," whereby "receptivity should be directly related to vital interests" of time, place, community, and interests. The simple truism that people rarely attend to issues that do not affect them should be a guiding principle in assessing rhetoric's effects.[55] Finally, rhetoric's effect can be gauged by assessing its effectiveness in reaching an audience. Here Mouat found Kenneth Burke's identification a helpful conceptualization as well as a possible merging of effect with effectiveness. Specifically, Mouat pointed to the consideration of "rhetorical concepts that produce effectiveness," an assessment that can benefit from the relationship "established between societal orders and methods of identification." For Mouat, identification connects invention to audience reception in as much as proposals are developed such that they resonate with the audience's beliefs, desires, and aversions and ultimately lead to instructions about future courses of action.[56]

Edwin Black, of course, famously stands out among rhetorical critics for formulating an alternative approach to rhetorical criticism, the kind that could overcome the evidentiary constraints of assessing effect. His tectonic attack on neo-Aristotelian criticism in 1965 sought to overcome the constraints of those pursuing an Aristotelian application to rhetorical criticism, including the scholars mentioned earlier. His discussion of rhetoric's effect is related primarily to the inadequacies of the neo-Aristotelian method of criticism and not to any concern with effect per se. Black argued that neo-Aristotelian criticism (his coined term) could not account for the effect of a speech and the way it is received by the audience. Black found difficulties in the neo-Aristotelian critic's work on historical speeches, asking whether it was "even possible, for any critic, for any contemporary, to experience a reaction to a substantially dead speech?"[57] At best, the critic can suggest the effects a speech may have had.[58]

By and large, the neo-Aristotelian critic, Black argued, is concerned with the immediate audience of the discourse and, "unless he deals with a contemporaneous rhetorical object, can have no comparable experience with the discourse."[59] The very distinction Black made between the pragmatic and the formalistic judgment of rhetoric centers on effect, with the pragmatic judgment being concerned with the immediate effect of the speech and the formalistic ignoring the audience altogether, preferring instead a "timeless standard."[60] However, when the critic moves away from the consideration of immediate effect and accounts for "all the differences a rhetorical discourse has made in the world and will make," and "insofar as these effects are consequences of a wide range of human experience, there can be no separating them [the practical and the formalistic] from any abstract 'quality' that solicits our humane interest." Thus, "understanding effect so broadly would dissipate the formalist-pragmatist dichotomy and tend to resolve the differences between the positions of Parrish and Wichelns."[61] Yet, given the focus of neo-Aristotelian criticism on immediate effect, the merging of the two perspectives, argued Black, was not likely.

Instead, Black suggested that we modify the notion of effects and consider in its place the more practical notion of probable effects. To exemplify the point, he presented his essay on Chapman's *Coatesville Address,* a speech heard by only three individuals that was assessed nonetheless as compelling, suggesting that such a judgment would have been impossible under neo-Aristotelian criticism since the speech simply "did not fetch results."[62] Black's perspective gave most of the weight to the rhetorical text and an assessment of its probable effects, timeless effects, and even unrealized effects.

Perhaps, with the passage of some three decades, the earlier postulations of rhetoric's effects were somewhat unsettling, for Black offered a corrective in the form of a collection of essays published in 1992, *Rhetorical Questions: Studies of Public Discourse.* Black admitted that his earlier focus was on the speech and not on its intended effect on an audience. But, alas, new developments called for "the extension of its province" to include consideration of the audience; Black stated that "A speech, like a film or a play or a novel, is interpreted through its auditor's memory of comparable artifacts. Its meaning and effect will pivot on its alignments within the personal history of its audience."[63]

Black also wrote in 1992 that, though his monumental volume of 1965 sought to counter the stifling nature of neo-Aristotelian criticism, the book "has had a long life, as books go. It should probably be put to sleep now." Black specifically mentioned his critique of Chapman's *Coatesville Address,* stating that "the pages on the *Coatesville Address* were scarcely epiphanic, but they were not an embarrassment."[64] So what was in the *Coatesville Address* that required Black to claim that his critique was not an embarrassment? Perhaps, with hindsight, ignoring the full extent of rhetoric's effects had an undesirable impact on the discipline. As Carroll C. Arnold has suggested, perhaps in a hint of criticism of Black's analysis of the *Coatesville Address,* an oral presentation that does not engage an audience is not rhetorical. For Arnold, "contextual information must be supplied if oral rhetoric (or its printed remains) is to be open to full understanding," and oral rhetoric requires an active speaker and an active audience.[65] The essential principle Arnold advocated is that "rhetorical discourse that is intended to be oral is an instigative portion . . . of conception and attitude inducing interaction with a particular body of listeners, in whom, and only in whom, the final altering rhetoric can be generated and the purpose of the speaker realized."[66]

No doubt, Black's methodological attack on rhetoric's effects yielded new kinds of criticism that focused primarily on the text itself, moving away from the cookie-cutter approach of neo-Aristotelian criticism. With this significant paradigm shift, public-address scholars became inductive critics—Black later celebrated "emic" criticism—and as such they began to pursue textually related perspectives and methods. The study of effects was significantly reconceptualized as the study of probable effects, allowing the critic to, at best, guess what would or could have been the effects of a speech without direct evidence to substantiate any conclusion on the subject. This development clearly brought unintended consequences and limitations that constrained critics' work. Commenting on the same essay by Arnold, though not addressing the notion of effect per se, Joshua Gunn called for the recovery of "a more robust understanding of the object of speech" and suggested that perhaps "we have self-importantly erred on the side of text."[67] Perhaps we have.

The ongoing and historically lengthy controversy over rhetoric's effect yielded many explanations that reflect a contemporary perspective on rhetorical criticism. Thus, the focus from the 1930s to the 1950s was primarily on great speakers and their speeches, and methods of criticism were rather stilted and unimaginative.[68] With Edwin Black's "devastating assault on new-Aristotelianism," the door opened to new and varied perspectives on rhetorical criticism.[69] Critics lashed out against the heavy emphasis on immediate effect as necessary for forwarding a critical judgment of the speech.[70] The lamentations of several scholars regarding rhetorical criticism that covered everything but the text itself brought a shift in focus so that context was complemented by text, a perspective ushered in primarily by Michael Leff.[71] The survey of the history of rhetorical criticism brought Stephen E. Lucas to offer a revised perspective, the one he called *textual context,* in which "[m]eaning and effect are produced, not by the text as a static entity, but by the progressive interaction of the audience with the temporal flow of the ideational, dispositional, stylistic, and syntactical elements in the discourse." Yet this perspective is quite in line with Leff's central advocacy that at the center of rhetorical criticism is the text itself.[72]

Indeed, the discussion of text in context, which, taken at face value, appears to include the text's effect, has left the latter out of the discussion. For Zarefsky "[i]t seems self-evident that any rhetorical act is 'addressed' and hence evokes a 'public.'"[73] However, if it is so self-evident, why we have so consistently shortchanged the public to whom the speech was addressed? Zarefsky also opines that "any instance of public address occurs in some context and hence is susceptible to historical study."[74] Yet it is precisely the need for historical study that has often been limited and assigned a secondary or an external quality vis-à-vis the more important internal feature—the text.

Rhetoric's Effects Reexamined

The recent scholarship cited earlier that began a modest reconsideration of rhetoric's effects also brought scholars to reexamine the discipline's earlier conceptualizations. In 2006 David Zaresky added much clarity to the earlier studies in rhetorical criticism, suggesting that their work was rather mechanical and that effect was understood to mean the measuring of an audience's reaction to a single speech. The critic's task was rather complicated when effects were understood narrowly and empirically, requiring the critic to find empirical evidence for a speech's effect. The net result was bad scholarship, since "single speeches rarely have discernible effects; they work together with many other causal forces and as part of the broad social and cultural frame in which they are embedded. Moreover, the science of measuring effects of messages on audience attitudes and behavior is inexact at best."[75] Indeed, Zarefsky opined that scholarship on or about effects "usually out ran the evidence offered," forwarding rather superficial assessments about a given rhetorical act.[76]

In any event, Zarefsky argued, this is not what Wichelns intended, as his "concern, after all, was with criticism, not empirical measurement." As a critic, the focus Wichelns suggested was on the relationship between the text and its possible effect, and its practice meant an assessment of the effects the speaker contemplated and the construction of the text with specific effects in mind. Such considerations were to be viewed interpretatively and not as measurable qualities. The outcome the critic was to seek was reasoned argument, not empirical observation. An erroneous application of

Wichelns's guiding essay, claimed Zarefsky, resulted in rhetorical studies that sought a mechanical application to assessing rhetoric's effects, using categories from Aristotle's *Rhetoric*.[77]

For any student of rhetoric seeking to account for a chronological sequence of the development of rhetorical criticism, this is the point at which Edwin Black comes in with his criticism of the Aristotelian cookie cutter and mechanical forms of rhetorical criticism, relegating effects to the periphery and assigning to them, at best, some sense of probability. And, though the corrective to Wichelns is illuminating, the solution to the limitations of studying effects is still constrained. In other words, the larger philosophical and practical questions about rhetoric's effects are yet to be addressed.

But is it also possible that scholars have engaged in a narrow read of Wichelns's argument? Indeed, Wichelns called for rhetorical critics to study how orators convey ideas to audiences. But he also put the practice of rhetorical criticism within the larger framework of political discourse and stated that the essential objective of rhetoric is influence—and that the principal question the critic should ask is how the audience was influenced. In other words, we do read Wichlens to suggest not that studying effects was confined to textual evidence the critic offers but that it is more expansive and ought to include the interplay between speaker and audience.

Our concern with rhetoric's effects is capacious: one cannot teach the art of public speaking without a foundational assumption about a speech's effect. We cannot approach the study of political communication without assuming that communication affects others or that it is planned for effects and, more critically, that we can, at a minimum, assess the effect of rhetoric and preferably engage the locus of effects. Yet, when we seek to address effects, we are often told that our study should be limited to textual evidence or that we do not have access to gauging the "true nature" of rhetoric's effects. We seem to have insulated our critical work and limited its focus and scope while the considerations of effects are all around us, alive and well. As William L. Benoit and Mary Jeanette Smythe have aptly put it, "[t]raditional rhetorical theory adopts the perspective of rhetors rather than auditors," whereby we have privileged invention over reception and interpretation.[78]

A productive way of engaging a more recent approach to rhetoric's effects is to highlight the notion of agency and where in the rhetorical process it resides. Specifically, agency residing in the audience offers critics the view of effects not as a simplistic product of a cause but as the product or the results of a complexity of social and political situations that collectively allow an audience to engage a rhetorical text in multiple ways. Agency residing in the audience, as distinct from that residing in the agent/rhetor, opens up the consideration of effects that are not necessarily unified but varied and also the possibilities for their intended and unintended actions.

Karlyn Khors Campbell considers agency a rather ambiguous term that "can refer to invention, strategies, authorship, institutional power, identity, practices, and subject positions."[79] She suggests that agency be considered "a communal and participatory, hence, both constituted and constrained by externals that are material and symbolic," that it "is 'invented' by authors who are points of articulation," that it "emerges in artistry or craft," that it "is effected through form," and that it "is perverse, that is, inherently, protean, ambiguous, open to reversal."[80] Campbell suggests that, "from its beginning, there have been concept of rhetorical agency in Western rhetorical theory, by which I mean a sense that language mattered, that influence through symbolic action in speech and/or writing was possible and occurred, for good or ill, vividly expressed in the works of Gorgias, Isocrates, Plato and Aristotle."[81] To this we would sharpen the focus and argue that agency can reside not only in the speaker/writer but also in the audience/readers and that, as Erin Rand opines, both intended and unintended consequences can materialize as effects.[82]

Campbell argues that agency for the ancient Greeks "was [a] collective, of the *polis,* grounded in *endoxa,* the beliefs that either constituted common sense or were accepted as true because of the *arête,* the 'excellence' or talents of those with demonstrated prowess, as in military leadership."[83] If we take the "collective" as shared perception and understanding between rhetor and audience, then agency is not exclusive to the rhetor/orator but a reciprocal quality within the community. Indeed, Campbell does not equate agency with intentionality or with autonomy but asserts that "rhetors/authors, because they are linked to cultures and collectives, must negotiate among institutional powers and are best described as 'points of articulation' rather than originators.'"[84] Agency, then, is never a constant or unified variable in the rhetorical process, and hence speaker and audience are in constant interplay, which makes it all the more important to understand how audiences react and act as a link in the continuous chain of rhetorical exchanges.

Campbell also argues that "form is the foundation of all communication, but it is also a type of agency that has a power to separate a text from its nominal author and from its originary moment of performance."[85] It is on this particular point that we believe that rhetoric's unintended effects are effects nonetheless. It is the critic's job to figure out what brought about these particular effects and whether they can be traced to the rhetor's text or to other possibilities in the rhetorical context. Thus, Campbell cautions critics not to fall for the simplistic cause-and-effect approach to understanding agency; rather, "What is needed are synthetic, complex views of authorship as articulation, of the power of form as it emerges in texts of all sorts, of the role of audiences in appropriating and reinterpreting texts when they emerge and through time, and of the links of all these to the cultural contexts, material and symbolic, in which discourse circulates."

Following Campbell's lead, Rand seeks to move away from agency rooted in the speaker and in the direction of agency that can also reside in the audience and maintains that "neither texts nor rhetors 'have' agency separate from their contextual articulations."[86] Rand explicitly argues that, "In contrast to an understanding of rhetorical agency as the ability of rhetoric or texts to act, I view rhetorical agency as the capacity for words and/or actions to come to make sense and therefore to create effects through their particular formal and stylistic conventions."[87]

Likewise, Cheryl Geisler (following Hariman and Lucaites and Biesecker) contends, for instance, that iconic photographs can bring an "interplay of audience and media in constructing and being constructed by these images, an interplay that raises questions concerning who has agency—and therefore responsibility—for these repeatedly circulating cultural products."[88] Her definition of agency is "the complex process by which a communicative act materializes out of a combination of individual will and social circumstances."[89] Ultimately, Geisler argues that agency is "not a problem to be solved or trouble to be resolved, but a central object of rhetorical inquiry."[90] We couldn't agree more, but with the caveat that agency for this study means the possible actions and interactions audiences can potentially undertake in reaction to a rhetorical act. As Geisler argues, rhetoric "as a productive art" and that "rhetoric . . . is concerned with the art of *doing* in language."[91]

Like Campbell, Christian Lundberg and Joshua Gunn clarify that the movement from effects to a "rhetorical agent" that caused it is too simplistic if not altogether problematic.[92] They also challenge Geisler's view of "agency as a kind of substance," contending that "every act of speaking is an act of response."[93] Thus, they suggest a circulation model in which agency residing in the audience creates a response that generates rhetoric that then produces/constructs another audience, and the chain continues, *perpetuum mobile*. They advocate the more conventional account of agency possessing the agent rather than the agent possessing agency as a way to understand that effect is generated by a combination of structures, forces "that *might* precede or produce it."[94]

Our friends in Composition Studies talk not about effects but about reception, but, conceptually, they mean exactly what we mean—effects, or how a message is received by an audience. While some rhetorical scholars have abandoned the study of effects to the privilege of the text, composition scholars have engaged in the study of effect for decades, seeking to understand the reception of texts by their audiences. Though the study of reception carries its own struggles and has both proponents and critics, the principal notion that the text is never always just a probability is important for rhetoric scholars to understand. Even the most rudimentary discussion about a text's effect accounts for the author generating commentaries and assessment from friends, reviewers, and formal critics.[95] Thus, effect is conceived not only as the consequence of the rhetorical act but as its antecedent, as well. More recent developments in reception studies have moved away from focusing on the author's conception of his readers to a more purposeful disregard of how the author sought to shape results, giving the weight in reception studies to how audiences received the text despite the author. This move also gives greater credence to the text's larger sociohistorical contexts.[96]

The approach to reception assessment, then, is its interpretation by a community of scholars, a standard not too different from the community of rhetorical scholars who possess the tools to address the effective and affective nature of rhetorical texts. Jack Bratich argues that "the audience is a product of discursive construction but that these constructions themselves draw on the ontological domain of what may be called 'audience powers' or 'mediated multitudes.'" At the intersection of audience and reception, Bratich borrows from Michael Hardt and Antonio Negri's shift from epistemology to ontology, whereby an audience member is considered a subject-in-action, "constituted through desires, affects, and relations."[97]

The analogy between a text's reception and rhetoric's effect goes only so far. While the text of a poem or novel may speak to the sentiments of readers and may touch them in various ways, it usually does not seek specific action. By contrast, rhetoric's role is instrumental if not instructive (often construed in political terms)—it seeks to move audiences in the direction suggested by the speaker. Yet, what is important for the discussion about rhetoric's effect is that composition scholars have not disregarded and do not disregard the audience, whereas some rhetoric scholars do. Composition scholars also consider two kinds of audiences: the expert and the popular, assuming that the popular reception of a book or a novel should not be confused with that of the critic or the expert.[98] This distinction between two audiences ought to guide rhetorical critics who, likewise, might productively consult the effect of a rhetorical act on audiences but also generate an independent assessment of its effect thereon.

One need only consider various examples of censorship to gauge the importance of rhetoric's effect and the potential risks of specific contents in the eyes of political operatives with no insights into theorizing about rhetoric's effects. Consider the Austrian censorship battle over Giuseppe Verdi's opera *Nabucco* (1842). Censors feared that the biblical story of Hebrew exiles in Babylon yearning for their return to Jerusalem and freedom would incite a similar longing for their native country among Italians under Austria's rule. No survey, interviews, ethnographies, or reception assessments were necessary for the Austro-Hungarian authorities to conclude that Verdi's opera was a national outcry in the guise of a biblical story. In short, the opera's story and its nationalistic allusion were conceived as such by the composer and interpreted accurately by the authorities and the people of Italy as a call to freedom. The ultimate evidence of the opera's effect was plain when the "Chorus of Hebrew Slaves—'Va, pensiero'—was swiftly adopted as a surrogate national anthem."[99] When the rhetorical text and its context and audience assessment are consistent with the overall plot, the critics can and should generate an assessment of rhetoric's effect and can do so with the confidence that a textual analysis, audience assessment, and an overall understanding of situational constraints can yield a fairly accurate appraisal of rhetoric and its effect.

And, although we are encouraged by the renewed interest in and the utilization of rhetoric's effects that we see in several scholars, the predominance of textual focus cannot be overstated. In viewing rhetoric as addressed, we opted as a discipline over the past forty years not to address those addressed. We now believe that unless we assess rhetoric's effect, we will continue to generate scholarship that is not altogether convincing or credible. We are also of the opinion that without a conscious and visible move toward the study of audiences, scholars have become more literary critics than rhetorical critics, the very distinction Herbert Wichelns sought to establish in 1925.

We take claims of rhetoric's effect(s) to be precisely that: interpretive claims made by a rhetorical critic that link a rhetorical act to some sort of reaction—behavioral, attitudinal, textual—to that act. Contra Edwin Black's concern that a preoccupation with effect might render the critic some sort of empirically obsessed automaton, we see just the opposite: a concern with effect asks critics to engage directly with questions of what the rhetoric under discussion is doing—and how we know that. We should emphasize that "effects" don't typically have demonstrable "causes" lurking explicitly in a text, such that the critical and/or theoretical task is simply to discover both, à la Plato and, later, his student Aristotle. No, what we're advocating, and what we feature in this anthology, is a careful engagement with what exactly might constitute effects, how those effects relate to the text in question, and how effects circulate and come to alter our understanding of the original text. Frankly, without a recalibration and reconceptualization of what constitutes effect, we'll be forever stuck in the same tired "prove it to me" game of effects, causes, and measurements more fit for a laboratory than a dynamic polis unceasingly and rather seamlessly engaged with a 24/7 news cycle. Letters and editorials are rather quaint in an age of "like" icons and "comment" buttons—and where countless rhetorics are visible for all to see, share, alter, and recirculate in something approximating real time.

The Case for Rhetoric's Effects

We have divided our project into three parts. In part I, we probe theoretical issues of rhetoric's effects. In part 2, we cover case studies of public address. In part 3, we extend the boundaries of rhetoric's effects. We conclude the project with a summary and reflecting essay.

We begin with Carole Blair's period essay, first published in the *Prospect of Rhetoric Project* in 1996 in greatly truncated form. The essay was written for the Rhetoric Society of America conference in 1996. The title of that conference was "Making and Unmaking the Prospects of Rhetoric," marking the twenty-fifth anniversary of The Prospects of Rhetoric: Report of the National Development Project. Blair kept the original essay tucked away, seeing no prospects for the full version to get a public read. We are grateful to her for allowing us to present it here as is. As a period piece, Blair's essay provides a detailed survey of the discipline's historical struggle with the praxis of criticism and its impact on the study of effects. Its perspective and insight are temporal and thus significant for its reflective quality as well as for its contemporary advocacy. Blair's piece resonates today because it reflects on the discipline's move that many took for granted, specifically, the conceptual move toward symbolicity as a development that did much to stifle rhetoric's more crucial purpose—that of yielding results. Equating rhetoric "unproblematically" with symbolism and theory building became the primary goal of rhetorical criticism, Blair argues, ignoring "rhetoric's capacity to *do* things, rather than simply *mean* something." Scholars, argues Blair, began to turn away from the study of effect to an appreciation for rhetoric's epistemological status. Through the study of speech act theory and French poststructuralism, Blair finds in these domains a renewed focus on rhetoric's material consequences—its effects. Blair's essay looks back and looks forward critically, reflecting, projecting, and challenging the simple truism of rhetoric as action that yields results and the critic's responsibility to ascertain it.

Robert C. Rowland tackles the kinds of evidence available to the critic in gauging the resonance of rhetoric. The premise that drives his argument is that the controversies over effect are primarily over purpose and evidence rather than over theory or method. Rowland laments the focus on textuality that is divorced from how a real audience responds to being addressed. Scholars of rhetoric, he argues, need to discover the circumstances for the success or failure of a specific rhetorical act, and "rhetorical analysis of the resonance or influence or scope of ideological, cultural or psychological patterns requires evidence of some kind that relates to real audiences." Rowland illustrates that, to a great extent, rhetorical criticism, whether explicit or implied, carries some focus on how audiences understand rhetoric, but evidentiary validation is needed. Specifically, Rowland calls on critics to focus on what is in the message that establishes resonance but maintains that a close textual analysis alone is rather suspect in such an endeavor. Ultimately, the critic is called on to provide evidence that the critical perspective taken "explains how real people are influenced by messages."

With Pat J. Gehrke, the discussion moves from the important consideration of rhetoric's effects to how critics can take up this question in a productive way. For Gehrke, such criticism is global in essence, seeking to account for the occasion of the rhetoric, its audience, and its historical underpinnings, ideas, and thoughts. The praxis of such a critical perspective requires attention to causation as the conditions that brought the rhetoric in question. Gehrke argues for considering rhetoric as event with all its complexities, accounting for relevant archival material and the need to connect related rhetorical events to the history of ideas. Gehrke calls on critics to understand rhetoric as a conditional and contributory cause as well as its relevant effects, such that critics produce "inquiry into rhetorical events as probabilistic conditional contributory causes of other subsequent events." Focusing primarily on two case studies, Kenneth Burke's "Rhetoric of Hitler's *Battle*" and Davis W. Houck and Mihaela Nocasian's study of Franklin D. Roosevelt's first inaugural address, Gehrke points to criticism that accounts for much more than just the speaker and his or her speech and is obliged to study also the scope of the event at hand, events of thought, and events of economy. In short, the critic needs to account for traditional historical material (archive1) and Foucault's concern with discourse that includes limits on what is sayable, conversation, memory, reactivation, and appropriation (arhive2). Archives as source and archives as subject and their manifestation in rhetorical events are necessary since the study of effects is the "study of practices of enunciation, of expression, or relation and of differentiation." Ultimately, offers Gehrke, "the study of effects is bound to the study of histories of thought."

David Frank advocates the study of rhetoric's effects primarily for its moralistic essence. He focuses on Chaim Perelman and Lucy Olbrechts-Tyteca's New Rhetoric project as a foundational treatise on rhetorical theory in the twentieth century and argues that the New Rhetoric's objective is to transform rhetoric's effects into a coherent rhetorical philosophy. On the heels of World War II and the Holocaust, Frank argues that Perelman saw the urgent need for a return to rhetoric to counter the positivist paradigm of the prewar period. Out of moral necessity, understanding and assessing rhetoric's effects became an essential instrument to stop future genocide, especially given the effective use of rhetoric to promote the death of millions of European Jews. The New Rhetoric was Perelman's as well as Arendt's answer to the totalitarianism they faced. Action, or *vita activa,* was the concept both scholars advocated, postulating that rhetoric's effects have profound moral implications. *Vita activa* was forwarded to replace the *vita contemplativa* of the post–World War I period and the resultant collapse of moral reason. In pursuing this line of thinking, states Frank, Perelman and Olbrechts-Tyteca modified Aristotle's epideictic rhetoric whereby audiences merely applauded values orated within a genre that reinforces "values producing action." Frank calls for an appreciation for rhetoric's effects that can yield moral argument and maintains that rhetoric's ethical imperative is inherent to its concern with audience.

As we move to specific case studies, we open with Stephen H. Brown, who opines that the discipline associated with the interpretation of human symbolic behavior is obliged to come to terms "with the question of how or whether communicative acts solicit certain effects." Brown is not interested in the social scientific conception of effects, which he sees as not very illuminating or very informative. The perspective he takes centers on the temporal as essential in tying text to context. To illustrate the concept of temporality in the assessment of rhetoric's effects, Brown investigates three case studies, each producing a different measure of effect and each affecting other rhetorics: short term (Thomas Paine's "Common Sense"), mid-term (George Washington's Farewell Address), and long term (Thomas Jefferson's Declaration of Independence). While "Common Sense" produced immediate and significant effects in hastening the circumstances of revolutionary America, Washington's Farewell Address, especially its warning against alliances with foreign powers, was invoked at the conclusion of the nineteenth century and into the years leading to the Great War of 1914, allowing for competing as well as differing interpretations of the illustrious document. Thomas Jefferson's Declaration of Independence, though designed for immediate effect, has had the longest effects, for it has been and continues to be cited or referenced domestically and internationally. Its lasting effect is without question, even to those of different cultures, languages, and political experiences. Brown's primary argument is that the so-called tension between text and context is fallacious and that the "life line" to bridge these two constructs is what we often refer to as "effect."

Sara A. Mehltretter Drury investigates the case of President George W. Bush's attempts at immigration reform and its legislative failure. Though the House passed comprehensive immigration reform, the Senate closed the debate without a vote. On the face of it, Bush failed to enact immigration reform, yet, claims Drury, his efforts, and especially his May 15, 2006, address, invited effects nonetheless. Drury looks at who responded to the president and the range of reactions, arguing that Bush succeeded in framing the public conversation on immigration. She examines those agents that engaged the call for immigration reform, rejected it, and/or transformed it as examples of the ability of critics to use Bush's rhetoric to generate significant effects, including those related to the outcome of the public policy debate. Despite the policy failure, Bush succeeded in framing the immigration reform significantly as an issue of national security and invoked the American narrative of the American Dream to justify the creation of a path toward legal status for undocumented immigrants. Bush's focus on national security concerns resonated with both political sides of the debate, but xenophobic and even racist sentiments against immigrants largely defeated the policy. In accounting for these multiple responses, Drury argues that rhetoric's effects should be understood as fluid, circulatory, and interwoven, allowing us to understand the responses of multiple audiences in assessing the complex issue of rhetoric's effects.

Adam J. Gaffey examines the U.S. Senate's annual ritual of reading George Washington's Farewell Address, a practice that began during the Civil War but that has been followed most consistently since 1900. Gaffey also looks at the added ritual of commentary and reflection on the address by senators entrusted to read it, a practice that began in 1947. Collectively, these two rituals, argues Gaffey, are indicative of the transcending and transforming function of Washington's Farewell Address. Rhetoric's effects in this case point to the value of a text's second life whereby effect is not limited to an isolated instance of a speech and its auditors but is created as the speech is revisited in a variety of differing contexts and with different listeners. The Senate reading of the speech performs Washington's effects via repetition, appropriation of the speech's message, circulation, and renewal and interpretation across time. As each senator reads and reflects on the address, its effects lie in its ability to function as a corrective, as a political guide, and as an affirming ideal. Washington's Farewell Address, "read aloud to all, but *understood* and *remembered,* and *rationalized* to the present through internal reflection," becomes the tangible data of its effect.

Amos Kiewe takes up the case of Franklin D. Roosevelt's First Fireside Chat, the very example that Edwards criticized as not producing effects, and laments presidential rhetoric scholars' inattentiveness to their own claims. Kiewe forwards economic indices that clearly prove how the banks returned to solvency quickly after being on the verge of collapse. Significantly, Kiewe focuses on the letters sent to Roosevelt by thousands of citizens as testimony of their sentiments and their reception of the radio address. The citizens wrote that the address was *reassuring,* that it *inspired* many and brought others to have *faith* and *confidence* in the presidency; others appreciated the *heart-to-heart* talk as well as the president's visit to their parlor. The First Fireside Chat was designed for immediate effect—to build confidence in the nation's banks when they reopened eleven hours after the speech. The banks reopened, and money and gold were quickly brought back into circulation, thus restoring the banks' solvency. That a very plain speech, largely technical, could produce such diverse sentiments, ranging from gratitude to the perception of divine inspiration in the new president, helps us understand the material effect of Roosevelt's First Fireside Chat. Its long-range effects cannot be ignored, as well, ranging from the built-in anticipation of future fireside chats during the Roosevelt presidency to the stability of the banking system, which lasted all the way to the banking crisis of 2008. The case for rhetoric's effects is not just about accounting for the reaction to the chat in a simplistic cause-and-effect process but in understanding its agency in engaging the audience and their interaction with a text that led many to construct their own rhetoric as a direct reply to the president.

Erin Rand discusses rhetoric's effects from the perspective of polemics, specifically those of Larry Kramer, the gay activist, and his charges of irresponsible behavior among gay men in the midst of the AIDS crisis. Kramer's provocative and inflammatory rhetoric yielded unpredictable effects that "emerge across a range of different sites," opines Rand. Yet, she finds that such polemics can carry productive possibilities to affect change, although control of the effects cannot be guaranteed. Agency, in particular, is among the polemic's more significant effects, not necessarily because of the substance of the polemics but more likely because of its form. Rand casts the polemic as a queer rhetorical form, not suggesting that it suits queers or gendered or sexual differences but using the term to describe the tenuous if unpredictable relationship between the intending agent and the effects of speech or action. In the context of Kramer's polemics, Rand contends that in the "undecidability of agency" lies the potential for rhetorical action; she also maintains that the characteristics of the polemic are specifically prone to unforeseen effects and that such effects cannot be determined solely if at all by the text itself. Queerness, then, can be both the source for rhetorical agency and the excess of unpredictable effects.

In extending the boundaries for studying effects, Anne T. Demo takes an expansive view of rhetoric's effects to include photojournalism and documentaries as rhetorical acts. New scholarship that addresses the effects of visual rhetoric has challenged the more traditional views of media scholars. Indeed, media coverage of social events such as political resistance and open-source circulation studies are challenging traditional views of media effects. Demo explores how a participatory culture that combines on- and offline activism functions in the age of social media as emerging markers of rhetorical effects. Demo's operative principle is that the potential interplay between audiences and rhetors during the inventional and production process, and not just after a text circulates in its finished form, is crucial for extending the study of rhetoric's effects. From YouTube to Google Maps, political controversies can generate real-time coverage and continuous effects that in turn circulate to produce new cycles of rhetoric and effects. The case study Demo explores is a 2007 YouTube *9500 Liberty* project, in which some one hundred videographers documented how a Northern Virginia community responded to the passage and later revisions of a controversial immigration enforcement ordinance. The *9500 Liberty* YouTube segments were significant to the debate on immigration reform, leading Demo to argue that "participatory media platforms like YouTube create the possibility of generating measurable rhetorical effects during the production process" and that "the 'finished product' may be displaced as the lone unit of analysis within the study of rhetorical effects." Demo argues that online activism can impact offline organizing and that new critical insights are required to understand the impact of new social media on political issues.

Aaron Hess takes rhetoric's effect into the ethnography of drug education by literally immersing himself in the work of DanceSafe, an advocacy campaign. Hess presents his work with this group, which provides information about the health and consequences of drug use, as an effective alternative to the failing War on Drugs campaign. In becoming part of the advocacy movement and delving into the exigency at hand, Hess engages in a critical-rhetorical ethnography in which effects are viewed not as textual products but as a process. The objective of DanceSafe is to allow for a nonjudgmental approach to drug use and to settle for the lesser objective of harm reduction rather than "victory" in a metaphoric war on drugs that has failed. DanceSafe tables and booths at various raves provide information about drugs and their risks in a setting that allows ravers a choice about continued drug use. As a participant-observer and following *phronesis* as practical judgment, Hess assessed the effect of DanceSafe by observing the setting as well as by conducting interviews over a two-year period. Rhetoric's effects in this case study were taken as an "*in situ* reception of an active campaign," allowing the researcher to engage ravers in positive and nonjudgmental drug education. Ravers reported that DanceSafe messages resonated with them and brought some of them to modify their drug use by engaging in the advocacy's primary objective—focusing on ravers' personal responsibility. The effects of rhetoric, for Hess, lie in the materiality of modifying individuals' drug use as well as in the advocate's own modification of praxis relative to the drug culture.

Greg Dorchak offers a view of rhetoric's effects as applied to the performance of music, specifically, the virtuosity of fiddling on Cape Breton Island in Nova Scotia, Canada. An important cultural feature of life on Cape Breton is its longstanding musical heritage, which underwent significant changes in technique and aesthetic, the effect of one virtuoso, Winston Fitzgerald. The performance and demonstration of musical judgment motivated others to implement changes to this practice in ways that cannot be quantified but that can nonetheless be assessed over time. The effects of rhetoric in this case are illustrated in the ways a community modified its collective understanding of agency with regard to musical virtuosity. The highland music transplanted in the early nineteenth century, with its emphasis on the solo virtuosity of one fiddler and the dancing it accompanied, remained intact until the 1950s, when improved communication and transportation ended the island's isolation. Fiddling performed via radio and television allowed Fitzgerald's virtuosity to influence future generations of fiddlers. His heightened technical skills as well as his formulation of a new aesthetic understanding brought others to refine their style accordingly. The Cape Breton community's judgment of Fitzgerald's style gradually changed the community's taste and identity beyond the musical performance alone. His "clean" style relative to the older gritty one asserted a new aesthetic judgment, creating new musical possibilities and a larger context for discourse about music. Rhetoric's effects in this case have evolved over some sixty years, allowing one person to create the space for others to grow and change. The materiality of such effects cannot be assessed empirically, but they are significant and observable nonetheless.

In the concluding chapter, Davis W. Houck takes us back and looks forward. He brings us back to Wichelns's seminal essay and the ways scholars have interpreted the direction outlined at the foundation of the discipline. Houck specifically challenges David Zarefsky's readings of Wichelns, especially in lieu of the challenges posed by George C. Edwards III. The crux of the matter, argues Houck, centers on Wichelns's calls in more than one publication for uncovering empirical evidence for effect, which Zarefsky appears to deny. The larger context for avoiding the study of effects centers on Edwin Black's dissertation and the resulting 1965 seminal challenge to the neo-Aristotelian perspective. The "effect" of Black's project was detrimental to the discipline, argues Houck, in that largely ignoring situated audiences prevented the critic from "taking seriously the evidence of an audience's reaction." If effects were meaningful to Black, they were only those that affected the critic—not the audience. In his "second persona" essay, Black makes it clear that it is sufficient for the critic to assess what a rhetor would have the audience become—not what, in fact, it actually becomes. And though the feedback and reaction of an audience to rhetorical acts can offer the critic a new way of seeing the speaker and the speech, the discipline opted for symbolic inducement as the primary critical perspective for assessing rhetorical acts. Following Carole Blair's criticism of the symbolic turn in rhetorical theory, Houck opines that the focus on meaning cannot and does not correspond to the work a rhetorical act "does" with a given audience. And though the critic who appreciates effects may have to get a bit "dirty" in his or her work, where the evidence exists, it is essential that we understand what rhetoric does to audiences.

The contributors to this volume (as well as those in the discipline) who have lamented the neglect of scholarship that addresses rhetoric's reception and effects argue here that such a turn is much needed. The essays in this volume do not offer a one-size-fits-all effect formula. On the contrary, our call for studies of rhetoric's effects has taken a range of perspectives covering traditional as well as newer approaches. We offer here multiple ways of looking at rhetoric's effects, but the common thread among these essays is the engagement of the audience in the production and reception of rhetorical texts and the varying degrees of interplay. The authors presented in this volume consider the engagement of the audience important to the study of rhetoric. They also note challenges to the study of effects but agree that the study of rhetoric's effects is doable, that the sources and resources are plentiful, and, crucially, that the value of such a perspective lies primarily in validating the conclusions rhetorical critics make—however tentative.

Notes

1. George C. Edwards III, "Presidential Rhetoric: What Differences Does It Make?," in *Beyond the Rhetorical Presidency,* ed. Martin J. Medhurst (College Station: Texas A&M University Press, 1996), 200.

2. Edwards, "Presidential Rhetoric," 210.

3. Edwards, "Presidential Rhetoric," 216.

4. Edwards, "Presidential Rhetoric," 216 (italics in original)

5. George C. Edwards III, *On Deaf Ears: The Limits of the Bully Pulpit* (New Haven: Yale University Press, 2003), 23.

6. Edwards, *On Deaf Ears,* 26.

7. Ezra Klein, "The Unpersuaded," *The New Yorker* 38, no. 5 (March 19, 2012).

8. Edwards, *On Deaf Ears,* 79.

9. Martin J. Medhurst, "Afterword: The Ways of Rhetoric," in *Beyond the Rhetorical Presidency,* ed. Martin J. Medhurst (College Station: Texas A&M University Press), 225.

10. David Zarefsky, "Presidential Rhetoric and the Power of Definition," *Presidential Studies Quarterly* 34 (2004): 607.

11. Zarefsky, "Presidential Rhetoric and the Power of Definition," 608–609.

12. Zarefsky, "Presidential Rhetoric and the Power of Definition," 618.

13. Michael Leff, "Lincoln at Cooper Union: Neo-classical Criticism Revisited," *Western Journal of Communication* 65 (2001): 231–248; Leah Ceccarelli, "Polysemy: Multiple Meanings in Rhetorical Criticism," *Quarterly Journal of Speech* 84 (1998): 395–415, especially 400–403; Leah Ceccarelli, "Rhetorical Criticism and the Rhetoric of Science," *Western Journal of Communication* 65 (2001): 314–329; Davis W. Houck and Mihaela Nocasian, "FDR's First Inaugural Address: Text, Context, and Reception," *Rhetoric and Public Affairs* 5 (2002): 649–678; Amos Kiewe, *FDR's First Fireside Chat: Public Confidence and the Banking Crisis* (College Station: Texas A&M University Press, 2007).

14. Leff, "Lincoln at Cooper Union," 240.

15. Leff, "Lincoln at Cooper Union," 246.

16. Ceccarelli, "Rhetorical Criticism and the Rhetoric of Science," 326.

17. Erin J. Rand, "An Inflammatory Fag and a Queer Form: Larry Kramer, Polemics, and Rhetorical Agency," *Quarterly Journal of Speech* 94 (2008): 308.

18. Houck and Nocasian, "FDR's First Inaugural Address," 650.

19. Houck and Nocasian, "FDR's First Inaugural Address," 651.

20. Carole Blair and Neil Michel, "The Rushmore Effect: Ethos and National Collective Identity," in *The Ethos of Rhetoric,* ed. Michael J. Hyde (Columbia: University of South Carolina Press, 2004), 159.

21. Blair and Michel, "The Rushmore Effect," 183.

22. Robert Hariman and John L. Lucaites, *No Caption Needed: Iconic Photographs, Public Culture, and Liberal Democracy* (Chicago: University of Chicago Press, 2007), 2.

23. Hariman and Lucaites, *No Caption Needed,* 8–9.

24. Hariman and Lucaites, *No Caption Needed,* 10.

25. Hariman and Lucaites, *No Caption Needed,* 20.

26. Carole Blair, "'We Are All Just Prisoners Here of Our Own Devices': Rhetoric in Speech Communication after Wingspread," in *Making and Unmaking the Prospects for Rhetoric: Selected Papers from the 1996 Rhetoric Society of America Conference,* ed. Teresa Enos, Richard McNabb, Carolyn Miller, and Roxanne Mountford (Mahwah, N.J.: Lawrence Erlbaum, 1997), 33.

27. "Research Report," *Quarterly Journal of Public Speaking* 1 (1915): 30.

28. Houck has speculated that one outcome of Wichelns's emphasis on effect was to steer rhetoricians toward the study of prominent politicians and their oratory. Why? If for no other reason than effects might be recorded or preserved. See Davis W. Houck, "Textual Recovery, Textual Discovery: Returning to Our Past, Imagining our Future," in *The Handbook of Rhetoric and Public Address,* ed. Shawn Parry-Giles and J. Michael Hogan (Walden, Mass.: Blackwell, 2010), 111–132.

29. Herbert A. Wichelns, "The Literary Criticism of Oratory," in *The Rhetorical Idiom: Essays in Rhetoric, Oratory, Language, and Drama,* ed. Donald C. Bryant (New York: Russell and Russell, 1966), 23.

30. Wichelns, "The Literary Criticism of Oratory," 35.

31. Wichelns, "The Literary Criticism of Oratory," 41.

32. Wichelns, "The Literary Criticism of Oratory," 37.

33. Wichelns, "The Literary Criticism of Oratory," 26.

34. Wichelns, "The Literary Criticism of Oratory," 27.

35. Wichelns, "The Literary Criticism of Oratory," 39.

36. Wichelns, "The Literary Criticism of Oratory," 6–7.

37. Martin J. Medhurst, "The Academic Study of Public Address: A Tradition in Transition," in *Landmark Essays on American Public Address,* ed. Martin J. Medhurst (Davis, Calif.: Hermagoras Press, 1993), xvii.

38. Ernest J. Wrage, "Public Address: A Study in Social and Intellectual History," reprinted in *Readings in Rhetorical Criticism,* ed. Carl R. Burgchardt (State College, Pa.: Strata, 1995), 30.

39. Wrage, "Public Address: A Study in Social and Intellectual History," 33.

40. Wayland Maxfield Parrish, "The Study of Speeches," reprinted in *Readings in Rhetorical Criticism,* ed. Carl R. Burgchardt (State College, Pa.: Strata, 1995), 38 (italics in original).

41. Wayland Maxfield Parrish and Marie Hochmuth, *American Speeches* (New York: Longmans, Green, 1954), 3.

42. Parrish and Hochmuth, *American Speeches,* 7.

43. Parrish and Hochmuth, *American Speeches,* 7–8.

44. Parrish and Hochmuth, *American Speeches,* 5–6.

45. Wayne N. Thompson, "Contemporary Public Address as a Research Area," *Quarterly Journal of Speech* 33 (1947): 274.

46. Thompson, "Contemporary Public Address as a Research Area," 275.

47. Thompson, "Contemporary Public Address as a Research Area," 277.

48. Thompson, "Contemporary Public Address as a Research Area," 278.

49. Thompson, "Contemporary Public Address as a Research Area," 279.

50. A. Craig Baird, *American Public Address, 1740–1952* (New York: McGraw-Hill, 1956), 13.

51. Baird, *American Public Address,* 11.

52. This moral judgment seems problematic as it ignores the possibility that a demagogue such as Hitler could succeed nonetheless, despite a lack of moral or ethical guidance.

53. L. H. Mouat, "An Approach to Rhetorical Criticism," in *The Rhetorical Idiom: Essays in Rhetoric, Oratory, Language, and Drama,* ed. Donald C. Bryant (New York: Russell and Russell, 1966), 162.

54. Mouat, "An Approach to Rhetorical Criticism," 163.

55. Mouat, "An Approach to Rhetorical Criticism," 168–170.

56. Mouat, "An Approach to Rhetorical Criticism," 171–172.

57. Edwin Black, *Rhetorical Criticism: A Study in Method* (New York: Macmillan, 1965), 56.

58. Black, *Rhetorical Criticism: A Study in Method,* 56.

59. Black, *Rhetorical Criticism: A Study in Method,* 59.

60. Black, *Rhetorical Criticism: A Study in Method,* 73–74.

61. Black, *Rhetorical Criticism: A Study in Method,* 74.

62. Black, *Rhetorical Criticism: A Study in Method,* 82.

63. Edwin Black, *Rhetorical Questions: Studies of Public Discourse* (Chicago: University of Chicago Press, 1992), 13.

64. Black, *Rhetorical Questions,* 17.

65. Carroll C. Arnold, "Oral Rhetoric, Rhetoric, and Literature," *Philosophy and Rhetoric* 1 (1968): 191, 203.

66. Arnold, "Oral Rhetoric, Rhetoric, and Literature," 204.

67. Joshua Gunn, "Gimme Some Tongue (On Recovering Speech)," *Quarterly Journal of Speech* 93 (2007): 363–364.

68. Stephen E. Lucas, "The Renaissance of American Public Address: Text and Context in Rhetorical Criticism," *Quarterly Journal of Speech* 74 (1988): 241.

69. Lucas, "The Renaissance of American Public Address," 241.

70. Lucas, "The Renaissance of American Public Address," 242.

71. Lucas, "The Renaissance of American Public Address," 248.

72. Lucas, "The Renaissance of American Public Address," 254.

73. David Zaresfky, "The State of the Art in Public Address Scholarship," in *Text in Context: Critical Dialogues on Significant Episodes in American Political Rhetoric,* ed. Michael C. Leff and Fred J. Kaufeld (Davis, Calif.: Hermagoras, 1989), 13.

74. Zarefsky, "The State of the Art in Public Address Scholarship," 23.

75. David Zarefsky, "Reflections on Rhetorical Criticism," *Rhetoric Review* 25 (2006): 384.

76. Zarefsky, "Reflections on Rhetorical Criticism," 384.

77. Zarefsky, "Reflections on Rhetorical Criticism," 384.

78. William L. Benoit and Mary Jeanette Smythe, "Rhetorical Theory as Message Reception: A Cognitive Response Approach to Rhetorical Theory and Criticism," *Communication Studies* 54 (2003): 96.

79. Karlyn Kohrs Campbell, "Agency: Promiscuous and Protean," *Communication and Critical/Cultural Studies* 2 (2005): 1.

80. Campbell, "Agency: Promiscuous and Protean," 2.

81. Campbell, "Agency: Promiscuous and Protean," 2.

82. Rand, "An Inflammatory Fag and a Queer Form," 313–314.

83. Campbell, "Agency: Promiscuous and Protean," 3.

84. Campbell, "Agency: Promiscuous and Protean," 5.

85. Campbell, "Agency: Promiscuous and Protean," 7.

86. Rand, "An Inflammatory Fag and a Queer Form," 299.

87. Rand, "An Inflammatory Fag and a Queer Form," 299–300.

88. Cheryl Geisler "How Ought We to Understand the Concept of Rhetorical Agency? Report from the ARS," *Rhetoric Society Quarterly* 34 (2004): 11.

89. Geisler "How Ought We to Understand the Concept of Rhetorical Agency?," 14.

90. Geisler "How Ought We to Understand the Concept of Rhetorical Agency?," 13.

91. Geisler "How Ought We to Understand the Concept of Rhetorical Agency?," 9, 16.

92. Christian Lundberg and Joshua Gunn, "'Ouija Board, Are There Any Communications?' Agency, Ontotheology, and the Death of the Humanist Subject, or, Continuing the ARS Conversation," *Rhetoric Society Quarterly* 35 (2005): 88.

93. Lundberg and Gunn, "'Ouija Board, Are There Any Communications?,'" 96.

94. Lundberg and Gunn, "'Ouija Board, Are There Any Communications?,'" 97.

95. Philip Goldstein and James l. Machor, "Reception Study: Achievements and New Directions," in *New Directions in American Reception Study,* ed. Philip Goldstein and James L. Machor (New York: Oxford University Press, 2008), xii.

96. Goldstein and Machor, "Reception Study: Achievements and New Directions," xii.

97. Jack Bratich, "Activating the Multitude," in *New Directions in American Reception Study,* ed. Philip Goldstein and James L. Machor (New York: Oxford University Press, 2008), 34.

98. Amy Blair, "Main Street Reading *Main Street,*" in *New Directions in American Reception Study,* ed. Philip Goldstein and James L. Machor (New York: Oxford University Press, 2008), 155.

99. Matthew Boyden, *A Rough Guide to Opera,* 4th ed. (New York: Penguin, 2007), 216.

Part I

Theoretical Probes

"We Are All Just Prisoners Here of Our Own Device"

Rhetoric in Speech Communication after Wingspread

CAROLE BLAIR

Preface, 2011. This is a paper written in 1996, a period of some turmoil in the disciplinary matrix we knew then as "Speech Communication." I have retained that and other terminology so as to preserve the sensibilities of the time in which the paper was written, even though it probably seems alien in parts or at least dated to many who have known the discipline only as communication or communication studies. "Communication" then typically referred to empirical studies, as contrasted to, rather than inclusive of, rhetoric. This paper was prepared for the Rhetoric Society of America Conference in May 1996, the theme of which was "Making and Unmaking the Prospects for Rhetoric," to mark the twenty-fifth anniversary of a milestone in rhetoric's contemporary history: the publication of The Prospect of Rhetoric: Report of the National Developmental Project. *This edited collection contained papers from two related conferences, one, in January 1970, at the Wingspread Conference Center in Racine, Wisconsin, and the second, in May 1970, at Pheasant Run Resort in St. Charles, Illinois. The editors of* The Prospect of Rhetoric, *Lloyd F. Bitzer and Edwin Black, were the keynote speakers at its twenty-fifth anniversary commemoration by RSA. Four of us—Patricia Bizzell, Mary Garrett, Steven Mailloux, and I—were asked to offer, according to the program, "New Perspectives on the Prospect of Rhetoric." My paper, like the others, was published in a much condensed form in the selected conference proceedings.[1] This is the first public "outing" of the full paper. Since that is the case and since I cannot reproduce the mid-1990s version of myself, I have edited only lightly the draft of the paper I wrote then. It certainly has been tempting to correct for some excesses and to put new words and ideas in the repertoire of that former self, but I have resisted. I have taken the liberty, though, of editing for grammar, clarity, and some misbegotten phrases, since it was but a draft that I believed would never see print. Still,*

I view the paper's value, if any now, as a period piece of sorts and one that I shouldn't tinker with too much so many years later.

As matters of clarification and inclusion, I should mention that I was then an associate professor of American Studies at the University of California, Davis. The original acknowledgments on the paper read as follows: "I would like to thank Thomas S. Frentz, William L. Nothstine, and Greg Dickinson for their willingness to discuss the ideas for this draft during its formulation. I am also grateful to James J. Murphy for his generous offer to me of his compilation of Wingspread and Pheasant Run materials; as a member of the Steering Committee for the National Developmental Project, he had accumulated considerably more material than that finally published in The Prospect of Rhetoric." *Here I would like to update that acknowledgment to include Amos Kiewe and Davis Houck for inviting a resurrection of this thing so many years later; they didn't know when they made their request that there was a more fulsome version (than that in the proceedings volume) that had been residing idly in a filing-cabinet drawer that hadn't been opened in years. It was amusing not only to find a copy after so long but the more so to read it again for the first time since the mid-1990s. I am grateful to them also for dealing with the copyright and royalty issues having to do with the song lyrics of "Hotel California" that animate the paper. And with that, now, a temporal shift to 1996. . . .*

I can complete this historical rumination on post-Wingspread rhetoric only if I begin by securing your indulgence on three important matters. First is the obvious and probably non-controversial assumption that rhetorical study in the past twenty-five years has taken two very different directions, depending on the disciplinary affiliations of its scholars. That is, rhetorical scholarship in English and that in Speech Communication have taken different paths for very important, if not always apparent, reasons. What I have to say will be about rhetorical studies as pursued within Speech Communication; while my purview is therefore limited, the topic is still rather broad, and so I hope you will excuse my departure from rhetoric-at-large to rhetoric in Speech Communication.

A second assumption looms large in what I have to say about *The Prospect of Rhetoric* and its formation in the Wingspread and Pheasant Run conferences. That assumption is that *The Prospect of Rhetoric* marked a watershed in rhetorical studies in Speech Communication; it functioned as a manifesto for valuing particular kinds of pursuits and not others in rhetorical theory and criticism. However, that is not to suggest that Wingspread, Pheasant Run, or the documents produced by those conferences "caused" or initiated those pursuits. In fact, I believe and will assume throughout this paper that *The Prospect of Rhetoric* simply validated or authorized choices many rhetoricians already had made and that were beginning to have profound effects upon rhetorical studies in Speech Communication. That is not at all to devalue *The Prospect of Rhetoric* or the contributions of those who participated in Wingspread and Pheasant Run. It simply is to parry the twin risks of granting too much credit and assigning too much blame to a single document or to its contributors. In any case, I hope you will excuse my tendency here to treat *The Prospect of Rhetoric* as one, albeit one very important, event among many others of its time.

Third, I would like to ask that we be a bit loose here in our understanding of "theory." This matter probably is a little more difficult than the first two concerns, and certainly more subject to contestation. But I hope that, at least for the sake of a historical-critical argument, we can foreground for the moment certain views of "theory" and place others to the side. Specifically, I hope we can understand "theory" as discursive—not as a particular kind of language or as a genre but as a specific kind of *use* to which languages of various kinds can be put. To wit, I believe that language practice may become "theory" when it is used as such, as an exemplary, interpretive, authorizing, or interventionist instrument of other discourse or of extradiscursive practices. In that sense, I think it unwise to limit "theory" to particular kinds of statements that purport to be or are judged by their capacity as accurate or empirically verifiable, generalizing accounts. My invitation to hold such an ordinary view of "theory" in abeyance and to privilege a view of "theory" as use or functionality facilitates my goal of using a popular song as a heuristic vehicle for my attempt to understand post-Wingspread rhetoric in Speech Communication. Songs and theories typically strike us as occupying radically different spaces within the landscape of discourse. But *used* theoretically, that is, as an interpretive, metadiscursive construction, I believe the Eagles' 1976 mega-hit "Hotel California" might offer us some interesting insights on our recent intellectual history.

"Hotel California" tells an allegorical tale of a traveler in the desert who grows weary and stops at a place he has glimpsed as a "shimmering light" in the distance—the Hotel California. He is greeted at the door by a woman and by distant voices declaring the hotel to be a lovely place with plenty of room at any time of the year. But not everything is as it seems. The woman who greeted the traveler seems to have some problems, as do "a lot of pretty, pretty boys that she calls friends." As they dance in the courtyard, some "dance to remember," but others dance to forget. The traveler calls for the Captain to bring his wine but is informed that "We haven't had that spirit here since nineteen sixty-nine." The faraway voices continue, but now they not only declare the hotel a lovely place but also suggest bringing "your alibis." The scene is transformed from one of vague discomfort to near vertigo with images of mirrors on the ceiling and pink champagne on ice, as the mysterious woman tells the traveler: "We are all just prisoners here of our own device." The most unsettling scene is "in the master's chambers," where those gathered for a feast "stab it with their steely knives, but they just can't kill the beast." At that point the traveler looks desperately for a way out: "Last thing I remember, I was running for the door. I had to find a passage back to the place I was before." But the song ends with the night man telling him that "You can check out anytime you like, but you can never leave."[2] The listener is left uncertain about the fate of the traveler and whether he was able to escape this hauntingly appealing but disturbing retreat. Although the final words suggest that he is trapped, the mysterious woman suggests that everyone at the hotel is responsible for his or her own imprisonment and thus, presumably, for the possibility of escape.

When I began work on this paper, I couldn't get that lyric out of my mind: "You can check out anytime you like, but you can never leave." I don't know *why* it kept running through my mind; I hadn't thought of the song or even heard it for some time. But the image wouldn't be banished, so I surrendered to it, dug out my copy of *Hell Freezes Over,* and played the song. And since it gave me inspiration toward thinking in a particular way about post-Wingspread rhetoric, I decided that perhaps its use as a heuristic should be shared here, rather than suppressed, for reasons I will discuss toward the end of the paper.[3] In any case, there are a number of striking images in "Hotel California" that tempted me to play with them in an intertextualization with *The Prospect of Rhetoric*. We could read the woman at the door, for example, as Dame Speech, who succeeds, at least for a time, in deceiving the traveler whose guard is down. I feel a particular temptation also to take note of her friends—the "pretty, pretty *boys*" (emphasis added). I'm tempted because we should not forget the seductive potential of rhetorical practices or even of the study of rhetoric to promulgate selective and sometimes narrow views of the world. I also think it important to remember that Wingspread and Pheasant Run, like the "Hotel California," were male strongholds and that *The Prospect of Rhetoric* speaks only of a ubiquitous male subject in its discussions of those who would engage in rhetorical scholarship. But I find other aspects of the intertextualization more inviting, if not perhaps as obvious. Specifically, I'd like to attend to what made the Wingspread blueprint for rhetoric so enticing but the actual edifice vertiginous, what its mysterious beast is, how it is that we might find a way of dealing with the beast (since stabbing it doesn't seem to work), and how we might find an exit from the strange vertigo of the intellectual scene that has characterized rhetorical studies in Speech Communication in the wake of *The Prospect of Rhetoric* (an aftermath that I will refer to also as "post-Wingspread").

"Plenty of Room at the Hotel California": The "Shimmering Light" in the Desert of Traditional Rhetoric

The story is familiar to most rhetoricians: the study of rhetoric and public address in midcentury Speech departments had become dry and lifeless. Stewart described rhetorical criticism in the decade 1935–1944 as one of "hardening of the arteries." He elaborated: "Accepted subject matter was a well-known but dead speaker, preferably a politician. Contemporary studies were frowned upon as unscholarly. Methodology was a rigid application of principles outlined in Wichelns's 1925 essay."[4] In the ensuing decades, there was increasingly vocal complaint about "traditional" rhetorical study, even as such work continued to accumulate. Leff and Procario summarized it well:

> [I]solated complaint gave way to a general clamor for revision [by the end of the 1950s]. The attack centered on scholarship in public address. Existing studies were regarded as "undistinguished" and "unimaginative" (Baskerville, 1957, p. 117); they were dismissed as "stereotyped" and "banal" (Clark, 1957, p. 84); they were attacked because their focus on extrinsic details moved critics out of, rather than more deeply into, their own subject (Redding, 1957); and they were condemned as responsive to only one critical approach, which often was applied in a sterile and mechanical way (Hochmuth, 1957, p. 89).[5]

Rhetoric, as the story goes, had become a desert—barren, infertile, desiccated. If the rhetorician, like the traveler in "Hotel California," found his head growing heavy and his sight growing dim, he could be forgiven. There was, as Donald Bryant suggested, "widespread weariness and disillusionment."[6] The hand of classical rhetoric was declared dead or, perhaps more precisely, deadening.[7]

However, barely visible in the distance was the hope of a "new rhetoric." Fogarty saw the possibility, as did Marie Hochmuth, as early as the 1950s.[8] By the 1960s at least the outlines of this new configuration must have been visible to most rhetoricians. Its chief architect was Kenneth Burke, but I. A. Richards and Count Alfred Korzybski's General Semantics group were enlisted, too. Consulted as well were such noteworthies as Richard Weaver, Suzanne Langer, Northrup Frye, Stephen Toulmin, and John Dewey. And while they were not centrally involved in the design of the "new rhetoric," one could detect, upon close inspection, the influences of Warren Weaver, Carl Hovland, Bernard Berelson, Charles Morris, and Charles Osgood. Of course, there had been no collaboration among any of these individuals. Their designs were appropriated, amalgamated, allied, and occasionally force-fitted to construct the edifice, for a result that might be described as energetic or even emphatic, if artificial in its strained unity. There were many hard-working and enthusiastic builders—all but the most recalcitrant, "traditional" rhetoricians, and these detractors were all but silenced by the publication of Edwin Black's groundbreaking book, *Rhetorical Criticism: A Study in Method,* in 1965. It would become the role of the Wingspread and Pheasant Run groups, particularly the latter, to validate and even promote the new edifice.

The "new rhetoric" seems to have been a welcome sight for weary rhetoricians' eyes, for any number of reasons. Certainly the "new rhetoric" was new, and that alone must have contributed to its allure. We can only imagine backward to think how resplendent and rich an asylum it must have appeared to those traversing what was deemed the monotonous desert landscape of traditional rhetoric. But it certainly was appealing as well because of its capaciousness. Indeed, there was "plenty of room." Rather than accommodating only those who would contemplate the persuasive speaking of historically prominent men of British and U.S. politics and pulpit, the "new rhetoric" promised access to others as well. First on the list of recommendations made by the Committee on the Advancement and Refinement of

Rhetorical Criticism and approved by the full group of Pheasant Run conferees was this mandate: "Rhetorical criticism must broaden its scope to examine the full range of rhetorical transactions; that is, informal conversations, group settings, public settings, mass media messages, picketing, sloganeering, chanting, singing, marching, gesturing, ritual, institutional and cultural symbols, cross cultural transactions, and so forth."[9]

Its second recommendation was equally inclusive, but in a different way: "Rhetorical criticism should continue to examine, insofar as it can, contemporary rhetorical movements; that is, the rhetoric of the black power movement, the Chicano movement, student protest movements, the women's liberation movement, and so forth."[10] In the Committee's view, "rhetorical criticism may be applied to any human act, process, product, or artifact, which in the critic's view, may formulate, sustain, or modify attention, perceptions, attitudes, or behaviors."[11]

The general rubric under which expansiveness was possible was a reformulation of rhetoric itself. According to the Committee on the Scope of Rhetoric and the Place of Rhetorical Studies in Higher Education, "Rhetorical studies are properly concerned with the process by which symbols and systems of symbols have influence upon beliefs, values, attitudes and actions, and they embrace all forms of human communication not exclusively public address nor communication within any one class or cultural group."[12] The focus here upon "symbols" provided the ground for expanding the reach of rhetoric to nonplatform-speaking venues. It also represented a radical shift in how it is that rhetoricians would understand and conduct their work.

That the characterization of rhetoric under the sign of "symbols" marked a clear historical turning point is evident in the very different ways rhetoric was described before, during, and after Wingspread. It would be misleading, I believe, to see the Wingspread participants themselves as having redefined rhetoric in this fashion. In fact, most did *not* link rhetoric explicitly or exclusively to the symbolic. However it is clear from the "Reflections" addresses of both Carroll Arnold and Lloyd Bitzer, delivered at Pheasant Run, that it had been the sense of the Wingspread conference that rhetoric should expand its scope.[13] The Pheasant Run participants complied, as have most rhetoricians since 1970. A few examples should suffice. Ehninger, writing in 1972, enlarged Bryant's classic formulation of rhetoric as the "rationale of informative and suasory discourse" to "the rationale of symbolic inducement."[14] Johannesen argued that rhetoric is concerned with "the use of verbal and nonverbal symbols by man and his institutions to influence human behavior."[15] Scott and Brock defined rhetoric as the "human effort to induce cooperation through the use of symbols."[16] Foss, Foss, and Trapp defined rhetoric as "the uniquely human ability to use symbols to communicate with one another."[17] Hauser described rhetoric as an "instrumental use of language," suggesting the entailment that "one person engages another in an exchange of symbols to accomplish some goal."[18] Medhurst and Benson suggested that when critics address how a text functions as rhetoric, they are inquiring about the text "as a symbolic form whose structure and context lead the audience to think, feel, believe, understand, or act in an arguably predictable way."[19] Foss described rhetoric as the "use of symbols to influence thought and action."[20] While it is not impossible to find a post-Wingspread rhetorician defining rhetoric without the term "symbol" attached somewhere, it is more than a bit unusual.[21]

By contrast, the tendency to equate rhetoric with the occurrence of symbols was not at all typical for pre-Wingspread rhetoricians, or at least pre-"new rhetoric" rhetoricians.[22] Even Marie Hochmuth, writing three years *after* her introduction of Kenneth Burke to the *Quarterly Journal of Speech* audience as a representative of the "new rhetoric," took rhetoric as "verbal activity primarily concerned with affecting persuasion, whether it be done by writing or speaking."[23] Even by 1963, she seemed hardly to have changed her view, defining rhetoric as "the theory and practice of the verbal mode of presenting judgment and choice, knowledge and feeling. As persuasion, it works in the contingent, where alternatives are possible."[24] Hoyt Hudson earlier had equated rhetoric not with symbol use but with persuasion, labeling it a "technique of power."[25] And Donald Bryant, defining rhetoric as "the rationale of informative and suasory discourse,"[26] explicitly rejected the notion that rhetoric should be defined in the more expansive sense of symbolicity. These earlier definitions have in common two features of note. First, they deal with oral and written language rather exclusively. Second, they link rhetoric to persuasion or influence but not to symbol use.

What seems clear in this admittedly incomplete but arguably quite representative review of definitions and descriptions of rhetoric before and after 1970 is that rhetoric became more expansive in the objects of critical and historical analysis that would be admitted under its rubric. That expansion, however important and even (for some of us) laudable, is only the most obvious entailment of the 1960s and 1970s redefinition of rhetoric. Unprobed, I think, perhaps because the understanding of rhetoric as symbolic seems so very obvious to us in the post-Wingspread era, is the consequence of shifting from a focal interest in persuasion or influence to symbolism and its attentive consort—meaning. Prior to attending to that shift, though, it would be useful to look at the conditions that prompted it.

"We Haven't Had That Spirit Here since 1969": The "Alibis" of Theory and Symbolicity

The transformation of rhetoric from persuasive discourse to symbolic conduct certainly was overdetermined. However, two conditions stand out as the most obvious and probably most consequential.[27] The first seems already clear in the Pheasant Run plea to expand the range of discourses available for rhetorical criticism. If we attend to the examples they named—picketing, marching, singing, and so forth—as well as to the larger social movements they named as targets of rhetorical study, it seems obvious that these rhetoricians sought a means of understanding, perhaps even exerting an influence upon, the kinds of social action that were being displayed prominently outside their campus windows at the time. That was, of course, evident in the historical record before Wingspread and Pheasant Run, for example, in Griffin's 1952 appeal for rhetoricians to study social movements—however, the signs of it are so prominent in both conferences' documents that one hardly need look elsewhere.[28]

Among the more chilling reminders of the context in which the Wingspread and Pheasant Run conferees worked is the notation in the Foreword of *The Prospect of Rhetoric* that Phil Tompkins could not attend Pheasant Run "because of the tragic events on his campus immediately prior to the conference."[29] Tompkins, at that time, was at Kent State; ten days before the start of the conference, Nixon had announced the Cambodian incursion, and less than a week after that, thirteen students at Kent State were gunned down, four of them killed, by National Guardsmen during an antiwar demonstration on campus. The notation of Tompkins's absence is not the only marker, however. Perhaps the most poignant is Booth's description at Wingspread of his so-far failed attempts to write a letter to a promising student who had joined the "Weatherman crowd" (99). And a large portion of the statement forwarded by Pheasant Run's Committee on the Scope of Rhetoric and the Place of Rhetorical Studies in Higher Education is given over to an assessment of the wrenching cultural conflicts of the time, not to mention a rather impolite rendering of "establishment rhetoric."[30] Especially in these two latter cases, there are clear indications that rhetoricians could and should be involved in these contemporaneous conflicts and that rhetoric had something to offer within the public arenas of conflict generated by the Vietnam conflict, the civil rights movement, and so forth.

But, to offer anything, the rhetoricians would have to understand rhetorical practice more broadly than before, for many of the vehicles of influence in the contemporary domestic movements were not platform speeches. To expand the range of rhetorical practices to include virtually any symbolic gesture would allow rhetoricians the capacity to deal directly with the jarring events that threatened to (if not actually did) engulf their campuses, as well as potentially larger domestic spheres, in warfare. It may be possible to forget now, as we reside in the relative tranquility of our campus habitats, that rhetoric's transformation was in part the result of the 1960s political unrest, disruption, and domestic struggle. Perhaps "we haven't had that spirit here since 1969," or at least since the early 1970s, but the character of our disciplinary work was profoundly reshaped by that spirit of real struggle over political and ethical action in the world. In any case, we became students of symbols, not just students of public platform speaking, partly because of the spirit and political action of those times.

But there was another prominent condition that also influenced rhetoricians in their decision to mark their area of study as symbolic activity. That was the postwar combat between rhetoric and communication within the field still named "Speech." This conflict was itself a rather complex phenomenon. And for those of us not around to witness its most hostile battles, it is possible to recover the sense of it only from its consequences and from the documents that represent it, not from documents that were actual instruments of the warfare. Although there are a few of the latter, most of the hostilities apparently were waged away from the printed page—in conference meeting rooms, department hallways and office, and so forth.[31]

It seems clear in retrospect, and pertinent to my point here, that rhetoricians saw at least some value in rapprochement with their more scientifically inclined colleagues. And the ways in which the two sides constructed their truce show us some of the means of rapprochement. Two are relevant here. First, the particular professional ideology pursued by those interested in communication demanded that knowledge be unified under the sign of a disciplinary group.[32] Thus, whatever rapprochement could be achieved between rhetoric and communication scholars, should they wish to remain within the same professional disciplinary group, would have to be accomplished not by granting difference but by declaring mutual interest and common cause. To the degree that this factor held, the second factor—the communication scholars' delineation of their own area of study as concerned with symbolic behavior—would be utterly definitive. And it was. It certainly is uncontentious to claim that communication scholars of the 1960s and since have claimed symbolic behavior as their principal territory. In fact, the participants in the 1967 New Orleans Conference on Research and Instructional Development posited as the first line of the preamble to recommendations "concerning issues and responsibilities in Speech-Communication" that "The conferees recommend acceptance of the following description of the area of study in speech-communication: *Spoken symbolic interaction is the central focus of study in the speech communication area.*"[33] That was not terribly surprising, especially given the influence of General Semantics and information theory on communication studies. The emphasis for them was on communicators' capacity to transmit information accurately. As Ehninger and Hauser suggest, "Given their concern to produce a reliable picture of the world as a set of physical entities or events, it was perhaps natural that the General Semanticists should come to think of good communication as essentially descriptive or reportorial . . . the General Semanticists directed the bulk of their efforts toward discovering ways in which descriptive or referential language might be made more dependable."[34]

If anything, information theory's influence was even more profound, offering the principal model of communication that would be used, adapted, and forwarded to students for decades—the Shannon-Weaver model, originally a representation of how telephone communication worked and thus concerned with the transmission of information from one location to another.[35] Although Shannon and Weaver understood "information" as clear sound, undistorted by "noise" or interference, communication scholars adapted the concept to reference *meaning*—the referential resources of symbols.[36] To my knowledge, communication scholars have rarely, if ever, wavered from the description of their focal concern offered at the New Orleans conference in 1967. Nor have post-Wingspread rhetoricians strayed far from their self-descriptions as students of things symbolic.[37]

That rhetoricians' acceptance of this description would have consequences far beyond those of expanding their area of study is a claim to which I will return. Before taking up those consequences, though, I wish to address one final set of terms for the truce between rhetoric and communication scholars, because it contributed to the same effects. That is, rhetoricians in the 1960s and particularly in the 1970s (in the wake of Wingspread and Pheasant Run) began to cast their goals differently; after that time, the focal goal of rhetorical study in Speech Communication became "contributing to theory." Nothstine, Blair, and Copeland trace this impulse in rhetorical criticism to a wholesale acceptance on the part of these rhetoricians of a scientized understanding of intellectual work, borrowed in large measure from their communication compatriots.[38] The tendency is obvious in *The Prospect of Rhetoric,* although it certainly did not originate there. The Committee on the Advancement and Refinement of Rhetorical Criticism put the case this way: "Whether rhetorical criticism ought to contribute to theory seems to us to be beyond question."[39] A similar statement, if not a stronger one, is found in almost every rhetorical criticism text written in the past twenty-five years. Even in a book Andrews described as hewing to a "traditional" perspective is this statement: "Another primary function of criticism, in a sense, subsumes all others: The criticism of rhetoric contributes to the development and refinement of rhetorical theory."[40]

Represented in these statements is a reconfiguration of an older theory-practice affinity articulated or assumed in earlier formulations of rhetoric. Perhaps the most prominent pre-Wingspread example is Thonssen and Baird's characterization of this relationship: "Rhetorical criticism helps to interpret the function of oral communication in society. It serves as an effective link between the theory of public address and the outside world."[41] Rather than suggesting that rhetorical criticism must always contribute to theory or that theory refinement is the principal goal of criticism, Thonssen and Baird suggested that "criticism helps to reveal the operation of theory in practice, thus clarifying its meaning and perhaps in some cases even formulating new theory."[42] Although criticism might lead to theory construction, in their view, it neither always did nor necessarily should. By contrast, Foss took the position in her popular 1989 text on rhetorical criticism that "rhetorical criticism *must* begin with the asking of a research question *so that the critic is able to contribute to rhetorical theory* as a result of the study."[43]

The re-understanding of rhetoric as principally symbolic, coupled with the revaluing of theory and practice, would have consequences. Certainly among those was the positive effect of putting an end, at least apparently, to the disciplinary battles in the field renamed at the time as "Speech Communication."[44] Another was to expand the study of rhetoric into areas functionally closed to it before. However, these twin moves essentially assigned rhetorical practice and its effectivity—its political capacity to do things in the world—to disciplinary oblivion, a consequence that was almost inevitable to the extent that rhetoricians took rhetoric to be unproblematically equated with symbolicity and posited theory building as the only and unquestioned goal of rhetorical criticism.

An exclusive focus on symbolicity diverts us from rhetoric's capacity to *do* things, rather than simply *mean* something. That distinction was as clear as it could be in Marie Hochmuth's characterization: "The new rhetoric which arises is a rhetoric concerned not with persuasion as a specific end, but with the meanings of statements in any type of discourse."[45] Despite rhetoricians' tendency to speak in the language of symbolic *action,* following Kenneth Burke, they have been far more engaged by the symbolicity component than by the action component, or than by the extraordinarily complex relationships between the two. In fact, the relationship is murky at best in Burke's own deeply philosophical inquiry into human motivational structures.[46] But virtually all post-Wingspread rhetoricians in Speech Communication appear to assume, rather than to explore, a clear and direct relationship between the symbolic production of meaning and the activity of that production in the world.[47] Their focus deflects attention from the fact that rhetoric does things and from the ways it does them—in other words, it diverts our attention from politics and civic affairs.

Perhaps the best evidence of rhetoricians' turn away from the political because of its consumption by symbolicity was the shift from a concern with rhetoric's effects to a concern with its epistemological status. Modern rhetorical studies assumed a close alignment with philosophy at about the time of Wingspread. Otis Walter's classic essay was at least a prod to rhetoricians to take such a direction, and the initiation of the journal *Philosophy and Rhetoric* was surely the clearest sign that it had done so.[48] Robert L. Scott's generative essay, "On Viewing Rhetoric as Epistemic," was published in 1967, and the debates that ensued over rhetoric's fundamental character as representing versus creating realities have consumed much theoretical discussion since.[49] My own reading suggests that this too is, in part, a response to the remaking of rhetoric as symbolic. Cherwitz and Hikins's definition of rhetoric as "the art of describing realty through language" requires little interpretation in this regard.[50] In fact, it epitomized the focus on symbolicity to the exclusion of effectivity. The only criterion that one could reasonably assume for evaluating rhetorical practice under Cherwitz and Hikins's definition is accuracy or clarity of representation—the same one that emerged two decades before, for those interested in General Semantics and what we might now consider naïve versions of communication theory. As Thompson put it succinctly in 1963, "for the communicationist to react favorably to an unclear speech is unthinkable. Clarity is the criterion, not a criterion; it is itself the end, not a means. In the satisfactory act the message sent and the message received are identical."[51] But the understanding of a message cannot be equated with that message's consequences or its effectivity; these latter concerns have been slighted, if not completely deferred, in the post-Wingspread bargain.

Theory construction diverts the rhetorician from the capacity of rhetoric to do things in another way: by disarticulating rhetorical study from the civic and pedagogical tasks rhetoric had formerly taken to be its own—those of having voice in civic affairs and assisting others to be so enabled.[52] As I have argued elsewhere, "When theory production and refinement become the central objectives of rhetorical criticism, critical 'method' had to be aligned as a precept and system. When such objectives became most entrenched, they functionally proscribed others, such as critical refusal, intervention, and advocacy."[53] Put most simply, when the rhetorician's task becomes the construction of theory, her or his audience will become almost exclusively academics. And to the extent that rhetoric is taught merely as a tool of theory construction, students will be equipped for academic understanding, less so to be articulate, thoughtful, or even critically receptive citizens.[54] Even more important, the rhetorical practices we study become merely "data" upon which to build generalizations, rather than concrete and consequential events to which we might respond in kind.[55]

In sum, when rhetoricians decided to stop for the night at their version of the "Hotel California," they brought their alibis, named Symbolicity and Theory Construction. There can be little doubt that those alibis were self-defeating. It is very clear, particularly in the documents from Pheasant Run but also those from Wingspread, that the participants were overwhelmingly concerned with the political dimensions of rhetoric. But that interest would be virtually impossible to pursue because of the singular goal of theory construction posited for rhetorical study and the definitive symbolic character assigned to rhetorical practice.

"Some Dance to Remember, Some Dance to Forget": A Personal Interlude

In almost every respect, my professional academic identity has been constructed by what Wingspread and Pheasant Run represented. I have been literally surrounded by Wingspread and Pheasant Run participants from the time I was a freshman in college. No fewer than eight of the participants in the two conferences were my teachers or people I talked with regularly in the hallway when I was a student. Others I have been privileged to work with as departmental colleagues. And with still others I've developed intellectual friendships over the years. It seems fair to suggest, excusing the imperfect analogue, that I'm one of the intellectual progeny of the Wingspread generation. But there has been something missing, even in the series of wonderful intellectual experiences I and other members of my generation have had in our special proximity to that group of people who revolutionized the study of rhetoric.

After numerous conversations with others of my academic cohort, I'm confident that I do not speak only for myself. Something really *was* missing. Many of us, I believe, have managed to find some of the missing puzzle pieces. But I think it fair to say that the character of rhetorical studies in Speech Communication in the 1970s and 1980s was not what we thought it would be when we chose to involve ourselves in it. There was no doubt a component of self-deception involved. But there was more—everything we had learned as undergraduates suggested to us that rhetoric was a means of engagement in the world, that it made a difference. The realm of the political intruded into our lives at very young ages—with President Kennedy's assassination, civil rights marches, Vietnam, student demonstrations, second-wave feminism,

Watergate. We were a politically invested generation; even those who had less genuine engagement found themselves at least interested. And the study of rhetoric appeared to offer us a way to perpetuate and focus our interest and involvement. But, during my years as a graduate student and subsequent years as a faculty member, I have found that my professional investment is conversely related to my political involvement. To the extent I follow the professional dictates of rhetorical studies as they were articulated during the 1960s, 1970s, and well into the 1980s, I can hardly engage in satisfying ways with the affairs of the world. Tom Farrell's statement strikes a familiar and uncomfortable chord: "this [academic humanist] world still seems oddly disconnected from the world of hunger, poverty, crime, drugs and genuine scarcity."[56] I find it remarkable, very sadly remarkable, that rhetoricians, of all people, would be led to make such statements or to harbor such misgivings.

Short of a few lucky accidents, among them running headlong into speech acts theory, and then, more important, French poststructuralism, I probably would not have located the source of my vague frustration with rhetoric. It was in those domains, not in rhetoric, that I remembered that rhetoric was about doing things, about politics, and about the world. In other words, I remembered the dimensions of rhetoric that drew me to it to begin with, but I did the remembering in the most unlikely of places—outside the area of study named for it. The point is that it really was accidental; at the very least, it was virtually tangential to work being done in the disciplinary core of rhetoric in Speech Communication.

I do not mean to suggest that my experience is everyone's, that it is all that important, or that it is identical to that of others of my generation. Nor do I wish to suggest that the version of rhetoric represented by Wingspread and Pheasant Run should now be abandoned wholesale for another. It is not without merit to understand rhetoric as symbolic. It is, though, *utterly* without merit to insist that rhetoric is only and exhaustively symbolic. Similarly, theoretical understandings in rhetoric are important. But we err if we think that generating them should be the only, or even the most important, function of our work.

The interesting thing about all this for me, beyond the level of my own idiosyncrasies, is that we post-Wingspread rhetoricians seem to have forgotten that our perspective is only one in a long history of perspectives on rhetoric and that "ours" is very likely an aberration. I can think of no other group of historical rhetoricians who focused their attention restrictively on symbolicity or who have understood their work as so exclusively theoretical. Forgetting is sometimes productive, but it has its disadvantages. The *Prospect of Rhetoric* is now out of print, apparently no longer necessary to tell us what we should do or even where we have been. That is unfortunate, not merely because a few good essays have almost disappeared but also because forgetting about the positions taken, the disagreements, and even the perceived need at the time for those two conferences makes it far less likely that we will remember that the recommendations forwarded by the Pheasant Run conference represented not necessities but *choices*. They encouraged particular directions and not others. It may be difficult to remember that alternative objectives and constructions are possible, because the choices represented by Wingspread and Pheasant Run became so naturalized. My generation has few means of remembering the grounds of choice making represented by *The Prospect of Rhetoric;* those entering the field more recently have even fewer.[57] Perhaps we should make the effort to suspend the dance of forgetting and attempt the dance of remembering, even though it may be more complicated and challenging.

"They Stab It with Their Steely Knives, but They Just Can't Kill the Beast": Rhetoric Still *Does* Have Consequences

No matter the degree to which the academic study of rhetoric has internalized and naturalized the depoliticizing, insulating implications of defining rhetoric as symbolic and of taking its task to be theory building, there is no denying that rhetorical practices continue unabated and that they continue to have material consequences. No matter how many times the beast of "effect" (or its variants of consequence and effectivity) is stabbed, it will not die. In fact, with all the apparently deadening consequences of definition and goal articulation by rhetoricians of the past twenty-five years, the "beast" still raises its head time after time, occasionally even in the Speech Communication literature. And, despite the beating taken by "effects studies" in midcentury, we are fundamentally stuck with the fact that rhetoric, however, it might be defined, still does things. Some of us might even go so far as to suggest that that is rhetoric's definitive characteristic. Bryant's injunction remains among the clearest articulations of this point: "In very general terms, the distinction I mean is that between the treatment of artifacts as significant primarily for what they *are* and the treatment of them as primarily significant for what they *do*."[58]

Bryant thus warned rhetoricians, even in 1973, against the abandonment of the exploration of rhetoric's "effects."[59] His injunction would fall on deaf ears. In retrospect, that seems unsurprising. The notion of effect as the standard concern of rhetoric had been articulated in Wichelns's groundbreaking essay in 1925. There he characterized rhetorical criticism as "not concerned with permanence, nor yet with beauty. It is concerned with effect."[60] Effect would never prove a comfortable focal point for rhetoricians, nor was it explored sufficiently to be a very well understood standard until its various applications and interpretations in critical practice had come under such fierce attack that there seemed hardly any way of salvaging the notion at all.

A number of issues arose in the 1950s in particular that prefigured Sproule's certainly accurate contention that "Wichelns presented an effect standard of the narrowest possible kind."[61] Although the most thorough analysis of the problems with effect would await Black's scrutiny in 1965, one issue seems to be among the most troubling; it was raised by Nilsen in 1956: "It is the viewing of the social act, the speech, so predominantly from the point of view of the individual—the speaker and his purposes—rather than from the point of view of society . . . that has led to much of the conflict and confusion about effects as an object of criticism."[62] Indeed, there were other problems as well, not the least of which was how to locate or account for the effect of a speech as a discrete force in society. Still, Nilsen's complaint, had it been taken up and explored, rather than being used as another knife plunged into the beast of effect, might have gotten rhetoricians to some of those other issues as well.[63]

Nilsen had identified a distinction that remains important—that between effect understood as the fulfillment of a rhetor's specific goal and effect rendered as social consequence. That distinction seems to locate the problem of the beast that will not be killed. "Effects studies" as interpreted by Wichelns may have been mercifully put down, but the question of effect remained (and remains) very much alive. As Cherwitz and Theobald-Osborne suggest, "[D]espite the problems associated with traditional effects studies, the speech communication discipline never may have relinquished the concept and assumption of effect."[64] However, they make the equally telling point that "There has been insufficient exploration of the concept theoretically or meta-critically; in short the concept of political effect has not been informed by nor kept pace with sophisticated advances in other aspects of rhetorical and communication theory."[65]

Perhaps the clearest difficulty with the concept of effect is its traditional imbrication with liberal humanism. If the speaker, the humanist subject, remains such a focal figure, there is an almost automatic emphasis on her or his goals and on her or his degree of success in accomplishing them. And if Cherwitz and Theobald-Osborne are correct in their argument that effect has remained an assumption of rhetorical studies throughout the twentieth century, including the post-Wingspread era, then we have an even more peculiar and complex difficulty in the wake of defining rhetoric as symbolic. To the extent that rhetoric was equated with the persuasive, the rhetor's goals were taken to be clear and could be judged as to failure or success, at least presumably. But, once we have reconceived rhetoric as symbolic, assessment of effect must be narrowed even further—to the question of whether the meaning of a symbolic construction is sufficiently clear to be understood by an audience. To pose the question of understanding does not necessarily or even frequently entail a question of other effects.[66] Audiences can perfectly well understand a message and not act on it, refuse to believe it, suffer little material influence at the hands of it, or even be profoundly affected by it without being aware of it. Hence, even in the redefinitions of rhetoric as principally symbolic in character, there is a reintroduction of humanist purpose. Each of the exemplary definitions—from Ehninger, to Scott and Brock, to Foss—include within them a goal orientation attached to symbol use. It is used to "induce," to "induce cooperation," to "accomplish some goal," to "influence," and so forth. But a better understanding of effect does not follow from an analysis of meaning—what the analyst gets by theorizing rhetoric as symbolic—even if we filter the issue back through the goals of the humanist subject. That we might be able to identify the wealth of meanings harbored by a symbolic construction does not entail that we have been able to identify what happens when that symbolic construction is mobilized in a social context, even if we know (or think we know) why it was mobilized.

The beast of effect is still very much alive. That it is can hardly be declared an idiosyncratic observation. There are any number of hints throughout our literature that the steely knives have failed to do their intended work. The beast certainly showed up at Pheasant Run. The Committee on the Scope of Rhetoric and the Place of Rhetoric in Higher Education suggested that, "For the student concentrating in either English or Speech-Communication, the study of what is happening when he talks or listens is rarely available, or when it occurs, it is unsystematic and superficial."[67] Karl Wallace seems to have seen the beast that year, too. In his book *Understanding Discourse,* he posed a series of questions about effect that suggest real possibilities for investigation, imploring the rhetorician to "think again about the value of 'effect' as it appears in the context of communication and his favorite model of it. Does 'effect' carry the same meanings as the concept does when one thinks of a cause and effect relationship? Does one distinguish between the effect and the consequence of an act of communication?"[68] Wallace seems to imply here not only that our predecessors thought less than they might have about effect but that there are ways of thinking about it that may be productive.[69]

In the 1980s and 1990s, the beast lived on and seemed to make even more frequent appearances. Edwin Black remarked in 1980 on the "remarkable poverty of our vocabulary about rhetorical experience." He explained the difficult of assessing rhetoric's functions: "Of course the functions for rhetoric are not available to us for direct observation. These functions are in the experiential realm. They are subcutaneous. I know that some rhetorical communications affect me because I experience the effects; but that you, too, have similar experiences is, for me, no more than a working hypothesis."[70] Rod Hart too experienced a sighting:

> A difficulty I label the *deterministic fallacy* also threatens theoretical understanding of the interplay of rhetoric and values. The determinist holds that rhetoric is all powerful, that it directly impinges on the affairs of people, and that rhetorical scholars should become watchdogs for society as a result. . . . The determinist fails to sense that many of us do not listen to what we hear even when the voices around us area loud and insistent. Those of us who do listen often do not believe. Those who believe may fail to do anything about it. . . . Rhetoric is extraordinarily powerful, but the existence of a plea does not ipso facto make a cultural or social reality.[71]

If rhetoricians as different as Black, Hart, and Michael Calvin McGee could recognize essentially the same problem, and be joined in the recognition by Tom Farrell and even by a self-professed communication scientist, there must be some reason to believe the "beast" is still with us. McGee forwarded the concept of the ideograph in

1980—a language construction that is understood, as Leff and Procario observe, "in respect to its usage [more than] its alleged idea content."[72] Farrell complained in 1993 of a trend he saw as the "textualizing of politics" and suggested a move away from understanding rhetoric as a product to understanding it as an activity; hence his suggestion that we attend to the "utterance" rather than the text.[73] Perhaps the most surprising, though, was John Waite Bowers's introduction of the "pragmeme" in the mid-1980s in his Speech Communication Association presidential address. While recognizing the interdependence of communication with other fields of intellectual work, Bowers insisted that, "we have our own unique domain. That domain is, in a semiotician's view of the universe, 'pragmatics': the study of the mutual influence between and among people and their signs and symbols."[74] He proposed that we take up a specific unit of analysis—the pragmeme—in a program he called pragmemics, suggesting analogues with phonemics and morphemics in the syntactic and semantic branches of semiotics. He even went so far as to suggest that issues like power and status "are probably important features for a theory of pragmemics."[75]

These observations were made in different contexts, each with its specific concerns and solutions, but they all have this in common—they recognize that effect is a problem that has been only inadequately addressed. While none of these authors goes so far as to suggest that the focus on symbolicity is the difficulty, enough of them propose other "units of analysis"—speech act, pragmeme, utterance, ideograph, and so on—to make the case even more plausible. That is, their proffered alternative constructions for understanding instances of rhetorical practice imply that the notion of the symbol is not coterminous with rhetoric. They also suggest that, instead of continuing the futile attempts to kill that beast, we take a different approach. If effectivity is a definitive dimension of rhetoric, it seems more productive to acknowledge and study it, not attempt at every turn to domesticate, subdue, and finally mangle it. If Foucault is correct, that may be a natural tendency—to quell a very a particular anxiety: "as to just what discourse is, when it is manifested materially, as a written or spoken object, but also uncertainty faced with a transitory existence, destined for oblivion—at any rate, not belonging to us; uncertainty at the suggestion of barely imaginable powers and dangers behind this activity, however humdrum and grey it may seem; uncertainty when we suspect the conflicts, triumphs, injuries, dominations and enslavements that lie behind these words, even when long use has chipped away their rough edges."[76] The anxiety is appropriate. The beast is dangerous. To ignore it is, however, both vain and futile.[77]

"You Can Check Out Any Time You Like, but You Can Never Leave": Can We Find a Passage [Back]?

The edifice of post-Wingspread rhetoric is chaotic—a collage of designs that barely hold together. Any attempt to find our way through the bewildering compound is bound to produce vertigo. The pieces don't all fit, and some aren't functional. Some corridors lead to dead ends but aren't marked as such; some of the rooms are still construction zones, but we're inside before we realize that. The residents don't seem to notice anything amiss, or if they do, they invite others in without warning them. It may be worthwhile to seek a passage out, if not back to where we were before.

There are a number of reasons, I believe, for not trying to go *back*. Finding our way out of the disarray that marks post-Wingspread rhetoric may be possible, but a mere return to the pre-Wingspread space is neither desirable nor even conceivable. It is not desirable because the "new rhetoric" represented by Wingspread and Pheasant Run has given us at least two things we should take with us when we leave—an expanded view of the range of rhetorical practices we address (even if we no longer or only occasionally label them as symbolic) and probably a clearer sense of why we need to explore carefully ideas and concepts we are prone to take for granted. It is also undesirable because of the many aspects of pre-Wingspread rhetoric that were mistaken or misguided; it would be unwise to attempt to go back to that desert, though we have learned a great deal from our time there, just as surely as we have in the lovely edifice of the "new rhetoric."

But it probably is impossible to go back anyway. It is unlikely that we could forget what we have learned from the "new rhetoric" or *The Prospect of Rhetoric,* even if we had some perverse desire to do that dance of forgetting. Moreover, while we have been inside the rhetorical version of the Hotel California, the terrain outside has changed sufficiently to suggest that there is no "there" to go back to. The desert has been fertilized, irrigated, and planted by an upstart, interdisciplinary outfit, going loosely under the name of "cultural studies." The territory rhetoric began to explore in the early part of the twentieth century and then abdicated—a territory marked by the political vectors of rhetoric—has been occupied by this group, in some cases, with great productivity and to great advantage.[78] When we leave the edifice of the "new rhetoric," we certainly will encounter this group. That is not to suggest that we must join it; it simply is to suggest that we might learn to live and work with this and other groups that share some of rhetoricians' goals, assumptions, and interests.

Finding our way out of the vertiginous structure we have all lived and worked within for years probably will not be easy. But we do have clues as to where the passages are and how to do more than "check out." What we should avoid are passages that lead us toward always building theory and the rooms decorated only with symbols. And if we lose our way, we can simply follow the beast—he's going with us, hardly damaged by twenty-five years of steely knife wounds. We know rhetoric is consequential, and we need to remember and explore its character as such.

The night man is wrong—we really *can* leave when we check out. In fact, we had already left the building at the beginning of this paper. My invitation to suspend disbelief for a time about what could count as theory, to the degree it received even grudging or contingent consent, suggested that we had made it out the door. The invitation resulted in an almost precise reversal of what the "new rhetoric" would have us do. Within that edifice, one would never use a song to study theoretical or historical formulations; one might use theory to study songs and contribute to theory in so doing. But my invitation out was not whimsical; it was quite serious. Among the issues the "new rhetoric" left unsettled was how critics and historians of rhetoric do their work, but the unsettledness did not much (and arguably could not, given the scientistic timbre of the position) entice rhetoricians to explore the character or practices of their own intellectual labor. That investigation is under way now, and among the things we may learn from it is a very different view of theory. If we can believe the reports of some rhetoricians, theory has become either a tertiary support for their work (rather than the prize they seek at the end of it) or merely a normed requirement of their writing processes.[79] Some argue that we do not really choose our theories by any systematic or rational process but that we end up choosing them for what they allow us to say.[80] These views suggest that "theory" is a function of discourse or a use to which we put it, not a more-or-less accurate hypothesis about a defined range of objects. These positions eschew the fetishizing of theory—or, importantly, a particular view of theory—and an attachment to rhetoric as exclusively symbolic.

It is difficult to say what a post–"new rhetoric" might become, but if this return and tour through post-Wingspread rhetoric have served to mark out issues that matter now, certainly the most urgent ones seem to be how to deal with rhetoric as a consequential practice of power and how to re-understand theory. Other issues are entailed, too, such as serious concerns about the uses to which rhetoric is put. Perhaps, too, we should be concerned about our own positions as rhetoricians vis-à-vis our area of study—what our relationships are to the practices we study and the audiences implicated by those practices. Such work already has begun in particular quarters, another indication that it is possible to slip past the night man after all.[81]

Equally important, as we leave, we should bid a fond farewell to the structure and its inhabitants who have generously supported and nourished us for twenty-five years. The "new rhetoric" did represent a welcome retreat for a time for our predecessors who sought relief from the desert. It is possible that rhetoric might not have survived in Speech Communication without the shelter of the "new rhetoric," even with its attendant alibis. If we have been prisoners, we have been so principally "of our own device," at times, happy and increasingly learned residents because of the resources offered by the "new rhetoric." If we are to leave the comfort of our own version of the Hotel California, we should be equipped with two of the most important admonitions offered in *The Prospect of Rhetoric*. One came from Brockriede as a suggestion of what we might prepare ourselves for as we leave: "What was not understood was feared."[82] There already has been plenty of that recently, and there probably will be more. More important, though, was Bryant's reminder to the Pheasant Run participants, one that resonates just as clearly in the 1990s: "Change is opportunity for improvement, but no guarantee of it."[83]

Notes

1. Carole Blair, "'We Are All Just Prisoners Here of Our Own Device': Rhetoric in Speech Communication after Wingspread," in *Making and Unmaking the Prospects for Rhetoric: Selected*

Papers from the 1996 Rhetoric Society of America Conference, ed. Theresa Enos, Richard McNabb, Carolyn Miller, and Roxanne Mountford (Mahwah, N.J.: Lawrence Erlbaum, 1997), 29–36.

2. Don Felder, Don Henley, and Glenn Frey, "Hotel California," Cass County Music/Red Cloud Music, ASCAP, 1976; The Eagles, *Hotel California,* Elektra/Asylum/Nonsuch Records, 1976; reproduced in The Eagles, *Hell Freezes Over,* Geffen Records, 1994.

3. For the moment, it seems reasonable to suggest only that critical-historical work has sometimes been predicated in this sort of prevarication for the sake of maintaining the ruse of "distance" or "impartiality." This is a recurrent theme of the commentaries written by critics about their own work in William L. Nothstine, Carole Blair, and Gary Copeland, eds., *Critical Questions: Invention, Creativity, and the Criticism of Discourse and Media* (New York: St. Martin's Press, 1994). See also Carole Blair, Julie R. Brown, and Leslie A. Baxter, "Disciplining the Feminine," *Quarterly Journal of Speech* 80 (1994): 383–384.

4. Charles J. Stewart, "Historical Survey: Rhetorical Criticism in Twentieth Century America," in *Explorations in Rhetorical Criticism,* ed. G. P. Mohrmann, Charles J. Stewart, and Donovan J. Ochs (University Park: Pennsylvania State University Press, 1973), 10.

5. For citations for Leff and Procario's sources, see the Works Cited lists in these works: Barnett Baskerville, "Selected Writings on the Criticism of Public Address," *Western Speech* 21 (1957): 110–118; Robert D. Clark, "Lessons for the Literary Critics," *Western Speech* 21 (1957): 83–89; W. Charles Redding, "Extrinsic and Intrinsic Criticism," *Western Speech* 21 (1957): 96–102; and Marie Hochmuth, "Burkeian Criticism," *Western Speech* 21 (1957): 89–95.

6. Donald C. Bryant, "Opening Remarks to the Conference [Pheasant Run]," in *The Prospect of Rhetoric: Report of the National Developmental Project,* ed. Lloyd F. Bitzer and Edwin Black (Englewood Cliffs, N.J.: Prentice Hall, 1971), 190.

7. Wayne N. Thompson, "A Conservative View of a Progressive Rhetoric," *Quarterly Journal of Speech* 49 (1963): 3.

8. Daniel S. J. Fogarty, *Roots for a New Rhetoric* (New York: Teachers College Bureau of Publications, Columbia University, 1959); Marie Hochmuth, "Kenneth Burke and the 'New Rhetoric,'" *Quarterly Journal of Speech* 38 (1952): 133–144; Marie Hochmuth, "I. A. Richards and the 'New Rhetoric,'" *Quarterly Journal of Speech* 44 (1958): 1–16.

9. Thomas O. Sloan et al., "Report of the Committee on the Advancement and Refinement of Rhetorical Criticism," in *The Prospect of Rhetoric: Report of the National Development Project,* ed. Lloyd F. Bitzer and Edwin Black (Englewood Cliffs, N.J.: Prentice Hall, 1971), 225.

10. Sloan, "Report of the Committee on the Advancement and Refinement of Rhetorical Criticism," in *The Prospect of Rhetoric: Report of the National Development Project,* ed. Lloyd F. Bitzer and Edwin Black (Englewood Cliffs, N.J.: Prentice Hall, 1971), 226.

11. Sloan, "Report of the Committee on the Advancement and Refinement of Rhetorical Criticism," in *The Prospect of Rhetoric: Report of the National Development Project,* ed. Lloyd F. Bitzer and Edwin Black (Englewood Cliffs, N.J.: Prentice Hall, 1971), 220.

12. Douglas Ehninger et al., "Report of the Committee on the Scope of Rhetoric and the Place of Rhetorical Studies in Higher Education," in *The Prospect of Rhetoric: Report of the National Development Project,* ed. Lloyd F. Bitzer and Edwin Black (Englewood Cliffs, N.J.: Prentice Hall, 1971), 208.

13. Carroll C. Arnold, "Reflections on the Wingspread Conference," in *The Prospect of Rhetoric: Report of the National Development Project,* ed. Lloyd F. Bitzer and Edwin Black (Englewood Cliffs, N.J.: Prentice Hall, 1971), 194–199, and, in the same volume, Lloyd F. Bitzer, "More Reflections on the Wingspread Conference," 200–207.

14. Donald C. Bryant, "Rhetoric: Its Function and Its Scope," *Quarterly Journal of Speech* 39 (1953): 401–424; Douglas Ehninger, "Introduction," in *Contemporary Rhetoric: A Reader's Coursebook,* ed. Douglas Ehninger (Glenview, Ill.: Scott, Foresman, 1972), 3.

15. Richard L. Johannesen, "Editor's Introduction: Some Trends in Contemporary Rhetorical Theory," in *Contemporary Theories of Rhetoric: Selected Readings,* ed. Richard L. Johannesen (New York: Harper and Row, 1971), 1.

16. This definition has remained consistent through two subsequent editions of the text. See Bernard L. Brock and Robert L. Scott, eds., *Methods of Rhetorical Criticism: A Twentieth-Century Perspective,* 2nd ed. (Detroit, Mich.: Wayne State University Press, 1980); and Bernard L. Brock, Robert L. Scott, and James W. Chesebro, eds., *Methods of Rhetorical Criticism: A Twentieth-Century Perspective,* 3rd ed. (Detroit, Mich.: Wayne State University Press, 1989).

17. Sonja K. Foss, Karen A. Foss, and Robert Trapp, *Contemporary Perspectives on Rhetoric* (Prospect Heights, Ill.: Waveland, 1985), 11.

18. Gerard A. Hauser, *Introduction to Rhetorical Theory* (Prospect Heights, Ill.: Waveland, 1986), 2.

19. Martin J. Medhurst, and Thomas W. Benson, "Rhetorical Studies in a Media Age," in *Rhetorical Dimensions in Media: A Critical Casebook,* ed. Martin J. Medhurst and Thomas W. Benson (Dubuque, Iowa: Kendall/Hunt, 1984), xx.

20. Sonja K. Foss, *Rhetorical Criticism: Exploration and Practice* (Prospect Heights, Ill.: Waveland, 1989), 4.

21. One rare example is Hart's characterization of rhetoric as the "art of using language to help people narrow their choices among specifiable, if not specified, policy options." Roderick P. Hart, *Modern Rhetorical Criticism* (Glenview, Ill.: Scott, Foresman/Little, Brown, 1990), 4.

22. As one example of the atypical, Brockriede, writing in 1966, suggested that the study of rhetoric commits one to "explain how contemporary man interacts symbolically and purposively with other men." Wayne Brockriede, "Toward a Contemporary Aristotelian Theory of Rhetoric," *Quarterly Journal of Speech* 52 (1966): 34.

23. Marie Hochmuth, "The Criticism of Rhetoric," in *A History and Criticism of American Public Address,* vol. 3, ed. Marie Kathryn Hochmuth (New York: Russell and Russell, 1955), 8.

24. Marie Hochmuth Nichols, *Rhetoric and Criticism* (Baton Rouge: Louisiana State University Press, 1963), 7.

25. Hoyt Hudson, "The Field of Rhetoric," *Quarterly Journal of Speech* 9 (1923): 167–180, reprinted in *Historical Studies of Rhetoric and Rhetoricians,* ed. Raymond F. Howes (Ithaca, N.Y.: Cornell University Press, 1961), 5, 11.

26. Donald C. Bryant, *Rhetorical Dimensions in Criticism* (Baton Rouge: Louisiana State University Press, 1969), 18, 19.

27. Thanks to Jerry Murphy's kind offer, I was able to borrow the materials he had saved from his experience as a steering committee member for the National Developmental Project, which eventuated in Wingspread, Pheasant Run, and, finally, *The Prospect of Rhetoric.* I have not dealt with the unpublished materials extensively in this paper, because I do not want to stray too far afield from the material published as *The Prospect of Rhetoric.* Still, here, I feel compelled to note that the two conditions I have specified for discussion—the political activities of the 1960s and the rhetoric-communication tiff—are primary topics in almost all of the position papers submitted by would-be participants of Pheasant Run. In fact, it is a rare case in which both of the topics don't make an appearance and an even rarer event in which neither appears. Although I am convinced that there really were other conditions that may also have contributed to rhetoric's definitional transformation, those submitted position papers convince me that the two factors addressed here were the two most important ones. The papers also convince me that a careful historical reading of them and other primary documentation related to the National Developmental Project would be a worthy and worthwhile undertaking.

28. Leland M. Griffin, "The Rhetoric of Historical Movements," *Quarterly Journal of Speech* 38 (1952): 184–188.

29. Edwin Black and Lloyd F. Bitzer, "Foreword," in *The Prospect of Rhetoric: Report of the National Development Project,* ed. Lloyd F. Bitzer and Edwin Black (Englewood Cliffs, N.J.: Prentice Hall, 1971), vi.

30. Ehninger et al., "Report of the Committee on the Scope of Rhetoric and the Place of Rhetorical Studies in Higher Education," 209–211.

31. It should be noted here how difficult it may be to determine in retrospect whether a document was read as inflammatory at the time of its publication. To read Bowers's "Pre-scientific Function" essay that way, for example, would be to ignore some details of its reception. It seems remarkable to me, even now, that rhetoricians would cite and appropriate this essay with seeming approval, but they did so at Wingspread, continued to do so afterward, and probably still do. See John Waite Bowers, "The Pre-scientific Function of Rhetorical Criticism," in *Essays on Rhetorical Criticism,* ed. Thomas R. Nilsen (New York: Random House, 1968), 126–145, reprinted in Douglas Ehninger, ed., *Contemporary Rhetoric: A Reader's Coursebook* (Glenview, Ill.: Scott, Foresman, 1972), 163–173; Wayne Brockriede, "Trends in the Study of Rhetoric: Toward a Blending of Criticism and Science," in *The Prospect of Rhetoric: Report of the National Development Project,* ed. Lloyd F. Bitzer and Edwin Black (Englewood Cliffs, N.J.: Prentice Hall, 1971), 136; and Roderick P. Hart, "Theory-Building and Rhetorical Criticism: An Informal Statement of Opinion," *Central States Speech Journal* 27 (1976): 70. Similarly, Thompson's essay "A Conservative View," although it generated not altogether agreeable responses, was reprinted in the two most prominent anthologies on contemporary rhetorical theory of the 1970s—Ehninger's *Contemporary Rhetoric* and Richard L. Johannesen, ed., *Contemporary Theories of Rhetoric: Selected Readings* (New York: Harper and Row, 1971). In most respects, I believe these facts of surprisingly positive reception tell us less about rhetoricians' unwillingness to wage disciplinary turf war in public than they do about rhetoricians' own general views, shared widely in U.S. culture, that science was the wave of the intellectual future. There is some reason to believe that the scientization of rhetorical criticism (and, I think, rhetoric more broadly) was undertaken willingly by rhetoricians at the time, not by coercion or force on the part of their communication colleagues. See, for example, William L. Nothstine, Carole Blair, and Gary A. Copeland, "Professionalization and the Eclipse of Critical Invention," in *Critical Questions: Invention, Creativity, and the Criticism of Discourse and Media,* ed. William L. Nothstine, Carole Blair, and Gary Copeland (New York: St. Martin's Press, 1994), 15–70. For other sources useful in reconstructing some of this historical dispute, see Thomas W. Benson, "History, Criticism, and Theory in the Study of American Rhetoric," in *American Rhetoric: Context and Criticism,* ed. Thomas W. Benson (Carbondale: Southern Illinois University Press, 1989), 1–17; Herman Cohen, "The Development of Research in Speech Communication: A Historical Perspective," in *Speech Communication in the 20th Century,* ed. Thomas W. Benson (Carbondale: Southern Illinois University Press, 1985), 282–298; Herman Cohen, *The History of Speech Communication: The Emergence of a Discipline, 1914–1945* (Annandale, Va.: Speech Communication Association, 1994); Jesse G. Delia, "Communication Research: A History," in *Handbook of Communication Science,* ed. Charles R. Berger and Steven H. Chaffee (Newbury Park, Calif.: Sage, 1987), 20–98; and W. Barnett Pearce, "Scientific Research Methods in Communication Studies and Their Implications for Theory and Research," in *Speech Communication: Essays to Commemorate the 75th Anniversary of the Speech Communication Association,* ed. Gerald M. Phillips and Julia T. Wood (Carbondale: Southern Illinois University Press, 1990), 255–281.

32. Nothstine, Blair, and Copeland, "Professionalization and the Eclipse of Critical Invention," 46–47.

33. Robert J. Kibler and Larry L. Barker, "Recommendations Formally Adopted by the Conference," in *Conceptual Frontiers in Speech Communication: Report of the New Orleans*

Conference on Research and Instructional Development, ed. Robert J. Kibler and Larry L. Barker (New York: Speech Association of America, 1969), 18.

34. Douglas Ehninger and Gerard A. Hauser, "Communication of Values," in *Handbook of Rhetorical and Communication Theory,* ed. Carroll C. Arnold and John Waite Bowers (Boston: Allyn and Bacon, 1984), 723.

35. Claude E. Shannon and Warren Weaver, *The Mathematical Theory of Communication* (Urbana: University of Illinois Press, 1949).

36. For a concise review of the proliferation of communication models, see Carroll C. Arnold and Kenneth D. Frandsen, "Conceptions of Rhetoric and Communication," in *Handbook of Rhetorical and Communication Theory,* ed. Carroll C. Arnold and John Waite Bowers (Boston: Allyn and Bacon), 6–9.

37. In fact, some have taken great pains to maintain the equation of communication (with rhetoric understood either as a type of communication or as a synonym, however archaic, for communication) with symbolic content. For example, Gary Cronkhite wrote in 1986: "My thesis is that there is a discipline whose *focus* is directly upon human symbolic activity, whose *scope* in practice includes little if anything that is not related to such activity, and whose *coherence* can be achieved by recognition of the study of human symbolic activity as its defining characteristic. Surely it will come as no surprise to readers of this journal that the discipline to which I refer is that generally represented by the rubrics 'speech,' 'communication,' 'rhetoric,' or some combination of these terms" (232). No, it didn't come as a surprise. In fact, one could only wonder why Cronkhite would see any need to write an essay defending this claim in 1986. But, as the second half of his essay makes rather clear, he saw the discipline's unity on this issue "threatened on many fronts" (237). He names four conflicts among communication scholars, any of which might harbor the potential for understanding rhetoric (or communication) as not exclusively symbolic in character: "rhetorical versus communication studies," "constructivism versus logical empiricism," "relational/pragmatic approach versus cognitivism,"and "rules versus laws." The perception that unity of purpose and of guiding concept is necessary for the health and well-being of a discipline certainly undergirds Cronkhite's plea, but it reads very much like the pleading of a lost cause. See Gary Cronkhite, "On the Focus, Scope, and Coherence of the Study of Human Symbolic Activity," *Quarterly Journal of Speech* 72 (1986): 231–246.

38. Nothstine, Blair, and Copeland, "Professionalization and the Eclipse of Critical Invention," 24–25, 40–41.

39. Thomas O. Sloan et al., "Report of the Committee on the Advancement and Refinement of Rhetorical Criticism," in *The Prospect of Rhetoric: Report of the National Development Project,* ed. Lloyd F. Bitzer and Edwin Black (Englewood Cliffs, N.J.: Prentice Hall, 1971), 222.

40. James R. Andrews, *The Practice of Rhetorical Criticism,* 2nd ed. (New York: Longman, 1990), xi, 12.

41. Lester Thonssen and A. Craig Baird, *Speech Criticism: The Development of Standards for Rhetorical Appraisal* (New York: Ronald Press, 1948), 21.

42. Thonssen and Baird, *Speech Criticism,* 21.

43. Foss, *Rhetorical Criticism,* xi, emphasis added.

44. Most units had been designated simply as Departments of Speech until around this time.

45. Hochmuth, "I. A. Richards and the 'New Rhetoric,'" 9.

46. Kenneth Burke, *A Grammar of Motives* (Berkeley: University of California Press, 1969); and Carole Blair, "Symbolic Action and Discourse: The Convergent/Divergent Views of Kenneth Burke and Michel Foucault," in *Kenneth Burke and Contemporary European Thought: Rhetoric in Transition,* ed. Bernard L. Brock (Tuscaloosa: University of Alabama Press, 1995), 133.

47. There were some attempts to combat this tendency, among them Benson's differentiation between rhetoric and semiotics—a laudable distinction, but one that hardly ever played out in practice. He suggested that "A rhetorician attends to symbolic *actions,* a structuralist to symbolic *forms.*" See Thomas W. Benson, "The Senses of Rhetoric: A Topical System for Critics," *Central States Speech Journal* 29 (1978): 242n.

48. Otis Walter, "On Views of Rhetoric, Whether Conservative or Progressive," *Quarterly Journal of Speech* 49 (1963): 367–382. There were other, earlier signs, as well, including the influential essays by Natanson and Eubanks and Baker. See Maurice Natanson, "The Limits of Rhetoric," *Quarterly Journal of Speech* 41 (1955): 133–139; and Ralph T. Eubanks and Virgil L. Baker, "Toward an Axiology of Rhetoric," *Quarterly Journal of Speech* 48 (1962): 157–168.

49. Robert L. Scott, "On Viewing Rhetoric as Epistemic," *Central States Speech Journal* 18 (1967): 9–17.

50. Richard A. Cherwitz and James W. Hikins, *Communication and Knowledge: Investigations in Rhetorical Epistemology* (Columbia: University of South Carolina Press, 1986), 62.

51. Thompson, "A Conservative View of a Progressive Rhetoric," 6.

52. As Cohen suggests of the early years in Speech, "The profession viewed the teaching of speech as a means of providing students with the tools of democracy." See Cohen, *The History of Speech Communication,* xi.

53. Blair, "Symbolic Action and Discourse," 152.

54. Nothstine, Blair, and Copeland, "Professionalization and the Eclipse of Critical Invention," 43.

55. This tendency, to subsume the "details" and specificities of rhetorical practices to theoretical generalization is quite evident in *The Prospect of Rhetoric.* See, for example, Samuel L. Becker, "Rhetorical Studies for the Contemporary World," in *The Prospect of Rhetoric: Report of the National Development Project,* ed. Lloyd F. Bitzer and Edwin Black (Englewood Cliffs, N.J.: Prentice Hall, 1971), 41, and, in the same volume, Brockriede, "Trends in the Study of Rhetoric," 128.

56. Thomas B. Farrell, "On the Disappearance of the Rhetorical Aura," *Western Journal of Communication* 57 (1993): 147.

57. I was reminded of that recently, as I discussed this paper with a former student and valued colleague, Greg Dickinson (personal correspondence, April 8, 1996), who had recently earned his doctorate. He suggested to me a "generation gap," in that the positions of the Wingspread participants, what was at stake for them, and so forth were not very clear to him or probably to others who had completed graduate work in recent years. Greg thought I actually knew a lot, which seemed to me to be both hilarious and scary. To the extent that we allow documents like *The Prospect of Rhetoric* to slip out of print and to the degree that we do not avail ourselves or our students of the opportunities to understand this component of our relatively recent history, we do ourselves and them a disservice.

58. It seems worth our attention that Bryant, in the same discussion, opposed the shift of rhetoric to encompass symbolicity at large. See Bryant, *Rhetorical Dimensions in Criticism,* 27.

59. Bryant was not alone. Simons attempted a differentiation between the approaches offered by communication theory in the 1960s and what was distinctively rhetorical: "Not all present day concern with the communication process is new or necessarily rhetorical. . . . Rhetoric is intrinsically normative; it utilizes observational research, not simply in order to describe what is, but as a basis for claims about what should have been or ought to be. . . . By the above standards, telecommunication theory, cybernetics and descriptive theory, although new, are not rhetorical in that they neither focus on attempts at discursive influence nor contribute directly to normative judgment." See Herbert W. Simons, "Toward a New Rhetoric," *Pennsylvania Speech Annual* 24 (1967): 7–20, reprinted in Johannesen, *Contemporary Theories of Rhetoric,* 50–62.

60. Herbert A. Wichelns, "The Literary Criticism of Oratory," in *Studies in Rhetoric and Public Speaking in Honor of James Albert Winans,* ed. Alexander Magnus Drummond (New York: Century, 1925), reprinted in *Methods of Rhetorical Criticism: A Twentieth-Century Perspective,* 2nd ed., ed. Bernard L. Brock and Robert L. Scott (Detroit, Mich.: Wayne State University Press, 1980), 54.

61. J. Michael Sproule, "The New Managerial Rhetoric and the Old Criticism," *Quarterly Journal of Speech* 74 (1988): 476.

62. Quoted in Martin J. Medhurst, "The Academic Study of Public Address: A Tradition in Transition," in *Landmark Essays on American Public Address,* ed. Martin J. Medhurst (Davis, Calif.: Hermagoras, 1993), xxix.

63. There were those at Wingspread who suggested that the rejection of all things traditional, including the assessment of effect, was hasty. See Barnett Baskerville, "Responses, Queries, and a Few Caveats," in *The Prospect of Rhetoric: Report of the National Development Project,* ed. Lloyd F. Bitzer and Edwin Black (Englewood Cliffs, N.J.: Prentice Hall, 1971), 159, 164, and, in the same volume, Bryant, "Opening Remarks to the Conference [Pheasant Run]," 190.

64. Richard A. Cherwitz and John Theobald-Osborne, "Contemporary Developments in Rhetorical Criticism: A Consideration of the Effects of Rhetoric," in *Speech Communication: Essays to Commemorate the 75th Anniversary of the Speech Communication Association,* ed. Gerald M. Phillips and Julia T. Wood (Carbondale: Southern Illinois University Press, 1990), 72–73n.

65. Cherwitz and Theobald-Osborne, "Contemporary Developments in Rhetorical Criticism," 58.

66. Aune puts the case and its consequences clearly in his characterization of a group of readings of Lincoln's Second Inaugural: "Paradoxically, neither the Lincoln critics nor the other authors (with the possible exception of Hogan) provide much evidence about the way in which audiences had their perceptions of reality shaped by the documents in question. Nor do they demonstrate why rhetoric—as opposed to other, more 'material' factors such as class interest—is a useful means of historical explanation. Moreover, they neglect interpretation. The traditional distinction between the sciences as providing 'explanation-theory' (*Erklären*) and the humanities as providing 'interpretation-theory' (*Verstehen*) seems to disappear, and as a result public address studies come to occupy an uneasy middle-ground between Explanation and Interpretation." See James Arnt Aune, "Public Address and Rhetorical Theory," in *Texts in Context: Critical Dialogues on Significant Episodes in American Political Rhetoric,* ed. Michael C. Leff and Fred J. Kauffeld (Davis, Calif.: Hermagoras Press, 1989), 47–48.

67. Douglas Ehninger et al., "Report of the Committee on the Scope of Rhetoric and the Place of Rhetorical Studies in Higher Education," 212.

68. Karl R. Wallace, *Understanding Discourse: The Speech Act and Rhetorical Action* (Baton Rouge: Louisiana State University Press, 1970), 20.

69. It is worth noting that Wallace's book, which explored the possibility of incorporating the notion of a "speech act" within rhetoric as its principal "unit of analysis," seemed to disappear rather quickly. It was cited infrequently, rarely showed up on reading lists for graduate courses, and so on. In fact, one might wonder if it was "disappeared" by those interested in maintaining the symbol as the principal "unit of analysis" of rhetoric and Speech Communication. Of course, that speculation seems overly conspiratorial in tone, but it *is* remarkable that almost any book by a rhetorician would so quickly vanish from public view, given that there were so few books of any kind on rhetoric published in the early 1970s. And it is the more remarkable when we consider the reputation of its author, Karl Wallace. Regardless, it is fair to say that this early attempt to displace symbolicity as the exclusive model of rhetorical activity had little impact.

70. Edwin Black, "The Mutability of Rhetoric," in *Rhetoric in Transition: Studies in the Nature and Uses of Rhetoric,* ed. Eugene E. White (University Park: Pennsylvania State University Press, 1980), 82–83, 72.

71. Roderick P. Hart, "The Functions of Human Communication in the Maintenance of Public Values," in *Handbook of Rhetorical and Communication Theory,* ed. Carroll C. Arnold and John Waite Bowers (Boston: Allyn and Bacon, 1984), 779.

72. Michael C. Leff and Margaret Organ Procario, "Rhetorical Theory in Speech Communication," in *Speech Communication in the 20th Century,* ed. Thomas W. Benson (Carbondale: Southern Illinois University Press, 1985), 25; Michael Calvin McGee, "The 'Ideograph': A Link between Rhetoric and Ideology," *Quarterly Journal of Speech* 66 (1980): 1–16

73. Farrell, "On the Disappearance of the Rhetorical Aura," 148, 152. I disagree with Farrell's assessment of the problem as "text." He is correct, I believe, in his view that "text" as a term might imply an inert product. His complaint seems to overlook the numerous theorizations of "text" over the past twenty or so years; they hardly can change the everyday sense of the term, but they do address the problem of considering it strictly as a completed product.

74. John Waite Bowers, "On the Pragmeme," Presidential Address, Speech Communication Association Convention, November 2, 1984, reprinted in *Spectra* 21 (January 1985): 2.

75. Bowers, "On the Pragmeme," 3. Also see John Waite Bowers and James J. Bradac, "Contemporary Problems in Human Communication Theory," in *Handbook of Rhetorical and Communication Theory,* ed. Carroll C. Arnold and John Waite Bowers (Boston: Allyn and Bacon, 1984), 871–893.

76. Michel Foucault, *The Archaeology of Knowledge and the Discourse on Language,* transl. A. M. Sheridan Smith (New York: Pantheon, 1972), 216.

77. McGee's suggestion that we are unable safely to ignore rhetoric because of its materiality is instructive here. See Michael Calvin McGee, "A Materialist's Conception of Rhetoric," in *Explorations in Rhetoric: Studies in Honor of Douglas Ehninger,* ed. Ray E. McKerrow (Glenview, Ill.: Scott, Foresman, 1982), 29–31.

78. There are some who might argue that cultural studies deals with a set of issues different from those that have concerned rhetoricians. Judging by the extent to which rhetoricians have allowed their fetishizing of theory and their self-definitions as students of the symbolic to foul their ability to deal with the material power of rhetorical practice, they might be technically correct. However, as I have tried to show throughout, the directions that post-Wingspread rhetoric have taken were not the only possible directions; they represented choices. And, in fact, it is striking, having read the position papers written by those who applied to participate in the Pheasant Run conference, how very much the questions of cultural studies resemble some of those raised by the Pheasant Run applicants. For example, Ehninger suggested that it was incumbent upon rhetoricians to deal not only with the techniques of "cajoling or persuading those who are like us in background and values" but also to learn to "speak across class, race, age, and culture lines to those who are in some way 'different.'" Douglas Ehninger, Unpublished, Untitled Position Paper, compiled with others as "Statements by Conference Participants," Pheasant Run Conference, May 10–15, 1970, 4. Arthur L. Smith posed as the most important task for Pheasant Run to address the question of whether rhetoric is a uniquely Western phenomenon. Arthur L. Smith, Unpublished, Untitled Position Paper, compiled with others as "Statements by Conference Participants," Pheasant Run Conference, May 10–15, 1970, 24. Although issues of "the other" are not the only ones cultural studies pose, they are certainly among the most prominent. And they have to do, of course, with power and with what rhetoric (or communication, as they might prefer) *does.*

79. See Elizabeth Walker Mechling and Jay Mechling, "Commentary: The Campaign for Civil Defense," 120; Thomas S. Frentz and Janice Hocker Rushing, "Commentary: The

Frankenstein Myth in Contemporary Cinema," 157–158; Bonnie J. Dow, "Commentary: Feminist Criticism and The Mary Tyler Moore Show," 100; and Thomas W. Benson, "Commentary: Rhetorical Structure and Primate," 186, all in *Critical Questions: Invention, Creativity, and the Criticism of Discourse and Media,* ed. William L. Nothstine, Carole Blair, and Gary Copeland (New York: St. Martin's Press, 1994).

80. See Barry Brummett, "Rhetorical Theory as Heuristic and Moral: A Pedagogical Justification," *Communication Education* 33 (1984): 97–107; Brian C. Taylor "Commentary: Reminiscences of Los Alamos," in *Critical Questions: Invention, Creativity, and the Criticism of Discourse and Media,* ed. William L. Nothstine, Carole Blair, and Gary Copeland (New York: St. Martin's Press, 1994), 418–419; and, in the same volume, Mechling and Mechling, "Commentary," 120, and Benson, "Commentary," 186.

81. Not surprisingly, there is little agreement as yet about what a post–"new rhetoric" should be, and perhaps there need be no such agreement. Generally speaking, however, there are two very general "camps." One values the return to and reformation of public address studies, in the narrow sense of formalist or structuralist readings of public, persuasive speeches. The other values readings of situated rhetorical practices and has as its patrons poststructuralism, American and British cultural studies, race theory, feminist studies, and so forth. The two camps do not agree on very many specific issues, for example on the nature of audience, symbolicity, or political effectivity of rhetoric. However, it is interesting to note that both tend to place traditional notions of theory in a subordinate position to engagements with rhetorical practices. The former group is represented by works like the following: Stephen H. Browne, "Edmund Burke's Letter for a Noble Lord: A Textual Study in Political Philosophy and Rhetorical Action," *Communication Monographs* 55 (1988): 215–29; Stephen H. Browne, "Generic Transformation and Political Action: A Textual Interpretation of Edmund Burke's Letter to William Elliott. Esq.," *Communication Quarterly* 38 (1990): 54–63; Stephen H. Browne, "Encountering Angelina Grimké: Violence, Identity, and the Creation of Radical Community," *Quarterly Journal of Speech* 82 (1996): 55–73; Robert S. Iltis and Stephen H. Browne, "Tradition and Resurgence in Public Address Studies," in *Speech Communication: Essays to Commemorate the 75th Anniversary of the Speech Communication Association,* ed. Gerald M. Phillips and Julia T. Wood (Carbondale: Southern Illinois University Press, 1990), 81–93; Michael Leff, "Textual Criticism: The Legacy of G. P. Mohrmann," *Quarterly Journal of Speech* 72 (1986): 377–389; Michael Leff, "Things Made by Words: Reflections on Textual Criticism," *Quarterly Journal of Speech* 78 (1992): 223–231; Michael Leff and Andrew Sachs, "Words the Most Like Things: Iconicity and the Rhetorical Text," *Western Journal of Speech Communication* 54 (1990): 252–273; Michael C. Leff and Fred J. Kauffeld, *Texts in Context: Critical Dialogues on Significant Episodes in American Political Rhetoric* (Davis, Calif.: Hermagoras Press, 1989); and Stephen E. Lucas, "The Renaissance of American Public Address: Text and Context in Rhetorical Criticism [review essay]," *Quarterly Journal of Speech* 74 (1988): 241–60. The latter is represented by works like the following: Barbara A. Biesecker, "Towards a Transactional View of Rhetorical and Feminist Theory: Rereading Hélène Cixous's The Laugh of the Medusa," *Southern Communication Journal* 57 (1992): 86–96; Carole Blair, Marsha S. Jeppeson, and Enrico Pucci Jr., "Public Memorializing in Postmodernity: The Vietnam Veterans Memorial as Prototype," *Quarterly Journal of Speech* 77 (1991): 263–288; Celeste M. Condit, "Hegemony in a Mass-Mediated Society: Concordance about Reproductive Technologies," *Critical Studies in Mass Communication* 11 (1994): 205–230; Dwight Conquergood, "Rethinking Ethnography: Towards a Critical Cultural Politics," *Communication Monographs* 58 (1991): 179–194; Greg Dickinson, "Landscapes of Memory, Landscapes of Consumption: The Rhetoric of Twentieth-Century Urban Consumption," Ph.D. dissertation, University of Southern California, 1995; Raymie E. McKerrow, "Critical Rhetoric: Theory and Praxis," *Communication*

Monographs 56 (1989): 91–111; Elizabeth Mechling and Jay Mechling, "The Atom According to Disney," *Quarterly Journal of Speech* 81 (1995): 436–453; Thomas K. Nakayama and Robert L. Krizek, "Whiteness: A Strategic Rhetoric," *Quarterly Journal of Speech* 81 (1995): 295–309; Kent A. Ono and John M. Sloop, "The Critique of Vernacular Discourse," *Communication Monographs* 62 (1995): 19–46; Laura Sells, "'Where Do the Mermaids Stand?' Voice and Body in The Little Mermaid," in *From Mouse to Mermaid: The Politics of Film, Gender, and Culture,* ed. Elizabeth Bell, Lynda Haas, and Laura Sells (Bloomington: Indiana University Press, 1995), 175–192; Raka Shome, "Postcolonial Interventions in the Rhetorical Canon: An 'Other' View," *Communication Theory* 6 (1996): 40–59; Martha Solomon, "The Things We Study: Texts and Their Interactions," *Communication Monographs* 60 (1993): 62–68; Bryan C. Taylor, "*Fat Man and Little Boy:* The Cinematic Representation of Interests in the Nuclear Weapons Organization," *Critical Studies in Mass Communication* 10 (1993): 367–394; and Douglas Thomas, "Burke, Nietzsche, Lacan: Three Perspectives on the Rhetoric of Order," *Quarterly Journal of Speech* 79 (1993): 336–355, as well as the vital, formative work by Mike McGee.

82. Brockriede, "Trends in the Study of Rhetoric," 128.

83. Bryant, "Opening Remarks to the Conference [Pheasant Run]," 190.

Purpose, Evidence, and Pedagogy in Rhetorical Criticism

ROBERT C. ROWLAND

From the founding of rhetoric as discipline in the classical era through most of the twentieth century, the dominant purpose of critical analysis and rhetorical history of all kinds was to explain how a given work or series of works functioned or failed to function for a situated audience. The study of rhetoric was recognized as important precisely because of the power of words and other symbols to move people to action. Rhetorical theory was justified with a similar rationale, and for that reason scholars tried to develop theories that explained how and why rhetoric functioned to influence audiences and also why it often failed to do so. In that way, rhetorical agency was in a sense shared by the rhetor and the audience. It was the speaker or writer who initiated the rhetorical exchange, but ultimately it was the audience that determined whether the rhetoric achieved its purpose, whether producing action, reflection, or some other result. Ethical and ideological theories were justified on the principle that rhetoric had great power to move people to achieve great ends but also could unleash the furies. It was the potential for good or ill that made ethical and ideological analysis essential.

Until quite recently, almost all rhetorical criticism, public address, studies of movements, campaigns, and genres, as well as more theoretical works, fit within the purpose of explaining how or why rhetoric worked (or failed) to work for an audience. The role of audience in shaping criticism is quite evident, for example, in Stephen Lucas's discussion of the controversy between advocates of rhetorical history and supporters of rhetorical criticism. In the conclusion of his essay, Lucas noted an important point of commonality between the approaches, observing that "Critics and historians alike typically work with at least some conception of audience in mind." In the last paragraph of his essay, Lucas added that "Rhetorical historians, like rhetorical critics, are concerned above all with what messages do rather than what they are, and the central office of each is to explicate how rhetorical communication works."[1] Clearly, Lucas assumed that students of rhetoric were concerned with audience-based interpretation, an assumption that reflected the general practice of the field.

It is important, however, not to reduce a concern with how rhetoric "works" to a simplistic focus on short-term effect as measured in applause, public opinion polls, or some other means. Only rarely does a single speech or essay or other rhetorical act produce immediate changes in public opinion. More often, a series of speeches and other rhetoric produces gradual changes in how an audience or set of audiences views a question, and this redefinition of the world in turn produces over time significant changes in public opinion.[2]

The larger point is that, as Lucas observed, the core purpose fulfilled by most rhetorical analysis from the classical age until quite recently was to in some way explain how and why a given work resonated or failed to resonate with an audience. Even when the focus was not on how the message was adapted to a specific audience, such as in some very close textual criticism, the underlying analysis was still tied to audience in the sense that the critic used theories that were audience based to explain the stylistic patterns found in the text. The work of Michael Leff provides the best illustration of this approach.[3] Leff was concerned with textual analysis not for its own sake but to explicate textual patterns as an "invitation to meaning" with an audience, including an understanding of how the text was received by its audience.[4]

In contemporary criticism, the critical consensus about the importance of audience-based interpretation has collapsed, and many critics no longer focus on explaining how a work functioned for a situated audience.[5] This shift began with attacks on neo-Aristotelian criticism, one part of which was a rejection of a focus on short-term effectiveness as simplistic.[6] Reporting about audience reaction, applause produced, and so on was viewed correctly as both uninteresting and not very revealing. In recent years, the critique of audience-based critical analysis has been heavily influenced by poststructuralist theory and criticism on one hand and by a social science critique of the power of rhetoric on the other.

The focus of contemporary criticism that has been heavily influenced by poststructuralist theories of symbolicity is on teasing out of a given text an understanding of complex linguistic patterns in the text. Whether the particular approach has been inspired by Freud or Foucault, Derrida or Lacan, or other theorists, the focus is often on textuality largely independent of the actual audiences that read, heard, or watched the rhetoric. In contrast, social scientists, notably George Edwards, have critiqued rhetorical studies for failing to provide adequate evidence proving cause and effect in making claims of audience impact.[7] As a consequence, apart from some of those scholars who are participating in the renaissance in public address, a focus on audience and influence is out of fashion.[8] In fact, this approach is sometimes labeled as mere sterile reporting of "what people already know."[9] Even within public address, some criticism is focused on very close textual analysis of linguistic patterns without any clear indication that any particular audience was aware of these patterns. In fact, some critics reject focusing on "any particular meaning,"[10] arguing that a focus on audience-based meaning stifles the critical enterprise.

A few critics clearly have recognized the shift away from audience-based analysis and made it clear that their criticism is not focused on audience. For example, Robert Terrill, in his analysis of Barack Obama's so-called race speech, delivered in March 2008, during his campaign for the presidency, made this point quite clear when he said, "Rather than an attempt to explain its appeal, the concern here is the specific contribution that this speech makes to contemporary public discourse, the ways of speaking that Obama enacts and that he urges his auditors to emulate."[11] Terrill placed agency entirely in Obama's hands, focusing on the patterns that "he urges his auditors to emulate" but ignoring the question of whether those patterns actually might produce such emulation. One difficulty is that while in many cases the focus of the analysis is on textuality, the critique is still justified as a way of explaining the influence, or resonance, or impact of the rhetoric. Even Terrill, a very careful critic, later characterized aspects of the speech as "particularly potent" and "especially powerful" (380, 381), comments that indicate how literally centuries of focusing on audience impact have shaped thinking in the field, creating in essence a terministic compulsion to discuss resonance even when that is not really the focus of the analysis. Of course, many critics are not as careful as Terrill in specifying their purpose.

It is widely known that purpose plays a crucial role in shaping the way that humans talk. Many scholars have made that point over the centuries.[12] At the very dawn of the study of rhetoric, Aristotle's distinction among deliberative, epideictic, and forensic was based in the purpose that works fulfilled for an audience.[13] In my own research, I've noted that purpose has great influence in shaping how arguers confront epistemic problems.[14] Precisely the same point applies to rhetorical criticism.

In the remainder of this essay, I weave back forth among three closely related arguments: works of rhetorical analysis that make claims about resonance, or influence, or potency, or some other synonym for effect need evidence appropriate to such claims of influence; works of rhetorical analysis focused on a purpose other than explaining audience resonance or ethical/ideological critique on the basis of the potential resonance of a text should include a justification of that critical purpose; and the forms of evidence used to support any critical analysis should be appropriate for the purpose of the critical analysis. My conclusions are that critical purpose should shape the process and product of criticism, explaining the resonance or lack of resonance of works of rhetoric remains an important critical purpose, and it is important to cite evidence appropriate for fulfilling a given critical purpose.

Influence and Agency in Rhetorical Analysis

A thought experiment is helpful in explaining why it is important to focus on potential or actual audience influence when analyzing rhetoric. Why has there been so much analysis of the rhetoric of Abraham Lincoln, Franklin Delano Roosevelt, and Ronald Reagan? Why is there so much contemporary focus on the rhetoric of Barack Obama? Why has there been so little focus on the rhetoric of Millard Fillmore or, in the contemporary era, of Fred Thompson? The obvious answer is that Lincoln, Roosevelt, Reagan, and now Obama used words to great effect to move the nation. Fillmore did not, and Thompson's rhetoric was so ineffective that after exciting a few pundits he quickly withdrew from the 2008 Republican primary campaign. Rhetoric is an important field of study in large part because of its role in shaping human society. And the fact that rhetoric often has vast influence, as in the case of Reagan or Lincoln, makes it also important to consider case analyses of rhetorical failure, particularly when that failure was unexpected or reveals something about the limits of rhetoric in producing short- or long-term influence.

One possible objection to this view would be to argue, as has George Edwards, that words in fact rarely move audiences to any great extent. Initially, it is important to note that a strong consensus among scholars from multiple fields concludes that rhetoric sometimes makes a very great difference. Is it possible to dispute that Lincoln, Franklin Roosevelt, Reagan, and Obama, along with many others, rose to prominence in large part because of their rhetorical skill? It is more than an odd coincidence that so many of the presidents remembered as great or near great, presidents remembered for changing American politics, are also presidents remembered for their rhetorical skill. It also seems impossible to dispute that rhetoric sometimes makes a very great difference in the political campaigns that choose our elected leaders and shape the political environment in which they operate. The primary problem with Edwards's argument, as David Zarefsky has demonstrated,[15] is that Edwards defines impact too narrowly. It is certainly true that a single speech rarely changes audience opinion, although there are obvious exceptions to that rule, such as Obama's 2004 Democratic National Convention speech and his response to the Jeremiah Wright controversy, "A More Perfect Union," the impact of which have been well documented, as I note later. But the fact that a single speech rarely shifts opinion in no way denies the power of rhetoric over time to shape audience opinion on individual issues or, as Zarefsky notes, how an audience defines the world itself. Is it really possible to deny that Reagan used words to create what Sean Wilentz has labeled the Age of Reagan? Wilentz argues on this point that "Above all, Reagan and his supporters, unlike the battered Democrats and the disgraced Republican establishment, gave the voters a compelling way to comprehend the disorientating and often dispiriting trends of the 1970s."[16] Here, Wilentz comments on Reagan's enormous skill in presenting a conservative definition of the world in his rhetoric. As an aside, if Reagan's rhetoric actually had little influence, it is certainly odd that conservatives continue to revere or in some cases almost deify him, while the less rhetorically skillful conservatives of the 1970s and 1980s are long forgotten.

The real impact of Edwards's critique is not to deny that rhetoric sometimes makes a difference but to point out that rhetorical impact depends upon a host of factors and that changing entrenched audience attitudes can be very difficult, especially in the short term, conclusions familiar to any traditional rhetorical scholar. One reason that short-term effect is often difficult to prove is that rhetorical agency is shared between the audience and speaker, and both are heavily influenced by the particulars of the situation in which the rhetoric was presented. On the other hand, in combination with other factors, rhetoric often plays a key role in shifting public opinion. Careful analysis of social scientific data of the kind favored by Edwards backs up this conclusion. For example, a social scientific analysis of "conditions governing the success" of presidential rhetoric by Brandon Rottinghaus found that "presidents can succeed at leading public opinion" in certain circumstances.[17] And Edwards himself admitted that "presidents are facilitators who reflect, and may intensify, widely held views. In the process, they may endow the views of their supporters with structure and purpose and exploit opportunities in their environments to accomplish joint goals." He went on to add that "Ronald Reagan did this brilliantly in 1981."[18] When Edwards labeled presidents as "facilitators who reflect, and may intensify" audience views, he was saying something quite close to the point made by Zarefsky that skillful presidents define the political and policy word for their supporters and others. And when he said that they may "exploit opportunities," he made precisely the point, recognized by rhetorical scholars since Aristotle, that rhetoric must adapt to the audience and context in which it is presented. The skepticism that Edwards expressed about the impact of rhetoric should be read primarily as a reminder of the importance of focusing on how presidents and other leaders shape public opinion over the long term in relation to an audience or multiple audiences and also of the importance of understanding any given rhetorical artifact within the context of the time, audience, and culture in which it occurred.

A very different objection would be to critique a focus on effects by noting that sometimes rhetorical analysis is important precisely because the rhetoric failed. Edwin Black made this point in his widely cited commentary about the failure of the Coatesville Address.[19] And yet, while Black is credited for pointing out the sterility of a neo-Aristotelian focus on audience applause and other markers of short-term effect, his critique was itself effect based. Black's point about the Coatesville Address was that the underlying message and form of the address had great long-term power. The influence of a rhetoric of racial reconciliation similar to the message in the Coatesville Address across the second half of the twentieth century and the first two decades of the twenty-first is obvious. As Black observed, "It is through the speech that we know the moral crisis, and by the speech that we are persuaded of it." Black's critique was powerful because it explicated both the short-term failure and the long-term power of the address, not because it undercut the idea that critical analysis should be tied to audience.[20]

The Importance of Resonance in Rhetorical Analysis

Rhetoric is important because it both moves and sometimes fails to move audiences. For example, in the 2010 midterm election campaign, President Obama campaigned across the nation both to support his program and to maintain the

Democratic majority in the House of Representative. A study of his rhetoric in that campaign would be quite important, because, unlike what happened in his two successful campaigns for president, in 2010 his rhetoric did not succeed in achieving his core objective. Thus, instances of rhetorical success and failure both support the value of audience-based critical analysis.

Critics sometimes create theoretical markers, such as Edwin Black's discussion of the "The Second Persona," as a stand-in for analysis of a particular audience.[21] Such approaches are valuable to the extent that they accurately reflect (or reveal) how or why an actual audience reacted to (or failed to react to) a symbolic act, as Black did brilliantly in his essay. The larger point is that the purpose of explicating the resonance of rhetoric is important precisely because that resonance sometimes produces great or terrible results and also because failures of resonance also often have vast consequences.

Discovering the reasons behind the success or failure of a particular work or set of works of that rhetoric has always been at the core of the discipline. It is for that reason that critics focus so heavily on Lincoln, Roosevelt, Reagan, and Obama and also sometimes the reason that they focus on rhetoric that in the short term failed utterly, as in the case of the Coatesville Address. At the same time, while explaining resonance or lack of resonance for a situated audience is obviously important, rhetorical analysis serves other functions as well. The thought experiment suggests that rhetorical criticism serves four primary functions:

1. Explaining why a particular work or group of related works impacted or failed to impact an audience or group of audiences;
2. Analyzing rhetoric to reveal a symbolic pattern present in the larger society or in other discourse, as when ideological critics trace symbolic patterns in order to show the influence or resonance of those patterns on society or when a biographer or historian uses rhetorical analysis to make judgments related to intellectual history;
3. Ideological or ethical commentary on works of rhetoric that either help build a democratic society or threaten the structure of that society;
4. Critical analysis of underlying symbolic patterns unrelated to audience understanding for the purpose of illuminating the patterns or testing or applying a particular theory to the work, with various forms of cultural criticism as examples of this approach.

The first three purposes obviously relate to audience (and therefore issues of resonance) in some way. This is most obvious in relation to the first purpose. Much of the critical analysis of the rhetoric of Lincoln, FDR, Reagan, and Obama has clearly served this purpose, focusing on explaining why their rhetoric worked in many contexts and occasionally why it failed. This research has rarely focused on simply determining whether the rhetoric worked (usually success or failure was obvious) but rather has sought to explain why a particular symbolic pattern had resonance or why even a Lincoln or a Reagan might fail in a particular context.

Although the connection is not as obvious as it is for works fulfilling the first purpose, the second and third purposes implicitly relate to an audience-based understanding of rhetorical practice as well. Consider, for example, works that sketch the development of a given ideological perspective, such as the work of Michael McGee or his students on ideographs, or analyses that describe the evolution of an archetypal metaphor, as the seminal work of Michael Osborne.[22] In both cases, the critic is describing the way that the symbolic practice related to audiences. When Osborne noted that the archetypal sea evolved over time from a place of danger and fear to alternative meanings, he was tracing the way that people understood the meaning. For Osborne, rhetorical agency was largely in the audience, thus his focus on how the meaning of the archetypal sea evolved for them over time. The same point applies to McGee's work on ideographs. Thus, rhetorical analysis of the resonance or influence or scope of ideological, cultural, or psychological patterns requires evidence of some kind that relates to how audiences responded to or otherwise received those patterns. Critical projects such as those of Osborne and McGee were valuable precisely because they provided copious quantities of relevant evidence, indicating how the ideographs and the archetypal metaphors resonated over time in different ways for people.

Precisely the same point applies to many analyses that in some way critique the ethics of or case made in rhetorical practice. Karlyn Kohrs Campbell referred to this type of criticism as focused on the ethical and truth criterions, while Phillip Wander labeled such works as reflecting the "ideological turn" in criticism.[23] While ideological or ethical criticism does not inherently focus on audience-based understanding, it often implicitly relates to audience. For example, contemporary criticism focused on the way that symbolic practices oppress women, people of color, gays and lesbians, and other groups clearly makes a judgment based on audience resonance. Kenneth Burke's classic analysis, "The Rhetoric of Hitler's Battle," is a good illustration of this point.[24] Burke's analysis has been universally recognized as brilliant because he seemed prescient in diagnosing how the symbolic practices of the Nazis could lead to repression, mass murder, and war. What made Hitler so very dangerous was that his rhetoric resonated with millions of Germans. Similarly, early feminist rhetorical critics, most notably Campbell, illuminated the way that not just laws but also symbols oppressed women.[25] In all of these cases, the ideological or ethical critique depends in part upon evidence of audience influence of some kind.

The opposite point is also relevant. Absent evidence of audience resonance, ideological critique often seems unimportant. For example, one occasionally hears conservative commentators claim that there is now backlash against white men or that capitalism has been unfairly singled out for attack. The absolute lack of evidence of any kind that white men or elite business leaders are being oppressed casts serious doubt about the ideological critique. Absent evidence of influence, ideological critique is pointless, precisely because without resonance ideology cannot harm anyone.

To this point, I have argued that the first three purposes served by rhetorical analysis in some way require evidence of audience resonance. Put differently, these three forms of criticism are important precisely because rhetoric sometimes has great influence and sometimes fails on issues of enormous import, producing tragic results. In the next section, I take up the question of what counts for such evidence. Prior to considering that question, however, it is important to consider the fourth possible critical purpose, commentary unrelated to audience-based understanding, such as some (but not all) forms of cultural criticism or very close textual analysis. For example, a critic might explore the stylistic patterns present in the rhetoric of any of the great rhetorical leaders that I mentioned earlier. Garry Wills famously did just that in an analysis of the Gettysburg Address.[26] With my colleague John Jones, I carried out a similar project focused on Reagan's Cold War rhetoric as exemplified in his address at Westminster on June 8, 1982.[27] While neither of these projects was focused on the influence of a particular speech on a particular audience, they both were focused on audience-based understandings and the long-term resonance of symbols. Thus, they fit comfortably within the second and third purposes I identified earlier. The key question is to consider the importance of a focus on stylistic or other textual patterns unrelated to audience understanding.

One possible rationale would be that such patterns are important to explicate rhetoric as a work of art. Even here, however, issues of audience resonance are likely to bleed into the critical analysis. Why have literary critics focused so heavily on great writers or so strongly critiqued the literary canon? The answer is that both the defenders and the opponents of studying canonical texts recognized the power of the ideas in Shakespeare and other members of the canon and therefore focused on how that power was created, in some cases in order to praise the work and in others to critique it. Thus, even in cases of very close analysis of style, the underlying purpose is often to illuminate audience-based understanding or resonance of the style.

In others, the purpose may be purely to explicate artistic patterns to illuminate those patterns, without claiming that they influenced or even necessarily were perceived by those who heard or read or watched the rhetoric. In still others, the purpose may be cultural critique of some kind. If the purpose is this type of critical illumination, then there would be no need for audience-based data, and the only possible standard of judgment would be the degree to which the critic could build a case that the analysis explicated an important aspect of the text. Some might question the importance of the critical illumination if it didn't relate to how some actual or possible audience might be influenced by the text. The answer to that challenge is for the critic to justify the importance of the analysis of artistry or the cultural critique in the particular case, without making or implying claims about influence or resonance.

Alternatively, a critic might use a text to test or apply a theory of some kind. I think a great deal of contemporary criticism fulfils this purpose, often applying poststructuralist, postmodern, or psychoanalytic theories. It is important to recognize, however, that as soon as a word such as resonance, impact, or influence is used to justify the critique, audience-based data are needed. When a Foucauldian critic exposes the way that symbols construct power or a psychoanalytic critic traces the symbolic patterns in a contemporary film as representing larger social trends or otherwise influencing an audience, she is making judgments that go beyond the particular text to make claims about how actual audiences responded to the text. Thus, in rhetorical analysis that maps a given theory (whether from Marx, Lacan, Foucault, or any other) onto a discourse, an implicit claim of audience resonance often lies beneath the surface of the critique.

To this point, I have argued that, except in cases where the critic explicitly justifies the analysis as unrelated to audience understandings, nearly all criticism explicitly or implicitly is focused on audience-based understanding of rhetoric. Of course, that audience-based understanding may reflect enthymematic or subconscious understandings as well as more obvious surface features as long as evidence of some kind exists to validate the interpretation as reflecting the way some audience was influenced or could have been influenced in a different context by the symbols. So far, when discussing that evidence of influence, I've used quite vague phrases, such as "evidence of some kind." I now turn to what that evidence might look like.

Evidence in Rhetorical Analysis

If the particular purpose falls into the fourth category, critical insight or theory application unrelated to audience in any way, then the only evidence needed is explanation of the insight revealed from the textual pattern uncovered by the critic or application of a theory to the text. Under such an approach, a conception of audience is largely absent, and agency lies either with the critic or with the text itself. The real question in such cases is not about evidence but about why the critical analysis is important if it does not reflect how any actual audience might understand or be influenced by the text. As I've noted, even in the work of very careful critics such as Terrill, claims about resonance, influence, or impact are often present. If such claims are present, than some sort of audience-based evidence is needed to support the interpretation.

For audience-centered criticism, the purpose of explaining how the rhetoric influenced a given audience or resonated over time can be fulfilled with three kinds of evidence:

1. Evidence directly bearing on how and/or why a given audience reacted to a message;
2. Application of a theory of rhetoric based generally in how messages move audiences in particular contexts, such as perspectives that evolved over centuries out of classical theories of rhetoric;
3. Evidence that a particular psychological, literary, ideological or other theory explains the resonance or lack of resonance of a text in a given context.

Some might reject use of the first form of evidence as a reversion to the simplistic neo-Aristotelian focus on immediate audience response. Of course, the difficulties of using evidence of short-term effect or audience reception such as applause, letters to the editor, polls and other forms of public opinion data, and so forth, are well known. Moreover, in many cases, there may be very little information on how the audience responded. And where evidence is present, there may be multiple factors that could explain the situation. For example, polling data may reflect audience response to a candidate or a host of other factors. In addition, a focus on short-term effect can blind the critic, preventing him from seeing much more important long-term patterns or ethical or ideological abuses.

All of these problems are real and important. And yet, in some cases there are useful data bearing on how an audience responded to a speech or other work of rhetoric. For example, it is impossible to dispute the impact that Obama's 2004 keynote address at the Democratic nominating convention had on American politics. It is literally true that in twenty minutes Obama went from being an unknown state senator to someone mentioned as a possible future president. A similar point could be made about Obama's speech in Philadelphia in March 2008, commonly known as the race speech.[28] There is a great deal of evidence that the speech changed the dynamic of the campaign, staunching the wound that the viral videos of Jeremiah Wright saying things that shocked many Americans had created. Obviously, cases such as these two Obama speeches are rare but hardly unique. For example, Davis Houck and Mihaela Nocasian used a careful analysis of letters and telegrams written by ordinary citizens following Franklin Roosevelt's first inaugural address to demonstrate the impact of the speech.[29] Such data may be difficult to find, but a critic would be foolish to ignore the evidence of audience resonance when it is present. Alternatively, the relevant factor may be the lack of evidence of any influence. Earlier, I mentioned the case of Fred Thompson. His presidential campaign began with great promise with strong praise from pundits. The campaign then went nowhere.[30] This is powerful evidence that the message did not resonate.

Thus, in the cases cited, the critic would link patterns identified in the text with audience response or lack of response. What would guide the critic in identifying the textual patterns? One answer is the general theories relating to audience influence that I discuss next. Another is that the audience response data may provide clues about what it was in the message that resonated. For example, there is overwhelming evidence that themes related to hope and change powerfully resonated for millions of people in Obama's 2008 presidential campaign.[31] A critical analysis that ignored how Obama created the hopeful feeling that real change might be possible would miss the mark in explaining the power of his rhetoric in the campaign. The comment of Houck and Nocasian that "Audiences matter in rhetorical acts; as such they should also matter in rhetorical criticism" is exactly on target.[32]

It is important to recognize that a simple judgment about the effectiveness or lack thereof of rhetoric is rarely the point. A book focused on judging whether the

Obama 2008 presidential campaign was effective would be a very short book. Hillary Clinton was the overwhelming favorite going into the Democratic primary battle, and Obama had to overcome strong public doubts about both his race and whether he could connect with ordinary Americans. The judgment that his rhetoric worked to overcome these barriers is both obvious and by itself trivial. The question is not whether his rhetoric worked (apart from a few cultural critics, everyone agrees on this) but to describe the political context and audience characteristics over time in the campaign and show how Obama's evolving message eventually overcame the very significant barriers he faced.

However, as I noted earlier, in most cases the critic will lack the kind of direct evidence of influence that is present for the Obama speeches I've discussed. In this case, the critic can build an audience-based critique based on general theories about what kinds of rhetoric resonate with audiences and contextual data indicating the applicability of the theory in the particular case. Until recently, virtually all rhetorical theory focused on explicating the way that strategy categories, rhetorical forms, and genres influenced audiences in particular contexts. Certainly, classical theory was developed on the premise that the theoretical principles described how audiences could be moved through rhetoric in a given situation. The implied situational focus is important. In identifying three modes of persuasion, Aristotle was not arguing that logos, ethos, and pathos were strategies that always moved an audience; rather, his concern was with identifying the factors that explain when such strategies will be successful in influencing an audience. Many theories about how genres, movements, and campaigns function are based on a similar premise. Much contemporary theory takes a similar approach. For example, when Kenneth Burke wrote of the power of identification or of how symbol systems can act as terministic screens that shape how people understand the world, he was developing an audience-based theory about how symbols move audiences in particular situations.

There is a great deal of evidence that rhetoric that creates a sense of shared identity and therefore a feeling of consubstantiality often strongly resonates with an audience, as it did in Obama's 2004 convention speech.[33] Similarly, solid support for the power of terministic schema to influence audiences can be found in recent research on framing in political communication.[34] On the other hand, in addition to focusing on symbolic forms that clearly produce strong responses in many instances, Burke also often conducted detailed and sometimes quite idiosyncratic analyses of particular aesthetic patterns, including punning. The evidence base that such patterns often influence audiences is much less obvious than in the case of identification or terministic framing strategies.

What this means is that a critic often can draw upon Burkean, classical, movement theory, or other audience-based theories to build an argument that textual patterns resonated or failed to resonate in a given context. The critic can draw on this material to show why in a given case a textual pattern might resonate strongly for a particular audience. Precisely the same point applies when the critics cites classical and other audience-based rhetorical theories to explain rhetorical influence. Clearly, the critical analysis would be stronger if it were based on actual evidence about a situated audience, as well as application of the audience-based theory. It is that evidence, the fact that we know that the patterns Burke identified did lead to scapegoating and ultimately genocide, that gives such power to Burke's critique of *Mein Kampf.* But even before the most terrible events of the Nazi era occurred, Burke's critique was a powerful one because he based it in important theories explaining how people respond to messages in particular situations. Much contemporary public address takes a similar approach. The critic makes a claim that the rhetoric resonated or failed to do so on the basis of textual citations that are linked to theories about how rhetoric functions in particular types of situations and then shows the application of the theories to the particular case.

The third kind of evidence that might be cited is similar in some ways to the second. Much contemporary criticism builds an argument about audience resonance by tying textual features to a preexisting theory. It differs from traditional audience-based criticism in that not all of its theories were developed for the purpose of explaining audience resonance (or lack of resonance). For example, Marxist, Foucauldian, deconstructionist, and psychoanalytic criticism is commonly used to explicate rhetoric. When relying on theories that were developed not to explain how situated audiences are influenced by rhetoric but for some other purpose, however, the critic needs to do more than merely map the theory onto the discourse and situation. The difficulty is that, unlike theories of rhetoric that were developed to explain how words influence people in particular situations, the theories I've mentioned and others were developed for other reasons and may not reflect particular audience understandings. We know that classical theories of rhetoric and the theories that evolved from them explain the general ways that people are influenced by rhetoric in broad and narrow situations because we have more than two thousand years of experience with these theories. Similarly, there is an enormous amount of evidence that Burkean theories of identification and terministic screens elucidate how symbols often influence people. In the case of the other theories that I have mentioned, this evidence base is not obviously present. Thus, the critic needs to both show how the theory can be mapped onto the discourse (and situation) and also demonstrate that the theory illuminates the way that people are impacted by messages of some type.

What is not enough, however, is to cite only from the text and from the theory itself. Another thought experiment may make this point clearer. Imagine that someone conducted a critical analysis of speeches by President Obama using Robert Graves's theory that much European and Middle Eastern myth in facts refers not to the explicit story being told but to an underlying cult of what he called the "White Goddess."[35] As a work of theory matching, such an analysis conceivably could be justified. However, a claim that Graves's theory of the White Goddess explained the resonance of Obama's rhetoric would depend upon additional evidence that Obama's audience in contemporary America was influenced by implicit references to a mythological pattern from a period prior to the classical age. While such a claim would strain credulity, the key point is that it would require support of a very different kind from simply matching Graves's theory onto Obama's rhetoric. It seems clear that, in at least some cases, there is a lack of evidence that theories often cited in contemporary criticism have any application to explaining resonance or lack of resonance of rhetorical patterns for situated audiences.

The case of psychoanalysis is revealing. A recent review of scholarship across the humanities by Patricia Cohen found that psychoanalytic theories were commonly applied in humanistic research, something that clearly is the case in rhetorical studies.[36] Even a cursory review of contemporary rhetorical criticism reveals that many critics apply broadly psychoanalytic theories in order to illuminate particular texts. In some cases, the critic applies Freud or Freudian theories, but other theorists, notably Jacques Lacan, are also commonly cited.[37] More broadly, psychoanalytic criticism in general and Freudian criticism in particular have had significant influence across the humanities in influencing cultural criticism, especially as they relate to sexuality. No one disputes the importance of the theories for that critical purpose. In fact, there is strong evidence supporting the cultural approach because, as Cohen noted, "psychoanalytic ideas have shaped the culture," and critics have found the work of Freud "particularly useful for gaining insights into questions of human existence."[38] However, there is a difficulty if the justification for the criticism is shifted from critiquing cultural practice to a focus on audience influence. The key point is that psychoanalytic and Freudian theory have been largely discredited for explaining the psychological functioning of ordinary people.

Admittedly, many of the core ideas in Freud—the existence of an unconscious, the idea that people lead conflicted lives, and so forth—have been strongly supported. But these ideas are so general that they are not especially useful for criticism. And, beyond the most general, psychoanalytic theories have been largely rejected by psychologists because they don't work for the purpose of explaining human psychological reactions. The evidence supporting this claim is overwhelming. Patricia Cohen noted in the *New York Times* that "A new report by the American Psychoanalytic Association has found that while psychoanalysis . . . is alive and well in literature, film, history and just about every other subject in the humanities, psychology departments and textbooks treat it as 'desiccated and dead,' a historical artifact, instead of an ongoing movement." Marci McDonald observed that "Freud's pioneering methods of psychoanalysis has been largely banished from medical studies" and added that "Traditional Freudian analysis is practiced today by only an estimated 2 percent of psychotherapists." Writing about a meeting of the Psychoanalysis section of the American Psychological Association, Joseph Brean argued that psychoanalysis "is indeed gravely wounded, unable to attract new talent," and is "dying a slow death on the margins of academia, where it is maligned by mainstream psychologists as unscientific, sex-obsessed, postmodern witchcraft." The science historian Frank Sulloway commented that Freud's "model of the mind and notion of dreaming are in total conflict with modern science." Writing in *The Guardian,* James Wood argued that "all of the available evidence points the other way [against the efficacy of psychoanalysis]." Usha Lee McFarlint noted that "the emerging consensus among scientists, including psychiatrists, about Freud is that he was wrong. About almost everything." His granddaughter Sophie Freud, a professor of psychology herself, has labeled his theories as "outdated."[39] Perhaps Richard Webster puts it best when he observed that Freudian theory "fails to do the only thing we ultimately have a right to demand of explanatory theories—it fails to explain."[40]

The key point is that psychoanalysis in general and Freudian theories in particular have been rejected by professionals who study the psychology of ordinary people because the theories don't work for explaining those people. Does this mean that rhetorical theorists should reject such theories outright? No, it means that a critic using such a theory should either make it clear that the theory is being applied for purpose of cultural critique unrelated to how situated audiences react or that in a particular case strong evidence exists to support the argument that psychoanalytic theory illuminates how an audience was influenced (or not influenced) by a text or texts. Absent that specific evidence, the consensus of researchers that psychoanalytic theories fail to explain how people think or act creates a presumption against the use of such theories for audience-based criticism. However, such theories might still be useful for cultural critique, where there is also a consensus about the utility of the theory. I am reminded of a comment by Forbes Hill in his debate with Karlyn Campbell when he praised Herman Stelzner's interpretation of Nixon's Vietnamization address for revealing "facets of its artistry I had not dreamed of before."[41] Hill's point was that there are purposes other than explaining audience response. For those purposes, psychoanalytic theory may be very powerful. However, given the consensus about the failure of psychoanalysis as an explanatory theory, merely citing Lacan or Freud or some other theorist to explain textual features is unlikely to reveal anything about actual audience response.

Another implication that comes from the argument developed here is that audience resonance is most likely to be explained by major textual features, rather than by details of language or argument. Implicitly, I made this point earlier in noting that there was strong support for using some but not all of Burke's theories for explaining audience resonance. It is well known that ordinary people are often quite poorly informed about the issues and rarely focus on the details of either policy or rhetoric. Moreover, the attention span of the public is notoriously short. Given these characteristics of audiences, approaches that attempt to explain audience resonance on the basis of very close analysis of language seem suspect. Stelzner's famous analysis of FDR's war address illustrates this point.[42] It is one thing to claim that the analysis identifies important stylistic patterns in the speech. It is altogether another thing to say that the details of these stylistic patterns had a demonstrable effect on audiences. I think this explains why classical theorists focused on ethos, logos, and pathos as the modes of proof and treated style as important primarily for supporting the larger strategy categories.

My point is not to claim that style and language never matter. In some cases a particular phrase may be enormously important; an example is the famous rhetorical question at the end of John F. Kennedy's inaugural. And a stylistic blunder such as Howard Dean's scream may undercut a message. But in these cases where the details of language matter, there generally will be a wealth of audience-based data to support the claim. For example, it would be easy to find many citations of Kennedy's famous call on the audience to "ask not what your country can do for you. Ask what you can do for your country." In other cases, however, a close analysis of style may be useful primarily to show how the style made larger textual features more or less compelling.

It is important to recognize that the approach developed here does not rule out use of theories that have been developed in contexts other than audience-based rhetorical theory. For example, there is a wealth of evidence that contemporary brain-imaging studies provide insights about how people process information.[43] Similarly, there is a vast research base in anthropology explaining how humans use myths to answer a number of basic questions about life and culture.[44] There is also a great deal of evidence supporting framing as a way of approaching how people are influenced by messages.[45] The key point is that when a critic maps a theoretical principle onto a text, that act of mapping is not enough per se to demonstrate that the theoretical application helps explain how or why the message resonates. In addition, the critic needs evidence of some kind that the theory explains how people are influenced by messages, either generally or in particular contexts.

The foregoing suggests the importance of thinking about the particular purposes served in rhetorical criticism and about what kinds of evidence are appropriate for fulfilling those purposes. The evidence that is needed to fulfill one purpose may not work if another purpose is being fulfilled. In particular, any time a critic makes a claim of resonance or influence, she needs to supply evidence that is tied to how audiences react in particular circumstances. That evidence need not be a simplistic report of applause, and it may simply be citation of textual (and contextual) features that can be tied to audience-based theories about the kinds of strategies that move audiences in particular circumstances, but it needs to be evidence either directly related to audience response or indirectly related to that response.

Summary

Critical pluralism and the polysemic approaches that come out of it are tied to the multiplicity of purposes served by criticism. It is crucial to note in that regard that there is in principle no way to choose among the various possible critical purposes. There is wide consensus that what I've labeled audience-based criticism is important, but so are other forms of critical analysis. However, if the stated or implied purpose is to explain the resonance of a message, that purpose limits the kinds of evidence that are appropriate. Thus, while there are no principled limits on critical purpose, once the purpose is chosen, that choice may sharply restrict the kind of evidence that is appropriate to fulfill the purpose.

One implication of the foregoing is that many critical controversies are really about purpose and evidence rather than about theory and method. The case of mythic criticism illustrates the importance of this point. Twenty years ago, I defended a narrow audience-based approach to mythic criticism.[46] The basic idea was that the anthropological literature indicates that myths are the most basic stories in any culture and are treated as fundamentally true in some way. Specific characteristics of form, such as a hero who stands larger than life, a setting in a place of great power, and often some sort of return to origin times, add to the impact of the stories. These formal characteristics play an essential role in the societal functioning of the myth, giving it great power. To say the least, these views were controversial, and many readers objected that the approach was too narrow.[47]

Janice Rushing was and remains the leading scholar defending a broader approach to myth than the one I supported. She was quite well versed in the anthropological, sociological, and literary literature on myth, the same literature that I had drawn on in building my argument. Yet, she came not only to a different conclusion but to one that was diametrically opposed to the conclusion I had drawn. For years, I was confused by how she and I could come to such different conclusions on the basis of the same theoretical evidence base. I knew that what I was saying reflected the anthropological consensus on the way that myths functioned in primitive societies and that the same kinds of stories still were present today. What I could not understand was why we came to such different interpretations. I kept asking myself what I was missing.

What I was missing was that we weren't serving the same critical purpose. I was focused on the way that modern examples of the anthropological version of myths continue to influence human society. While sometimes she used language that implied an audience-based standard, I think that Rushing really was focused on revealing cultural patterns that were linked primarily to psychological theories of myth. In a sense, we didn't disagree about myth at all; instead, we were in different subfields, focused on different critical purposes. If I could revise my essay today, I would draw a distinction between anthropological myth and cultural/psychological myths and argue that different kinds of evidence were appropriate for making claims in the two subfields. I very much wish that I could have shared that idea with her.

As I've noted, some scholars now argue that a focus on audience-based interpretation is outdated, producing criticism that merely reports how an audience reacted to a message. I think this judgment is quite wrong. The purpose of explaining how texts work for situated audiences is an important one and is by no means intellectually sterile. While merely judging the effectiveness of a given speech is often uninteresting, discovering the reasons why a given work resonated or failed to resonate is quite important and in most cases not a simple task at all. I suggest, for example, that the reasons behind the successes (and subsequent decline) of Sarah Palin and the Tea Party movement are by no means obvious.

A similar point can be made about any number of speeches by first Senator and now President Barack Obama. It isn't always clear why many of these works succeeded or failed. To illustrate this point, consider the roughly two-hundred-word statement that Obama made at the very height of the financial crisis during the 2008 campaign, immediately following the announcement of Senator John McCain that he was suspending his campaign. In his statement McCain called on Obama to join him in suspending the campaign and come to Washington, D.C., to work on the crisis. In his memoir of the campaign, Obama's campaign manager, David Plouffe, describes how, when Obama and his advisers met, their digital communication devices were vibrating as messages came in telling them that they had to suspend the campaign and follow McCain. Obama did not take that course. Instead, he issued a short statement, in which he said:

> With respect to the debates, it's my belief that this is exactly the time when the American people need to hear from the person who, in approximately 40 days, will be responsible for dealing with this mess.
>
> And I think that it is going to be part of the president's job to deal with more than one thing at once.
>
> I think there's no reason why we can't be constructive in helping to solve this problem and also tell the American people what we believe, and where we stand, and where we want to take the country.
>
> So in my mind, actually, it's more important than ever that we present ourselves to the American people and try to describe where we want to take the country and where we want to take the economy, as well as dealing with some of the issues of foreign policy that were initially the subject of the debate.[48]

In essence, Obama called McCain's bluff.

With this statement, Obama defused a potential campaign crisis. But he did more than that. After Obama's statement, McCain was forced to back down, and the first presidential debate occurred as scheduled. In addition, Obama's statement clearly put McCain on the defensive. In particular, his comment that a president needed to be able "to deal with more than one thing at once" struck a nerve. David Plouffe noted that Obama's comment "Presidents need to be able to do more than one thing at a time" "played over and over next to McCain suggesting postponement. We looked strong, confident, and steady. McCain looked erratic and a bit desperate."[49] With this statement, Obama exposed McCain's call for suspending the campaign as a stunt. As a result, according to Dan Balz and Haynes Johnson, McCain's "'brilliant political gambit had turned into a nightmare.'"[50] Hendrik Hertzberg observed that in his press briefing, Obama "looks and sounds like a president of the United States. He is preternaturally calm." He added that "Obama handled the situation perfectly. He didn't have to point out that McCain's cheap gambit was a cheap gambit. Surrogates, supporters, and perhaps, the press would do that for him. And by treating the debate-postponement ploy as a detail, he slipped the trap McCain had set for him: either be bullied into obeying McCain's order or be seen as putting politics above country."[51]

What had seemed a brilliant political ploy failed, and from this point McCain rapidly lost ground to Obama in the polls.[52]

While the impact of Obama's statement is now clear, it was not obvious at the time that Obama's response was the right one. As noted, many operatives advised the campaign to take another approach. The point is that discovering why a given message worked, even a short two-hundred-word statement, is often not a simple thing. In such cases, it is crucial that rhetorical critics make the effort to figure out how and why the message resonated as it did. In a way, this example illustrates the reasons that the Greeks made the study of rhetoric the first of the liberal arts. They understood that rhetoric was both powerful and essential in a democratic society, but they also recognized that rhetoric is an art and that therefore explaining the way that symbols influence audiences is often not easy or obvious. Their insight remains true today.

Additionally, a focus on audience provides an appropriate starting point for addressing two of the most endemic problems in rhetorical criticism. On the one hand, there is always a danger that the method will drive the criticism, that one will always find a narrative, a myth, an argument, or other pattern in critical analysis because one started with that theoretical perspective. The difficulty with this approach is obvious. If all symbolic action is viewed through the lens of myth, argument, narrative, or any other theory, then distinctions among different symbolic constructions will be lost.

At the same time, the most common corrective to theory-driven criticism, use of an inductive approach in which the method emerges from the text, also has drawbacks. While inductive criticism has much to recommend it, critics need guidance on how to apply theory and method to works and where to seek those theories and methods. Telling a young (or old, for that matter) critic that the theory or method should emerge from the text doesn't provide much guidance on where to seek that theory or method.

However, a focus on audience provides critics, especially students at both the undergraduate and the graduate level, with a starting point—not an end point but a starting point—for the critical process. In particular, the idea of solving a critical puzzle in order to explain why a situated audience either was influenced or was not influenced by a given work of rhetoric provides a good place to begin the analysis. Here, the focus is not on judging effectiveness per se. Rather, the beginning point is usually a confusing situation in which rhetoric either succeeded when that result seemed unlikely or failed when success would have been expected. The student then considers dominant characteristics of the message and the rhetorical situation as clues suggesting the most appropriate theory or method to explain the confusing state of affairs. Under this perspective, critical approaches that are often thought of as methods (mythic criticism, narrative criticism, and so forth), are really bounded theories explaining how forms of rhetoric work to achieve particular purposes in particular situations. The focus on a critical puzzle relating to a given text (or texts) and a situated audience provides the critic with a starting point for conducting the analysis and helps them avoid the problems associated with purely inductive or deductive method-centric approach to criticism.

The ultimate lesson is that critics need to be much clearer about laying out their critical purposes, justifying the importance of those purposes in a particular case, and justifying the proper form of evidence for fulfilling those purposes. I am not arguing for monistic criticism or a focus on audience alone. There are no necessary limits on the purposes served by rhetorical analysis, and, in any given case, a critic might argue for a number of different approaches.

At the same time, from the perspective of a given critical purpose, the available interpretations that sensibly can be defended may be much more limited. Consider the example of a very brief work written by General Tony McAuliffe during the Battle of the Bulge. In late December 1944, the 101st Airborne held the town of Bastogne against the German offensive that threatened to break through Allied lines and delay the end of the war. After the Germans surrounded the town, their commander sent in a note demanding surrender. In response, General McAuliffe wrote "Nuts" with three exclamation marks and then triple underlined the brief message. The Germans were befuddled by the response. According to Lieutenant General Harry W. O. Kinnard, who was there, the German officer who was given the note asked what it meant. The officer who was escorting them, a Colonel Harper, explained, "If you don't know what 'Nuts' means, in plain English it is the same as 'Go to Hell.'"[53]

While McAuliffe's one-word response is atypical in its brevity, it is an appropriate example of a rhetorical act produced in response to a highly constraining situation. If the critical purpose in considering the rhetoric is to explain how the message worked for the situated audience, there is limited ground for interpretation. It clearly functioned as an insult that was designed to raise the morale of the American forces. In terms of the German and American audiences, the message was purely monosemic. On the other hand, it is easy to imagine a number of critics taking alternative approaches in order to fulfill purposes other than explaining how the work functioned on December 22, 1944, at Bastogne. For example, a critic might consider the message from the vantage point of cultural criticism in order to gauge what the message revealed about American or military culture. Ideological criticism of decision making in military culture or feminist criticism of arrogance and machismo in the army also easily could be justified.

Three key points are revealed in this very brief analysis of an even briefer work of rhetoric. First, one of the primary justifications for rhetorical analysis is the importance of explaining how messages work for situated audiences. Even in the case of a one-word text, that purpose remains important. Second, a focus on audience provides an appropriate starting point for teaching students how to apply theory and method in critical analysis. It gives the critic a place to begin considering his critical purpose and the available theoretical and evidentiary basis for fulfilling it. Finally, while there are no principled limits on the purposes served by critical analysis, the nature of the purpose in a particular case may set quite narrow limits on what counts as evidence in that case and on what kinds of critical interpretations reasonably can be supported

Notes

1. Stephen E. Lucas, "The Schism in Rhetorical Scholarship," *Quarterly Journal of Speech* 67 (1981): 18, 20.

2. See David Zarefsky, "Presidential Rhetoric and the Power of Definition," *Presidential Studies Quarterly* 34 (2004): 607–619. Later in this essay, I discuss the various ways that a critic sensibly can discuss such influence.

3. See for example Leff's analysis of temporarily in Lincoln in Michael Leff, "Dimensions of Temporality in Lincoln's Second Inaugural," *Communication Reports,* 1 (1998), 26–31; Michael C. Leff, "Rhetorical Timing in Lincoln's 'House Divided' Speech," The Van Zelst Lecture in Communication, Northwestern University School of Speech, Evanston, Ill., May 1983.

4. Michael Leff, "Lincoln at Cooper Union: Neo-classical Criticism Revisited," *Western Journal of Communication* 65 (2001): 240.

5. In what follows, I describe what I think are well-known and obvious patterns in contemporary scholarship. To validate the accuracy of these patterns, I reviewed roughly the past decade of articles published in the *Quarterly Journal of Speech* and in *Rhetoric and Public Affairs.* The purpose of this essay is not to indict any particular scholar or scholarly purpose. I am quite cognizant, however, of the risk that a number of the theoretical claims developed here could be viewed as a form of critique. For that reason, I cite individual essays only for the purpose of illustrating the larger patterns and have focused on particularly careful examples of scholarship that fulfill each of the purposes I discuss, as in my citation of Robert Terrill's work on the "race" speech by then Senator Obama. I encourage the skeptical reader to look at recent issues of the journals I mentioned. Even a very brief review will reveal the textual patterns that I describe in the remainder of the essay.

6. The most important critique of a focus on effects alone is found in Edwin Black, *Rhetorical Criticism: A Study in Method* (1965; repr., Madison: University of Wisconsin Press, 1978), 36–90.

7. George C. Edwards III, "Presidential Rhetoric: What Differences Does It Make?," in *Beyond the Rhetorical Presidency,* ed. Martin J. Medhurst (College Station: Texas A&M University Press, 1996), 199–217; George C. Edwards III, *On Deaf Ears: The Limits of the Bully Pulpit* (New Haven: Yale University Press, 2003).

8. As Leah Ceccarelli noted in a discussion of polysemy, "Most critics do not currently focus on how texts were received by their contemporary audiences." See "Polysemy: Multiple Meanings in Rhetorical Criticism," *Quarterly Journal of Speech* 84 (1998), 407. For a discussion of the renaissance in public address see Stephen E. Lucas, "The Renaissance of American Public Address: Text and Context in Rhetorical Criticism," *Quarterly Journal of Speech* 74 (1988): 241–260; David Henry and Richard J. Jensen, "Social Movement Criticism and the Renaissance of Public Address," *Communication Studies* 42 (1991): 83–93.

9. Barry Brummett, "How to Propose a Discourse: A Reply to Rowland," *Communication Studies* 41 (1990): 129.

10. Michaela D. E. Meyer, "Utilizing Mythic Criticism in Contemporary Narrative Culture: Examining the 'Present-Absence' of Shadow Archetypes in *Spider-Man*," *Communication Quarterly* 51 (2003): 527.

11. Robert E. Terrill, "Unity and Duality in Barack Obama's 'A More Perfect Union,'" *Quarterly Journal of Speech* 95 (2009): 365.

12. Stephen Toulmin strongly makes this point that the ultimate force guiding the evolution of ideas is purpose in context. See Stephen E. Toulmin, *Human Understanding: The Collective Use and Evolution of Concepts* (Princeton: Princeton University Press, 1972).

13. George Kennedy notes that Aristotle's discussion of epideictic, deliberative, and forensic rhetoric begins with the audience since "A hearer of a speech must be a judge or not a judge." The other distinctions flow from the work that the speech does for the audience. See George A. Kennedy, *Classical Rhetoric and Its Christian and Secular Traditions: From Ancient to Modern Times* (Chapel Hill: University of North Carolina Press, 1980), 72–73.

14. See for example Robert C. Rowland, "Purpose, Argument Fields, and Theoretical Justification," *Argumentation* 10 (2008): 235–250.

15. Zarefsky, "Presidential Rhetoric and the Power of Definition."

16. Sean Wilentz, *The Age of Reagan: A History, 1974–2008* (New York: HarperCollins, 2008), 6.

17. Brandon Rottinghaus, *The Provisional Pulpit: Modern Presidential Leadership of Public Opinion* (College Station: Texas A&M University Press, 2010), 78.

18. Edwards, *On Deaf Ears*, 74.

19. See Black, *Rhetorical Criticism*, 78–90.

20. Black's comment about the importance of the speech as a reflection of the audience is on p. 89, but the analysis of the speech in the context of its time on pp. 83–90 speaks to the same issue.

21. Edwin Black, "The Second Persona," *Quarterly Journal of Speech* 56 (1970): 109–119.

22. Michael C. McGee, "The 'Ideograph:' A Link between Rhetoric and Ideology," *Quarterly Journal of Speech* 66 (1980): 1–16; John Louis Lucaites and Celeste Michelle Condit, "Reconstructing <Equality>: Culturetypal and Countercultural Rhetorics in the Martyred Black Vision," *Communication Monographs* 57 (1990): 5–24; Michael Osborn, "Archetypal Metaphor in Rhetoric: The Light Dark Family," *Quarterly Journal of Speech* 53 (1967): 115–126; Michael Osborn, "The Evolution of the Archetypal Sea in Rhetoric and Poetic," *Quarterly Journal of Speech* 63 (1977): 347–363.

23. Karlyn Kohrs Campbell, *Critiques of Contemporary Rhetoric* (Belmont, Calif.: Wadsworth, 1972), 34–38; Philip Wander, "The Ideological Turn in Modern Criticism," *Central States Speech Journal* 34 (1983): 1–18.

24. Kenneth Burke, "The Rhetoric of Hitler's Battle," in *Philosophy of Literary Form: Studies in Symbolic Action*, 3rd ed., ed. Kenneth Burke (Berkeley: University of California Press, 1967), 191–220.

25. Karlyn Kohrs Campbell, "The Rhetoric of Women's Liberation: An Oxymoron," *Quarterly Journal of Speech* 59 (1973): 74–86.

26. Garry Wills, *Lincoln at Gettysburg: The Words That Remade America* (New York: Simon and Schuster, 1992).

27. Robert C. Rowland and John M. Jones, *Reagan at Westminster: Foreshadowing the End of the Cold War* (College Station: Texas A&M University Press, 2010).

28. There is no question about the impact of the speech in the campaign. The overwhelming evidence on this point is discussed in Robert C. Rowland and John M. Jones, "One Dream: Barack Obama, Race, and the American Dream," *Rhetoric and Public Affairs* 14 (2011): 125–154.

29. Davis W. Houck and Mihaela Nocasian, "FDR's First Inaugural Address: Text, Context, and Reception," *Rhetoric and Public Affairs* 5 (2002): 649–678.

30. See Dan Balz and Haynes Johnson, *The Battle for America 2008* (New York: Viking, 2009), 272–275.

31. See Michael Grunwald, "How Obama Is Using the Science of Change," *Time,* April 13, 2009, 28; Nancy Gibbs, "This Is Our Time!" *Time,* November 17, 2008, 28; David Brooks, "Combat and Composure," *New York Times,* May 6, 2008, A27.

32. Houck and Nocasian, "FDR's First Inaugural Address," 675.

33. Robert C. Rowland and John M. Jones, "Recasting the American Dream and American Politics: Barack Obama's Keynote Address to the 2004 Democratic National Convention," *Quarterly Journal of Speech* 93 (2007): 425–448; David A. Frank and Mark L. McPhail, "Barack Obama's Address to the 2004 Democratic National Convention: Trauma, Compromise, Consilience, and the (Im)possibility of Racial Reconciliation," *Rhetoric and Public Affairs* 8 (2006): 571–594.

34. See for example, Geoffrey Nunberg, *Talking Right: How Conservatives Turned Liberalism into a Tax-Raising, Latte-Drinking, Sushi-Eating, Volvo-Driving, New York Times-Reading, Body-Piercing, Hollywood-Loving, Left-Wing Freak Show* (NewYork: Public Affairs, 2006).

35. Robert Graves, *The White Goddess,* rev. ed. (New York: Farrar, Straus and Giroux, 1966). William G. Doty describes Graves's claims that the explicit story in Greek and other myths actually referred to an "earlier historical strata" as lacking "wide acceptance" and observes that one "tires rather quickly" of such almost cryptographic criticism aimed at discovering an underlying monomyth. See *Mythograph: The Study of Myths and Rituals,* 2nd ed. (Tuscaloosa: University of Alabama Press, 2000), 244–245.

36. Patricia Cohen, "Freud Is Widely Taught at Universities, Except in the Psychology Department," *New York Times,* "Week in Review," November 25, 2008.

37. My point is not to attack particular works of criticism or individual critics but to make a larger point about evidence needed to make claims of audience resonance. For that reason, I am not citing examples of such criticism. A five-minute search of recent issues of journals in the field would reveal examples of the approach I am describing.

38. Cohen, "Freud Is Widely Taught at Universities."

39. Cohen, "Freud Is Widely Taught at Universities"; Marci McDonald, "Burying Freud and Praising Him," *U.S. News and World Report,* October 19, 1998, 60; Joseph Brean, "Will Freud Finally Slip? Pushed to the Fringes of Academia, Psychoanalysts Are Concerned Their Practice Is Dying," *National Post,* April 21, 2007, A8. Sulloway is quoted in John Leland, "The Trouble with Sigmund," *Newsweek,* December 18, 1995, 62; James Wood, "The Good Freud Guide," *The Guardian,* August 25, 1990, 3 (Lexis Nexis); Usha Lee McFarling, "If Freud Was So Wrong, Why Is He Still So Irrepressible?," *Ottawa Citizen,* May 16, 2000, A7. Sophie Freud is quoted in Judy Gerstel, "Freud Goes up in Smoke," *Toronto Star,* November 14, 2003, C1.

40. Richard Webster, *Why Freud Was Wrong: Sin, Science, and Psychoanalysis* (New York: Basic Books, 1995), 3.

41. Forbes Hill, "The Forum: Reply to Professor Campbell," *Quarterly Journal of Speech* 58 (1972): 460.

42. Herman Stelzner, "War Message, December 8, 1941: An Approach to Language," *Speech Monographs* 33 (1966): 419–437.

43. See for example, Marcia Clemmitt, "Lies and Politics," *CQResearcher* 21 (February 18, 2011): 147.

44. I discussed this evidence in Robert C. Rowland, "On Mythic Criticism," *Communication Studies* 41 (1990): 101–116.

45. See Jim A. Kuypers, "Framing Analysis," in *Rhetorical Criticism: Perspectives in Action,* ed. Jim A. Kuypers (Lanham, Md.: Lexington Books, 2009), 181–203.

46. Rowland, "On Mythic Criticism."

47. See especially Martha Solomon, "Responding to Rowland's Myth or In Defense of Pluralism—A Reply to Rowland," *Communication Studies* 41 (1990): 117–120; Janice Hocker Rushing, "On Saving Mythic Criticism—A Reply to Rowland," *Communication Studies* 41 (1990): 136–149.

48. "In Their Own Words: The Debate Dispute," *New York Times*, September 25, 2008, A23.

49. David Plouffe, *The Audacity to Win: The Inside Story and Lessons of Barack Obama's Hstoric Victory* (New York: Viking, 2009), 340.

50. Balz and Johnson, *The Battle for America 2008*, 349.

51. Hendrik Hertzberg, ¡Obámanos!: The Birth of a New Political Era (New York: Penguin Press, 2009), 262, 263.

52. Frank Newport et al., *Winning the White House 2008: The Gallup Poll, Public Opinion, and the Presidency* (New York: Checkmark, 2009), 510, 524.

53. See 'Nuts!' Revisited: An Interview with Lt. General Harry W. O. Kinnard," http:www.thedropzone.org/eurogpe/bulge/kinnard.html, no date (downloaded June 10, 2010).

What Rhetoric Can Do

Criticism as Critique

PAT J. GEHRKE

Influence is an extraordinarily difficult thing to establish, much less to measure.

Barnett Baskerville, "Must We All Be Rhetorical Critics?"

One can trace a number of arcs across the history of rhetoric, but in our current age one story commonly tracks the emergence and development of the criticism of rhetoric from 1925 to the present.[1] The relatively standard narrative places the birth of the criticism of rhetoric with Herbert Wichelns's 1925 "The Literary Criticism of Oratory" and takes as punctuations and turns the 1933 "Rhetoric of Hitler's Battle" by Kenneth Burke, Ernest Wrage's 1947 study in social and intellectual history, Ed Black's 1965 monograph on methods of rhetorical criticism, Lloyd Bitzer's 1968 "Rhetorical Situation," and Barnett Baskerville's 1977 query, "Must We All Be Rhetorical Critics?" I might add more recently, Martha Cooper's 1988 essay on Foucault's philosophy of the discursive event and the 2002 piece on Franklin Delano Roosevelt's first inaugural by Davis Houck and Mihaela Nocasian. If this list is not too idiosyncratic, and I believe in the main our current anthologies and syllabi endorse its reasonableness, then a relatively constant theme in this narrative of rhetorical criticism is a struggle with questions of what rhetoric can do or, to put it more precisely, how scholars of rhetoric can (if they can) take up questions of effect.

While Houck and Nocasian are certainly right that Wichelns's 1925 essay specifically defines "rhetorical criticism" as concerned with effect, that is, as Wichelns put it, "It regards a speech as a communication to a specific audience, and holds its business to be the analysis and appreciation of the orator's method of imparting his ideas to his hearers,"[2] Wichelns likewise offers a more complex and sophisticated view of what is entailed in that call than critics on either side of the effects question have tended to acknowledge. Indeed, the appeal by Wichelns to an art and science of rhetoric that would study, in his terms, "persuasion," "influence," or "moving" to assent or action produced far-reaching obligations for rhetoric scholars. These burdens, to occasion and to audience, to historical study and to sources, to ideas and to thought, to politics and to social life, have been mainstays of rhetoric from Wichelns forward, even if not all have acknowledged their presence.

To argue that Wichelns had a kind of simple billiard-ball cause-and-effect relationship in mind when he advocated the study of effects in criticism of rhetoric would be a rather naïve reading. Sadly, if Baskerville's characterization of rhetorical studies in the mid-twentieth century is correct, that is if indeed William Norwood Brigance and his cohorts were looking for direct and clear lines of influence, then certainly they missed much of the cautionary warning and broader concern afoot in Wichelns's essay. There is good evidence to support Baskerville's concerns, especially in his appeal back to Wrage's 1947 essay, which paints a bleak picture of the quality of work being done in public address at the time. Hence, one can understand why the perceived deficiency of prior rhetorical studies of effect might cast a dark pall over the entire enterprise and give much weight to those who would disavow the study of influence or persuasion in rhetoric.

My interest lies in the extent to which rhetoric scholars' return to explicit questions of effect and related methodologies, such as with Houck and Nocasian, might also reinvent the kind of complexity that Wichelns himself recognized as intrinsic to a concern with effects.[3] That is, if one chooses to take up the task of the study of effects, I believe those burdens originally laid out by Wichelns and then later articulated and transformed by rhetoric scholars such as Burke, Wrage, Bitzer, Baskerville, and Cooper hold a special kind of importance and offer guidance in method and scope. These obligations are not unique to critics of rhetoric but may likewise hold promise for historians of rhetoric and teachers of rhetoric, should we, as we occupy or move between these roles, take interest in issues of effect, of influence, or of persuasion. My goal is not to argue that everyone should study effects, that we all should be concerned with influence or persuasion, for I have no qualms with the idea of studying rhetoric without such a vocabulary and often enjoy reading scholarship that nary once deploys these terms. Instead, I merely wish to argue that once one has crossed the threshold of being concerned with effect, influence, or persuasion, one encounters four general obligations embedded in those endeavors:

1. Specifying causation, or, the typology of causes and conditions;
2. Attention to rhetoric as event, and corresponding complexities;
3. Studying archives as relevant to the event; and,
4. Relating the rhetorical event to the history of ideas or the history of thought.

None of these a revolutionary insight into the study of rhetoric and they may even be quite rudimentary and perfunctory principles. If there is a bold claim to be found in this somewhat timid essay, it may be that what has often occurred in recent decades (and we may lay the calendar mark of blame too precisely, somewhat unfairly, and rather arbitrarily around 1965) is not so much that critics of rhetoric gave up studying effects as it is that many gave up doing criticism. At least, they gave up doing criticism in the way that Burke and Wichelns depicted it. The surrender was so complete that by 1977 criticism had been redefined not to exclude effects but to narrow the kind of effects considered such that what became a common mode of criticism was, to be blunt, no longer critical; criticism was no longer put to the task of critique. Thus, I hold out hope that our current consideration of effects in rhetoric might reactivate the obligations of Wichelns, the restraint of the early Burke, and the scope of Wrage while infusing them with the insights of Bitzer, Cooper, and other more recent theorists of rhetoric.

Effect and Cause

To begin an inquiry into questions of effect in rhetoric, we need to start with a clarification of what we are looking for when we seek an effect. To elucidate this matter requires a brief tangent into theories of causes and conditions. While claiming a simple symmetry between the terms *cause* and *condition* in logic would be reductive, their problems and literature overlap significantly enough to warrant some cautious equivocation. Logicians and philosophers have been for centuries grappling with the typologies and categories of causes and conditions, so what can be offered here is not comprehensive but instead merely a prefatory and practical consideration to enable our forward movement back into the question of what rhetoric can do.

At the risk of being pedantic, we can begin with a rudimentary distinction between necessary, sufficient, and contributory causes. As Andrew Brennan put it when he was tasked with writing a summary of the scholarship, "there is no straightforward way to give a precise and comprehensive account of the meaning of the term 'necessary (or sufficient) condition' itself."[4] Hence, we will settle for how the story is generally told, which begins with the claim that a necessary cause is a particular condition required for the possibility of a specific effect. To place it in a relatively mundane syntax, the necessary cause is expressed as, "only if X is Y possible." This is not to say that X alone will be enough to cause Y but merely that X is prerequisite to Y, that is, X is a necessary condition for Y. In his 1906 *Introduction to Logic*, H. W. B. Joseph opposed the necessary to the accidental in this way: "Sir Robert Peel was killed by a fall from his horse, and we say his death was accidental. Why? He was a man, and for a man it is necessary to die, and for any one who falls in that particular way it may be necessary to die; but it is not necessary that a man should fall in that way; that is not predicable universally of man."[5] Thus, the accidental cause has a nonessential role in its effect, the necessary cause an essential one.

Inversely, we generally refer to the sufficient cause as that which, without need of aid from any other conditions or factors, is sufficient for causing a particular effect. In general syntax, it would be the simple claim that "if X, then Y." That is, the existence of X is sufficient itself for the production of Y. This is not to say that the sufficient cause is required for the effect but instead that it can be, in itself, enough to produce the effect, even if other causes could likewise alone or together produce that same effect. Joseph offers this example of a sufficient but accidental (not necessary) cause: "as when we say that the explosion of a powder magazine under the place where he is standing is the cause of a man's death."[6] Hence, the sufficient cause may not be essential to its effect, but it needs no additional conditions to aid in the production of the effect.

Before moving on to the third type of cause, I want to pause for a moment to consider the extent to which these first two types of causes might be of interest to critics and scholars of rhetoric. Setting aside the dream of a cause that would be both necessary and sufficient, at this point the answer appears to me that pursuit of either necessary or sufficient causes is at once both too mundane to be worthy of our efforts and beyond the scope of our capacities.

In the case of the necessary cause, we would have to ask whether a particular event of rhetoric was necessary, essentially required, for an event that followed. Let us touch back on two significant essays, one older and one newer, that discussed the effects of specific events of rhetoric: Kenneth Burke's "Rhetoric of Hitler's Battle" and Houck and Nocasian's "FDR's First Inaugural Address." If one asks the question of the necessity of Hitler's rhetoric in Burke's essay or of FDR's address in Houck and Nocasian's to their corresponding effects, it seems a simple logical tautology, not needing scholarly intervention, to say that if the rhetoric had never occurred there would be no effect of that rhetoric. In mathematical terms, one could say that there can be no $f(x)$ if there is no x (which is not the same as $x = 0$). Hence, the obvious claim is that the occurrence of any event is de facto a necessary condition for that event to have any effect. Yet, this mundane claim can offer no insight into any specific event of rhetoric and can be demonstrated as an abstract principle once and for all rhetorical events, thus hardly being worthy of scholarly intervention.

A more interesting inquiry might ask whether the specific form or content of a particular event of rhetoric was a necessary condition for whatever responses occurred, but this would require an accounting for the total of all possibilities absent that specific form or content, a universal knowledge of all possible events in the absence of the suspected cause. Indeed, the counterfactual logic of establishing necessary cause posits first this hypothesis: *If X had not occurred, Y would never have happened.* The obligation for testing that hypothesis is an extraordinary knowledge of all possible worlds without X, which is at once mundane (without X there would be no effects of X) and omniscient (in all possible worlds without X condition Y would never happen). Neither of these seems either worthy of or within the scope of rhetorical study. This choice of either making a mundane claim or needing god-like knowledge is only further complicated by the fact that one could not merely ask whether, if Hitler's rhetoric had been other than it was, the rise of Nazism, the Second World War, and the Holocaust would have possibly occurred. Instead, one would have to be able to isolate the specific necessary condition in his rhetoric that was required for those later events. Likewise with FDR's address: are there any other possible forms or contents his inaugural could have taken to achieve similar results? Certainly we might make arguments about forms that seem unlikely to have produced the subsequent historical events that we can document, but to say this particular condition is the one and only form of rhetoric that could have possibly produced these specific effects (the burden of necessary causality) is at least as unbearable a demand upon the scholar of rhetoric as it is upon the epidemiologist. Hence, I must conclude that when we concern ourselves with effect, it is to establish not a necessary cause but another form of cause entirely.

Likewise, with sufficiency, we find another kind of double bind, this time between the exceedingly simplistic and the impossibly arhetorical vacuum of single causes. In the first case, the mundane abstract claim is that any and every particular event of rhetoric is sufficient, in itself, for producing *some kind* of a response or effect, even if that is silence or nonacknowledgment. To the extent that, in the case of rhetoric, no effect is itself a significant effect, the question of any rhetorical event's sufficiency to produce an effect is not only mundane but logically ordained. On the other hand, one is hard pressed to find in even the longest and widest view of rhetoric a theory that does not, in some way, require an interaction with surrounding conditions, circumstances, situations, and events to produce whatever effects it might. From Aristotle to Atticus, from Fred Newton Scott to Robert L. Scott, a relation to a given situation might be the one nearly universal theoretical claim in the study of rhetoric. To ask whether a specific event of rhetoric produced specific effects requires a consideration of broader contributing factors that made that particular rhetoric, to borrow from Bitzer, the fitting (or unfit) rhetoric for that moment, which combined to give rise to the possibility of that potential effect. Indeed, Burke takes into consideration postwar German culture and society as well as the expansion of materialist capitalism when he analyzes Hitler's *Mein Kampf*. Likewise, Houck and Nocasian lay the assassination attempt at Roosevelt's speech in Miami just weeks before as backdrop for the inaugural. In both cases, what they demonstrate is that the event of rhetoric alone was insufficient for the results witnessed, as it operated out of a relationship with other factors, namely other events.

Thus we come to our final candidate, contributory cause, which might be the catch-all for those things that are not sufficient to produce the effect in themselves. A necessary but not sufficient cause would, by definition, rely upon other contributory causes to produce its effect. Yet, we have already ruled out the necessary cause, so when we look here to contributory causes we mean only those that had some hand in the production of the effect, though they may not have been required and were themselves alone insufficient for its emergence. Hence, we might say that event X contributes to the emergence of event Y but is neither necessary nor sufficient for the latter to occur. The inclusion of contributory cause can be especially perturbing, as isolating what events are contributory causes can be difficult, especially in the study of complex events and particularly those that rarely occur. More troubling is that when one asks after contributory causes one is usually seeking some kind of extent or degree of that contribution. In short, how much does the event of *Mein Kampf*'s publication and distribution or the event of FDR's inaugural account for the specific effects that followed in comparison with the scope of other conditions that contributed to those effects? Such questions call for a broad consideration of events just to begin to open the inquiry. One might be tempted to turn to quantitative social scientific methods, but scholars of rhetoric often study extraordinary events, and standard Bayesian statistical methods rely upon the law of large numbers, which is ill suited to situations that may be sui generis. Additionally, such methods tend to be more analytic than synthetic, making it difficult to apply them to broad complex social ecologies, which can shift radically from age to age and require a critic's sensitivity to the peculiarities of a given historical moment.

So, what we can claim with some confidence at this point is that what rhetoric can do is contributory and that its contributions are related to or dependent upon the surrounding conditions of the rhetorical event, which means that we are looking to rhetoric as a conditional and contributory cause—a cause that, given certain conditions, can contribute to particular effects. To say that a cause is conditional is certainly not to assert useless or even minor knowledge. After all, knowledge of the boiling point of water is quite useful knowledge and yet entirely conditional (100 degrees celsius, assuming normal atmospheric conditions at sea level on this planet). Yet, we should likewise note that what we have here is not a simple kind of condition and contribution. We find with rhetoric, unlike boiling water, that its causation is also probabilistic. The boiling point of water appears quite reliable given some basic conditions, but rhetorical events seem only probable in their production of effects, or it may be that the co-conditions of any rhetorical event are simply too complex for us to thoroughly consider, which would be effectively identical in practice to probabilistic cause.

So, we now have a somewhat laborious clarification of a basic foundation from which we can inquire about a method for studying effects in rhetoric. What we seek is inquiry into rhetorical events as probabilistic conditional contributory causes of other subsequent events. In this summary, all roads appear to lead in the direction of the broader consideration of rhetorical events as the first step in our analysis. Criticism of rhetoric begins by accepting a world of probabilistic relationships, in which a complex set of contributing factors within conditional constraints make possible the emergence of other events, perhaps even conditions and events that have never before occurred and will never converge in the same way again.

Rhetorical Events

At its birth in the modern American academy, criticism of rhetoric was already obsessed with the event of rhetoric's occurrence. In fact, one would be hard pressed to find the conditional and the contingent nature of rhetoric stated more strongly than how Wichelns himself put it. "The writer of rhetorical discourse is," he wrote, "in a sense, perpetually in bondage to the occasion and the audience."[7] It would be more than forty years before an inverse statement of that same proposition would become Bitzer's essay on the rhetorical situation. It was not a position of bondage, for Bitzer, but an exigence that opened a possibility for rhetoric. As he put it, "a particular discourse comes into existence because of some specific condition or situation which invites utterance."[8] The speaker is given both constraint and possibility by the event; whether one is in bondage or invited, the event governs the rhetorical house. This is not merely to say that one must be able to produce a reason for speaking, that the speaker must attenuate her or his claims to fit the audience and situation—a timidly neo-Aristotelean notion of adaptation. Quite to the contrary, Bitzer offers two considerations that refute the possibility of the rhetor providing his or her own exigence, originating rhetoric such that either rhetor or rhetoric might govern the event. First, Bitzer delineates between "real" rhetorical situations that hold true exigence in themselves and "sophistic" or "contrived" rhetorical situations.[9] Yet, more important, Bitzer posits that rhetoric emerges onto the scene only at the invitation of the situation, which means that the possibility for the rhetorical construction of an event requires an event's invitation for any event-constructing rhetoric. Even the contrivance of the "sophistic" event, in Bitzer's theory, would demand another prior or more encompassing event that would invite the rhetoric of contrivance. Indeed, in Wichelns's bondage and in Bitzer's invitation is the sheer fact that the event makes possible whatever rhetorical agencies might emerge, not only saying this or that is good or bad for the situation but also what might get to be said, who can say it, and how it may be said.

In 1947 Wrage expressed much this kind of understanding of the position of a speech or a writing within a rhetorical event. Unlike a strong sense of the rhetor-as-agent and rhetoric-as-agency, Wrage wrote that "a speech is an agency of its time, one whose surviving record provides a repository of themes and their elaborations from which we may gain insight into the life of an era as well as into the mind of a man."[10] While Wrage's concern here was speeches and he makes some concession to the then-dominant biographical and psychological traditions in criticism, he made clear that "the exclusive study of speeches would result in historical distortion unless related to a larger framework of life and thought."[11] A rhetorical event, then, is contained not merely in the moment of writing or speaking or in publication but in a whole of the epoch for which that rhetoric and that rhetor are agencies. Rather than saying that Wrage was not interested in questions of effect, it would be more precise to say that he expressed a more expansive and more complex understanding of effect than did many subsequent theorists and advocates of rhetorical effect.

We can see much of this in how both Burke and Houck and Nocasian treat their subjects. In the case of Burke's criticism of *Mein Kampf*, the essay is deep in its consideration of the psychology and biography of Hitler, insights into the "mind of a man," but it likewise is replete with the considerations of the ways in which Hitler's rise and the function of his rhetoric were made possible through a series of social, political, historical, or cultural shifts that both bound and invited Hitlerism in the 1930s. Perhaps most notable is Burke's constant return to the expansion of "materialist capitalism" and the corresponding weakening of religion as conditions that engendered a turn toward "dignity" in postwar Munich that could no longer be found in either work or God.[12] Burke goes to some pains to clarify that his concern is not with the fact that Hitler deployed a rhetoric of unity or unification, for Burke is quite a fan, at least at this point, of unification rhetoric. Instead, he asks what it was about this rhetorical event that made possible the emergence, distribution, and escalation of Hitler's specific kind of unification discourse. His answer is as complex as it is compelling; he locates that possibility in a confluence of the speaker's life, the historical events preceding *Mein Kampf*'s publication, the positions of the audiences, the economic structures and conditions in Germany, the literature and artistic work of the time, and rising scientific theories, as well as the political terrain and public sentiments about politics. The rhetorical event is all this together, which at once both binds what was possible and invites rhetorical practices. That is to say, the event makes speakers agencies of its epoch at least as much as it makes it possible for them to be agents in a struggle.

Likewise, Houck and Nocasian take up similar considerations in their study of FDR's inaugural. They situate their analysis of the speech by appealing directly to Thomas Benson's call that critics of rhetoric see "the three elements of production, text, and reception not only as sequential but also as mutually and inseparably part of the same larger text."[13] In this case, however, Houck and Nocasian situate the inaugural in a much broader understanding of rhetorical event than one might first expect from a focus on "production, text, and reception." For example, in the section entitled "God and Miami" they discuss the importance of the botched attempt on Roosevelt's life that occurred seventeen days before the inaugural. They then connect that event to the religious discourses that quickly swallowed up its reporting to tell of a divine destiny in the would-be-assassin's incompetence. Once those events entered into the discourses of God and country, a particular rhetorical agency opened before Roosevelt but also bound him. As Houck and Nocasian note, the religious vernacular entered the draft of the address after that moment, in the turn of the rhetorical event, and though we may laud the skill of the speech writer (Raymond Moley) or of Roosevelt in heeding the turn of events, it would seem a decidedly peculiar take on the central arguments made by Houck and Nocasian to claim that this speech was something other than one of Wrage's agencies of its time. Not only do Houck and Nocasian connect the reception of the inaugural to economic, religious, and journalistic discourses of the time, but, similar to Burke though by different evidences, they present the formation of the inaugural as itself an effect of the period.

In both these rhetorical studies, of rhetoric by Hitler and rhetoric by FDR, what we see repeated in practice is a primacy of the event that, in different ways, was called for by Wichelns, Wrage, and Bitzer. Indeed, it seems to go without saying that critics of rhetoric should, as Martha Cooper put it in 1988, "describe the event, its materiality, as a way of understanding what rhetoric itself is."[14] Perhaps, however, we have played a bit too loosely with this term, *event,* and if its slipperiness has caused equivocation we might ponder not how to constrain and define it for precision but instead ask whether that looseness has allowed us a broader consideration of the peculiarities and particularities of specific rhetorical events. After all, if we are asking about the possible effects and causes (admittedly probabilistic, conditional, and contributory) that might be entailed within a rhetorical event, we will need an openness to what we articulate as the space of an event to allow all those co-contributing, countervailing, and concomitant factors into our field of view. In both the cases of Burke and Houck and Nocasian they follow the event's unfolding out to where they see the scope of connections and relationships. They ask not only what this rhetorical event has wrought but also what made it possible, what made possible its singular emergence, which requires, as did Michel Foucault's work on events, "correlation with other previous or simultaneous events, discursive or otherwise."[15] Indeed, it bears noting that Cooper considered it Foucault's basic assumption that "discourse should be treated as an event," even if the finer points of those terms would require more parsing than is either practical or needed for the current inquiry.

So, the critic begins, then, with the rhetorical event and with speakers, writers, speeches, and texts as agencies of that event. We know that, as Byron Hawk put it, "no simple or linear cause-and-effect logic is adequate for describing the complexity of such discursive events,"[16] but what seems less clear is what resources we do have for asking after the probabilistic conditional contributory causes within the expanse of a rhetorical event and the agencies which that event binds and invites. Turning back again to Wichelns, we see an admonition particularly well heeded by both Burke and Houck and Nocasian. In 1925 Wichelns argued that "rhetorical criticism," most especially because it is concerned with questions of influence and effect, requires "a strong historical sense for the ideas and attitudes of the people (not merely of their leaders), and a full knowledge of the public opinion of the times."[17] Thus, the critic who studies effects will not be satisfied with either official or journalistic accounts but has an obligation to study the scope of events, events of thought, events of discourse, events of movement and economy, that might be related to the rhetorical event under study. That is to say, a kind of archival work will be required if one asks about the emergence of a rhetorical event and any kind of relationship of causation or effect.

Archives of Rhetorical Events

Certainly some studious critics of rhetoric frequently mine the historical archives, collected papers, and special collections that pertain to the rhetorical event under study. Some likewise come to context through the work of other historians, the publications of contemporaries, and similar sources. It certainly seems that Bitzer had all of this kind of work in mind when he wrote that "rhetorical works belong to the class of things which obtain their character from the circumstances of the historical context in which they occur."[18] Similarly, Wrage saw concern with archival and historical research intrinsic to rhetoric scholarship, for he wrote that "to adopt the rhetorical perspective is actually to approximate more closely a genuinely historical point of view when analyzing and interpreting speeches as documents of ideas in social history."[19] Such qualities of rhetorical inquiry make it logical that one who takes up the study of a rhetorical event would be concerned with what the archives hold, be those archives the physical collections of papers housed in quiet rooms where you are forbidden to bring a pen or any other kind of accumulation of what was said and written, what was allowable to say by whom and when, what was passed forward and what was left behind. In short, whether one comes to archives as would Jacques Barzun or as would Michel Foucault, calling for the study of a rhetorical event is to go to the archives. Indeed, joining something of the traditional historical treatments of archives (what we might call $archive_1$) with Foucault's conception of archives ($archive_2$) in what Linda Ferreira-Buckley has called "concomitant methodologies" may well be required in the study of rhetorical events.[20] This would not represent anything like a radical break from Wichelns, Burke, Wrage, Bitzer, or Houck and Nocasian but perhaps an amendment and a slightly increased complexity to some of what they all called for and practiced.

There is perhaps no clearer definition of terms in Foucault's work than the one he gives for an archive:

> The set of rules which at a given period and for a given society define:
> 1. The limits and forms of the *sayable*. What is it possible to speak of? . . .
> 2. The limits and forms of *conservation*. Which utterances are destined to disappear without a trace? . . .
> 3. The limits and forms of *memory* as it appears in different discursive formations. Which utterances does everyone recognize as valid, or debatable, or definitely invalid? . . .
> 4. The limits and forms of *reactivation*. Among the discourses of previous epochs or of foreign cultures, which are retained, which are valued, which are imported, and which are attempts made to reconstitute? . . .
> 5. The limits and forms of *appropriation*. What individuals, what groups or classes have access to a particular kind of discourse?[21]

Perhaps the only clarification required of these definitions, which seem quite straightforward, is that Foucault tended to deploy the term *discourse* as a very broad field of statements that, while finite, is not a specific conversation between given interlocutors or a single act of writing or speech. Instead of a specific act of rhetoric, a discourse is a broader field in which rhetoric occurs, an enabling dimension of the rhetorical event that makes possible a specific rhetorical act. Thus, Foucault tended to write histories of discourses such as a discourse of discipline, a discourse of madness, a discourse of surveillance, a discourse of science, with any particular epoch in history holding a range of interacting and overlapping discourses, each to varying degrees peculiar to that age. For the critic of rhetoric, such discourses manifest or interact within a rhetorical event as both an articulation of and the application of those rules that make up the archive$_2$ of that particular moment.

The concomitant methodology of the traditional archive$_1$ and the Foucaldian archive$_2$ can be said to glimmer in both Burke and Houck and Nocasian, though by no means would it be proper to call either of their essays "Foucauldian." Burke appealed to the notion of a "total worldview" found in Hitlerism and *Mein Kampf* that could account for every statement, a set of rules that made it possible or sensible to say this but not that, and that reactivated certain elements of prior discourses while making others unintelligible.[22] In this regard, through his reading of *Mein Kampf* he hints at some of the same kinds of concerns Foucault would invest in archive$_2$. Burke connects *Mein Kampf* not so much to other particular publications and speeches made at the time as to the operative discourses of sex, medicine, and race that would give Hitlerism its own kind of scientific reasoning. When Burke discusses Hitler's attack on the parliament it is not primarily in relation to specific documents from journalists and popular sources depicting parliament's excesses (something like a traditional archival connection); far more important is how the "Babel" of parliament connects to the "Babylon of Vienna" and the excesses and indulgences of parliamentary rhetoric become embroiled with discourses of prostitution, debauchery, and decadence. Finally, he concludes with the combination of conditions that made possible the emergence of a specific comingling of sciences and religion (natural law is God's law) with budding discourses of race and principles of survival-of-the-fittest that would ultimately enable the Holocaust. If Burke is light in archival work, it is in the appeal to archive$_1$, not archive$_2$, though certainly his consideration of historical and biographical detail must give him some credit for attending to the broad event.

The inverse might be said of Houck and Nocasian's essay, as their attention to archive$_1$ is impressive. Yet, they also present the comingling of those dusty documents from the FDR presidential library and the Moley papers with broader considerations of how particular discourses of the time made certain kinds of utterances possible while others were less so. First, as mentioned in the discussion of rhetorical events, Houck and Nocasian point to the connection between Roosevelt's position as divine savior and dominant Judeo-Christian discourses of salvation and faith in an interventionist God. They extend that thematic into what they call the "discourse of dictatorship" that was rising over the months prior to the inaugural. Their discussion of public support for a Roosevelt "dictatorship," in combination with the analysis of theologico-political themes of salvation and divine intervention, hints at the beginnings of an exploration of an archive$_2$ in understanding how the operative discourses and the rules that governed those discourses converged in the specific rhetorical event of an inaugural. While it would be overextending to say that Houck and Nocasian offer as rich an understanding of an archive$_2$ and its operative discourses as Burke did, their essay reflects a rich consideration of archive$_1$ with at least some indication of the ways in which archive$_1$ can lead us to ask the kinds of questions that Burke evoked with his focus on worldviews and rising discourses of science, directing us closer to archive$_2$.

As an amendment to these two examples of the comingling of archive$_1$ and archive$_2$ we might take guidance from Anne Laura Stoler's consideration of the relationship between the two archives. For Stoler, the official or physical archive embodied in archive$_1$ may well represent something of a text we can examine for a greater understanding of archive$_2$. After all, archive$_1$ is a site explicitly of conservation, memory, and reactivation—three of the four elements of archive$_2$. In this vein, Stoler argues that we consider archive$_1$ not only an "archive-as-source" but also an "archive-as-subject."[23] Thus, when a critic of rhetoric approaches an archive$_1$, if that critic is to seek after a rhetorical event, to inquire of its causes and effects, to fulfill that call from Wichelns, Wrage, and Bitzer that we take the historical moment of a rhetorical event seriously, then an archive$_1$ is not only rich source material but also a monument to practices of conservation, practices of memory, and practices of reactivation. What is present and absent from an archive$_1$ may be a vital insight, Stoler argues, into an archive$_2$. Thus, we might ask Houck and Nocasian what we can learn about the relevant archive$_2$ of their rhetorical event by how practices of conservation, memory, and reactivation are reflected in the presidential library or the Moley papers. Stoler's admonition likewise keeps those who ask after the questions of effect in rhetoric appropriately suspicious of their source materials, not so much to distinguish fact from fiction but, as she put it, "to track the production and consumption of facticities as the contingent coordinates of particular times and temperaments, places and purposes."[24] Such a duty thus folds back and burdens the rhetoric scholar who would examine an archive$_2$ to ground her or his analyses in the appropriate archives$_1$, both as source and as subject. Thus, rather than concomitant methods, archive$_1$ and archive$_2$ may hold an interdependent relationship.

Histories of Ideas and Thought

The combination of archive$_1$ and archive$_2$, with the now-dual function of archive$_1$ as both source and subject, returns us to the fundamental questions of the study of effects in rhetoric as articulated by Wichelns, Burke, and Wrage. When we investigate effects of rhetoric, we are, as the analysis up to this point has demonstrated, thrust into a broad consideration of the event and pushed into the examination of both archive$_1$ and archive$_2$, and we practice a history that is less about single rhetors and single texts than about rhetorical events comingling with discourses and historical conditions. We are not too far afield at this point from how Baskerville characterized Wrage's work: an "idea-centered" approach to "intellectual history," rather than a person-centered approach.[25] Baskerville contrasted a study of "influence" based on "the overpowering emphasis on personal persuasion" with Wrage's "attempt to learn what the *substance* of a speech, together with the rhetorical strategies, by means of which that substance is communicated to audiences, can tell us about the times out of which the speeches grew, the audiences to whom they were addressed, and the men and women who uttered them."[26] Note that both these projects share an interest in effects, in movement and action, but the scope and terrain in question and, more important, of allowable inquiry broadens significantly with Wrage's histories of ideas.

Many readers today may draw a distinction between histories of ideas and histories of thought, and in many contexts I think this quite reasonable. However, in the case of Wrage, the standard criticisms of histories of ideas—their focus upon great thinkers, the model of arborescent patrilineage, a tendency to posit ideas outside of time—all would be unfair. Wrage was careful to insist that when one studies the history of ideas, such ideas cannot be restricted "to a description of the great and noble thoughts uttered by accredited spokesmen for the edification of old and young."[27] Instead, he proposed a more "inclusive," method that "refers widely to formulations of thought as the product of expressions of social incentives."[28] In this way ideas could never be hypostasized or made transcendent but rather "are to be studied as a body of intricate tissues, of differentiated yet related thought."[29] For a scholar of rhetoric the study of the history of ideas is thus not the study of timeless philosophical concepts or of statements of great figures in history but is a study of practices of enunciation, of expression, of relation, and of differentiation. It is a study of something organic, changing, and distributed, something intricate, differentiated, and yet related, and its metaphor is not arborescent but rhizomatic. Both the essays of Burke and of Houck and Nocasian perform something of this broad concern with the tissues of thought that were the formulations and operations of the sayable within their chosen rhetorical events. They took their ostensible object of inquiry, Hitler's book for one and a president's inaugural in the other, and found that it called them to entire formulations of thought. Thus, their rhetorical criticisms were, in a way, performing Wrage's notion of a history of ideas.

Today we might more comfortably call Wrage's endeavor a history of thought, following Foucault's distinction, but this seems a semantic quibble in this specific case. We certainly should be comfortable enough to characterize Burke's work on Hitler and Houck and Nocasian's work on FDR as participating in histories of how certain behaviors, practices, and desires emerged, functioned, and circulated. Far more than being a history of the rise of the Third Reich or being a history of Roosevelt's early presidency, they are histories of how various factors converged into what could be said, remembered, reactivated, and conserved in two related yet differentiated rhetorical events. While it may be tempting to read the psychological profile of Burke's essay or the history of various versions of FDR's address as seeking out the "silently intended meanings" that Foucault tried to avoid, in both cases what they do far more is deploy those materials, in the biography of Hitler and in the transition of the inaugural across versions, to connect them to conditions of the manifest appearance of the rhetorical event that made *Mein Kampf* possible in one case and FDR's first inaugural possible in the other.

In seeking effects, a critic studies the rhetorical event in its breadth, requiring the combination of archive_1 and archive_2 as mutually dependent methodologies, which means that the study of effect is bound to the study of histories of thought, for no examination of an event as a rhetorical event can avoid the question of wide formulations of intricate, differentiated, yet related tissues of thought. I might add only this to the articulation of our method thus far: just as archive_2 interrogates archive_1 as a site of conservation, reactivation, and memory, so too must a history of thought ask not only what was sayable but what was not sayable or, perhaps even more important, what was so true that it would never need to be said. This is why a history of thought (or a history of ideas) can never be done by simply looking for the presence of a word or a cluster of words. Certainly thought is not simply isomorphic to a finite and static set of terms, but likewise what thought takes as most true may be entirely ellipsed from articulation. Does not the need to call something "political" belie that its status as political cannot be taken for granted? Those fields most political, that is, most naturalized in thought as being in the scope of politics, are those terrains in which the word "political" never need be written or spoken, because the political is already operative. Indeed, if one were to state it explicitly (for example, a political senate election), we would likely engage in contortions to give *political* a special function or meaning to explain its superfluous presence.

Finally, the rhetorical event folds back into the archives, becoming a part of the conditions and possibilities of future events. Whatever scope a critic gives to a rhetorical event in time and in discourse, that event likewise functions as a site of future potentiality. The event folds into archive_1 in its recording, collection, organization, and exclusion. Likewise, as a participant in the discourses of its epoch, a rhetorical event becomes a part of the archive_2, perhaps by iteration, perhaps by the interplay of transgression and limit, perhaps by practices of dissemination and reactivation. In so doing, every rhetorical event has the potential to contribute to the future conditions of possibility or impossibility; that is to say, each event participates in discourses and practices, participates in archive_1 and archive_2, to shape what in its own epoch and possibly in other epochs it may be possible to say or do.

To summarize, up to this point we have narrowed the scope of effects studies in rhetoric to probabilistic conditional contributory relationships, which pushed us into a consideration of the study of rhetorical events, a term intentionally left open to invite scholars of rhetoric to follow the shapes and contours of events as individual interventions require. The exploration of a rhetorical event demanded that we consider the function of the archives, both archive_1 and archive_2. Together not only do these archives give the scholar of rhetoric a way in which to trace out the practices, behaviors, and other events that would give shape to the rhetorical event under study, but the two archives mutually check each other's possible deficiencies or excesses. Finally, the study of the rhetorical event, reinvented from the examination of the two archives, inevitably involves the rhetorical critic in histories of thought.

Criticism as Critique

The question now appears to be what role *criticism* might play in such histories of thought. Given that our method has been teased out from Wichelns's own invention of rhetorical criticism, likewise bound to both Wrage's and Bitzer's insights, and demonstrated as practiced in different ways by Burke and Houck and Nocasian, what exactly does or can rhetoric scholarship concerned with effects do? Is its terminus the historical insight, recalling the distinction sharply invoked and mildly retracted by Baskerville in which critics are evaluative while historians are expository? In the context of Wichelns's description of rhetorical criticism and Wrage's argument for histories of ideas, that conclusion would appear most odd. If by "evaluative" Baskerville was referring to that easy move of applying a given aesthetic, moral, or political doctrine to a speech or speaker to stamp out approval or disapproval, then certainly the "evaluative" critics were not practicing criticism as Wichelns or Burke depicted it. Rather, for a critic to function as an agency of critique required a far more critical kind of criticism.

Here may be the critical distinction between Houck and Nocasian's essay on FDR's inaugural and Burke's study of *Mein Kampf.* Houck and Nocasian articulate the insight of their essay as both a richer understanding of the inaugural event and as an argument for the study of audience responses and more general effects of rhetoric. While the Burke's essay most certainly made an argument about approaches to criticism, his analysis was directed toward a more critical task of interrogating the operations of fascism. That is to say, while Houck and Nocasian provide broad analysis of a rhetorical event with keen attention to the archives and a connection to the history of ideas, if they offer a critique it is of those critics who eschew the study of effects. Burke, on the other hand, offers a deeper critique that encompasses both certain kinds of criticism and the rhetoric of fascism within a particular movement in the history of thought. Both represent forms of criticism, but I would contend Burke's critique offers more the kind of impact that Wichelns, Wrage, Bitzer, and Cooper were hoping criticism might be able to produce.

For Burke, criticism that wielded a given ethical or political principle and then bludgeoned a text with it was not criticism at all. When scholars and students today encounter Burke's "Rhetoric of Hitler's Battle" I have to wonder how much of Burke's polemic against easy moralistic judgment leaps to the fore of their reading and discussion of the essay. Certainly his position is peppered across the text, not always in subtle ways, and he even tips his hand right from the start, yet it still rarely receives commentary. When scholars mention the essay, Burke's arguments about what criticism can and should do are largely eclipsed by its other contributions. Two general readings tend to dominate this commentary. Most common is the position that the essay offers primarily a study of Hitler's rhetorical tactics in order to determine appropriate methods of defense and "inoculation" against such devices (see, for example, Robert Ivie).[30] Nearly as common and sometimes coexisting with this first reading is an approach that sees Burke's essay as offering a larger lesson, as Karlyn Kohrs Campbell wrote, about "the processes of symbolically transforming the mythic principles of one universe of thought, in this case Christianity, into a potent ideology, in this case Nazism."[31] These certainly seem quite reasonable interpretations of the essay, and I have no doubt Burke makes these moves in his analysis of *Mein Kampf*, but there is also a clear advocacy present about what Burke held to be the responsibilities of a critic. Briefly tracing out those elements of "Rhetoric of Hitler's Battle" not only casts doubt on Michael McGee's claim that the essay "does little more than demonstrate the moral polemical power of dramatistic methods"[32] but, more important, it gives us a picture of the responsibilities of critics of rhetoric who might choose to follow the path we have laid out thus far.

In the opening of the essay Burke condemns prior reviewers of *Mein Kampf* for "vandalistic comments" and accuses them of engaging in a type of book burning. He calls us to eschew the easy path of knocking off "a few adverse attitudinizings" and calling it a day, even though he says a reviewer of *Mein Kampf* who did so "would likely have guaranty in advance that his article will have favorable reception among the decent members of the population."[33] His complaint is strong, right from the first page, but here at the start of the essay he condemns this kind of criticism simply for turning away from a possible moment of enlightenment to seek instead easy gratification. He is a dozen pages into his analysis when he drives home the split between these two kinds of criticism with more fervor, positioning his own as "a harkening to the opposition and attempting to mature a policy in the light of counter-policies," which he opposed to the kind of criticism "Hitler wanted": "a pure and simple coefficient of power enabling him to go most effectively in the direction he had chosen."[34] This simple coefficient of power, this efficient movement to a given conclusion by application of force, describes well the kind of moralistic gratification Burke sets aside in his opening. Hitlerism and the easy attitudinizings of pious reviewers, for Burke, share this quality of seeking not to harken to what might be said or written but instead to consume everything as fuel for the "hasty" critic's established cause.

To refrain from that moralistic impulse and study *Mein Kampf* with all seriousness, not merely seeking in it the evil we already feel to be there, is no small task, but, as Burke insisted, doing so is prerequisite to asking, "What are we to learn from Hitler's book?"[35] This is what Burke performs in his criticism: a criticism and even a judgment that emerges by working through a text into a rhetorical event, across the archives, and into histories of thought. In other words, Burke offers a critical approach to criticism; he performs a kind of criticism as critique. Indeed, Burke is, in this essay, almost curiously analytic and restrained, consistently retreating back away from the easy moralizing to ask how Hitler's rhetoric functions and why it circulates so well.

Burke certainly comes to a judgment of *Mein Kampf,* but it is a judgment that comes from working through the book, not lording over it like a magistrate imposing law. That restraint and the eventual judgment are made possible first by his refusal to apply reductive, simple ideas of rhetorical cause that would lay the blame for Nazism solely on mob psychology or Hitler's rhetorical *pharmakon*. Second, he extends his analysis out not only to a book, or a speech, or a speaker, or even the whole of Nazi media and communications but across the scope of the rhetorical event, its placement in history, practices of work and religion, desires for dignity, and discourses of science and race. To do so required that he build something of an archive$_2$, working with texts available, trying to build a map that would outline the multiple lines that intersected across this rhetorical event and converged in the space of *Mein Kampf*. Finally, he connects that rhetorical event and its convergence, along with the broad related events in Hitler's rhetoric, to the history of thought, to thinking about politics, about capitalism, and about public discourse. Only then does he give us a picture of what we can say of this text, lay out a lesson to be learned from *Mein Kampf,* though by this point the lesson is more about a broad event and not just one of its rhetorical agencies.

Yet, one of the most important lessons that I draw from Burke's study is not about Hitler, or Nazi rhetoric, or even symbolic transformation of principles into ideology. Instead, for today, I see in "Rhetoric of Hitler's Battle" this lesson: criticism can do more than give us the easy gratification of passing righteous judgment, if it first opens itself to asking what is to be learned and what is at work in an event and if it engages judgment as a working through that event to seek the broad network of probabilistic, conditional, and contributory conditions that made it possible at this time that this was said and not that. That is to say, criticism can withhold that kind of judgment that operates as the establishment of a violation of given law in order to make a space for asking first what we can learn from this rhetorical event. Wichelns seemed to have precisely this in mind when he wrote that the critic of rhetoric's first concern is not with the valuation of beauty or the imposition of timeless standards. What Burke performed only shortly after Wichelns's call was a criticism that not only asked about effect but also was an opening into an exploration of thinking, of our possibilities and options for thought and life. Burke demonstrated how critical judgment is made possible only after one refuses to vandalize or burn even *Mein Kampf*. In this way, "Rhetoric of Hitler's Battle" was perhaps the most profound critique of fascism possible. That, I believe, is what rhetoric scholarship can do. It can study effects and events in a way that is at once rigorous and valuable, working through those events, across the related archives and histories, to produce critiques that offer more than merely the easy gratification of repeating our political and ethical platitudes.

Notes

1. Barnett Baskerville, "Must We All Be Rhetorical Critics," *Quarterly Journal of Speech* 63 (1977): 114.

2. Herbert A. Wichelns, "The Literary Criticism of Oratory," in *Landmark Essays on Rhetorical Criticism,* ed. Thomas W. Benson (Davis, Calif.: Hermagoras Press, 1993), 26.

3. The editors of this volume document and explain well the concern with effect in the study of rhetoric in their introduction and their discussion of the debate among George Edwards, Martin Medhurst, and David Zarefsky. While not necessarily models for the methods discussed in this essay, readers may also take interest in recent works that explicitly consider the effects of rhetoric, such as Christine Harold and Kevin Michael DeLuca, "Behold the Corpse: Violent Images and the Case of Emmett Till," *Rhetoric and Public Affairs* 8 (2005): 263–286; Jennifer Rose Mercieca, "Did the 2008 Election Change Everything?" *Rhetoric and Public Affairs* 15 (2012): 717–735; and Erin J. Rand, "An Inflammatory Fag and a Queer Form: Larry Kramer, Polemics, and Rhetorical Agency," *Quarterly Journal of Speech* 94 (2008): 297–319. Likewise, more implicit assumptions or arguments of effect are frequently found in the criticism of rhetoric, such as Samuel McCormick, "Mirrors for the Queen: A Letter from Christine de Pizan on the Eve of Civil War," *Quarterly Journal of Speech* 94 (2008): 273–296; and Laura Johnson, "(Environmental) Rhetorics of Tempered Apocalypticism in *An Inconvenient Truth*," *Rhetoric Review* 28 (2009): 29–46.

4. Andrew Brennan, "Necessary and Sufficient Condition," in *The Stanford Encyclopedia of Philosophy* (Spring 2009 edition), ed. Edward N. Zalta, Uri Nodelman, and Colin Allen, http://plato.stanford.edu/entries/necessary-sufficient (retrieved February 9, 2011), 2.

5. H. W. B. Joseph, *An Introduction to Logic* (London: Clarendon Press, 1906), 63–64.

6. Joseph, *An Introduction to Logic,* 459.

7. Wichelns, "The Literary Criticism of Oratory," 28.

8. Lloyd Bitzer, "The Rhetorical Situation," *Philosophy and Rhetoric* 1 (1968): 4.

9. Bitzer, "The Rhetorical Situation," 11.

10. Ernest J. Wrage, "Public Address: A Study in Social and Intellectual History," *Quarterly Journal of Speech* 33 (1947): 456.

11. Wrage, "Public Address," 456.

12. Kenneth Burke, "The Rhetoric of Hitler's Battle," in *Landmark Essays on Rhetorical Criticism,* ed. Thomas W. Benson (Davis, Calif.: Hermagoras Press, 1993), 41.

13. Davis W. Houck and Mihaela Nocasian, "FDR's First Inaugural Address: Text, Context, and Reception," *Rhetoric and Public Affairs* 5 (2003): 650; Thomas W. Benson, "'To Lend a Hand': Gerald R. Ford, Watergate, and the White House Speechwriters," *Rhetoric and Public Affairs* 1 (1998): 224.

14. Martha Cooper, "Rhetorical Criticism and Foucault's Philosophy of Discursive Events," *Central States Speech Journal* 39 (1988): 3.

15. Michel Foucault, "Politics and the Study of Discourse," in *The Foucault Effect: Studies in Governmentality with Two Lectures by and an Interview with Michel Foucault,* ed. Graham Burchell, Colin Gordon, and Peter Miller (Chicago: University of Chicago Press, 1991), 59.

16. Byron Hawk, *A Counter-History of Composition: Toward Methodologies of Complexity* (Pittsburgh: University of Pittsburgh Press, 2007), 266.

17. Wichelns, "The Literary Criticism of Oratory," 14.

18. Bitzer, "The Rhetorical Situation," 3.

19. Wrage, "Public Address," 455.

20. Linda Ferreira-Buckley, "Rescuing the Archives from Foucault," *College English* 61 (1999): 578.

21. Foucault, "Politics and the Study of Discourse," 59–60

22. See, in particular, Burke, "The Rhetoric of Hitler's Battle," 35.

23. Ann Laura Stoler, *Along the Archival Grain: Epistemic Anxieties and Colonial Common Sense* (Princeton: Princeton University Press, 2010), 44.

24. Stoler, *Along the Archival Grain,* 33

25. Baskerville, "Must We All Be Rhetorical Critics," 109.

26. Baskerville, "Must We All Be Rhetorical Critics," 113.

27. Wrage, "Public Address," 451.

28. Wrage, "Public Address," 451.

29. Wrage, "Public Address," 452.

30. Robert L. Ivie, "Productive Criticism Then and Now," *American Communication Journal* 4 (2001), http://acjournal.org/holdings/vol4/iss3/special/ivie.pdf (retrieved February 9, 2011).

31. Karlyn Kohrs Campbell, "Criticism: Ephemeral and Enduring," *Speech Teacher* 2 (1974): 11–12.

32. Michael Calvin McGee, "The 'Ideograph': A Link Between Rhetoric and Ideology," *Quarterly Journal of Speech* 66 (1980): 4.

33. Burke, "The Rhetoric of Hitler's Battle," 33.

34. Burke, "The Rhetoric of Hitler's Battle," 45.

35. Burke, "The Rhetoric of Hitler's Battle," 48.

Rhetoric's Effects, the *Vita Activa*, and the Rhetorical Turn in Twentieth-Century Thought

DAVID A. FRANK

Kiewe and Houck's historical survey of the effects of U.S. twentieth-century rhetoric begins with Herbert Wichelns and ends most recently with David Zarfesky. Rhetoric's effect, they observe, was "hailed as the key focus of rhetorical criticism but later dismissed, its scope narrowed then elevated, later impugned and then recently resurrected by several prominent scholars."[1] As they rightly note, "the story of rhetoric's effects has a tormented history in rhetorical studies."[2] The "tortured history" of rhetorical effects in what Hobsbawm calls the "short twentieth century" commences with the beginning of World War I in 1914 and ends with the fall of the Soviet Union in 1991.[3] This context helps explain why rhetorical effects were both rendered taboo by many philosophers and embraced by professors of speech. My intent is to confront this history by placing the thinking about rhetoric's effects in its twentieth-century context. I join Kiewe and Houck in urging rhetorical scholars to place rhetoric's effects at the center of their studies. The "resurrection" of rhetoric's effects as a focus of study will help the field face the truly big questions confronting humanity.

To accomplish these aspirations, I use Perelman and Olbrechts-Tyteca's new rhetoric project as the "representative anecdote" of twentieth-century rhetorical theory. The new rhetoric project is an appropriate selection given it is seen as the "most complete contemporary rhetoric"[4] and "the single most important event in contemporary rhetorical theory."[5] And the new rhetoric project explicitly attempts to fold rhetoric's effects into a coherent rhetorical philosophy by yoking the *vita contemplativa* with the *vita activa*.[6] Actions taken as a result of rhetoric and rhetoric's effects are at the center of the project; both result from the assumption that language, argument, persuasion, as expressions of reason, have an influence on the world.

The new rhetoric project explicitly joins its philosophy of rhetorical action to the empirical study of rhetoric's effects. Perelman and Olbrechts-Tyteca cite a host of quantitative studies on the impact of messages on audiences, including those offered by Asch, Bach, Festinger, Hovland, Kelman, Knower, and a host of other prominent social scientists.[7] They nest these studies of the effects of persuasion within a larger rhetorical constellation justifying action as a subject of study and a consideration of rhetoric's effects as the focus of empirically oriented social science. We must keep in mind their audience and their intent, which was to confront the constrictive definition of reason held by many philosophers in the pre- and postwar period that explicitly ruled out the study of action and the effects of argumentation.

The trajectory of the new rhetoric project provides a good illustration of rhetoric's effects in the twentieth century as Perelman began his intellectual life as a logical positivist, rejecting rhetoric, metaphysics, and the possibility that reason and values might inform action. After experiencing and witnessing the horrific consequences of the Holocaust and World War II, Perelman saw the need to extend reason beyond the confines established by the logical positivists and turned to rhetoric. This turn was prompted by the need to take rhetoric's effects seriously and to anchor the actions taken as a result of persuasion in a system of reason-based responsibility. Although the 1958 French and the 1969 English editions of Perelman and Olbrechts-Tyteca's magnus opus, *Traité de l'argumentation: La nouvelle rhétorique,* elevated the focus on persuasive action, this effort yielded to subsequent attempts to sideline an emphasis on rhetoric's effects, and thus the potential of the new rhetoric project has yet to be fully developed and realized.

Discussion of rhetoric's effects in the context of the twentieth century has a profoundly moral subtext. Rhetoric was used as an instrument to promote and carry out genocide. Indeed, the origins of twentieth-century rhetorical theory in the United States and Europe and the exigence for a thorough account of rhetoric's effects can be traced to Kenneth Burke's confrontation with *Mein Kampf,*[8] Chaïm Perelman's reflections on the Holocaust,[9] and Hannah Arendt's post–World War II writings on totalitarianism.[10] Kenneth Burke, as Ann George and Jack Selzer have written, "immediately" subjected Hitler's book to a rhetorical analysis after the English translation was introduced on February 18, 1939, finishing the essay "The Rhetoric of Hitler's Battle" in March 1939.[11] Burke, recognizing that Americans were "trained in pragmatism," called them to "inspect" the "magic" of Hitler's appeals to prevent Nazi Germany from acting out his vision. The essay provides an initial introduction and synthesis of the critical methodology Burke developed over time, including the "historical criticism attentive to Hitler's rhetorical situation," and an analysis of Hitler's use of antitheses, identification, and scapegoating.[12]

On October 8, 1949, Perelman delivered an address to his students at the Université Libre de Bruxelles and explained that between the two wars,

> there were no positive doctrine(s) to fascist slogans, to dogmatism, to fanaticism, to the appeal to force that these doctrines advocated. And among a large

> number of us, who were young at the time, one saw a skepticism appear that could too easily degenerate into cynicism, a lack of discipline that could turn into anarchy, an indifference that too often could resemble cowardice. You see the theoretical crisis that tormented your elders during the period between the two wars: it resulted from the fact that the end of scientism, the limitation of the scientific method to scientific problems, left us without rules of action, without conviction that one could honestly accept outside science itself.[13]

Perelman's turn to rhetoric was a direct response to the diagnosis he presented to his students, and the new rhetoric project is designed as a theory of proper action, the result of persuasion, against the absolutism represented by the totalitarianism he faced.[14] Similarly, Hannah Arendt turned to the rhetorical tradition for her analysis of Hitler's anti-Semitism and construction of the Third Reich's ideologies.[15]

Arendt, in her *Origins of Totalitarianism,* begins her analysis with a consideration of Plato's confrontation with the Sophists on the status of rhetoric.[16] Noting that the ancient sophists were concerned primarily with persuasion rather than truth, the modern sophists (the totalitarians who are the subject of her book) were, she continued, concerned primarily with the destruction of freedom in service to totalitarian ends. Arendt argued that the ancient sophists "destroyed the dignity of thought whereas the others destroyed the dignity of human action."[17] The link Arendt draws here between rhetoric and human action speaks directly to the questions raised by Kiewe and Houck's introduction.

Burke, Perelman, and Arendt feature rhetorical action in their theories. This is a critical, if unappreciated, theme joining their efforts to explain symbolization. All three distinguished between the freedom offered by rhetoric and the determinism of the totalitiarian and material universes. Their focus on the freedom afforded by rhetoric is a function of their rhetorical situation; they were confronting Hitler and totalititarian thought.[18] To illustrate: Burke juxtaposes nonsymbolic motion with symbolic action.[19] The former takes place without conscious intent and is rooted in biology or formal systems in which freedom is not a value, whereas the latter is expressed in speech, suggesting freedom and choice. Perelman, before making his rhetorical turn in 1948, sought a philosophy that could create the contexts necessary for freedom.[20] Similarly, Arendt identifed within totalitarian movements the impulse to destroy freedom in service to immutable and impersonal laws outside the reach of time and experience. Speech and rhetoric were alternatives.[21]

After World War II, Burke, Perelman, and Arendt challenged the dominant philosophical movement in Europe and the United States, which had subordinated rhetoric to formal logic and the *vita activa* to the *vita contemplativa.*[22] This subordination was enforced by analytic philosophers with the doctrine of logical positivism and Heidegger's philosophy of being.[23] The twentieth century's "rhetorical turn," which emerged as a philosophical movement in 1958, was essentially a shift from speculative and abstract metaphysics to a rhetorically inflected sense of human/humane action, one bringing reason and rhetoric into a rapprochement.[24] My intent here is to provide the historical context for the rhetorical turn in twentieth-century thought, marking the years of 1929, 1948, 1958, 1962, and 1969 as key dates in this turn. I then conclude with this argument: Perelman worked through what Kiewe and Houck have accurately captured as the dilemmas of rhetorical effects by nesting it within the *vita activa.*

Rhetorical Effects and the *Vita Activa* in the Twentieth Century

Action, a concept that shares much with rhetorical effects, has roots in the Greco-Roman notion of the *vita activa.*[25] The latter, however, is joined to a philosophical tradition, one that can be traced to the invention of the liberal arts and the Western university system by Roman and Christian rhetoricians.[26] This tradition linked rhetorical action to the *vita contemplativa,* insisting that the effects of rhetorical behavior have a moral and reflective grounding. The brief against rhetoric and rhetoricians, as articulated by Plato and other ancient philosophers, was that it was concerned primarily and only with rhetorical effects, that it was merely an amoral "knack," an expression of magic, not an art but a tool of manipulation. Plato and many thinkers who followed him advanced speculative philosophy to the problem of rhetorical effects, an approach leaving human time, opinion, and values for the sanctity of the timeless, eternal, and the language of math and geometry.

The horrific consequences of World War I prompted the rise of logical positivism, a movement against "mysticism, romanticism, and nationalism."[27] Affected by the Ramist division of reason and rhetoric and the reduction of rhetoric to style, if logical positivists did acknowledge rhetoric, they did so by conflating it with the irrationalism of World War I. Logical positivism advanced a thorough empiricism as a doctrine and declared values meaningless. A movement beginning in Europe, it was designed to counter Hegel's philosophy of absolute idealism and to challenge Heidegger's speculative metaphysics.[28]

The frame offered by the logical positivists and Heideggerian metaphysics produced an intellectual climate between the World War I and II that either declared values unworthy of reason or moved philosophy inward, away from public deliberation and argument. Given rhetoric's concern with values and the persuasion of audiences to action, rhetoric became as irrelevant as its effects. The year 1929 is a touchstone as it marks the convergence, in Kiewe and Houck's words "the narrowing scope," of rhetoric before World War II. Indeed, Perelman witnessed the removal of rhetoric from Belgian secondary and higher education in 1929 and thought rhetoric "was dead."[29]

The death of rhetoric in Europe was accompanied by the moral collapse of reason in Western Europe and the rise of totalitarian movements anchored in the Burkean notion of motion.[30] In 1948, philosophers and other thinkers gathered for the first post warconference on philosophy. There, the president of the conference,

H. S. Pos, invited his colleagues to broaden the realm of philosophy to include action and values.[31] He claimed that European philosophy had been unduly limited to speculation, which deprived postwar philosophers and citizens of using reason in their daily lives.

The American context in 1948 hosted philosophers who shared the European speculative impulses and the discipline of speech, which anchored its purpose in rhetoric's effects. The same year, Robert D. Clark, who had served a president of the Western Speech Association, published his article "These Truths We Hold Self-Evident" in the *Quarterly Journal of Speech*.[32] Clark, who understood, as did Burke, that Americans were "trained in pragmatism," lamented the speech field's narrow focus on rhetoric's effects: "We are so close to our subject, we become so engrossed in the immediate results which we achieve—the awkward, timid boy who gains sudden confidence and efficiency; the loud, aggressive girl who develops poise and charm—we are so frequently rewarded by gratifying results that we give our attention ever to refining the process of getting immediate results—of getting them more quickly, more efficiently, and on a higher level of skill."[33] Clark argued that speech teachers of the era held as a self-evident truth "that the purpose of training in speech is to make more effective speakers," that the field should help people "win" the desired response to a message.

This self-evident truth, Clark continued, is partial and "based on a faulty concept of truth," one that was "socially dangerous in a democratic society" that would justify denying speech a role in the liberal arts.[34] Clark's complaint was not intended to urge his colleagues to ignore rhetoric's effects; rather, he suggested that these effects should be placed in the social contexts and that the truth claims made in persuasive efforts should be a focus of the rhetorical critic. Clark called as witnesses the pragmatists William James and John Dewey, who, he argued, sought a pragmatism that would be in service to the "welfare of the group and not simply that of the individual as antagonistic to the group."[35]

Unfortunately, Clark's appeals did not affect the trajectory of the speech field, as the truncated and partial focus on rhetoric's effects remained in place through the 1950s. Robert Oliver, in his retrospective on Chaïm Perelman's visit to Pennsylvania State University in 1962, noted the divide between philosophy and speech: that philosophy concerned itself with "methodological considerations," whereas speech was concerned primarily with persuasion and the "achievement of pragmatic effects.[36] For fifty years, the speech field, according to Oliver, who referred to his coedited volume published in 1959 on the history of the speech profession, sought to study how the "great orators" influenced their audiences "through oral discourse."[37] The only philosopher, Oliver observed, cited by speech scholars in this era was William James.[38]

Oliver detected in Perelman's new rhetoric the possibility of a rapprochement between philosophy and rhetoric, one that would join the philosopher's concern with "methodology" and the speech profession's concern with rhetoric's effects. American philosophy, however, remained under the influence of the analytic tradition, refusing to consider within its province questions of effects, values, and politics. As McCumber has written, American philosophy in this era was "traumatized" by the politics of the period, leading it to avoid contemporary events and experience.[39] The retreat to a sterile form of analytic philosophy allowed philosophers in this period to navigate beyond questions of value, effectively circumventing what McCumber terms the "Academic McCarthyism" philosophers faced. By the mid-1950s, the speech discipline's restricted view of rhetoric's effects and philosophy's traumatized analytic agenda yielded to a series of books and articles that attempted to work through the postwar intellectual problems with a turn to rhetoric.

The evidence suggests that a turn took place in 1958 with a number of seminal publications, including Chaïm Perelman and Olbrechts-Tyteca's *Traité de l'argumentation: La nouvelle rhétorique,* Arendt's *The Human Condition* and a revised edition of *Origins of Totalitarianism,* Stephen Toulmin's *Uses of Argument,* Ong's *Ramus,* Polanyi's *Personal Knowledge,* and a number of other publications that would become influential.[40] For the purposes of this piece, I will discuss Arendt's *Human Condition* and Perelman and Olbrechts-Tyteca's *Traite* as foundational attempts to bridge rhetoric's effects with philosophy. The notion of the *vita activa,* best articulated by Arendt, folds rhetoric's effects into a rhetorical philosophy thoroughly explicated by Perelman and Olbrechts-Tyteca.

In notebooks Perelman kept of the readings he conducted immediately after the war he noted, "Philosophy deals with matters of contemplation, not action."[41] Perelman's declaration reflected the dominant European and American philosophical assumption. After his rhetorical turn in 1948, a result of an encounter with Latini's rendition of Cicero's rhetoric, Perelman came to see rhetoric as the bridge between contemplation and action.[42] Arendt did, as well, and provided the philosophical rationale for bridging the gap between the *vita activa* and the *vita contemplativa.*

Rhetoric's Effects and the *Vita Activa*

"We have relegated the study of effects to a secondary position" write Kiewe and Houck, and, in so doing, we miss an important component of rhetoric. Similarly, Hannah Arendt in 1958 found that the *vita activa* had been trumped by the *vita contemplativa* in Western thought. Although giving great value to thinking, Arendt sought to recover the *vita activa* as a touchstone for civil society and returned to the rhetorical tradition. Speech is at the center of her recovery effort.[43] Arendt identifies three expressions of the *vita activa:* labor, work, and action. She devotes *The Human Condition* to these topics.

Directly confronting the determinism of totalitarianism, the limitations of "motion," and Heidegger's philosophy of mortality, Arendt's theory of action offers humans the possibility that judgments can be made in a community ruled by pluralism.[44] Action, according to Arendt, allows humans the freedom to begin again through speech. Unlike in totalitarian societies, dominated by terror and absolute control by a central authority, the *vita activa* creates a public sphere that provides the space for the judgments necessary for political action. The funeral oration of Pericles provides Arendt with a key illustration. Pericles used this speech to persuade his audience to act on the basis of an authentic history of mixed impulses and a future in which humans have some agency. Rhetoric's effects, in Arendt's vision, are yoked to the *vita contemplativa* and the *vita activa*. They constitute far more than the pragmatic implications of speech at the center of Clark's critique.

Perelman and Olbrechts-Tyteca in their *New Rhetoric* develop their own version of the *vita activa,* and a major theme of their work is to develop a philosophy for rhetoric's effects. In his 1958 "The theoretical Relations of Thought and Action," Perelman offers the same critique developed by Arendt in her *Human Condition*. Here, Perelman condemns Western thought for failing to include action in the realm of reason.[45] Indeed, the intent of the new rhetoric project was to overturn the Cartesian view of reason that limited it to the *vita contemplativa,* which, they complained, was a "*perfectly unjustified and unwarranted limitation*" of reason from the "*domain of action.*"[46] The new rhetoric project sought to extend a rhetorically inflected sense of reason into the domain of reason.

What seems to be an idiosyncratic interpretation of the persuasion-conviction binary, the epideictic, and the role of time in argumentation is a function of Perelman and Olbrechts-Tytca's effort to develop an expression of reason suitable for the "plane of action." Philosophy, they note, had been limited to contemplation and conviction and that no follow up action is necessary or required thereof.[47] Persuasion, on the other hand, leads to action. Persuasion produces rhetoric's effects; Perelman and Olbrechts-Tyteca seek to fold both into a larger system of informal logic and reason.[48]

To accomplish this objective, Perelman and Olbrechts-Tyteca thoroughly recast Aristotle's notion of the epideictic, creating a profoundly different orientation to rhetoric than that offered by the ancient Greeks and Romans. According to Perelman and Olbrechts-Tyteca, the Classical tradition of the epideictic consisted of speeches delivered to an audience that "merely applauded and went away."[49] In their reconceptualization of the epideictic, Perelman and Olbrechts-Tyteca define it as a genre that creates or reinforces values that produce action. They explain, at some length, that the epideictic is linked directly to rhetoric's effects. To illustrate, Perelman and Olbrechts-Tyteca suggest the the French in London failed to fully develop an appeal intended to enlist their compatriots in France in efforts to resist the occupation. Had this happened, preexisting values might have been triggered, leading to more action against the Nazis.[50]

In addition to the reordering of the conviction-persuasion binary and the redefinition of the epideictic, Perelman and Olbrechts-Tyteca also develop, in a 1958 article, their theory of time and rhetoric. They suggest that argument itself is an action resulting in effects: "The action of the orator is an aggression, because it always aims to change something or to transform the listener. Even when it strives to reinforce the established social order, argument undermines and threatens the tranquility of the person to whom it is addressed and whose beliefs it strives to support. This action intends to cause another action; the desired adherence will be rendered by an action or at least by a disposition to action."[51] Unlike demonstration, apodictic logic, conviction, and the Classical view of the epideictic, argumentation takes place in human time and has material effects. In contrast, in the *vita contemplativa,* apodictic logic, and demonstration, human time (*durée*) plays no role. In the new rhetoric project, rhetoric's effects are important philosophically as they deal with plural truths and what Perelman and Olbrechts-Tyteca term "confused notions." Contrary to Descartes's position that knowledge is and should be "clear and convincing," which can justify violent action, truth assumes a humble stance. Truth itself is contested, often ambiguous, rooted in pluralism. Conviction is important to the extent it serves as a prelude to action.

Perelman and Olbrechts-Tyteca identify moral checks on rhetoric and its effects by detailing in the *Traité* and subsequent works the moral, epistemological, and ontological modesty of the rhetorical approach. While persuasion is a critical goal in the new rhetoric, the authors are careful to limit its reach.[52] There are moments, the authors write, that are not appropriate for persuasion. Because damage might be done to an audience moved to action because of persuasion, Perelman and Olbrechts-Tyteca write that it may be improper and immoral to achieve a persuasive effect; those who are subjected to persuasion have the freedom to resist. Not all audiences are open to persuasion as a method, and some are not capable of understanding rational argumentation. These moral limits are necessary, Perelman and Olbrechts-Tytca note, because of the rhetorical effects of persuasion.

The rhetorical method of persuasion and argumentation is limited, as are the value truths and knowledge claims it produces. Rhetoric, Perelman and Olbrechts-Tyteca maintain, does not produce immutable truths, beyond the pale of human time and experience. "Rhetorical proof," they write "is never compelling."[53] Rhetoric offers good but not absolute reasons for action. Such reasons can justify choice, decisions, and the placement of one value over another in a hierarchy. Since actions take place in a world of flux and indeterminacy, it allows for the value pluralism necessary for rhetoric to flourish.

Perelman and Olbrechts-Tyteca offer a philosophical justification of reasoned action, which they yoke to rhetoric's effects. They title section 10 of part one of the *New Rhetoric* "The Effects of Argumentation."[54] Here, they outline a pragmatic rationale for the study of reasoned action. Perelman's target audience at first consisted of European philosophers; later, he expanded his vision to include American professors of speech and philosophy. Tindale's carefully written history of the new rhetoric's reception reveals much about rhetoric's effects history.[55] In 1958 Perelman met with a group of philosophers to engage issues raised by the Anglo-Saxon and Continental expressions of thought. The dialogue failed because the philosophers from Oxford, according to Charles Taylor's review, did not give value to experience and history, seeking instead to study questions of language.[56] Tindale concludes his survey by noting the mixed reception accorded the new rhetoric in England and Europe.[57] The undertows of the speculative tradition, the bias in favor of the *vita contempletiva,* and the general prejudice against rhetoric served as constraints on the efforts made by Perelman and Olbrechts-Tyteca to persuade their target audience of philosophers.

For speech professors in America, the new rhetoric project served to validate their focus on rhetoric's effects. When Perelman visited the United States in 1962 at the joint invitation of the philosopher Henry W. Johnstone and the speech professor Robert T. Oliver of Pennsylvania State University, he brought with him the new rhetoric project. Johnstone, who had met Perelman in Belgium during the 1950s and had written a modestly favorable review of Perelman's efforts to study philosophical argument, most likely suggested Perelman's name to Oliver. In turn, Oliver saw in Perelman a distinguished European philosopher, one endorsing the study of persuasion and rhetoric's effects, who could be called an advocate for the American speech discipline.[58] Perelman provided Oliver and his colleagues with a "reluctant witness," a recovered logical positivist who justified the study of rhetoric and persuasion from within the Classical and Western philosophical traditions.

Perelman, who worked hard to move the *Traité* into English, understood there were a significant number of speech scholars interested in his ideas, more so than philosophers. As a result, he proposed to Emily Schossberger, the editor at University of Notre Dame Press who supervised the production and publication of the translation, a modification of the title from the French *Traité de l'argumentation: La nouvelle rhétorique* to the English *The New Rhetoric: A Treatise on Argumentation,* declaring that the title would better persuade scholars of speech to embrace the book.[59] With the publication of the English translation of the *Traité* in 1969, the American scholarly audience could now read and digest the new rhetoric project.

The reception of the new rhetoric in America, with its emphasis on action and rhetoric's effects, was decidedly mixed. First, the work of another Belgian, Paul De Man, and a number of other writers, including Jacques Derrida, developed a line of thinking in the 1970s and 1980s designed to deconstruct meaning and to question the relationship between reason and action, a critique undermining the very purpose of the new rhetoric.[60] Many humanists were attracted to this line of thought given the cultural contexts, which included the Vietnam War and the misuse of reason and rhetoric during this era. Perelman and Olbrechts-Tyteca's new rhetoric, viewed through the lens of the postmodern critique, is conservative in its assumptions, which include the possibility of communion and the idea that reason might serve the cause of justice. Peter Goodrich, well known for his advocacy of postmodern jurisprudence, argues that Perelman's new rhetoric program was "positively conventional and politically conservative in the extreme."[61]

One influence of postmodernism on the fields of rhetorical studies has been, as Kiewe and Houck note, the "predominance of textual focus" to the exclusion of the context and audience. There is literally nothing outside the text in the most extreme versions of postmodernity. By adopting a primarily textual approach, rhetorical scholars have become, as Kiewe and Houck rightly note, more literary than rhetorical critics. The rhetorical critic should be interested in both the literary construction of a text and how it moves (or fails to move) an audience to action. For both functions, the new rhetoric serves as an important foundation.

Second, the notion of the "universal audience" has produced misreadings, suggesting that the new rhetoric project seeks a transcendent standard of truth. One of the most cited critiques of Perelman's new rhetoric in the speech literature, John Ray's 1979 article in the *Quarterly Journal of Speech*, centers on the universal audience. Ray, and some subsequent scholarship in the field, finds the universal audience to be a distillation of abstract, transcendent truths, effectively lifting the principles needed to judge rhetorical behavior out of time and context.[62] Lise Ede, in an article in the *Central States Speech Journal*, would rehearse this complaint, as would Charles Willard in his 1996 book.[63] Authors of the entries in the 2009 *SAGE Handbook of Rhetorical Studies* that address the new rhetoric find the universal audience "arbitrary" or possibly "relativistic."[64]

In his 2010 review of the new rhetoric's reception, Tindale writes:

> Perelman did not simply bring rhetoric into philosophy: on the contrary, his reworking of principles from both disciplines necessitated a fusion that produced something quite new. It was the full nature of this newness that was lost on most of his contemporaries.
>
> What was lost on many readers of the new rhetoric was the focus on action and the aspiration to bring rhetoric's effects into a rhetorical system.[65]

Tindale explains why many philosophers have resisted or have misread the argument of the new rhetoric: "Standing in the way, perhaps, is the philosopher's 'innate' resistance to matters rhetorical." An explanation of this resistance can be traced to a heritage of speculative and analytic philosophy. In addition, as Blackburn writes, "Most contemporary philosophers think of their subject in an entirely unhistorical way."[66]

Tindale acknowledges that, in the past fifty years, there "has been the serious recovery of rhetorical themes and concepts, seen in part in the moves philosophers have made toward greater interdisciplinarity. If Perelman's work has not been a major cause of that recovery, it at least supports it, standing as a resource and inspiration for the future."[67] I agree, and I devote the rest of this essay to considering how the new rhetoric might serve as a resource and an inspiration for the agenda for rhetoric's effect as set forth by Kiewe and Houck.

The New Rhetoric and Rhetoric's Effects

As Clark and Oliver noted, scholars of speech did have a concern for rhetoric's effects through most of the century, one emanating from rudimentary—if not crude—expressions of pragmatism. Philosophers fled rhetoric's effects, seeking instead the security of speculation and the *vita contemplativa*. Perelman's new rhetoric project seeks to bring the two impulses into rapprochement. Like Tindale, Wayne Booth sees great potential in the new rhetoric for combating the problems of "absolutism."[68] Booth concludes that Perelman's work is "sadly neglected."[69]

The focus on rhetoric's effects may help complement efforts to place rhetoric and the work of Perelman in service to the creation of moral action, the inoculation of humanity against barbaric behavior, and the development of the cognitive habits necessary to understand and prevent mass violence. Indeed, because the new rhetoric project was designed in response to genocide and mass murder, it offers a means of working through and beyond twentieth-century trauma. Accordingly, lessons about twentieth-century rhetoric and rhetoric's effects should help us identify three goals in the twenty-first century. First, rhetoric should sponsor moral action and deter immoral action. Jonathan Glover, in his history of morality in the twentieth century, identified, without using the term *rhetoric,* the moral implications of rhetorically inflected methods of child rearing and culture.

The evidence suggests that those who rescued victims of the Nazis had not been given a rigidly disciplined upbringing. When they were children, parents had shown them respect, giving them reasons rather than orders. Respect may create a climate where moral identity can grow. Evidence from Nazi-occupied countries suggests that cultures may have climates that vary in their support for the growth of moral identity.[70]

Rhetoric, in contrast to logical positivism, analytical philosophy, and the corruption of totalitarianism, places the audience at the center of attention. In so doing, rhetoric calls for a communion and an identification with others.

Glover's assessment of the evidence is validated by the research conducted by the Oliners, who, after interviewing seven hundred rescuers and nonrescuers of Jews during the Holocaust, found that parents who disciplined by using questions, arguments, and were much more likely to rescue Jews than children whose parents disciplined their children by using corporal punishment.[71] The relationship between rhetoric, properly defined and taught, and moral action is a result of the freedom given to the audience. As Perelman and Olbrechts-Tyteca note, "The use of argumentation implies that one has renounced resorting to force alone, that value is attached to gaining the adherence of one's interlocutor by means of reasoned persuasion, and that one is not regarding him as an object, but appealing to his free judgment."[72] The rhetorical attitude and disposition encourages empathy, a key factor in genocide prevention.

Second, rhetorical criticism, such as that provided by Kenneth Burke, can and should unveil how rhetoric is and can be used to promote genocidal behavior. Burke in his "The Rhetoric of Hitler's Battle" displayed the characteristics of genocidal discourse, which was both effective and horrifically immoral. Burke's analysis helps us understand the symbolic characteristics of genocidal discourse, helping to inoculate audiences against its use. Rhetoric was used immorally by Hitler to justify and encourage genocidal behavior. Science and religion were also both bent and distorted to achieve the same ends. Rhetorical criticism can help provide the symbolic immunization against the toxic discourse of totalitarian and genocidal movements.

The recent genocide in Rwanda illustrates the existence of symbolic precursors to mass killing in which symbolic dehumanization is often a prelude to genocide.[73] In Rwanda, the Hutus labeled the Tutsis cockroaches, and this representation was used repeatedly in radio broadcasts. In turn, more than 800,000 Tutsis were murdered, in part because of the symbolic climate that reduced them to insects. The use of symbols to frame people as less than human requires a robust rhetorical criticism.

Rhetorical theory and rhetorical criticism can and should be joined with the discipline of social psychology to help construct a genocide pedagogy, a third goal rhetorical scholars might pursue to help students and others better think about genocide. Toward this end, I joined the social psychologists colleagues Paul Slovic and Daniel Vasfjall in publishing an article in the *Journal of Advanced Composition* that draws on both disciplines.[74] Our objective was to examine the roles played by rhetorical psychology, presence, and psychic numbing in genocide pedagogy.

Slovic, well known for his collaborations with the Nobel laureate Daniel Kahneman, has written extensively on the social psychology of genocide.[75] What is striking about his work and what attracted me to our collaboration was his belief that the burden of responding to genocide must be a function of international law and "moral argument."[76] Our resulting collaboration demonstrates the importance of accounting for rhetoric's effects in moving audiences to act against genocide.[77]

The research in social psychology reveals that people do not act unless they are engaged emotionally and are able to comprehend particular rather than global tragedies. Psychic numbing sets in when audiences are faced with numbers that are large. Though audiences can comprehend individuals who suffer, it is much more difficult to empathize with thousands or millions who might need relief. Slovic and other social psychologists attribute the response to individual rather than mass suffering to be a condition of human cognitive functioning. If audiences are to act, they should receive messages that achieve presence and engage emotion and the intellect. What social psychologists have offered, in turn, is an explanation of how audiences interpret messages. They have identified two systems of reasoning, one intuitive and the other deliberative. The two are intertwined; the deliberative system brings rational systems of judgment to bear on its more impulsive and emotional counterpart. Moving people to action through moral argument and rhetoric requires careful attention to both.

Perelman and Olbrechts-Tyteca's theory of rhetoric complements and embellishes the theoretical explanation offered by my colleagues in social psychology and offers unique insight into the function and role of moral argument to produce moral action. Deliberate reasoning and moral argument, using the principles of rationality, can help correct errors of thought. Moral argument, combined with the value premises established by international law, may help to prompt action against those who commit genocide. Slovic intuits the value of moral argument. The field of rhetoric has not only intuited this value but has established both philosophical and empirical bases for the relationship between moral argument and action.

Summary

Born as a response to twentieth-century war and genocide, the new rhetoric of Perelman and Olbrechts-Tyteca (as well as the theories of Burke and Arendt) seek to offer visions of a human community at ease with limits, degrees of uncertainty, and the tilling of civil society with rhetoric. Rhetoric's effects are of central concern in these theories, for they deal with the world of experience, one with a history and unfolding future, and with the direct material consequences for human beings. Rhetoric's effects, as Kiewe and Houck argue, should be tethered directly to almost any textual analysis. Beyond this, there is an ethical imperative in the study of rhetoric's effects.

This ethical imperative is a function of rhetoric's concern with audiences. The point Kiewe and Houck make about the "torturous history" of rhetoric's effects in the twentieth century is crucial. Rhetorical scholars have declared the importance of the audience and have also yielded to the temptations of close textual studies. Too often, as they point out, the text has trumped the audience. Many philosophers in the twentieth century engaged in ahistorical studies of language, reflective of the analytical tradition, and did not consider audiences and their opinions and emotions within the jurisdiction of reason. As Pos, Judt, Arendt, Perelman, and others noted, the pre-Holocaust and pre–World War II landscape reflected the flight of reason to the *vita contemplativa,* leaving intellectuals and thinkers with few resources to battle the rise of fascism and totalitarianism.[78]

The discipline of rhetoric, broadly conceived, can prepare audiences to resist the appeals of fascism, provide audiences with the skills of rhetorical criticism to evaluate the appeals of demagogues, and check the intuitive and emotional mode of reasoning with the one that is more deliberate and rationale. Textual analysis should complement but not substitute for a focus on the audience. Certainly, as Kiewe and Houck note, "textual analysis, audience assessment, and an overall understanding of situational constraints can yield a fairly accurate appraisal of rhetoric and its effect,"[79] but our focus should remain on the audience and on rhetoric's influence on the actions taken by the audience.

As Kiewe and Houck conclude in their introduction to this volume, "we opted as a discipline over the past forty years not to address those addressed."[80] Considering the "torturous history" of rhetoric's effects in the twentieth century, their chronology would date the discipline's choice to opt out of the concern with audiences sometime around 1971, close to the publication of *The New Rhetoric.* I am hopeful that the discipline can respond to Wayne Booth's observation that Perelman had been "sadly neglected" and Tindale's claim that the new rhetoric project remains a "resource and inspiration for the future" by drawing from the new rhetoric project and other similar efforts to construct an ethical and empirical foundation that can host the study of rhetorical influence and rhetoric's effects.[81]

Notes

1. Amos Kiewe and Davis W. Houck, Introduction to *The Effects of Rhetoric and the Rhetoric of Effects* (this volume).

2. Kiewe and Houck, Introduction to *The Effects of Rhetorics and the Rhetoric of Effects.*

3. E. J. Hobsbawm, *The Age of Extremes: A History of the World, 1914–1991* (New York: Vintage Books, 1996).

4. Walter Jost, *Rhetorical Investigations: Studies in Ordinary Language Criticism* (Charlottesville: University of Virginia Press, 2004), 303 n48.

5. James Crosswhite, *The Rhetoric of Reason: Writing and the Attractions of Argument* (Madison: University of Wisconsin Press, 1996), 35.

6. Chaïm Perelman and Lucie Olbrechts-Tyteca, *The New Rhetoric: A Treatise on Argumentation* (Notre Dame, Ind.: University of Notre Dame Press, 1969); Chaïm Perelman and Lucie Olbrechts-Tyteca, *Traité de l'argumentation: La nouvelle rhétorique,* 1re éd. Logos: Introduction aux Études Philosophiques (Paris: Presses Universitaires de France, 1958); Chaïm Perelman, "The Theoretical Relations of Thought and Action," *Inquiry* 1(1958): 130–136; Michelle K. Bolduc and David A. Frank, "Chaïm Perelman and Lucie Olbrechts-Tyteca's 'On Temporality as a Characteristic of Argumentation': Commentary and Translation," *Philosophy and Rhetoric* 43 (2010): 315–336; David A. Frank and Michelle K. Bolduc, "Chaïm Perelman's 'First Philosophies and Regressive Philosophy': Commentary and Translation," *Philosophy and Rhetoric* 16 (2003): 177–207; David A. Frank and Michelle Bolduc, "From *Vita Contemplativa* to *Vita Activa:* Chaïm Perelman and Lucie Olbrechts-Tytca's Rhetorical Turn," *Advances in the History of Rhetoric* 7 (2004): 65–86; David A. Frank, "1958 and the Rhetorical Turn in the Twentieth Century," *Review of Communication* 11 (2011): 239–252; David A. Frank, "After the New Rhetoric," *Quarterly Journal of Speech* 89 (2003): 253–261.

7. See the footnotes in Perelman and Olbrechts-Tyteca, *The New Rhetoric,* 49, 50, 57, 317, 481.

8. Kenneth Burke, "The Rhetoric of Hitler's Battle," in *The Philosophy of Literary Form: Studies in Symbolic Action,* 3rd ed. (Berkeley: University of California Press, 1973), 191–220.

9. Chaïm Perelman, "Le libre examen, hier et aujourd'hui," *Revue de l'Université de Bruxelles* (1949): 39–50.

10. Hannah Arendt, *The Origins of Totalitarianism* (Cleveland: World, 1958).

11. Ann George and Jack Selzer, *Kenneth Burke in the 1930s* (Columbia: University of South Carolina Press, 2007), 201–202.

12. George and Selzer, *Kenneth Burke,* 202.

13. Perelman, "Le libre examen, hier et aujourd'hui," 46–47.

14. Frank and Bolduc, "Chaïm Perelman's 'First Philosophies and Regressive Philosophy'"; Frank and Bolduc, "From *Vita Contemplativa* to *Vita Activa*"; Frank, "1958 and the Rhetorical Turn in the Twentieth Century"; David A. Frank, "A Traumatic Reading of Twentieth-Century Rhetorical Theory: The Belgian Holocaust, Malines, Perelman, and De Man," *Quarterly Journal of Speech* 93 (2007): 308–43; Frank, "After the New Rhetoric"; David A. Frank, "The New Rhetoric, Judaism and Post-Enlightenment Thought: The Cultural Origins of Perelmanian Philosophy," *Quarterly Journal of Speech* 83 (1997): 311–331.

15. Bolduc and Frank, "Chaïm Perelman and Lucie Olbrechts-Tyteca's 'On Temporality as a Characteristic of Argumentation.'"

16. Arendt, *The Origins of Totalitarianism.*

17. Arendt, *The Origins of Totalitarianism,* 9.

18. Frank, "A Traumatic Reading of Twentieth-Century Rhetorical Theory."

19. Kenneth Burke, *A Grammar of Motives* (Berkeley: University of California Press, 1969), 232.

20. Chaïm Perelman, "Les deux problèmes de la liberté humaine," in *Library of the Xth International Congress of Philosophy*, ed. H. J. Pos, E. W. Beth, and J. H. A. Hollak (Amsterdam: North Holland Publishing, 1948); Chaïm Perelman, "Le problème du bon choix," *Revue de l'Institut de Sociologie* 3 (1948): 383–398.

21. Arendt, *The Origins of Totalitarianism*, 465.

22. Hannah Arendt, *The Human Condition* (Chicago: University of Chicago Press, 1958).

23. See Christian Delacampagne, *A History of Philosophy in the Twentieth Century* (Baltimore: Johns Hopkins University Press, 1999).

24. Dilip Parameshwar Gaonkar, "Rhetoric and Its Double: Reflection on the Rhetorical Turn in the Human Sciences," in *The Rhetorical Turn: Invention and Persuasion in the Conduct of Inquiry*, ed. Herbert W. Simons (Chicago: University of Chicago Press, 1990); Frank, "1958 and the Rhetorical Turn in the Twentieth Century."

25. Arendt, *The Human Condition*, 5–6.

26. Bruce A. Kimball, *Orators & Philosophers: A History of the Idea of Liberal Education* (New York: Teachers College Press, Columbia University, 1986).

27. Peter Godfrey-Smith, *Theory and Reality: An Introduction to the Philosophy of Science* (Chicago: University of Chicago Press, 2003), 24.

28. Godfrey-Smith, *Theory and Reality.* Heidegger was seen as an "especially important key rival" of the logical positivists.

29. Chaïm Perelman, "The New Rhetoric and the Rhetoricians, Remembrances and Comments," *Quarterly Journal of Speech* 70 (1984): 188–196.

30. See Tony Judt, *The Burden of Responsibility: Blum, Camus, Aron, and the French Twentieth Century* (Chicago: University of Chicago Press, 1998); Tony Judt, *Past Imperfect: French Intellectuals, 1944–1956* (Berkeley: University of California Press, 1992); Delacampagne, *A History of Philosophy in the Twentieth Century.*

31. H. J. Pos, "Speech by Mr. H. J. Pos," in *Library of the Xth International Congress of Philosophy*, ed. H. J. Pos, E. W. Beth, and J. H. A. Hollak (Amsterdam: North Holland Publishing, 1948), 3–10.

32. Robert D. Clark, "These Truths We Hold Self-Evident," *Quarterly Journal of Speech* 34 (1948): 445–50.

33. Clark, "These Truths We Hold Self-Evident," 445–46.

34. Clark, "These Truths We Hold Self-Evident," 446.

35. Clark, "These Truths We Hold Self-Evident," 448.

36. Robert T. Oliver, "Philosophy and/or Persuasion," *Logique el analyse* 6 (1963): 571–580; Robert Tarbell Oliver and Marvin G. Bauer, *Re-establishing the Speech Profession: The First Fifty Years* (New York: Speech Association of the Eastern States, 1959).

37. Oliver, "Philosophy and/or Persuasion," 578.

38. Oliver and Bauer, *Re-establishing the Speech Profession*, 578.

39. John McCumber, *Time in the Ditch: American Philosophy and the McCarthy Era* (Evanston, Ill.: Northwestern University Press, 2001), xix.

40. Perelman and Olbrechts-Tyteca, *Traité de l'argumentation: La nouvelle rhétorique*; Stephen Edelston Toulmin, *The Uses of Argument* (Cambridge: Cambridge University Press, 1958); Walter J. Ong, *Ramus: Method, and the Decay of Dialogue: From the Art of Discourse to the Art of Reason* (Cambridge, Mass.: Harvard University Press, 1958); Michael Polanyi, *Personal Knowledge: Towards a Post-Critical Philosophy* (Chicago: University of Chicago Press, 1958); Arendt, *The*

Origins of Totalitarianism; Arendt, *The Human Condition*. See Frank, "1958 and the Rhetorical Turn in the Twentieth Century."

41. "Logique 1944–1945," Notebook, in Archives, "Chaïm Perelman," Universite Libre de Bruxelles, Brussels.

42. Frank and Bolduc, "From *Vita Contemplativa* to *Vita Activa*."

43. Arendt, *The Human Condition*, 12–17.

44. Rüdiger Safranski, *Martin Heidegger: Between Good and Evil* (Cambridge, Mass.: Harvard University Press, 1998), 383.

45. Perelman, "The Theoretical Relations of Thought and Action."

46. Perelman and Olbrechts-Tyteca, *The New Rhetoric*, 3. Italics in original.

47. Perelman, "The Theoretical Relations of Thought and Action," 26–28.

48. Frank and Bolduc, "Chaïm Perelman's 'First Philosophies and Regressive Philosophy'"; Frank and Bolduc, "From *Vita Contemplativa* to *Vita Activa*"; Frank, "1958 and the Rhetorical Turn in the Twentieth Century"; Frank, "After the New Rhetoric."

49. Perelman, "The Theoretical Relations of Thought and Action," 48.

50. Perelman, "The Theoretical Relations of Thought and Action," 53.

51. Bolduc, "Chaïm Perelman and Lucie Olbrechts-Tyteca's 'On Temporality as a Characteristic of Argumentation,'" 317.

52. Perelman and Olbrechts-Tyteca, *The New Rhetoric*, 54–56.

53. Perelman and Olbrechts-Tyteca, *The New Rhetoric*, 59.

54. Perelman and Olbrechts-Tyteca, *The New Rhetoric*, 45–46.

55. Christopher W. Tindale, "Ways of Being Reasonable: Perelman and the Philosophers," *Philosophy and Rhetoric* 43 (2010): 337–361.

56. Charles Taylor, *La philosophie analytique* "Review of Cahiers de Royaumont." *Philosophical Review* 73 (1964): 132–135.

57. Tindale, "Ways of Being Reasonable 359.

58. Oliver, "Philosophy and/or Persuasion."

59. Chaïm Perelman, in *Letter to Emily M Schossberger. 29th November 1967. File: Traité de l'argumentation* (Chaïm Perelman Papers, Archives, Université Libre de Bruxelles, Bruxelles, Belgium).

60. I develop this claim at some length in Frank, "A Traumatic Reading of Twentieth-Century Rhetorical Theory."

61. Peter Goodrich, *Legal Discourse: Studies in Linguistics, Rhetoric and Legal Analysis* (London: Macmillan, 1987), 111.

62. John W. Ray, "Perelman's Universal Audience," *Quarterly Journal of Speech* 64 (1978): 361–375.

63. Lisa Ede, "Rhetoric vs. Philosophy: The Role of the Universal Audience in Chaïm Perelman's *The New Rhetoric*," *Central States Speech Journal* 32(1981): 118–125; Charles Arthur Willard, *Liberalism and the Problem of Knowledge: A New Rhetoric for Modern Democracy* (Chicago: University of Chicago Press, 1996), 82.

64. Andrea A. Lunsford, Kirt H. Wilson, and Rosa A. Eberly, eds., *The SAGE Handbook of Rhetorical Studies* (Sherman Oaks, Calif: Sage, 2009), 114, 93.

65. Tindale, "Ways of Being Reasonable," 337–361.

66. Simon Blackburn, "Being and Time," *New Republic* 241 (2010): 36–39.

67. Tindale, "Ways of Being Reasonable," 356–357.

68. Wayne C. Booth, *The Rhetoric of Rhetoric: The Quest for Effective Communication* (Oxford: Blackwell, 2004), 73.

69. Booth, *The Rhetoric of Rhetoric*.

70. Jonathan Glover, *Humanity: A Moral History of the Twentieth Century* (New Haven: Yale University Press, 2000), 403.

71. Samuel P. Oliner and Pearl M. Oliner, *The Altruistic Personality: Rescuers of Jews in Nazi Europe* (New York: Free Press, 1988).

72. Perelman and Olbrechts-Tyteca, *The New Rhetoric*, 55.

73. Philip Gourevitch, *We Wish to Inform You That Tomorrow We Will Be Killed with Our Families: Stories from Rwanda* (New York: Farrar, Straus and Giroux, 1998).

74. David A. Frank, Paul Slovic, and Daniel Vastfjall, "'Statistics Don't Bleed': Rhetorical Psychology, Presence, and Psychic Numbing in Genocide Pedagogy," *Journal of Advanced Composition* (2011): 609–624.

75. As an illustration, see Paul Slovic, "The More Who Die, the Less We Care," in *The Irrational Economist: Making Decisions in a Dangerous World*, ed. Erwann Michel-Kerjan and Paul Slovic (New York: PublicAffairs, 2010), 30–40.

76. Paul Slovic and David Ziontis, "Can International Law Stop Genocide When Our Moral Intuitions Fail Us?" in *Understanding Social Action, Promoting Human Rights*, Derek Jinks, Ryan Goodman, Andrew K. Woods, eds., 100–134 (Oxford: Oxford University Press, 2012).

77. Frank, Slovic, and Vasfjall "'Statistics Don't Bleed.'

78. Perelman, "Le libre examen, hier et aujourd'hui."

79. Kiewe and Houck, Introduction to *The Effects of Rhetoric and Rhetoric of Effects.*

80. Kiewe and Houck, Introduction to *The Effects of Rhetoric and Rhetoric of Effects.*

81. Booth, *The Rhetoric of Rhetoric*, 73; Tindale, "Ways of Being Reasonable," 357.

Part II

Case Studies of Public Address

Rhetoric, Text, Effect

STEPHEN H. BROWNE

"One event follows another," David Hume famously posited, "but we can never observe any tie between them. They seemed conjoined, but never connected." As a result, he explained, "the necessary conclusion seems to be that we have no idea of connexion or force at all, and that these words are absolutely without meaning, when employed either in philosophical reasonings or common life." Now, Hume was scarcely the first or the last thinker to trouble himself with the vexed issue of the relationship between cause and effect. He was, however, the first to state in such stark terms the skepticism with which we ought to approach the matter. As the editors of this volume so amply demonstrate, rhetoricians have struggled, with mixed results, to resolve what appears to be an intractable problem: while we cannot empirically and without qualification lay claim to understanding such a relationship, we nevertheless believe that it must exist, that it is somehow ingredient to our understanding of how the world works. Indeed, Hume himself finally resorts to what we might now call a socially constructed understanding of how one act imposes itself in demonstrable ways upon another. To reject such a conception is to invite pathology of a kind.[1]

But all this lets us off the hook not at all. Of all the disciplines associated with the interpretation of human symbolic behavior, rhetorical critics, historians, and theorists would seem among the most obliged to come to terms—yet again—with the question of how or whether communicative acts solicit certain observable effects. In this I agree with our editors; other matters, I suspect, are better left open for further discussion.[2]

The central aim of this project, however, cannot and should not be ignored. As the editors make clear in their interrogation of Professor Edwards's concerns, we very much need to clarify what it is when we talk about the consequences of rhetoric—what it does and how we know when it is doing something. To that end, a brief discussion of what we might mean when we talk about effects will help set this essay's coordinates. For the purposes of illustration, we can imagine a range of judgments available to us in the face of any given rhetorical act. On one end of the spectrum, we might conclude that there is no evidence of effect: it's just not there. Now, this itself might lead to interesting insights (why no effectivity? What happened to make it so?), but, as to any noticeable consequence, well, it's just not there. Shifting along a bit, we might observe that, indeed, certain effects might be observable but that they are by conventional standards just not very relevant. Here we may allude to the work of Hannah Arendt or Lawrence Rosenfield or Edwin Black, who press very hard, if not always consistently, on the revelatory character of language. That is to say, we have perhaps pushed too hard on the instrumental nature of language use, at the cost of understanding how language operates as a medium of disclosure for the agent. Another, more blunt way of putting the point is to examine how language says more about the speaker/author than it does about much else. So a given speech act may produce effects, but that is not really the most interesting thing about it. A third shift along our continuum takes us to matters of degree. To claim that a symbolic act has effected something is in this sense not to say very much; the reader wishes to know, how much? With what level of intensity has it been effected? A shrug, after all, is every bit as much an effect as profuse sweating, a yawn as much as a yelp. We will not have gone very far in our analysis until we can develop a vocabulary for discerning degrees of response.[3]

We then come to that point on the spectrum that seems to have exercised the distinguished presidential historian in College Station. Edwards's chief complaint, as I understand it, is that no empirical data convincingly indicate that presidential messages, broadly construed, have few if any effects on their auditors. Without rehearsing the critique already advanced by Professor Kiewe, it is still worth reminding ourselves that the conception of effects applied by Edwards is resolutely social scientific, with all the investments in quantitative empiricism that implies. If I may invoke an example familiar in my own work on Edmund Burke, we would on this basis be obliged to concede that the British statesman proved an inconsequential orator because, as a member of the loyal opposition, he was routinely defeated in his efforts to restore harmony with the American colonies. This much, of course, disregards the enormous fund of arguments he installed in the public domain when it came to negotiating imperial relations, not only with America but also with India, Ireland, and other venues for international diplomacy. Burke may have lost his battles, but can we really say he lost his wars?[4]

Three Texts: An Introduction

I wish to occupy the remainder of my space by dwelling on the opposite pole of our imagined line of thinking about effects. My aim is not to displace the company it keeps but, I hope, to deepen as well as broaden our subject, specifically by entering into the calculus considerations of time. How might we integrate temporal dimensions into the question of rhetoric's relationship to causality and effectivity? The question is prompted by the suspicions that by doing so we can, in a sense, have our cake and eat it too. That is to say, I suspect that if we take time and timing seriously, we can at once make good on certain (modest) obligations to demonstrate effectivity, without conceding that opinion polls and other empirical means necessarily exhaust our options. My approach is confessedly synoptic and is designed as much to encourage further enquiry as to conclusively demonstrate the case. Here then is my proposal: one productive way of thinking about how rhetorical acts (and here I will limit such acts to certain canonical texts) are effective is to ask how they effect other texts. Put another way, rhetoric doesn't just effect "others" (that is, other people); it also effects rhetoric. Language shapes language. To calibrate the point more tightly, I argue in the following that we can see how this process works by observing how a given text effects its immediate reception (effectivity in the short term); how another text's effects extend its influence across several generations (effectivity in the mid-term); and how a given text continues to make itself felt in our own time (effectivity in the long term).

A cautionary note: I do not claim that anyone of these texts is limited to such effects; indeed, they all persist as touchstones in the American political imagination. I mean only to suggest that they respectively illustrate the ways in which rhetorical acts can be seen operating on immediate circumstances, in more distant contexts, and in realms more distant still. Presumably, then, we will arrive at an admittedly generalized but perhaps useful way of comparing different modes of textual effectivity, as those texts negotiate and get negotiated by their temporal exigencies. At this point, allow me to introduce them in turn—though they need little such introduction—and turn then to the analysis at hand.

Seven months prior to the composition of the Declaration of Independence, an obscure English artisan published in Philadelphia an anonymous tract of forty-eight pages that one estimable historian in our own time has called "the most incendiary and popular pamphlet of the entire revolutionary era." No one had quite seen anything like it, but people could not keep their eyes off it. Its first year saw sales of a half million and twenty-five editions. Its author did not remain anonymous for long: Thomas Paine rapidly became a bellwether for revolution at a time when many—more than is usually recognized—still held out hope for an amicable restoration of relations with the mother country. Everything about the pamphlet seemed new: its style was popular, not to say impertinent; it was openly contemptuous of monarchy and unblinkingly self-confident in its claims; and it seemed utterly confident in American's capacity to "make the world over again." *Common Sense* was, in this sense, anything but: granted, many of its tenets were no doubt whispered about in smoky alehouses and by furtive patriot cabals, but here was something altogether novel: a brazen, public, and open-throated call to throw off the chains of oppression and assume a free people's rightful place in the commonwealth of nations. Within the year, the author and his many, many readers had their wish. Could one ask for a more ideal case study in the immediate effectiveness of rhetorical discourse?[5]

When the nation's first president set his mind to something, he almost always made good on his resolve. Thus in June 1792 George Washington professed every intention of ending his administration with a few words of gratitude and advice to his fellow countrymen. James Madison concurred with this Cincinnatus of American politics and even assisted in composing a rough draft of a document laying out such sentiments as seemed consistent with the president's sentiments. In this, however, both the present and the future chief executives failed. Others, including Jefferson and Hamilton, prevailed upon Washington to extend his office by at least one more term; whether he turned out grateful for the change of course remains doubtful in view of the rough-and-tumble years that occupied his second administration. But there could be no dissuading Washington from insisting that his second tenure be his last, and in the fall of 1796 he published what soon became known as the Farewell Address.[6]

Washington was no orator, as he well understood, and thought it best to have the document published in the *American Daily Advertizer* on September 17. But while the ideas were not especially novel and the tone didactic, the text was, in the words of one historian, "soon elevated to the status of a sacred document," while Jared Sparks later referred to the "vigor of its language, the soundness of its maxims, and its pure and elevated sentiments." No one, however, would mistake its author for that of *Common Sense,* and it came nowhere near effecting the immediate enthusiasm aroused by that earlier text. We have in the Farewell Address, however, an excellent example of a rhetorical effort that occupied the American political imagination well beyond its original exigence, and while the Address could be many things for many people, there can be no doubting John Marshall's assessment that it represented an "act which might be at the same time, suitable to his own character and permanently useful to his country."[7]

Of our third text no state paper has been written about more save the U.S. Constitution. The Declaration of Independence has been subject to as many interpretive approaches as might be imagined, from popular invocations to scholarship in political science, history, philosophy, literature, psychoanalysis, and rhetorical studies. Virtually every president has found in its words such sentiments as to inspire and, it must be said, justify their own political aspirations. Thus Lincoln: "it gave promise that in due time the weights should be lifted from the shoulders of all men, and that all should have an equal chance." Thus Wilson: "Every man who signed the Declaration of Independence believed, as Mr. Jefferson did, that free men had a much more trustworthy capacity in taking care of themselves than any government had ever shown or was ever likely to show, in taking care of them; and upon that belief American government was built." Thus Reagan: "Go into any schoolroom, and there you will see children being taught the Declaration of Independence, that they are endowed by their Creator with certain unalienable rights—among them life, liberty, and the pursuit of happiness—that no government can justly deny—the guarantees in their Constitution for freedom of speech, freedom of assembly, and freedom of religion." Thus Obama: "What is required is a new declaration of independence, not just in our nation, but in our own lives—from ideology and small thinking, prejudice and bigotry—an appeal not to our easy instincts but to our better angels." It is enough here to remind ourselves that however partisan its appeal—evidenced most recently by Obama's inadvertent omission of "our creator" from a public speech and the outcry it prompted—the Declaration remains an urtext of American collective identity.[8]

Together, these three texts—*Common Sense,* the Farewell, and the Declaration—serve to illustrate my thesis that rhetorical acts may indeed to be shown to be consequential in important ways. More specifically, I aim to ask how and in what ways Paine's tract effected immediate responses in an immediate context; how Washington's text asserted itself well into nineteenth-century American politics; and how the Declaration in our time continues to shape global aspirations for freedom and national self-determination.

Common Sense in Its Time

We live in a time when revolutions and other major upheavals may be catalyzed with breathtaking speed, when Twitter, Facebook, and Google can help bring down regimes of three and more decades. Needless to say, it has not always been thus. The time of revolution has changed, and so has its timing. Historically, that is to say from roughly the late eighteenth to the early twenty-first century, such dramatic transformations have in fact been, in the main, terribly wordy affairs, and that means it took a while to get things really under way. The processes that led from talk to arms took time, sometimes a long time. The reasons for this can be complex, but a few of the more obvious factors help explain the novelty of Paine's achievement. Among them: the lack of what we now call "social media"; the challenges posed by space and distance; and the long-established rituals of deference and loyalty that shaped pretentions to collective resistance. I treat each briefly in turn.

American colonists in the late eighteenth century—that is, white subjects of the crown—were the most literate people on the planet. This was especially the case among white, male Northerners above the Mason-Dixon line. The reasons for this date back to early New England and include commitments to education for the young, relatively high levels of prosperity, and the importance placed on reading scripture and devotional tracts. The capacity to read naturally entails an appetite for things to read, and colonists were more than happy to churn out all manner of printed material, including bibles, sermons, almanac, pamphlets, ephemera, and, of course, newspapers. Colonists in fact produced and consumed newspapers at an astounding rate—again, more than any other recorded population of which we are aware. True, many of these works—most—did not survive long, but there seemed always to be another ready to fill any perceived public need. We are familiar perhaps with the *New England Courant, the South Carolina Gazette, the Virginia Gazette,* and of course the redoubtable Benjamin Franklin's *Pennsylvania Gazette,* but we know of literally hundreds of lesser organs that dotted the cities and towns of the era.[9]

Among the results of this print culture is what Benedict Anderson has called an "imagined community," a network of mediations that makes it possible for people who do not know one another to imagine that they are part of some sort of shared, collective identity. Importantly, too, it created and sustained a means through which ideas—great and small—could be aired and debated, sometimes at length and over considerable periods of time. This is why, in part, the American Revolution, when it came, arrived after an enormous amount of print had been expended in deliberating upon various issues, strategies, legacies, fears, and aspirations. It was, in short, why it took more than fifteen years—say from the 1765 Stamp Act Crisis—to get from the rumblings of discontent to the smoke and powder of Bunker Hill.

How an aggrieved people move themselves from words to guns is always a vexed question and admits of no single explanation. But how and why American seemed so quickly to stop debating and start marching must include the story of Paine's *Common Sense.* Having arrived in Philadelphia in 1774, Paine quickly insinuated himself among the leading patriots of the day, including Benjamin Franklin and Benjamin Rush. Within a few short years, he was coaxed to compose and then delivered a composition the rhetoric of which, as one notable historian has argued, has "become intrinsic to American political speech, and [is] now permanently embedded in the expressions of identity on which the culture depends." Less abstractly, the pamphlet proved a remarkable event in the history of American print culture. Although some debate remains about how just how many copies were produced and read, no one doubts that the impact of the text was immediate and palpable. Paine's friend Rush reported that it "burst from the press with an effect which has rarely been produced by types and papers in any age or country." Washington and Franklin concurred, and one delegate to the Second Continental Congress avowed that he "heard nothing praised in the course of his journey, but Common sense and independence." Praise for the author and his sentiments grew rapidly as word spread, as captured in the following letter to Paine from the *Connecticut Gazette:* "In declaring your own, you have declared the sentiments of Millions. Your production may justly be compared to a land flood that sweeps all before it. We were blind, but on reading these enlightening works the scales have fallen from our eyes; even deep-rooted prejudices take to themselves and flee away, tho' not as an eagle toward heaven. The doctrine of Independence hath been in times past, greatly disgustful; we abhorred the principle—it is now become our delightful theme, and commands our purest affections."[10]

Such encomiums may be listed at length, though all this is not to say Paine was without his critics. John Adams famously referred to the pamphlet as a "crapulous mass," and scholars continue to debate the sources, composition, and meaning of the text. In his astute and rhetorically sensitive treatment of the subject, for example, Robert Ferguson worries that Paine bequeathed to the American political imagination an enduring sense that "danger lurked from a hidden enemy within." Sophia Rosenfeld, on the other hand, insists that to understand *Common Sense* is to understand "common sense," with the result that both wind up in a confused and often inconsistent vocabulary for political action. Some historians are unfailing in their applause for the text—Bernard Bailyn, notably—whereas other are more skeptical of its coherence, style, sources, and implications. But while sea changes are rarely described as taking place rapidly, we seem to have here evidence of one such phenomenon, and I would like to argue that, for rhetorical critics, the question of effects could not be more relevant to the immediate circumstances of revolutionary America.[11]

Traditions of grievance against duly constituted authority took several forms in early modern England. From Magna Carta forward, these forms may have included the petition, epistolary exchanges, sermons, and broadsides, among others. This is not to say that the period wasn't marked by more informal, indeed popular and sometimes violent expressions—marches, funerals, sacking, tarring and feathering. But among political elites, convention held that, above all, objections were to be composed with the utmost deference to the monarch and his or her representatives. Such deference carried with it certain protocols of language and tonality central to its rhetorical function; thus, in article XI of the 1628 Petition of Right, we find the following:

> All which they most humbly pray of your most excellent Majesty as their rights and liberties, according to the laws and statutes of this realm; and that your Majesty would also vouchsafe to declare, that the awards, doings, and proceedings, to the prejudice of your people in any of the premises, shall not be drawn hereafter into consequence or example; and that your Majesty would be also graciously pleased, for the further comfort and safety of your people, to declare your royal will and pleasure, that in the things aforesaid all your officers and ministers shall serve you according to the laws and statutes of this realm, as they tender the honor of your Majesty, and the prosperity of this.[12]

Let us now fast-forward to July 5, 1775, when the colonists extended to the crown the so-called Olive Branch Petition, and we see that the protocols are still very much in place:

> To the King's Most Excellent Majesty:
>
> MOST EXCELLENT SOVERIEIGN: We your Majesty's faithful subjects of the colonies of New-Hampshire, Massachusetts-bay, Rhode island and Providence plantations, Connecticut, New-York, New-Jersey, Pennsylvania, the counties of New Castle, Kent, and Sussex on Delaware, Maryland, Virginia,

> North Carolina and South Carolina, in behalf of ourselves and the inhabitants of these colonies, who have deputed us to represent them in general Congress, entreat your Majesty's gracious attention to this our humble petition.[13]

Finally, let us now take a look at a passage from *Common Sense,* and the point will perhaps be made obvious: "England since the conquest hath known some few good monarchs, but groaned beneath a much larger number of bad ones; yet no man in his senses can say that their claim under William the Conqueror is a very honorable one. A French bastard landing with an armed banditti and establishing himself king of England against the consent of the natives is in plain terms a very paltry rascally original."[14]

The contrasts, of course, could not be more obvious. Paine's brief pamphlet ushered in not just a new way of thinking about politics but also a new way of talking about politics. Put another way, the author helped to set on foot a vocabulary in which deference took on an entirely new meaning; it authorized a people to speak in its own tongue, to voice its grievances unfettered from the traditions of royal ritual and all the constraints such rituals imposed. It is not too much to conclude, therefore, that he gave to republican ideology its own idiom: not one necessarily of contempt or disrespect—to be sure, the language of diplomacy retained a good deal of the ancient argot—but in a sense he gave to the colonists permission to confront unwonted authority in their own terms. To this extent, it may be said that the immediate effect of *Common Sense* was to effect a change in the rhetoric of political resistance.

Paine's revolutionary legacy turned out to be short and vexed. His deistical sentiments and outright anti-authoritarianism soon enough ensured the disfavor of those who thought they had unleashed democratic forces that threatened to exceed even the most adamant patriots of the new republic. But his ignominious end really had nothing to do with his famous pamphlet and everything to do with where its logic inextricably led him. He all but disappeared in the later years of his life, but for a brief moment he made good on his claim that the "world might be made new again." And at the heart of that achievement was the conviction that if Americans could just learn how to talk in a new way, that if they could free themselves from the slavery of an antiquated discourse, they might well free themselves from the past itself. That is the lasting *and* immediate effect of *Common Sense.*

Washington's Farewell Address and the Vagaries of Effect

That certain texts, though rare enough, command such rhetorical force as to reset the terms of debate is made evident by Paine's incendiary pamphlet. That such power is no guarantee of effecting the designs of their authors is the lesson drawn from the story of Washington's famed Farewell Address. As we noted, the first president's announcement of his retirement from public office was in truth a deferred performance, but if anything it took on additional weight during the vexatious years of Washington's second term. The address was delivered in print, not orally, and thus reached a broad and diverse audience in its own time; as we shall see, its influence was to extend well beyond the immediate exigencies of the moment and indeed reasserted itself dramatically in the decade of its centennial in the 1890s.

In one sense, Washington's final message contained nothing particularly novel, and his position with respect to its major themes was well known to Americans generally. Here he warned of sectional strife, the dangers of party alignments, and the inevitable strife these entailed; encouraged his countrymen to cultivate such virtues as were necessary to a free and new republic; to attend to the needs of educating young citizens; and to be vigilant about the dangers of credit and the imperatives of effectively managing the nation's precarious purse strings. But the enduring legacy of the address issued from his counsel regarding his new country's stance toward the commonwealth of nations it had so recently joined. Because of its significance to the conduct of foreign relation a century after its pronouncement, I quote the relevant passage at some length:

> The great rule of conduct for us in regard to foreign nations is, in extending our commercial relations to have with them as little political connection as possible. So far as we have already formed engagements let them be fulfilled with perfect good faith. Here let us stop.
>
> Europe has a set of primary interests which to us have none or a very remote relation. Hence she must be engaged in frequent controversies, the causes of which are essentially foreign to our concerns. Hence, therefore, it must be unwise in us to implicate ourselves by artificial ties in the ordinary vicissitudes of her politics or the ordinary combinations and collisions of her friendships or enemies.[15]

This passage, which is frequently bundled with Jefferson's admonition in his first inaugural address against "entangling alliances," remained a cornerstone of U.S. foreign relations well into the twentieth century. It thus affords us an opportunity to observe how a given text can be seen effecting itself somewhere toward the middle of our spectrum, between Paine's immediate influence and the Declaration's long-term reach. Again, this much is not to suggest that the Farewell had long to wait before being taken up as a warrant for administration policy: it clearly underwrites John Quincy Adams's composition of the Monroe doctrine and by the 1820s had settled into the canon of American state papers. Thus J. E. Hall, writing in the *Port-Folio* of 1825, expressed the almost universal sentiment respecting the Farewell: "I regret that any thing should be said or done to disturb our faith in this remarkable paper—a paper which, if future ages should become degenerate, posterity may recur as the Greeks repaired to the altar of Apollo, for a sacred spark to rekindle their household fires when they had been polluted by the invasion of the Persians."[16]

But time, of course, will have its way, with founding texts as with everything else, and the ensuing history of American foreign relations was bound to bend the meaning of Washington's Farewell toward its own ends. By the end of the nineteenth century, indeed, many thought that the age had indeed "become degenerate" and its household polluted, if not by Persians, then surely by those who would twist and distort the first president's words to their own unfortunate ambitions. To be clear: the text itself suffered from no loss of prestige. For all the wrangling over its proper application, most still agreed with William Phelps that "No archives contain another document embodying so much patriotism, displaying so much political wisdom, and expounding, with such fidelity and solicitude, the policies and principles which should regulate a nation's foreign relations." For some, like George Mott, the Farewell Address now deserved pride of place in the nation's pantheon of state papers. "The time has sufficed for eulogizing the Declaration of Independence," Mott declared, and he counseled that, "as we enter upon a new century, we should give to this Farewell a supreme significance equal to that which first thrilled every patriot's heart. The need of it is the prophecy of its coming. In this is the hope of deliverance."[17]

Few, then, denied the lasting significance of Washington's parting words. What mattered in the context of the 1890s was what those words meant and what they were capable of authorizing in the way of U.S. foreign policy. The reasons for this are not far to seek, but they are complex: the country was then confronting its emerging status as a major power in international affairs, and its role in managing that status was far from clear or uniformly understood. We cannot attend to details sufficiently here, but perhaps it is enough to be reminded of the conflicting pressures placed on its leaders from seemingly every corner of the globe. Upheavals in South America, dynastic challenges and strife in Europe, South African wars, and of course the contentious question of America's presence in the Pacific: these theatres and more demanded some sort of considered response on the part of U.S. leaders and the public; if no single rationale for action could be found that did not have its critics, most observers seemed agreed that in Washington they could find sufficient authority for whichever option might be chosen. It is well to recall, too, that the situation cannot be fairly reduced to whether America ought or ought not pursue imperialist ambitions; that question loomed large, to be sure, but others entered the picture as well: what constituted advantageous commercial terms and what price ought to be paid for such terms; when was intervention, military or otherwise, justly imposed to mitigate the domestic conflicts—and sometimes the massacre—of foreign peoples?

The history of Washington's address teaches us that although a text may retain its canonical status, it may at the same time yield itself up to differing and sometimes competing interpretations. In this sense, we may say that the meaning of the text is not so much polysemous as is its effects: no one doubted what the propositional content of Washington's language signified. At stake was how and to what ends that content was to be applied. Isolationists, peace advocates, and other critics of American expansionism certainly believed they understood what Washington would wish: "We should seek commercial, but not political, relations with the foreign world," wrote Phelps, for "this Washington declares to be our foreign policy. Controversies will arise in Europe, and as our peculiarly isolated position removes us from them, why bind ourselves by artificial ties that drag us into unnecessary difficulties?" In the event, such opponents of "entangling alliances" were forced to witness a decade of unprecedented intervention—military, commercial, and cultural—into the affairs of nations near and far. On reflection, they could only look back on the recent past and appeal again to the Founder's fondest hopes: "He would be among the strongest and most outspoken of the opponents of everything savoring in the least of imperialism," wrote the *Advocate of Peace* in 1903," in the current sense of the word, and over every movement toward great military and naval establishments for this country."[18]

Any given point in the past was once itself a future possibility. The reminder here is useful in warning us away from imposing on the eventual turn of events a sense of the ordained. As it happened, America in the decade of the Farewell's centenary opted to turn its face both east and west, and south for that matter, and in the process at least helped to set the course of international relations for the foreseeable—and unforeseeable—future. The reasons for this are complicated in the extreme, and it would be foolish to attribute such a turn to any single source. At the same time, we cannot ignore the extent to which proponents of American expansionism availed themselves of Washington's text in pursuit of global aspirations. For critics of such a policy, this work of appropriation could be nothing except tragic irony. For supporters, it made all the sense in the world—but some interpretive reassembly was required.

Underscoring the expansionists' program was the truism that the world was a different place from what it had been in Washington's time and that therefore, if his words were to still apply, they must be adjusted to the new realities facing an America very different from the one the president beheld. On this basis, sound enough, issued more specific lines of argument, some tendentious, perhaps, but some still resonant in our own time. One had only to pick up the papers then to read of depredations inflicted by despots upon their own people. Ought America, with all its resources and its claims to being a model new republic, sit idly by while innocents perished? Surely not, *The Independent* editorialized in 1896: "We may be sure that when he would forbid our country to intervene in the political disputes of the Old World, he did not mean to prevent us taking our fair part in the policing of the world and in putting down inhuman outrages." Here we have an instance of what might be called the humanitarian appeal to the Farewell as a warrant for U.S. intervention. A more aggressive variation was forcefully expressed in a well-known publication by the social commentator Robert Ellis Jones, who in 1899 dismissed any reservations about America's international role by stressing the chief executive's martial spirit. "Washington expected that, if it were necessary for reprisal upon a persistent European enemy, we might throw our sword into the European Balance," he wrote. "Washington was no gentle dreamer or theory-spinning humanitarian, but a warrior from his youth."[19]

Soon enough such sentiments were put to a test of truly epic proportions as America contemplated entry into the Great War. In spite of those voices still sounding

Washington's putatively pacifist counsel, events conspired to, in effect, render the Farewell Address all but irrelevant. The world had indeed changed, and if Washington could be invoked at all, it was simply to declare once again, with Roland Usher, that he would "be the last to hold that the American people are to-day to feel themselves bound to follow under present conditions a counsel regarding alliances explicitly based upon the fundamental problems of a small, weak, disorganized debt ridden country." As America stood at the precipice, it knew itself to be neither small nor weak, neither disorganized nor debt ridden; it was poised in the strongest possible way, rather, to "make the world safe for democracy." And so the Farewell Address began its long fade from American memory.[20]

Jefferson's Declaration in the Twentieth Century

Thomas Jefferson was a master of political expression, and he knew it. When he set out to give his thoughts maximum rhetorical force, he accordingly set his eye on the future, confident that what he had to say might well be held in trust by future generations. This, however, is not to say that his Declaration was designed *only* for the coming time: no one, then or now, would deny that the document was meant to effect immediate ends, including establishing international relations, rallying public sentiment, and sustaining martial commitment during the difficult years of the fight for independence. George Washington was confident "that this important event will act as a fresh incentive to every officer and soldier to act with fidelity and courage," and John Adams noted, "I am well aware of the Toil and Blood and Treasure, that it will cost Us to maintain this Declaration, and support and defend these States. Yet through all the Gloom I can see the Rays of ravishing Light and Glory. I can see that the End is more than worth all the Means. And that Posterity will triumph in that Days Transaction, even although we should rue it, which I trust in God We shall not."[21]

History and historians, however, have demonstrated time and again the multiple ways in which Jefferson's text slipped the bonds of its own time and continues to assert itself as a touchstone of enlightened political thought. Shortly before his death, indeed, the failing former president reflected on its legacy after fifty eventful years of American nationhood. "All eyes," he wrote in his last letter, "are opened or opening to the rights of man. The general spread of the light of science has already laid open to every view the palpable truth, that the mass of mankind has not been born with saddles on their backs, nor a favored few, booted and spurred, ready to ride them legitimately, by the Grace of God. These are grounds for hope for others; for ourselves, let the annual return of this day forever refresh our recollections of these rights, and an undiminished devotion to them."[22]

The first half of the nineteenth century found reasons aplenty to bear out Jefferson's final prayer. In addition to the annual fetes celebrating the Fourth of July and its founding text, American reformers, especially, found in the Declaration ample resources for advancing their own causes, including abolitionism, women's rights, and even Texas statehood. But what can we say of the effects of the Declaration in the twentieth century, when the founding generation had long past and, with it, any real sense of its immediate exigencies and aspirations? To ask this question is in fact to ask after the primal conditions that may be said to account for Jefferson's lasting influence both at home and abroad. Put another way: what traits ingredient to the text might plausibly be identified as lending themselves to the needs of distant heirs and unanticipated actors in the political affairs of our time, broadly construed? Here I suggest at least three such qualities that may account for the Declaration's continued effectivity: (1) its appeal to universal *norms* of political thought and action; (2) the distinctive *rhetorical form* that gives shape and force to that text; and (3) the Declaration's function as source of *legitimate authority*. I will treat each briefly in turn and proceed to offer examples of each as operating in the scenes of international affairs.[23]

While it is certainly the case that the balance of Jefferson's text is represented by a serial list of grievances against the British crown, it is no less true that such complaints have been subordinated to the more general propositions of the preamble. These propositions in turn are thoroughly familiar within Enlightenment contexts of political theory, and it is no small part of Jefferson's success that he manages to so efficiently wed the general and the particular into a coherent and compelling rationale for independence. It is nevertheless impossible to mistake the centrifugal force of the preamble, straining as it does to stretch the specifics of the colonial cause toward the broadest possible reaches of human aspiration. A quick survey of its language will readily make the point: "the course of human events"; "the powers of the earth"; "laws of nature and of nature's God"; "opinions of mankind"; "all men are created equal"; "unalienable rights"; "life, liberty, and the pursuit of happiness"; "any form of government"; "all experience hath shown that mankind"; "a candid world." This much is perhaps enough to illustrate a simple and familiar point but one that goes far toward explaining the lasting effect of the text. It stages the colonial case in the most accessible possible language and in the process helped establish a vocabulary that, even in translation, could be made to sponsor independence movements of seemingly every kind and cast. Jefferson thus not only used the Declaration to make an appeal but made the Declaration appealing to those who might not share in its immediate or particular concerns but who found in its language an ideal way to give expression to their own ambitions.

In addition to its universalizing language, the Declaration is notable for the form in which these expressions are given optimal effect. The author never claimed to have espoused a single novelty of political thought anywhere in the text; similarly, we ought to note that the form assumed by the Declaration was for many centuries an enduring resource for political expression. Declarations of one sort or another had of course asserted themselves into English law, letters, and politics since at least Magna Carta and as recently as colonial documents on the eve of armed conflict in 1775. But, though familiar, the Declaration as rhetorical form commands our attention for several reasons, which together may help us assemble our explanation for its lasting influence. Given the considerable variability declarations have evinced over time, we must be cautious about generalizations, but at a minimum we can observe that they tend to be relatively brief, direct, and unambiguous; as with its cousin the manifesto, the declaration does not so much invite argument as announce itself to the world; importantly, it marks itself off decisively from the more domesticated genre of the political petition. A declaration does not plead; it demands; it gives reasons but never excuses; it indicts but refuses to negotiate. Above all, it declares that behind and in front of all this is an incontrovertible "WE," a pronominal assumption that, fictional or not, a unified and resolute body of people stands prepared to act on behalf of its concerted rights.[24]

We must note, finally, a more general but nevertheless powerful set of indicators that help explain the lasting effects of Jefferson's text. To this end, it is worth reminding ourselves that, for better and worse, what we now refer to as "American exceptionalism" is scarcely the product of Americans alone. Whatever glories or afflictions may be laid at the feet of this abiding conviction, it is historically evident that other peoples, other nations, and other people who would be nations have looked to the American founding for inspiration, strength, and credibility. We have reason, then, to stretch the Aristotelian concept of ethos beyond its intended referent as an attribute of the individual and apply it to broader political contexts. In this sense, the Declaration may be seen as the textual embodiment of the American ethos; precisely because this ethos seemed to consist not in petty jealousies and imperial rivalries but in the more exalted language of rights, so much more could it be invoked as legitimately authorizing future independence movements. This is not to suggest, of course, that such appeals were then or now are always generous, disinterested, or motivated by unsullied ideals. The point is rather rhetorical: history shows us time and again that the U.S. Declaration funded the emancipatory aims of twentieth-century peoples because, in appealing to its values, they hoped thereby assume its probity, power, and promise.

Together, the language, form, and authority commended by Jefferson's text enable us to account for the perdurance of that document well beyond its initial appearance before the world. Without tracing each of these factors in great detail, we can usefully cite at least several examples where the Declaration explicitly made itself felt in the postcolonial eras of the twentieth century, notable with respect to Japan, Rhodesia, Palestine, Poland, and Vietnam. These examples are of course varied and come from diverse corners of the globe, and indeed that is part of my argument: that, however different the contexts and circumstances from which these people operated, they nevertheless found in the Declaration sufficient reason to invoke its rhetorical appeal to their respective ends. For reasons of space, I here take up briefly one such instance.

It would be difficult to locate a less promising scenario for the appearance of a late-eighteenth-century Anglo-American document than Japan. Barriers of language, vexatious imperial relations, and historical norms conspired to block passage of Jefferson's text from seemingly every direction. Nevertheless, historians of the subject note that at least two main junctures Japanese leaders and scholars turned their eyes to the West as they sought to forge new political commitments and gain for them popular support. The first such efforts occurred during the so-called Meiji Enlightenment of the late nineteenth century, when fledgling efforts toward democratizing Japanese culture faced serious obstacles from conservative defenders of traditional order. Fukuzawa Yukichi, in particular, early in the second half of the century espoused Western and, especially, American conceptions of rights as embodied in the Declaration. Thus in 1866 he introduced his compatriots to the text, the sense of which may be gathered from the translation into English by the Japanese scholar Tadashi Aruga: "When it becomes inevitable for one kin group of people, compelled by the course of events in human life, to leave the government of another nation, to join the ranks of the nations of the world and establish a separate nation in accordance with the nature of reason of the physical world and that of the way of heaven, they must explain the reasons for establishing a new nation and let them be known widely by a declaration out of consideration for [other] people's sentiments."[25]

The second major assertion of the Declaration arrived shortly after the cessation of hostilities with Japan at the end of World War II. Coupled with the Japanese Constitution of 1946–47, its language is explicitly invoked during the MacArthur-led attempt to fashion Western-style democracy into an acceptable form for the Japanese. In this he had considerable support from native opinion leaders, among them Takagi Yasaka, who similarly effected translations of the Declaration in 1931 and in 1952. Takagi's particular vision owed rather more to his Christian convictions than heretofore expressed, but he managed in 1946 to secure the text as a fixture in Japanese education for generations to come. For Takagi, "The Anglo-American founders of democratic ideas and institutions, Locke and Jefferson and the others, were at once rationalists and believers in the Christian faith." He stressed that "until we Japanese can appreciate the significance of this fact, we shall fail to grasp the meaning of democracy."[26]

In 1945 Ho Chi Minh delivered to his Hanoi audience a speech on the Democratic Republic of China. It began [in English translation]: "All men are created equal. They are endowed by their Creator with certain inalienable rights, among these are Life, liberty, and the pursuit of Happiness." This fact ought to give us pause. Aside from the obvious ironies of its source and future, the passage reminds us, in its very context, of the multiform ways in which certain texts take on a life of their own, indeed superannuate themselves to the point where their authors cannot possibly have expected where their words might land, by whom they might be spoken or for what ends. But however intransigent their career, such texts, rare enough, perhaps, nonetheless persist in shaping the rhetorical culture of our time.[27]

Summary

I have sought through the foregoing accounts to suggest at least one way in which rhetorical critics might address directly the question of effects. There are, of course, several other options: to ignore or deny the relevance of the question; to better demonstrate the intensity of a given effect; or, in attempt to satisfy the standards espoused by Professor Edwards, to provide a convincing test of effectivity through the rigors of empirical design. One might imagine circumstances in which one or another option might best be undertaken, and I have tried not to dismiss their legitimacy out of hand. I do think, however, that rhetorical critics have ample occasion to stretch their conception of effect to include considerations of time and to further complicate that conception by asking after the ways in which texts—certain texts, at least—may effect themselves in different ways over relatively discrete historical eras. Paine's *Common Sense,* for example, shows us how a text may in very short order recalibrate the very language of political resistance; Washington's Farewell illustrates the ways in which a text may be expropriated well beyond its situated aims to effect the work of policy a century after its original publication; and the Declaration reveals how, in language, form, and authority, a text may be used to further the ends of emancipation on a global scale.

If there is a more general claim about the role of effects in rhetorical criticism to be found here, it is that we need to be more mindful of posing dilemmas where they do not necessarily exist. By this I mean to suggest that the frequently alleged tension between text and context is in fact a pseudo problem, assuming as it does a fixed tension between the interiority of the text and the exteriority of the conditions within which it operates. There are several ways to expose the fallacy for what it is. For the purposes of this essay, I will simply conclude that the tension is resolved by running a lifeline, as it were, between the two constructs, and that lifeline is what we have, for better or worse, referred to as the matter of "effect." This study in rhetorical effectivity puts us in position to advance certain generalizations. We have observed that certain texts may be properly understood as shaping—and reshaping—the immediate contexts of their appearance, and we have treated one instance in which this is demonstrably the case. I have tried to suggest through additional case studies that as rhetorical critics we are uniquely situated to trace the career of texts as they are taken up in circumstances well beyond their birth in the immediate, that we can and should attend to the intermediate and long-term conditions through which they continue to assert themselves in public argument. We are fully warranted, that is to say, in claiming that such texts retain their force because we want them to matter still, because we care, and take care, that they not go away. Such texts will demand of each generation that their story be told again, for its own reasons and to their own ends.

Notes

1. David Hume, *An Enquiry Concerning Human Understanding* (La Salle: Ill.: Open Court Publishing Co., 1958): 80.

2. See editors' introduction to this volume.

3. Hannah Arendt, *The Human Condition* (Chicago: University of Chicago Press, 1958); Lawrence W. Rosenfield, "The Practical Function of Epideictic," in *Rhetoric in Transition: Studies in the Nature and Uses of Rhetoric*, ed. Eugene E. White (University Park, Pa.: Pennsylvania State

University Press, 1980): 131–155; Edwin Black, "Secrecy and Disclosure as Rhetorical Forms," *Quarterly Journal of Speech* 74 (1988): 133–150.

4. See especially George C. Edwards III, "Presidential Rhetoric: What Difference Does It Make?," in *Beyond the Rhetorical Presidency*, ed. Martin J. Medhurst (College Station: Texas A&M University Press, 1996), 199–217.

5. The relevant scholarship on *Common Sense* is of course vast; for work especially well attuned to its rhetorical dimensions, see Bernard Bailyn, "Common Sense," in *Fundamental Testaments of the American Revolution* (Washington, D.C.: Library of Congress, 1973), 7–22; Robert A. Ferguson, "The Commonalities of Common Sense," *William and Mary Quarterly* 57 (2000): 465–504; and J. Michael Hogan and Glenn Williams, "Republican Charisma and the American Revolution: The Textual Persona of Thomas Paine's *Common Sense,*" *Quarterly Journal of Speech* 86 (2000): 1–18.

6. George Washington, "Farewell Address," in *Washington's Farewell Address: The View from the 20th Century,* ed. Burton Ira Kaufman (Chicago: Quadrangle Books, 1969): 15–30; for background studies and interpretations, see also Felix Gilbert, *To the Farewell Address* (Princeton: Princeton University Press, 1970); Edward Pessen, "George Washington's Farewell Address, the Cold War, and the Timeless National Interest," *Journal of the Early Republic* 7 (1987); 1–25; and Matthew Spalding and Patrick J. Garrity, *A Sacred Union of Citizens: George Washington's Farewell Address and the American Character* (Lanham, Md.: Rowman and Littlefield, 1998).

7. Arthur A. Markowitz, "Washington's Farewell and the Historians: A Critical Review," *Pennsylvania Magazine of History and Biography* 94 (1970): 173.

8. Abraham Lincoln, "Speech in Independence Hall, Philadelphia, Pennsylvania (Feb. 22, 1861)," reprinted in *The Collected Works of Abraham Lincoln,* ed. Roy P. Basler (New Brunswick, N.J.: Rutgers University Press, 1953), 240; Woodrow Wilson, "The Author and Signers of the Declaration of Independence," in *Woodrow Wilson: The Essential Political Writings* edited by Ronald J. Pestrillo (Lanham, Md.: Lexington Books, 2005), 99; Ronald Reagan, *Speaking My Mind: Selected Speeches* (New York: Simon and Schuster, 1989), 378; Barack Obama, Speech in Philadelphia, May 2, 2011, http://www.npr.org/templates/story/story.php?storyId=88478467 (accessed August 19, 2013).

9. Benedict Anderson, *Imagined Communities* (London: Verso, 1991); and, still, Bernard Bailyn, *Ideological Origins of the American Revolution* (Cambridge, Mass.: Harvard University Press, 1965), provide useful background to the publication culture of colonial and early America.

10. Ferguson, "Commonalities," 467; quoted in Sophia Rosenfeld, "Tom Paine's Common Sense and Ours," *William and Mary Quarterly* 65 (2008): 637; *Connecticut Gazette,* March 3, 1776, 1.

11. Ferguson, "Commonalities," 467; Rosenfeld, "Tom Paine," 635–636.

12. "The Petition of Rights, 1628," http://www.constitution.org/eng/petright.htm (accessed August 17, 2013).

13. "The Olive Branch Petition; in Congress in Philadelphia, October 26, 1774," http://www.constitution.org/primarysources/olive.html (accessed August 17, 2013).

14. Thomas Paine, *Common Sense,* in *Thomas Paine, Common Sense, and the Turning Point to Independence,* ed. Scott Liell (Philadelphia: Running Press, 2003), 34.

15. Washington, "Farewell Address"; Gilbert, *To the Farewell Address,* 27.

16. J. E. Hall, "Washington's Farewell Address," *Port-Folio,* September 1825, 227.

17. William W. Phelps, "Washington's Valedictory," *American Magazine of Civics* 7 (1895): 466; George S. Mott, "Formation of Washington's Farewell Address to the American People," *Pennsylvania Magazine of History and Biography* 21 (1897): 408.

18. Phelps, "Valedictory," 473; "Washington's Anti-militarism," *Advocate of Peace* (March 1903): 39.

19. "Washington's Doctrine and Arbitration," *Independent,* February 20, 1896, 48; Robert E. Jones, "Washington's Farewell and Its Applications," *Forum* (September 1899): 20.

20. Ronald G. Usher, "Washington and Entangling Alliances," *North American Review* 24 (1916): 30.

21. Quoted in William Pencak, "The Declaration of Independence: Changing Interpretations and a New Hypothesis," *Pennsylvania History* 57 (1990): 226.

22. Pencak, "The Declaration of Independence," 229.

23. For a survey of the Declaration's global reach, see especially *The Journal of American History* 85, no.4, to which I am much indebted for the following remarks. For the best rhetorical analysis of the text, see Stephen E. Lucas, "Justifying America: The Declaration of Independence as a Rhetorical Document," in *American Rhetoric: Context and Criticism,* ed. Thomas W. Benson (Carbondale: Southern Illinois University Press, 1989), 67–130.

24. For a penetrating analysis of the rhetorical function of the pronominal "we," see Janet Lyon, *Manifestoes: Provocations of the Modern* (Ithaca: Cornell University Press, 1999).

25. Quoted in Tadashi Aruga, "The Declaration of Independence in Japan: Translation and Transplantation, 1854–1997," *Journal of American History* 85 (1999): 1411.

26. Argura, "The Declaration of Independence in Japan," 1410.

27. "Vietnamese Declaration of Independence, 1945," Internet Modern History Sourcebook, http://www.fordham.edu/halsall/mod/1945vietnam.html.

Responses to Rhetoric's Invitation

An Analysis of the Bush Presidency, the Immigration Debate, and Rhetoric's Effects

SARA A. MEHLTRETTER DRURY

One legacy of the George W. Bush administration's domestic policy is that it never achieved comprehensive immigration reform. This result transpired despite favorable conditions: Republican control in both houses of the Congress, tremendous news coverage, numerous speeches by the president and members of the White House staff, and public advocacy in support of the legislation. President Bush began the call for reform while running for re-election, in 2004. His plan included increased border security as well as a series of new policies governing how the United States defined and treated "illegal immigrants," individuals who were in the United States—sometimes for decades—without permission from the government.[1] Once re-elected, Bush continued to advocate for immigration reform, and in May 2006, Bush gave a nationally televised address arguing that Congress should pass comprehensive immigration reform. Each congressional body passed versions of immigration legislation (H.R. 4437 and S. 2611), but reconciliation failed; no comprehensive piece of legislation emerged from the Republican-controlled 109th Congress.[2] After the 2006 midterm elections and Democrats took control in both the House and the Senate, efforts to pass a comprehensive immigration reform act in 2007 were even less successful.[3] As the legislators of the 110th Congress left Washington for their 2007 summer recess, most commentators—and the politicians themselves—agreed that the time for action had passed. There would be no immigration reform under President Bush.

Many media outlets blamed presidential, rather than congressional, leadership for the failure to enact immigration reform. In the *New York Times*, a headline declared a "Defeat for Bush," elaborating that the "cornerstone of [Bush's] domestic agenda" had "collapsed Thursday in the Senate, with little prospect that it can be revived before Mr. Bush leaves office in 19 months."[4] The *Chicago Tribune* bemoaned that immigration reform "now lies in ruin." Its editorial, titled "The Speech Bush Didn't Give," blamed Bush's inability to "level with his fellow Americans" as causing the defeat of legislation in Congress.[5] Referring to the legislation as the president's proposal, Peter Baker of the *Washington Post* noted that Bush, after hearing that the Senate had failed to close debate and vote, "did something he almost never does: he admitted defeat."[6] Other papers noted the president's failure to lead his own party in the debate. Republicans, with a few exceptions, had largely denounced Bush's call for "amnesty" for illegal immigrants.[7] The *Chicago Tribune* wrote that Bush's party had "abandoned him" and suggested that Bush would be unable to "push major policy proposals through Congress."[8] Baker's *Washington Post* article made reference to Bush's "resounding defeat" and the "last, best chance at a major domestic accomplishment for his second term."[9] The *Miami Herald* editorialized, "The Senate's rejection Thursday of President Bush's immigration plan was the latest in a series of embarrassments that have exposed Bush's political weakness and shaken his hold on power."[10]

Even outlets that mentioned Congress as accountable for its failures placed some blame on the president. The *Los Angeles Times,* for example, wrote, "Although the provisions were worked out by a bipartisan group of lawmakers, and President Bush had made it a top priority, in the end neither he nor Majority Leader Harry Reid (D-Nev.) could persuade even a simple majority of the Senate to keep the bill alive."[11] The *Boston Globe* noted that Bush had used "his influence to revive" the immigration bill in the Senate, and yet, despite presidential pressure, there was a "failure of bipartisan compromise" in Congress.[12] Indeed, immigration had been rejected twice, by congressional leadership in each party—first by the Republicans in the 109th Congress in 2006 and then by the Democratic-led 110th Congress in 2007. According to the media accounts, this rejection seemed to be a failure in presidential leadership and effectiveness.

The idea that the president, rather than Congress, might inspire and create legislative policy is a more modern conception of presidential leadership and authority. In his book *The Rhetorical Presidency,* the political scientist Jeffrey Tulis argued that the twentieth-century president had the ability to violate constitutional norms of lawmaking by speaking to the people, rather than Congress (the traditional creator of legislation), to win support. Once the public supports the president, legislators are compelled to also support the president's agenda.[13] Analysis from this framework would suggest that since Bush did not pass his legislative agenda despite his public appeals, the policy failure was a failure of the bully pulpit—of presidential leadership and rhetoric.

Yet, despite these failures, Bush's discourse about immigration—most notably his address to the nation on May 15, 2006—did have effects on public discourse and public policy. In communication studies, scholars have consistently argued that presidential rhetoric—the president speaking to the public—has significant effects on politics. These effects of rhetoric, as David Zarefsky has contended, "are better understood as invitations to response" rather than a message-effects model of communication. In other words, rhetoric is "far more likely to suggest possibilities and issue invitations than it is to determine outcomes."[14] Zarefsky warned that looking at speeches as singular events with immediate effects considers only "one dimension of a rhetorical transaction" and reduces "the message to a verbal text and then to treat that text as a 'black box,' rather than seeing its dynamics as interesting and worthy of analysis in their own right."[15] When scholars consider the effects of rhetoric as not limited to the "black box" of immediacy and socially scientific validity, understanding of rhetoric's effects also expands. In his defense of this model of understanding, Zarefsky offered several case studies demonstrating how the "presidential use of the power to define" a particular reality through public discourse subsequently altered "public conceptions of political reality, thereby shifting the ground" of the debate.[16]

There is still much to be learned about the conditions of presidential rhetoric and its effects. The president has unparalleled access to audiences in that he (or she) can speak to the nation and have those remarks broadcast live on every major television network. Rhetorical critics who study the presidency have, as noted by Zarefsky, focused primarily on "the relationship between rhetor and text" as a historical matter, the motives of the rhetor as revealed in the text, and the text—here meaning beyond the verbal, or the "entirety of presidential performance"—as a departure point.[17] These perspectives underscore how rhetoric works to define reality—in other words, how the president might shape the qualities and character of national discussions on particular policies.

The broader understanding of the study of rhetoric's effects encourages the critic to search not solely in the speaker-text or speaker-audience relationship but also in the diffuse and diverse responses to the text and its fragments. Scholars have already begun this movement toward a broader understanding of effects in relation to the public discourse around and after a particular text's rhetorical moment. This is evident in the rich history of social movement rhetoric,[18] as in more recent case studies of public policy debates and deliberations.[19] More significant, critics might think of some scholarly projects as located not primarily in a single text but rather in what Kirt Wilson has called a "discursive field." Looking at a speech by Dr. Martin Luther King Jr., Wilson argued that a text, in some cases, "invites the critic to consider the interaction between rhetoric and hermeneutics." This interaction involves the text receiving and interpreting "a discursive field comprised of local history, folklore, private conversations, and public rhetoric."[20] Similarly, Nathan Stormer proposed that if rhetoric is a "historically contingent phenomenon," studying the effects of rhetoric requires identifying and analyzing the "wide variety of agents in 'a configuration of rhetoric.'"[21] In studying the anti-urban-sprawl movement in Austin, Texas, Jenny Edbauer argued that a critic may not be able to separate out a primary speaker, exigence, audience, and response. Instead, a "public scene" or debate "forces us into a rather fluid framework of exchanges—a fluidity that blends the elements of the rhetorical situation."[22] Furthermore, in a 2012 forum in *Rhetoric and Public Affairs,* several scholars suggested that the concept of "rhetorical circulation" might aid our understanding of the diffuse yet pervasive effects of rhetoric.[23] In her introduction to that forum, Mary Stuckey wrote that the theoretical and critical engagement of rhetorical circulation allows scholars to "examine questions of purpose and of repurposing," "explore the ways texts fragment and combine," and "attend to issues of authorship and audience."[24] The work of these scholars calls for a broader understanding of rhetoric's effects, including emphasizing a critical read of audience response—or lack of response—as well as broader circulation in public discourse.

This broader view of effects is appropriate for scholars interested in the presidency and public discourse. There is more to understanding the quality and character of public discourse than focusing primarily on the president's rhetorical framework as given to an audience at a particular time and place. Critics might expand the effects of presidential rhetoric to include the full "discursive field" of a public policy debate, answering questions of who responds to presidential rhetoric and detailing specific groups or actors over time and how those agents perceive, engage, reject, and/or transform public discourse. As Rod Hart has argued, rhetorical critics can and should become "smarter, more layered, and more precise about rhetorical effects."[25] It is not that rhetorical critics cannot make effects claims about how rhetoric—and, in this case, presidential rhetoric—influences public policy but rather that a broader understanding of rhetorical invitation and response might in turn broaden the ability of critics to make effects claims. Writing about rhetorical circulation, Stephen Heidt called for looking at the "fragmentation" of presidential messages, arguing that "presidential scholars can systematically understand how audiences receive presidential messages, the rhetorical work those messages perform on those audiences, and how the recirculation of those messages work on the president" by developing broader notions of rhetorical effects.[26] This includes studying notable instances of presidential rhetoric, examining both successes and cases when the president's invitation to respond was altered, countered, or rejected.

In this essay, I utilize the case study of the 2005–2007 immigration debate to demonstrate a broader notion of rhetorical effects, with a particular focus on Bush's 2006 speech on comprehensive immigration reform. In so doing, I aim to further our understanding of the presidency and rhetorical effects, moving beyond the success-failure model of public policy debates and considering the rhetorical circulation of Bush's speech across a fuller field of public discourse on immigration reform. Although President Bush's rhetoric failed to persuade his listeners to support his proposed immigration reform, his rhetorical appeals altered the scope of the debate on immigration, demonstrating circulation effects in the field of public discourse.

In this essay, I analyze the historical background of immigration rhetoric and the president's discourse, including White House official statements and a nationally televised address, as well as responses to those texts. I also take up the questions of how Congress and several political factions responded to Bush's invitation to see immigration a particular way. In his May 15, 2006, speech to the nation, the president offered an invitation to view immigration as a national security problem with clear legislative solutions, a framework that had circulation in the rhetoric of Congress and the public.

Following the opening of a broader understanding of rhetorical effects, I offer three subsequent effects claims about Bush's immigration reform rhetoric. First, within the speech itself, Bush advanced a framework of immigration that defined the problem primarily as a national security threat and offered solutions to that problem that recast a narrative of the American Dream for this generation of immigrants. The second and third claims look specifically at the effects of Bush's narrative being taken up on the one hand by Congress, and on the other hand opposed by the American public. Both of these effects reflect the study of rhetorical circulation, mapping the "residues of discourse" present in the broader debate.[27] The congressional debate, particularly in the U.S. Senate, reflected and responded to Bush's framework of immigration. Much of the broader discursive field of the immigration debate, however, opposed or rejected Bush's framing of immigration, articulating alternatives for public consideration. I begin my analysis with a critical look at immigration policy in the United States and then examine Bush's rhetoric and the varied responses to his discourse from Congress and the public. I end by arguing not just for the study of the invitations of presidential rhetoric but also for the consideration of responses, both favorable and unfavorable.

Immigration, the United States, and the President

Since the first colonists landed on the shores of Virginia and Massachusetts, immigration has commanded political attention. Aristide R. Zolberg has argued that the United States has frequently attempted to "violently eliminate" those individuals who were seen as unfit for citizenship.[28] The debate over who may enter the United States and become a citizen has resurfaced time and again, whether focusing on Germans in Pennsylvania, Italians in New York, Irish in Boston, Chinese in San Francisco, Hmong in Minnesota, or Mexicans in Houston.

Rhetorical scholars have emphasized how the dominant frames of the immigration debate often revolved around negative stereotypes and the burdens immigrants place on American society.[29] These narratives tend to focus on the economic costs of immigration, the criminality of immigrants, and cultural and ethnic stereotyping. In their book *Shifting Borders,* Kent A. Ono and John M. Sloop consider the dominant arguments in the debate over California Proposition 187, a referendum designed to limit or eliminate immigrants' access to government services in that state. Sloop and Ono argue that immigrants are often discussed as "economic commodities" or "human capital" that benefits or harms the United States.[30] Lisa A. Flores has examined the debate over immigration in California in the 1920s and 1930s and concludes that "immigrant and criminality" were "closely connected" in discourses of that era.[31] The negative stereotypes surrounding immigrants have not abated in the contemporary era. Anne Demo, through her analysis of Immigration and Naturalization Service (INS) videos from 1999 and 2000, argues that the INS inherently emphasized the lawlessness of immigrants. As Demo concluded, the "portraits of immigrant lawlessness and border violence" revealed "the physical and economic threats posed by ill-enforced borders," while deterrence of illegal immigration appeared to be achievable only through physical "security and order."[32] J. David Cisneros argued that immigrants are frequently compared to "a dangerous pollutant"; groups of immigrants were "unorganized, idle, and aimless—connoting a sense of accumulating danger" to U.S. society.[33]

Scholars have also noted the importance of the president in defining the characteristics of immigration. Michael Novak has argued that the president "is given great power over the symbolic lives of American citizens," particularly over the character and identity of the nation.[34] The president "represents the history and aspirations of the nation" and so has tremendous ability to influence public discourse, even suggesting who belongs in America. Presidents may construct situations where particular immigrant groups are included or excluded due to ethnic, racial, political, and/or cultural characteristics.[35] Presidential rhetoric yields effects because the president, in addressing the nation, is able to define the field of the debate, constructing a framework for discussion. Since the president may "shape the context in which events or proposals are viewed by the public,"[36] even when he or she fails in the policy realm, his or her rhetoric may have had circulation effects on American culture and public discourse.

The Renewal of the U.S. Immigration Debate

President George W. Bush began the process of redefining the immigration issue on October 18, 2005, when he spoke after signing a new Homeland Security Appropriations Act (HSAA).[37] Bush's remarks did not focus entirely on immigration, but the president dedicated roughly one-third of his speech to the need to improve border security. In his remarks, the president stated the connection between immigration and national security in simple, direct terms: "To defend this country, we've got to enforce our borders."[38] Yet, Bush still employed traditional immigration narratives in his remarks, describing some illegal immigrants as members of "violent criminal gangs" and calling for more detention facilities and quicker deportation of illegal immigrants.[39] According to Bush, the new HSAA provided ample funding to deal with these problems. The president's focus was on enforcing current laws, not creating new policies.

The president's visit to the U.S.-Mexico border in November 2005 signaled a change in the Bush administration's focus from enforcing old policies to creating new laws. The new law would be designed to both secure the border and create pathways for immigration. Over three days, Bush toured the southern border, giving two formal speeches on the need for immigration reform, meeting with border officials, and taking pictures at checkpoints. Bush's 2005 visit emphasized the centrality of the U.S.-Mexico border to the issue of immigration.[40] He was, according to the *New York Times*, at the "front lines of the fight" to alter immigration policy.[41] A *Boston Globe* editorial characterized the president as "wisely nudging Congress" toward legislative reform.[42] After the visit, the *American Spectator* commented that he had "fastened" the attention of the public on immigration.[43]

Meanwhile, the White House Press Office released a list of specific objectives for reforming immigration laws, including stricter penalties for illegal immigrants and the employers who hired them. But the White House also proposed a new temporary-worker program, under which immigrants—and, more specifically, Mexican immigrants—could legally enter the United States to be employed in what the official press release termed "jobs that no American is willing to take."[44] According to the White House fact sheet on the program, the new temporary-worker program would not be "an automatic path to citizenship or amnesty." Instead, it would "promote legal immigration" and "decrease pressure on the border."[45] This concession, however small it may seem, was a move toward an immigration policy that would be more friendly to illegal immigrants already in the United States.

The debate over immigration began in the House of Representatives, and Democrats and Republicans endorsed different parts of Bush's plan. Democratic representatives split over how best to handle illegal immigrants already in the United States. Those in more conservative or moderate districts represented voters who would likely oppose full amnesty for illegal immigrants. Some Democrats rallied around Bush's proposed guest-worker program in the hopes that the 12 million illegal immigrants already in the United States could move toward citizenship.[46] Many Republicans appreciated Bush's attention to penalties for illegal immigrants and those assisting them. Some conservatives also called for stronger border security. In the final stages of the House debate on immigration, in December 2005, Republicans pushed through an amendment mandating a new 698-mile security fence along the U.S.-Mexico border.[47] This added to the bill's harsh penalties against illegal immigration and employment of illegal immigrants. The House bill passed by a vote of 239–182 on December 16, 2006.[48] In the end, most Republicans voted for the bill and most Democrats against it, although thirty-six Democrats joined the majority and sixteen Republicans dissented.[49]

In the Senate, the debate did not proceed so rapidly. Immigration reform stalled in the Judiciary Committee during December and January. The "Securing America's Borders Act" [S.2454] finally came to the Senate floor in late March and was bitterly debated. Most senators in favor of creating a temporary-worker program and opening paths to citizenship emphasized the human factors of immigration. While Senator Bill Frist (R-Tennessee) echoed his House colleagues' call for stronger border security, Senator Judd Gregg (R-New Hampshire) challenged his colleagues and called for a "society that says we are open," with fewer restrictions on who could enter the country.[50] Similarly, Senator Dick Durbin (D-Illinois) encouraged the Senate to listen to the calls of immigration protestors: "Si se puede—yes we can . . . they love this country as much as almost any other citizen."[51] The more moderate Republican senator John

McCain (Arizona) acknowledged "the burdens illegal immigrants impose on our cities and counties and States" but called immigration reform a "Federal responsibility" that had to be addressed. McCain also asked his colleagues to "face honestly the moral consequences of our current failed immigration system,"holding the U.S. government responsible for those who died in the difficult crossing from Mexico to the United States. McCain suggested that comprehensive reform could slow illegal immigration and thus eliminate "desperate" and gruesome deaths under the desert sun.[52] As the Senate debate dragged on, the complexity of the issue became increasingly apparent, with senators on both sides of the issue debating the economics of illegal immigration, cultural issues like bilingual education, and the problems of drug trafficking and policies. National security issues arose occasionally during the debate, but few in the Senate discussed immigration primarily as a national security issue during early 2006.

Ultimately, debate culminated on April 7, 2006, with the Senate's failure to vote for cloture on "Securing America's Borders Act" and bring the legislation to a vote.[53] The finger pointing began. The *Washington Post* quoted Hillary Rodham Clinton (D-New York) blaming the Republicans: "Republican efforts to criminalize undocumented workers and their support networks would 'literally criminalize the good Samaritan and Jesus himself.'"[54] Senator Arlen Specter (R-Pennsylvania), on the other hand, accused the Democrats, telling the *Washington Post,* "It's not gone forward because there's a political advantage for Democrats not to have an immigration bill."[55] Senator Joseph Lieberman (D-Connecticut) attributed the stalemate to "trivial issues and partisan backbiting,"[56] while Senate Majority Leader Bill Frist (R-Tennessee) was quoted in the *Christian Science Monitor* expressing his frustration that nothing had come of the debate: "I'm here to solve problems, not stand around."[57] For a third time, the Senate bill was sent back to the Judiciary Committee for revisions. The *New York Times* editorialized that President Bush needed to "step up" and "get his party united behind him" on new legislation.[58]

Bush tried to do just that in his address to the nation on May 15, 2006. In a live televised address, Bush outlined a comprehensive plan for securing the borders, dealing with illegal immigrants already in this country, and reforming the processes by which immigrants could enter the country legally. Bush framed immigration as a national security issue, and, in so connecting immigration to national security, he increased the urgency of the issue, gained public attention, and invited responses to his rhetoric.

Bush's "Address to the Nation on Immigration Reform"

Bush's May 15, 2006, address came at a critical juncture in the ongoing immigration debate. The president began his speech by acknowledging the importance of the issue and the passions on both sides of the debate, acknowledging both those who "rallied in support of those in our country illegally" and those who "organized to stop illegal immigrants from coming in."[59] Addressing lawmakers in Washington, Bush then announced that the immigration debate had "reached a time of decision" and cast himself as a voice of reason and compromise after months of heated debate.[60]

In *The Rhetorical Presidency,* Jeffrey Tulis argued that the president possesses the unique "rhetorical power" to pressure Congress into passing legislation.[61] Bush directed his speech both to Congress and to the public, drawing on an ethos of presidential leadership and expertise to augment his case. In the introduction to the immigration speech, the president suggested that the purpose of the speech was, first, to "make it clear" where he stood and, second, to demonstrate where he wanted to "lead our country on this vital issue."[62] Throughout the speech, Bush emphasized his experience, noting that he had dealt with immigration during his time as governor of Texas and routinely using the first person as he introduced various initiatives. This framing suggested that the legislative solution should come from the president, rather than Congress. Later in the speech, Bush admonished Congress for its lack of solution, issuing a directive that the "Senate should act by the end of the month so we can work out the difference between the two bills, and Congress can pass a comprehensive bill for me to sign into law."[63] Although this might appear to give responsibility back to Congress, the placement of this statement toward the end of the address suggests that Congress needed to pass Bush's law, adhering to the president's plan for immigration reform. Furthermore, the sentence ended by affirming Bush as leader of policy—he would "sign [the bill] into law," giving it final approval and force. Tulis has criticized presidential appeals that put the president into the dual role of leader and legislator, arguing that these appeals may stifle congressional deliberations over a specific policy by "reshaping the political world in which that policy and future policy is understood."[64] In the case of Bush's appeal for immigration reform, his speech seemed to invigorate, rather than stifle, congressional and public debate. The effects of Bush's rhetoric may have not included persuading others to support his policy initiative but instead may have furthered public debate by circulating his framework of comprehensive, multifaceted immigration reform as a critical matter of national security.

Bush's speech outlined several objectives for comprehensive immigration reform: "securing our borders, creating a temporary worker program, making it easier for employers to verify employment eligibility and continuing to hold them to account for the legal status of workers they hire, dealing with the millions of illegal immigrants who are already here, and honoring the great American tradition of the melting pot."[65] At first glance, only the first objective appears relevant to national security. However, Bush reframed the debate in terms of that first objective, redefining the whole controversy of immigration reform in terms of national security and subsuming the earlier amnesty debate under a new discursive framework. He also constructed an image of the "ideal immigrant" in the twenty-first century, a new version of the American Dream narrative. Bush's discourse invited a favorable response to new national security initiatives—an invitation that would be accepted with reservations by some and countered by others.

National Security and Immigration

In Bush's narrative, the 9/11 terrorist attacks transformed the problem of immigration into a problem of national security. The president explained, "[F]or decades, the United States has not been in complete control of its borders."[66] Illegal immigrants were "beyond the reach and protection of American law"[67] and as such were untraceable and untrackable—a clear national security concern in a post-9/11 world. Using the word "secure" six times and "security" six more times in just the first ten paragraphs of the printed transcript, Bush reduced the whole immigration debate to the simple fact that, in the wake of the terrorist attacks, the United States needed to "secure its borders." Secure borders were what defined a "sovereign nation," and in the post-9/11 world border security had become "an urgent requirement of our national security."[68]

Elaborating on the security issue, Bush reinforced the criminality theme common to immigration narratives. For example, he emphasized that the borders of the United States must be "shut to illegal immigrants, as well as criminals, drug dealers, and terrorists."[69] The inclusion of "terrorists" as a potential threat is significant, of course, as it played on the post-9/11 fears and concerns of all Americans. Despite the 9/11 Commission's conclusion that the terrorists who attacked the United States in 2001 did not enter the nation illegally,[70] Bush tried to make the porous southern border the newest front in the War on Terror.

Bush spent the first ten minutes of his eighteen-minute speech—more than half of the entire address—proposing additional ways to secure the border. The organization clearly demonstrated Bush's prioritization of security within any comprehensive reform of immigration law. Bush's first step was to improve "manpower and technology at the border." He called for hiring an additional six thousand Border Patrol agents, and he argued that "motion sensors, infrared cameras, and unmanned aerial vehicles" could all assist in "preventing illegal crossings." Bush's most significant proposal, however, was to send "up to 6,000 [National] Guard members" to the "southern border." Bush committed the Guard only to "assist the Border Patrol by operating surveillance systems, analyzing intelligence, installing fences and vehicle barriers, building patrol roads, and providing training." Symbolically, the commitment of Guard troops to patrolling the border militarized the government's response to the problem, reinforcing Bush's redefinition of immigration reform as a national security concern—as another front in the War on Terror.

While militarizing the border connected immigration to national security, Bush also cast each of his other objectives for immigration reform in national security terms. Even the temporary-worker program became part of the larger effort "to secure our border." Describing most immigrants as good, freedom-loving people who would "do anything to come to the United States to work and build a better life," Bush argued that allowing some Mexican workers to work in the country legally would "add to our security" by "making certain we know who is in our country and why they are here." Bush also proposed "tamper-proof" digital identity cards to help keep track of those workers, demonstrating that the U.S. government would not only keep track of foreign workers but also eliminate the likelihood of illegal infiltration through counterfeit identity cards.

Bush's address of May 15 thus framed immigration as a security issue, directly connected to the War on Terror and even the war in Iraq. There were, of course, other issues to consider in the debate over immigration: economics, the impact of immigration on America's educational system, and questions of human rights, among others. In Bush's framing, however, immigration policies had become inextricably tied to what he viewed as the first obligation of government: to protect the nation from another terrorist attack. In the post-9/11 era, Bush argued, the United States could no longer live with unsecured borders and millions of illegal immigrants "living in the shadows" of American society. Bush did not return to a call for harsh punishment of illegal immigrants. Instead, he redefined the American Dream narrative around "good" illegal immigrants and called for the establishment of paths to citizenship as a means of enhancing national security.

The Ideal Immigrant Narrative Re-created

Bush's speech created a group of ideal immigrants for the new century out of those "living in the shadows." Since the concept of amnesty was politically volatile, Bush undertook great pains to recast immigrants—particularly Mexican immigrants—as a new generation of American Dreamers. The president was quick to point out that immigrants are "a part of American life," challenging the historical, often negative frames of illegal immigration. He articulated the characteristics of the ideal immigrant, creating an understanding of who deserved citizenship despite their illegal status. He emphasized that the illegal immigrants of today were courageous and hardy, like the pioneers of old. Despite their "forged documents" used "to get jobs," the president stressed that "the vast majority of illegal immigrants are decent people who work hard, support their families, practice their faith, and lead responsible lives." They risked their lives and broke the law because they would "do anything to come to America to work and build a better life." Even if they needed to "walk across miles of desert in the summer heat, or hide in the back of 18-wheelers," they would try to "reach our country."[71] In short, today's Mexican immigrants were trying to claim a new American Dream, just as European immigrants had in earlier parts of U.S. history. They were not a threat to national security—provided that these "honest immigrants" would "respect the law" by participating in temporary-worker and documentation programs.[72]

In depicting these immigrants, Bush characterized them as deserving of citizenship. Good immigrants were productive members of society, with "deep roots in the United States." They had created "a home, a family, and an otherwise clean record" in their new country, leaving their old country behind. Giving them pathways to legal work and even citizenship was not a sign of "amnesty," which Bush acknowledged would be "unfair to those here lawfully." Instead, a "middle ground" could be found where desirable illegal immigrants could stay, while others who did not contribute to society would be deported. Furthermore, even those "good" immigrants would still have to "pay their debt to society" for breaking the laws of immigration. In fact, those who were willing to take on extra burdens and seek legal immigration and citizenship would "demonstrate the character that makes a good citizen" of the United States.[73]

Bush concluded his speech with a story that demonstrated the importance of legal documentation programs for "good" immigrants while connecting his legal-worker program to national security initiatives. Reinforcing his argument that admitting immigrants of "good character" was good for the United States, Bush referenced a young Mexican immigrant he had met at Bethesda Naval Hospital, Master Gunnery Sergeant Guadalupe Denogean. Denogean, a Mexican immigrant who had come to the United States as a boy, spent most of his young life "picking crops with his family." As soon as he was old enough, he volunteered for the United States Marine Corp and was "seriously injured" in the "liberation of Iraq." When asked by the president if he had any requests, the sergeant had just two: "a promotion for the corporal who rescued him and the chance to become an American citizen."[74] The first request demonstrated that Denogean, as an example of "good" immigrants, cared about his fellow soldier, representing his fellow Americans. The second request reinforced Bush's argument that good immigrants would enhance national security—perhaps even, in the case of Denogean, risking their lives to promote U.S. security interests. Denogean became a representation of how even the process of granting work permits and citizenship can reinforce the security of the United States. The president described Denogean's citizenship ceremony: "And when this brave Marine raised his right hand, and swore an oath to become a citizen of the country he had defended for more than 26 years, I was honored to stand at his side." The United States would always, the president concluded, "be proud to welcome people like Guadalupe Denogean as fellow Americans." These immigrants were people willing to "risk everything for the dream of freedom" in the United States, the "great hope on the horizon . . . a blessed and promised land." Such individuals would only add to the quality, character, and most important, the security of the nation.

Bush's speech, therefore, made new immigrant groups part of the historical American Dream narrative and also demonstrated how temporary-worker and citizenship programs would enhance the national security goals of immigration reform. The president attempted to transform biases against some illegal immigrants, particularly hardworking Mexican immigrants, by emphasizing their quality of character and contribution to society, especially as those contributions relate to national security. In this way, Bush set up an expectation of how "good" immigrants behave to support the nation, one that public response to his speech would problematize.

The Broader Immigration Debate

The president's speech was only one aspect of the public policy debate on immigration. In examining rhetoric's broader effects, we might also consider responses to the speech by particular agents and groups, closely analyzing how Bush's frame was appropriated, reframed, and challenged in public discourse. Some of these responses are more directly tied to the speech itself, such as congressional debate in the months following Bush's address or blog posts about Bush's speech. Others muddy the field, as they were ongoing rather than direct responses. Still, these discourses can be located as part of the circulation of Bush's speech within the discursive field of the immigration debate.

The Congressional Debate over Immigration

In the days and weeks following Bush's speech, congressional legislators reoriented their discussion of immigration policy. Whereas national security had been one issue in the immigration debate, stressed by conservative legislators in favor of the "fence" initiative, it now was the primary focus when the Senate resumed debate shortly after the president's address. In March, senators had called for increased understanding of the human factors behind immigration—the poor working conditions in Mexico, the unfairness of punishing illegal immigrants, and the need to keep the United States open to those who sought the blessings of freedom. Two months later, immediately after the president's speech, the Senate resumed debate by considering an amendment that required border security before the government would consider any sort of guest-worker program or path to citizenship.

National security had become the top priority in the immigration debate, and even opponents of the president's original bill echoed that emphasis. The day after Bush's speech, the framing of the debate turned toward national security. Not everyone agreed with the president, but they responded to his arguments. Senator Johnny Isakson (R-Georgia) had authored the amendment to secure the border first and only then to allow other programs to take effect. In a speech before the Senate, Isakson examined the immigration issue broadly but then took his cue from Bush's speech, emphasizing the primacy of the national security narrative and stating, "The first thing the President said is to secure the border." Isakson proposed an amendment that would require that the border be secure before any amnesty programs could be enacted, justifying this amendment by quoting Bush from the previous night: "Last night, the President said we are a nation of laws. And we are a nation of laws. I submit to you that when laws are enforced, and they are enforced soundly, laws are obeyed and they are respected."[75] With his comments and "enforcement first" amendment, Isakson subtly opposed the president's call for more comprehensive immigration reform and demanded a postponement of guest-worker and citizenship initiatives while still demonstrating the effects of Bush's speech at a discursive level. Although the Isakson amendment was ultimately defeated by a vote of 55–40,[76] Isakson's framing of statements on broader immigration reform and his amendment demonstrated a response to Bush's speech the night before.

Other senators likewise emphasized military solutions at the border, addressing immigration almost solely as a national security issue. Those who placed priority on increased guest-worker or amnesty programs acknowledged the importance of national security. Senator Ken Salazar (D-Colorado), for example, stressed that national security had to be "at the heart of a workable immigration law."[77] Like Isakson, Salazar proposed an amendment as a response to the president's speech the day before. Salazar's alternative solution more reflected Bush's emphasis on strictly controlling of the border while implementing a guest-worker program, on the grounds that providing opportunities for immigrant workers was no less important to national security. Speaking in favor of the Salazar amendment, Senator Edward Kennedy (D-Massachusetts) called for the combination of stronger border security and more opportunities for immigrant workers as the "most effective way" to protect national security.[78] Speakers on all sides of the debate seemed to share the president's view that immigration reforms directly involved national security concerns.

The debate ended in a stalemate, however. Neither amendment passed, and Congress similarly failed to find a compromise. While the Senate was able to pass the Comprehensive Immigration Reform Act of 2006 on May 25, 2006, the bill differed substantially from its House counterpart. The Senate bill offered pathways to citizenship and more guest-worker cards, while the House bill—authored and supported by the conservative majority—focused solely on border protection and penalties for illegal immigrants. The two pieces of legislation went to conference committee. This left immigration reform in, as the *New York Times* put it on June 27, 2006, "legislative limbo."[79] More than a year later, the conference committee still had not been able to create a compromise bill. These two pieces of legislation expired when the 109th Congress ended, in January 2007. The new 110th Congress, with Democratic majorities in both the House and the Senate, once again took up the issue of comprehensive immigration reform. Another round of debate met a similar stalemate, and, in June 2007, the Senate closed debate on a compromise bill. The House never reintroduced immigration for debate.[80]

While Congress reached no compromise on immigration reform, Bush's speech and the responses to it offer implications for our understanding of presidential rhetoric and deliberative discourse in the United States. This analysis demonstrates that a president may be able to temporarily or permanently alter the framing of a public policy debate. The president may be limited in his intended effects yet still have wide-ranging circulation effects across subsequent pieces of discourse. Although Bush's speech seemed to have a strong influence on the terms and framework of the debate, the president did not control the outcome of that debate. While senators responded to Bush's framing of immigration as a national security initiative, they did not always support his policy proposal. By focusing on national security, Bush identified the common ground shared by both sides in the debate—securing the border. Yet an effect of this was that, as Congress focused on the specifics of immigration policy and national security, it also seemed increasingly unable to create a solution that satisfied the wide variety of opinions on guest workers and pathways to citizenship that were represented in the nation's legislative body.

The Public Responds

Unlike the Congress, which seemed to primarily focus on the primacy of securing the borders, public discourse took up more human questions of immigration and national security. The public debate was often related to whether audiences accepted or rejected Bush's ideal-citizen framework. Each time the president made a statement or Congress debated immigration reform, the opposing factions rallied their like-minded supporters.

Religious groups that supported reform continued to emphasize the human factors of immigration after the president's speech. The Catholic advocacy group Justice for Immigrants held prayer meetings throughout the debates, and Father Larry Snyder, head of Catholic Charities USA, upheld the commitment of the U.S. bishops to "point out the moral deficiencies in the immigration system and work toward justice until it is achieved."[81] The 75th General Convention of the Episcopal Church passed a resolution advocating for immigrant rights. This document proclaimed that the Episcopal Church would "deplore any action by the Government of the United States which unduly emphasizes enforcement, including militarization of the border between the United States and Mexico, as the primary response to immigrants entering the United States to work," and the Convention undertook "a campaign to educate Episcopalians as to the plight of refugees, immigrants, and migrants, which will include information about the root causes of migration." The Episcopal Church promised to "commit to welcoming strangers as a matter of Christian responsibility."[82] JSPOT.org, the blog of the group Jewish Funds for Justice, summarized its cautious hopes after the president's speech: If the president could use "his political influence in Congress (does he have any left?) to push a compromise that creates a path to citizenship for the 12 million undocumented workers already here that would be an enormous step in the right direction." The blog's writers cautioned, however, that they were concerned about Bush's call for assimilation. Immigrants should be valued, they explained, and allowed to "preserve cultural distinctiveness." The nation's culture would be "richer" for the "infusion of new talent" and "cultural particulars."[83] For these reform-minded religious groups, Bush's characterization of immigrations as hard workers seeking a better life and possessing something to offer U.S. society resounded as reasonable and true.

More moderate conservatives also embraced Bush's plan. For example, Andrew Sullivan, a prominent writer and blogger for *The Atlantic*, wrote that Bush's "insistence on both goals—border security and gradual legalization of millions of illegal immigrants already here—makes sense to me." Furthermore, the president's "eschewal of inflammatory rhetoric was welcome," and "[h]is enthusiasm for immigration and his empathy with immigrants are genuine."[84]

Bush's new American Dream narrative did, however, meet resistance from several groups interested in the public policy issue of immigration. For proponents of reform, including recent immigrants, Bush's invitation neglected political and economic reality. This group spoke out against what it saw as the inherent injustice of

U.S. immigration policy and the U.S. economic system. It argued that wealthy U.S. businesses denied immigrants access to the American Dream, since the businesses took advantage of illegal, cheap labor. As Benita Heiskanen has pointed out, immigrants in the United States illegally worked below minimum wage and without benefits, potentially saving U.S. businesses large amounts of money.[85] The Brookings Institute researchers Jeffrey D. Manze and Neil G. Ruiz described this process, writing that "[t]he American mindset has been to see guest workers as inputs to serve us at best or as parasites who take away American jobs."[86] To those who favored reform, the United States was economically benefiting from illegal immigration and continued to deny immigrants just, fair wages and citizenship status in order to preserve economic stability.

Meanwhile, the public protests against illegal immigrants rejected the characterization of the "good" immigrant, supporting security, law, and order, proposed by President Bush. Several blogs, including the Coalition against Illegal Immigration—which served as a common hub for many anti-immigration reform websites—accused the immigration movement of being aligned with "radical Marxists." This accusation portrayed immigrants very differently from the president's dutiful soldier-citizen example, and one can see how the demonization of "radical" factions challenged Bush's notion of good, hardworking American Dreamer immigrants.[87] Similarly, these groups portrayed immigration reform protests as closing down businesses, marching in the streets and disrupting order, and opposing U.S. culture. For such groups, Bush's suggestion that these immigrants could take part in the American Dream ignored the perception of immigrants as radical activists and usurpers of "American" jobs. The Coalition against Illegal Immigration criticized illegal immigrants as stealing jobs from earnest Americans: "Since when is masonry a job that Americans won't do? Masonry is a trade—a skilled labor trade—it's not some lowly job that Americans don't want. Actually, here in the Midwest, you'd be hard pressed to find any job that isn't filled by Americans. There are many Americans that take great pride in the skills of their hands. This is just one example of an American worker that has been displaced and couldn't obtain a job 'he wanted' because illegal immigrants will work for a fraction of the pay."[88] Although this narrative also emphasized the injustice of low wages for illegal immigrants, the solution was to deport immigrants and give jobs back to "American workers." Immigrants were not hardworking members of U.S. society, as Bush had suggested; instead, they were taking resources and jobs away from U.S. citizens.

More extreme conservatives rallied specifically against Bush's security narrative, arguing that moves toward worker programs and citizenship were unfair and unjust steps toward legalizing illegal behavior. The television host Bill O'Reilly, host of *The O'Reilly Factor*, initially condemned the Bush plan in 2006, stating that "an open border policy and the legalization of millions of Hispanic illegal aliens would deeply affect the political landscape in America," implying that any effects would not be positive.[89] The conservative Rush Limbaugh supported the president's plans to secure the border but blasted Democrats for supporting amnesty in order to secure a new Hispanic voting bloc: "The entire demographic makeup, the ethnic makeup, so many other aspects of our demography will change dramatically in ways that will make the country unrecognizable, and you have to know that people behind this are aware of it." Limbaugh described the Democrats as wanting "some voters" and "welfare state victims" to support their party.[90] O'Reilly and Limbaugh both supported the plan to secure the border, but their remarks took on familiar xenophobic, even racist, concerns common in anti-immigration rhetoric.

The president's narrative of "good" immigrants who deserve paths to citizenship challenged and invigorated extreme conservative factions, spurring them to promote their views of immigrants as dangerous, nonwhite criminals. Yet the responses of O'Reilly and Limbaugh, representative of other conservative talk show hosts, portrayed illegal immigrants not as a threat to national security but rather as a threat to civil society and American identity. The difference was important, as the type of threat suggests particular legislative options. Bush's proposals for additional security enforcement were not sufficient for O'Reilly, Limbaugh, and their political allies. Illegal immigrants already in the United States deserved to be punished because they had broken the laws and threatened American society.

Bush's immigration discourse and, more specifically, his May 2006 national address invited the public to reconsider its understanding of illegal—primarily Mexican—immigrants in the United States. The president's address prompted more public discourse, particularly among those groups that wanted to challenge his frameworks of immigration policy and the character of immigrants. These replies demonstrate that public responses are part of the way a president's speech invites continued public discussion and debate on a public policy issue. The effects of a president's discourse should include these responses, encompassing the circulation of a fuller discursive field.

Expanding Rhetoric's Effects

President Bush did not originate the discussion over immigration policy; his speech was shaped by contextual factors, as well. However, the president's speech articulated a particular viewpoint, changing the framework of congressional debate and bringing some groups on the left and the right to challenge his construction of the immigration problem. It would be easy to conclude that Bush's speech had little effect because Congress never enacted immigration reform, but this conclusion would overlook the substantial influence of his speech on public discourse. Moreover, analyzing the circulation of Bush's immigration reform rhetoric as effects highlights Zarefsky's comment that the redefinition of political reality may not always "work in the president's favor."[91] The speech on immigration did indeed alter the political imagination of both Congress and the public, though the effects were likely not what the Bush administration had aimed for. In looking at the responses to discourse—creating a larger discursive field for analysis—rhetorical critics might be able to better answer questions of how particular moments in presidential public address are integrated into broader patterns of public discourse.

The examples in this essay detail the reactions of only a few of the groups that responded to Bush's speech. There are many more responses that might be analyzed; clearly the difficult process of gathering the myriad responses to a presidential speech and to a public policy initiative is a limitation of this case study. A fuller investigation of presidential rhetoric's effects might include other media outlets, blogs and other new media, so-called vernacular discourses at protest rallies and public meetings, and so on. This is not easy work for rhetorical critics; it involves not only gathering a text and its initial responses but also collecting and analyzing responses from many textual sources. In any public policy issue, the loudest and more aggressive groups tend to come to the forefront. With newer technologies and social media available and accessible to researchers, the possibilities for finding more voices—more responses—increase. Yet at some point the critic still must apply an interpretative lens, considering the most relevant, influential, critical, or interesting voices for the particular case study of rhetoric's effects.

For scholars of presidential rhetoric, a crucial component of examining rhetoric's effects should be the full field of discourse, considering circulation in addition to production. In the case of presidential discourse, a single speech may still have great potential to create effects across public discourse. A presidential address on a major policy agenda item commands the attention of the nation's legislators and political leaders, the news media, and the public. Yet presidential rhetoric is not only that of the speech moment; instead, it is interwoven and complex, with multiple agents responding to the discourse, often simultaneously in different—or even virtual—settings. By studying both the president's rhetoric and the rhetoric of response, we can come to a better understanding of how presidential rhetoric is circulated in and through discursive fields of public debate on policy. Even in the limited discursive field detailed in this essay, the examination of rhetoric's invitation and responses can facilitate a fuller understanding of rhetoric's effects.

Notes

1. "Bush Calls for Changes on Illegal Workers," CNN.com, January 8, 2004, http://www.cnn.com/2004/ALLPOLITICS/01/07/bush.immigration/ (accessed July 1, 2010).

2. Library of Congress, "Bill Summary and Status, H.R. 4437 Border Protection, Antiterrorism, and Illegal Immigration Control Act of 2005," http://thomas.loc.gov/cgi-bin/bdquery/z?d109:h.r.04437 (accessed January 1, 2013); Library of Congress, "Bill Summary and Status, S. 2612 The Comprehensive Immigration Reform Act of 2006," http://thomas.loc.gov/cgi-bin/bdquery/z?d109:SN02611 (accessed January 1, 2013).

3. Robert Pearl and Carl Hulse, "Immigration Bill Fails to Survive Senate Vote," *New York Times*, June 28, 2007, http://www.nytimes.com/2007/06/28/washington/28cnd-immig.html?_r=1 (accessed July 1, 2010). In the Senate, supporters of the bill failed to pass a cloture motion, which would have ended debate and "move[d] toward final passage. Supporters fell 14 votes short of the 60 needed to close debate."

4. Pearl and Hulse, "Immigration Bill Fails to Survive Senate Vote."

5. "The Speech Bush Didn't Give" [editorial], *Chicago Tribune,* June 29, 2007. ProQuest Historical Newspapers, http://search.progquest.com/docview/462114009 (accessed July 1, 2010).

6. Peter Baker, "Bush May Be Out of Chances for a Lasting Domestic Victory," *Washington Post,* June 29, 2007. Newsbank, http://www.Newsbank.com/ (accessed July 1, 2010).

7. Peter Baker, "Bush May Be Out of Chances for a Lasting Domestic Victory," *Washington Post,* June 29, 2007. Newsbank, http://www.Newsbank.com/ (accessed July 1, 2010).

8. Jill Zuckman, "Immigration Issue Becomes Politics' Newest Third Rail ," *Chicago Tribune* [Chicago Edition], June 30, 2007. ProQuest Historical Newspapers, http://search.proguest.com/docview/459243905 (accessed September 5, 2010).

9. Jonathan Weisman, "Immigration Bill Dies in Senate—Bipartisan Compromise Fails to Satisfy the Right or the Left," *Washington Post,* June 29, 2007. Newsbank, http://www.Newsbank.com/ (accessed July 1, 2010).

10. "Bill's Defeat Points to Bush's Dwindling Clout" [editorial], *Miami Herald,* June 29, 2007. Newsbank, http://www.Newsbank.com/ (accessed July 1, 2010).

11. "The Grand Failure," *Los Angeles Times* [Home Edition], June 29, 2007. http://articles.latimes.com/2007/jun/29/opinion/ed-immigration (accessed February 9, 2014).

12. Susan Milligan, "Immigration Bill Dies in Senate," *Boston Globe,* June 29, 2007. Newsbank, http://www.Newsbank.com/ (accessed July 1, 2010).

13. Jeffrey K. Tulis, *The Rhetorical Presidency* (Princeton: Princeton University Press, 1987), 11.

14. David Zarefsky, "Presidential Rhetoric and the Power of Definition," *Presidential Studies Quarterly* 34 (2004): 607, 610.

15. Zarefsky, "Presidential Rhetoric and the Power of Definition," 608.

16. Zarefsky, "Presidential Rhetoric and the Power of Definition," 613.

17. Zarefsky, "Presidential Rhetoric and the Power of Definition," 609.

18. The study of social movements has been a crucial part of rhetorical studies since the early 1960s. An excellent anthology of critical articles is Charles E. Morris III and Stephen H. Brown, eds., *Readings on the Rhetoric of Social Protest* (State College, Pa.: Strata, 2001, 2006, 2013).

19. See Robert Asen and Daniel C. Brower, *Counterpublics and the State* (Albany: State University of New York Press, 2001); Robert Asen, *Invoking the Invisible Hand: Social Security and the Privatization Debates* (Lansing: Michigan State University Press, 2009); and Michael W. Shelton, *Talk of Power, Power of Talk: The 1994 Health Care Reform Debate and Beyond* (Westport, Conn.: Praeger, 2000).

20. Kirt H. Wilson, "Interpreting the Discursive Field of the Montgomery Bus Boycott: Martin Luther King Jr.'s Holt Street Address," *Rhetoric and Public Affairs* 8 (2005): 306.

21. Nathan Stormer, "Articulation: A Working Paper on Rhetoric and *Taxis*," *Quarterly Journal of Speech* 90 (2004): 275.

22. Jenny Edbauer, "Unframing Models of Public Distribution: From Rhetorical Situation to Rhetorical Ecologies," *Rhetoric Society Quarterly* 35 (2005): 19.

23. Mary E. Stuckey, "On Rhetorical Circulation," *Rhetoric and Public Affairs* 15 (2012): 609–612; Megan Foley, "Sound Bites: Rethinking the Circulation of Speech from Fragment to Fetish," *Rhetoric and Public Affairs* 15 (2012): 613–622; Stephen Heidt, "The President as Pastiche: Atomization, Circulation, and Rhetorical Instability," *Rhetoric and Public Affairs* 15 (2012): 623–633; Jason Edward Black, "Native Authenticity, Rhetorical Circulation, and Neocolonial Decay: The Case of Chief Seattle's Controversial Speech," *Rhetoric and Public Affairs* 15 (2012): 635–645; Darrel Allen Wanzer, "Delinking Rhetoric, or Revisiting McGee's Fragmentation Thesis through Decoloniality," *Rhetoric and Public Affairs* 15 (2012): 647–657; Brandon Inabinet, "Democratic

Circulation: Jacksonian Lithographs in U.S. Public Discourse," *Rhetoric and Public Affairs* 15 (2012): 659–666; Melody Lehn, "Jackie Joins Twitter: The Recirculation of 'Campaign Wife,'" *Rhetoric and Public Affairs* 15 (2012): 667–674; Nathan S. Atkinson, "Celluloid Circulation: The Dual Temporality of Nonfiction Film and Its Publics," *Rhetoric and Public Affairs* 15 (2012): 675–684; and Sean P. O'Rourke, "Circulation and Noncirculation of Photographic Texts in the Civil Rights Movement: A Case Study of the Rhetoric of Control," *Rhetoric and Public Affairs* 15 (2012): 685–694.

24. Stuckey, "On Rhetorical Circulation," 609.

25. Roderick P. Hart, "Thinking Harder about Presidential Discourse," in *The Prospects of Presidential Rhetoric,* ed. James Arnt Aune and Martin J. Medhurst (College Station: Texas A&M University Press, 2008), 244.

26. Heidt, "The Presidency as Pastiche: Atomization, Circulation, and Rhetorical Instability," 624.

27. Heidt, "The Presidency as Pastiche: Atomization, Circulation, and Rhetorical Instability," 629.

28. Artistide R. Zolberg, *A Nation by Design: Immigration Policy in the Fashioning of America* (New York: Russell Sage Foundation, 2006), 1–2.

29. See Vanessa Beasley, *You, the People: American National Identity in Presidential Rhetoric* (College Station: Texas A&M University Press), 2004; Anne Demo, "Sovereignty Discourse and Contemporary Immigration Politics," *Quarterly Journal of Speech* 91 (2005): 291–311; Lisa A. Flores, "Constructing Rhetorical Borders: Peons, Illegal Aliens, and Competing Narratives of Immigration," *Critical Studies in Media Communication* 20 (2003): 362–387; and Kent A. Ono and John M. Sloop, *Shifting Borders: Rhetoric, Immigration, and California's Proposition 187, Mapping Racisms* (Philadelphia: Temple University Press, 2002).

30. Ono and Sloop, *Shifting Borders,* 30–31.

31. Flores, "Constructing Rhetorical Borders," 363.

32. Demo, "Sovereignty Discourse and Contemporary Immigration Politics," 302, 306.

33. J. David Cisneros, "Contaminated Communities: The Metaphor of 'Immigrant as Pollutant' in Media Representations of Immigration," *Rhetoric and Public Affairs* 11 (2008): 578, 580.

34. Michael Novak, "President of All the People," in *Who Belongs in America? Presidents, Rhetoric, and Immigration,* ed. Vanessa B. Beasley (College Station: Texas A&M University Press, 2006), 22.

35. See Vanessa Beasley, "Immigration and Presidential Rhetoric of Shared Beliefs," in *You, the People: American National Identity in Presidential Rhetoric,* (College Station: Texas A&M University Press, 2004), 68–92; Robert H. Ferrell, "Immigration and the Red Scare," in *Who Belongs in America? Presidents, Rhetoric, and Immigration,* ed. Vanessa B. Beasley (College Station: Texas A&M University Press, 2006), 134–148; and Mary Anne Trasciatti, "Hooking the Hyphen: Woodrow Wilson's War Rhetoric and the Italian American Community," in *Who Belongs in America? Presidents, Rhetoric, and Immigration,* ed. Vanessa B. Beasley (College Station: Texas A&M University Press, 2006), 107–133.

36. Zarefsky, "Presidential Rhetoric and the Power of Definition," 611.

37. George W. Bush, "Remarks on Signing the Department of Homeland Security Appropriations Act, 2006," October 18, 2005, in *Weekly Compilation of Presidential Documents* 41 (no. 42): 1554–1558.

38. Bush, "Remarks on Signing the Department of Homeland Security Appropriations Act, 2006," 1555.

39. Bush, "Remarks on Signing the Department of Homeland Security Appropriations Act, 2006," 1556.

40. While the immigration debate certainly incorporated concerns over the northern border and port security, the majority of the debate centered around Mexican immigrants and the U.S. border with Mexico.

41. Richard W. Stevenson, "Bush, Touring the Border, Puts Emphasis on Enforcement," *New York Times*, November 30, 2005. LexisNexis Academic, http://www.lexisnexis.com (accessed August 21, 2011).

42. "Borderline Reform," *Boston Globe*, November 30, 2005, http://www.boston.com/news/globe/editorial_opinion/editorials/articles/2005/11/30/borderline_reform/ (accessed August 21, 2011).

43. R. Emmett Tyrrell Jr., "Our Immigration Imbroglio," *American Spectator*, December 1, 2005. LexisNexis Academic, http://www.lexisnexis.com (accessed October 25, 2006).

44. Office of the White House Press Secretary, "Fact Sheet: Securing America through Immigration Reform," November 28, 2005, http://georgewbush-whitehouse.archives.gov/news/releases/2005/11/20051128–3.html (accessed August 21, 2011).

45. Office of the White House Press Secretary, "Fact Sheet: Securing America through Immigration Reform."

46. Michael A. Fletcher, "President Hints at Bipartisan Shift," *Houston Chronicle*, December 20, 2006. LexisNexis Academic, http://www.lexisnexis.com (accessed August 21, 2011).

47. Rachel L. Swarns, "House Votes for 698 Miles of Fences on Mexico Border," *New York Times*, December 16, 2005. LexisNexis Academic, http://www.lexisnexis.com (accessed August 21, 2011).

48. Library of Congress, "Bill Summary and Status, H.R. 4437 Border Protection, Antiterrorism, and Illegal Immigration Control Act of 2005."

49. Jonathan Weisman, "House Votes to Toughen Laws on Immigration," *Washington Post*, December 17, 2005. LexisNexis Academic, http://www.lexisnexis.com (accessed August 21, 2011).

50. Judd Gregg, speaking on immigration reform, 109th Cong., 2nd sess., *Congressional Record* 152 (March 27, 2006): S2400.

51. Richard J. Durbin, speaking on immigration reform, 109th Cong., 2nd sess., *Congressional Record* 152 (March 27, 2006): S2403.

52. John McCain, speaking on immigration reform, S. 2454, 109th Cong., 2nd sess., *Congressional Record* 152 (March 30, 2006): S2560–S2561.

53. Library of Congress, "S.2454 Securing America's Borders Act, All Congressional Actions," http://thomas.loc.gov/cgi-bin/bdquery/z?d109:SN02454:@@@X (accessed January 15, 2013).

54. Jonathan Weisman and Jim VandeHei, "Immigration Debate Is Shaped by '08 Election," *Washington Post*, March 24, 2006. LexisNexis Academic, http://www.lexisnexis.com (accessed August 21, 2011).

55. "Immigration 'Nirvana,' Lost," *Washington Post*, April 8, 2006, http://www.washingtonpost.com/wp-dyn/content/article/2006/04/07/AR2006040701713.html (accessed August 21, 2011). Specter was at this time a Republican, though he would change party affiliation in 2009.

56. Carl Hulse and Rachel L. Swarns, "Blame and Uncertainty as Immigration Deal Fails," *New York Times*, April 8, 2006. LexisNexis Academic, http://www.lexisnexis.com (accessed August 21, 2011). Lieberman was at this time a Democrat, though he became an independent in the 2006 fall election.

57. Gail Russell Chaddock, "A GOP Faceoff over Illegal Immigration," *Christian Science Monitor*, March 29, 2006, http://www.csmonitor.com/2006/0329/p01s04-uspo.html?s=hns (accessed August 21, 2011).

58. "It's the President's Turn" [editorial], *New York Times*, April 9, 2006, http://www.nytimes.com/2006/04/09/opinion/09sun1.html (accessed August 21, 2011).

59. George W. Bush, "Address to the Nation on Immigration Reform," May 15, 2006, in *The Public Papers of the Presidents of the United States: George W. Bush, 2001–2009,* vol. 5, book 1 (Washington, D.C.: Government Printing Office, 2007), 928.

60. Bush, "Address to the Nation on Immigration Reform," 928.

61. Tulis, *The Rhetorical Presidency,* 203.

62. Bush, "Address to the Nation on Immigration Reform," 928.

63. Bush, "Address to the Nation on Immigration Reform," 931.

64. Tulis, *The Rhetorical Presidency,* 179.

65. Office of the White House Press Secretary, "Fact Sheet: Comprehensive Immigration Reform," May 15, 2006, http://georgewbush-whitehouse.archives.gov/news/releases/2006/05/20060515–10.html (accessed August 21, 2011).

66. Bush, "Address to the Nation on Immigration Reform," 928.

67. Bush, "Address to the Nation on Immigration Reform," 929.

68. Bush, "Address to the Nation on Immigration Reform," 929.

69. Bush, "Address to the Nation on Immigration Reform," 929.

70. *The 9/11 Commission Report* (New York: Norton, 2004), 215–231. While the details themselves are subject to interpretation and questioning, the 9/11 Commission concluded that the majority of the hijackers on September 11 not only obtained valid U.S. visas and were in the country legally but also had occasional interactions with law enforcement, used their true names, and were well documented.

71. Bush, "Address to the Nation on Immigration Reform," 930.

72. Bush, "Address to the Nation on Immigration Reform," 930.

73. Bush, "Address to the Nation on Immigration Reform," 931.

74. Bush, "Address to the Nation on Immigration Reform," 932.

75. Johnny Isakson, speaking on Comprehensive Immigration Reform Act of 2006, S. 2611, 109th Cong., 2nd sess., *Congressional Record* 152 (May 16, 2006): S4576.

76. Dave Montgomery, "Senate Strongly Supports Bush's Immigration Goals," *Philadelphia Inquirer,* May 17, 2006. Lexis-Nexis Academy, www.lexisnexis.com (accessed January 30, 2013).

77. Ken Salazar, speaking on Comprehensive Immigration Reform Act of 2006, S. 2611, 109th Cong., 2nd sess., *Congressional Record* 152, issue 60 (May 16, 2006): S4577.

78. Edward Kennedy, speaking on Comprehensive Immigration Reform Act of 2006, S. 2611, 109th Cong., 2nd sess., *Congressional Record* 152 (May 16, 2006): S4578.

79. Jim Rutenberg, "President to Push for Line-Item Veto Power," *New York Times,* June 28, 2006, http://www.nytimes.com/2006/06/28/washington/28bush.html (accessed August 21, 2011).

80. Fred Barnes, "Things Fall Apart," *Weekly Standard,* July 9, 2007. ProQuest Historical Newspapers, http://search.proguest.com/docview/232997808 (accessed July 10, 2010); "Nowhere to Hide: Illegal Immigration," *Economist,* July 9, 2007. ProQuest Historical Newspapers, http://search.proquest.com/docview/223997538 (accessed July 10, 2010).

81. Kaitlynn Reilly, "Death of a Bill," Catholic News Service, July 2, 2007, http://www.catholic.org/national/national_story.php?id=24577 (accessed September 7, 2010).

82. Episcopal Church, "Acts of Convention, Resolution 2006-A017," http://www.episcopalarchives.org/cgi-bin/acts/acts_resolution-complete.pl?resolution=2006-A017 (accessed August 31, 2010).

83. Jeremy Burton, "Dubya's Dubious Message," jspot, May 16, 2006, http://www.jspot.org/diary/210 (accessed August 31, 2010).

84. Andrew Sullivan, "Bush's Speech," *Daily Dish,* May 15, 2006, http://andrewsullivan.theatlantic.com/the_daily_dish/2006/05/bushs_speech.html (accessed August 31, 2010).

85. Benita Heiskanen, "A Day without Immigrants," *European Journal of American Studies,* Special Issue 2009 (December 1), http://ejas.revues.org/7717 (accessed July 10, 2010).

86. "Rethinking the Revolving Door for Immigration," http://www.brookings.edu/opinions/2007/0423immigration_ruiz.aspx (accessed July 10, 2010).

87. In these blogs, illegal immigration protests were connected to Marxist ideology. See "Activists Plan Immigrant Rights Campaign," cross-posted at Morning Coffee, http://morningcoffee.wordpress.com/2006/06/26/activists-plan-immigrant-rights-campaign/ (accessed July 10, 2010) and The Coalition Against Illegal Immigration, http://uncooperativeblogger.wordpress.com/2006/06/26/activists-plan-immigrant-rights-campaign/ (accessed July 10, 2010). See also "Who's Behind the Immigration Rallies, *FrontPage Magazine,* http://archive.frontpagemag.com/readArticle.aspx? ARTID=5022 (accessed July 10, 2010).

88. "The Great American Betrayal," posted on the website of the Coalition against Illegal Immigration, June 23, 2006, http://uncooperativeblogger.wordpress.com (accessed July 10, 2010).

89. Bill O'Reilly, "Talking Points Memo," transcript, May 17, 2006, http://www.foxnews.com/on-air/oreilly/2006/05/17/opposing-bush-border (accessed January 31, 2013). *The O'Reilly Factor* is an evening news and talk show hosted by Bill O'Reilly that is aired on FoxNews.

90. Rush Limbaugh, "Senate 'Compromise' Bill Must Change," transcript, May 16, 2006, http://www.rushlimbaugh.com/daily/2006/05/16/senate_compromise_bill_must_change_or_this_country_will_change_forever2 (accessed January 31, 2013).

91. Zarefsky, "Presidential Rhetoric and the Power of Definition," 613.

Giving "Timeless Effect to the Farewell Address"

Repetition and Reflection in the United States Senate

ADAM J. GAFFEY

"Read in accordance with resolution of the Senate by [signed] J. B. Foraker, Feb.22nd 1900."

First entry in the Senate's book of signatures on Washington's Farewell Address

The third week in February brings formal observance of George Washington's birthday in the United States Senate.[1] The ceremony, which has endured for more than a century, marks the first president's birthday with an institutional gift of declamation. As public memorializing goes, however, the display appears to be all for naught: a lone speaker recites the 1796 Farewell Address to a nearly vacant Senate chamber while printed copies of the text sit atop unattended desks.[2] Clocked at nearly one hour, the ritual is challenging for even the most accomplished speakers.[3] Senators begin smoothly—even confidently—but eventually succumb to the paragraph-long sentences that constitute the text's typographic style.[4] As the speaker rounds his or her way past Washington's praise of union, warning against parties, and advice on the national tenets of public virtue, the task is finally completed, and relief comes in the form of a well-deserved quaff of water. The text has been recited, and the ritual is complete—or so it seems. In the Senate cloakroom, outside the view of C-SPAN cameras, a second dimension of remembrance begins. Engaging a new text, the senator scrawls his or her name and personal response to the Farewell Address in a leather-bound notebook, adding a new page to an ongoing chronicle of prior speakers dating back to 1900. Alone again, our senator has concluded commemoration of George Washington's birthday in the deliberative body of the U.S. Congress. Both the Farewell Address and the chronicle of responses are retired until the cycle recommences the following year.

Unorthodox in form and neglected in historical observation,[5] the Senate's commemorative ritual nevertheless speaks to a distinctive question of effect. Indeed, next to the sparse display of reciting the words of Washington's well-known political adieu, the commemorative energy that constitutes the ritual's contemporary form is in the written reflection: a written text is orated; the act of speaking begets writing. While senators might occupy the discursive space of the Farewell Address through an open recital, it is in the expansive pages of the journal that we discover the meaning of the text as the practitioners of the ritual imagine it.

The Farewell Address notebook is an austere text, comprising blank pages with no formal instruction for use. Throughout the early decades of the twentieth century the text was a mere log noting who read the Farewell Address and when. The reading of the Farewell, at the time, spoke for itself. Since the late 1940s, however, the Senate has utilized the journal to revive the relevancy of its own institutional identity against the memory of Washington's iconic text. The ritual, in short, has become an opportunity to read and write effect into the text and to record a relational dialogue between the Senate and the memory of Washington.

The contents of this institutional palimpsest offer insight to the distinctive question of effect, namely that rhetorical effect can derive from what the editors of this volume call "agency residing in the audience" and the audience's continuation of a text's legacy.[6] Rather than scrutinize exact consequences achieved by the Farewell Address in later arguments (searching for evidence that the Farewell Address influenced senators' appeals, or effect as a noun), the Senate's ritual of recital and reflection invites analysis on the constructive interactions between reader and text (effect as a verb, or something done to a text via appropriation and interpretation).[7] Herbert Wichelns's well-known concern with "effect" over "permanence" or "beauty" relative to "speech as communication to a specific audience" has been a touchstone for gauging the impact of discourse.[8] However, this study seeks to expand an alternate premise offered by James Jasinski that "a one-dimensional view of rhetorical effect" is unlikely to remain predominant or useful to rhetorical studies.[9]

The Senate's example affirms the importance of studying extensional rhetoric and also expands our sense of how effect is utilized. As my analysis of the Senate's journal demonstrates, senators have increasingly turned attention away from potential conflicts with the Farewell Address and have opted instead to reaffirm the attachment to the text, even to the point of making the act of reading itself a statement both affirming Washington's memory in the Senate and celebrating the institutional and personal values of the reader. To interpret the effect inherent in the Farewell Address, in other words, is to also understand the institutional philosophy of the contemporary Senate emerging over time. Rhetorical effect is detectable by how responding rhetors utilize ideas of an author, as well as the degree to which they feel constrained to abide by the message despite their obvious aversion to faithfully maintaining its principles. In a related sense, the long-term potency of rhetorical effect, this study suggests, is equally attributable to a communal attachment to the memory of the author and to the text itself.

The remainder of this piece proceeds as follows. First, I present a general overview of Washington's Farewell Address and the emergence of the institutional ritual in the Senate. Next, I clarify the presumptions and premises of extensional constitutive rhetoric and clarify how the Senate's palimpsest of signatures fits into the act of expanding the meaning of Washington's text, followed by an analysis of the document itself. Finally, I consider the relevance of this case study against conceptions of effect and the relationship between institutional philosophies and the actualizing of a text.

Deliberative Epideictic: The Senate's Farewell

Congress, as can be seen in this remark, was meant to argue: "Read pursuant to the standing order of the Senate at the request of Vice President Curtis—February 22, 1933—[signed] Otis F. Glenn, Illinois." The bulk of the U.S. Senate's prescribed institutional protocol is to advise and consent on issues pertaining to public law and government appointments. In crucial cases, the upper house assumes a forensic position by ruling on articles of impeachment against the president. Designed to deliberate or determine past fact, the U.S. Senate is an unexpected environment for an epideictic encounter. Though senators participate in "end of session valedictories and eulogies," the annual tribute to George Washington remains the institution's "oldest non-legislative ritual" and a rare time of reflection and reaffirmation of collective values.[10] Epideictic rhetoric presents a way to establish a common sense of the present and to frame an occasion by wrapping "its participants in reminders of excellence and therefore to rescue it in memory."[11] Though rare, the "full potential of epideictic," Celeste Condit claims, arises from the presence of the following: speeches that explain understandings, "allow the sharing of community," and display "eloquence for the judgment of the community."[12]

Tensions between praise of the past and the presence of a community have defined the Senate's tradition of repeating the Farewell Address since the beginning. Like most occasions of remembrance, the annual reading of the text arose from neither institutional obligation nor Constitutional provision. In 1888, George Frisbie Hoar (R-MA) introduced the original resolution affirming the Farewell Address in the Senate with little debate or contest. Hoar would eventually propose a permanent resolution on reading the Farewell Address, which passed in 1901. The Senate's order, as it remains today, prescribes the following: "*Resolved,* That unless otherwise directed, on the 22nd day of February in each year, or if that shalt be on Sunday, then on the day immediately after the reading of the Journal, Washington's Farewell Address shall be read to the Senate by a Senator to be designated for the purpose by the presiding officer; and that thereafter the Senate will proceed with its ordinary business."[13] Hoar's 1901 resolution ensured that the Farewell Address would take oral form in the Senate in near perpetuity. What could not be determined, however, was the diminished interest and participation of the Senate as years progressed.[14]

What the Senate collectively lacked in communal commitment to witnessing the Farewell Address in performance, it made up for in the expressive energies recorded in written remembrances of individual participants. The motive for maintaining the notebook is unclear. Its centrality to the contemporary ritual of repetition is undeniable. The leather-bound text, embossed with the title "Washington's Farewell Address, Senate Official Copy," functions as a text in perpetual progress, always incomplete and awaiting a new page to collect the thoughts and insights of readers. Regardless of its origin or purpose, the significance of the text is undeniable to the evolution of the institutional ritual. Beginning in 1900, early entries reflect an objective, factual, and rudimentary acknowledgment of the Senate custom and the date of the recitation. Signatures of this sort are stacked upon one another, sometimes up to four on a single page. Beginning in the late 1940s and ever since, senators have taken to offering thoughtful, trite, and sometimes controversial observations about Washington, the relevance of the Farewell Address, and the appropriateness of recent political happenings in the text, often taking up a single page or more.

Did waning attendance to the Senate ritual trigger a greater use of the notebook as a repository of public remembrance? The historical record cannot sustain such a causal claim. What is clear, however, is that the notebook was a constant fixture in the ceremony and was also available to senators throughout major controversies of the early twentieth century that, one might expect, invited some perspective on resonant themes central to Washington's Farewell Address, such as the League of Nations debate, the Great Depression and New Deal legislation, or the lead-up to World War II. Did the Farewell Address fail to resonate in these public debates? We could not suspend such disbelief.[15] By simple observation, these historical eras are unaccounted for in any detail within the Senate's chronicle of participants. The more convincing explanation is that the notebook is a medium that became functionally important in commemorating Washington at a certain point in the Senate's institutional culture. This increased emphasis on private remembrance, I suggest, represents a material form of rhetorical effect: documented evidence of speakers' appropriation of the text.

The constructive effect of language as appropriation has been well established in rhetorical studies.[16] As James Jasinski has noted, the extensional constitutive capacity of language is apparent by reorienting the traditional roles assigned to speaker and audience. Audiences don't passively read a text but instead "actualize the constitutive potential of the text, thereby generating extensional force, without necessarily sharing in the intentions of the author or speaker."[17] If the Senate's effort to scrawl out interpretations of the Farewell Address counts as an extensional molding of the text in memory, then Washington's text was itself a lasting constitution of public virtue for citizenship for the young United States. Insomuch as citizens of the colonies saw their revolutionary struggle as an effort to break free from "the worse than Egyptian bondage of Great Britain," Washington was appropriately eulogized and admired as the "Moses of America."[18] The end of his two terms in the new country's presidency marked the end also of a new era of American time:

The letter declaring the voluntary conclusion of his public life would explain how "The PEOPLE of the United States" would carry on.

Following Washington's death, in 1799, the Farewell Address took on an important function in a country now deprived of guidance from its original leader. What remained through newspaper and print was a political testament for the future: "advice, which if scrupulously observed, might, under the smiles of Providence, ensure numerous blessings to this happy country for future ages."[19] Though Washington's address was clearly intended as an eloquent defense of Federalist policy,[20] its impact as a touchstone of American civic virtue is undeniable. Stephen Lucas and Susan Zaeske note that Washington's parting message ranks with the Declaration of Independence and the Gettysburg Address as "the most honored of American political discourses."[21] Garry Wills minces no words in his assessment: the text is Washington's "masterpiece."[22] As Matthew Spalding and many other students of the Farewell Address note, the text emphasizes "union at home and independence abroad," though each goal spoke to the larger message of the testament: "the development of what Washington called a national character."[23] Michael J. Hostetler defines the enduring quality of the Farewell through its timeless task: "Over two hundred years after its publication, it still calls Americans to the unfinished process of national character building."[24]

The gravity of the text is not lost on the Senate's readers. Multiple participants have attested to the spiritual euphoria of the reading experience. Senator John Rockefeller (D-WV) wrote in 1986 that "one is carried back in spirit to the first years of this great nation," further observing, "One feels, in reading his words aloud, the urgency of love and concern he felt for the fragile young nation." Senator Ralph Flanders (R-VT) went even further when he wrote, in 1951, "A careful reading discovers its wisdom as no recital of words taken out of context can do." Indeed, as Hubert Humphrey (D-MN) noted in 1956, the text is not only "immortal and enduring" but also accessible in performance. "Indeed, for a few moments, half way through the address, it was as if 'these councils of an old and affectionate friend' had come alive!" Bill Frist (R-TN) wrote in 1997.

Within this new euphoric dialogue with Washington, the journal reveals a keen insight into the institutional culture of the U.S. Senate: as political time and culture have moved further from Washington's council, the institutional response has been to increasingly forge association with the Farewell Address and Washington, even to the point of memorializing the personal fulfillment of reading the text when institutional practice have failed to match. The Senate's effect on the text, insofar as its commemorative ritual is concerned, has been to fortify institutional identity in reading the Farewell Address anew.

> February 24th, 1993. To read the words of our nation's first president on the floor of the U.S. Senate is a distinct honor. The fact that his words were written as a guiding light for the future of this nation makes the actual moment of the

delivery of the speech timeless. Thank goodness this has become a tradition because as citizens we must never lose our exposure and connection to the principles of wisdom of our founding fathers. The fact that Madison, Hamilton, and Jay all contributed to this speech reflects the sentiment of this group of dedicated patriots. God bless America! (signed) Dirk Kempthorne, USS Idaho.

Change from Washington: Relevance of the Farewell

Following the 1949 reading by Margaret Chase Smith several senators throughout the 1950s, 1960s, and 1970s represented a world of contrast to the themes of the Farewell Address and considered the text a corrective measure of political guidance. Exceptions exist, to be sure. Frank Moss (D-UT), for instance, wrote in 1960 how Washington's words "retain their vigor," elaborating that the "course he charted has served us well and we are today the great united and powerful nation of which he spoke." James Pearson (R-KS) offered a bland assessment of the address in 1965, noting a "hope that the words of Washington—heard again in the Senate of the United States," will serve the "purpose" of understanding the past to plan for the future.

The predominant theme of remembrance in the mid-twentieth century, however, was one of openly questioning the relevance of what the Farewell Address means in the context of the actions of the Senate. Though some found it fitting to read the Farewell Address not only on Washington's birthday but, more specifically, "in the Senate," as Prescott Bush (R-CT) wrote in 1955, others offered more pointed contrasts between the principles perceived in the text and the reality of the present. Reading the Farewell affirmed Senator Barry Goldwater's (R-AZ) belief in 1957 that the "troubles of mind and conscience" in the United States could be alleviated with "documents left to us" by the founding generation, foremost among them Washington's text. Frank Church (D-IN) defined the Farewell Address in 1958 as a set of "admonitions" that remain "ageless" and that the people must measure "against the living facts of our own times." For Gordon Allott (R-CO), Washington's Farewell Address offered sage advice for a moment "when the mind of the people seems confused and even frustrated" in the present. "His advice with respect to the dominance of Party over Union was never more appreciable than today," Allott continued in 1959. In more pointed contrast, Winston Prouty (R-VT), writing in 1963, perhaps responding to the Cuban Missile Crisis six months prior, contrasted the existing political context with the belief that, if Washington were alive, he would, among other things, "[r]ecognize that the luxury of isolation is no longer possible but that in formulating our relations with other nations the question must be asked: is this in the best interest of the United States of America?" Even when Washington's principles were revised to support a new ideology, his words clashed with modern occurrences.

Political unity also becomes a key concern for senators writing soon after the mid-twentieth-century turn toward elaborated interpretation of the text. Senator Lee Metcalf (D-MT), writing in 1966, dismissed the idea that the text embodies a vision "against foreign entanglements" and instead read the central theme as "national unity," an especially important observation in an age of "strife over civil rights": "This wise advice," he continued, alluding to political unity, "is to be heeded." The relationship between religion and government was also a key concern in some of the early decades of the Senate's elaborated form of commemoration through writing: "[W]hen Washington talks about religion," Senator S. I. Hayakawa (R-CA) penned in 1977, "it seems to me he was better able than any political leader living today to appeal to common understandings, common assumptions about morality and duty such as existed in his time but exist precariously, if at all, today." Last, the morality of political actors is read from the address, especially in moments when political virtue is in question. In the fallout of the Iran-Contra investigation in 1987, newly elected senator John McCain (R-AZ) noted the contrast between Washington's advice and the happenings in the present, defining the Farewell Address in a prescriptive light: "closer adherence to his words is the surest path to a restored institution of the presidency and a renewal of faith of the American people in their system of government."[25] What has been lost—or separated from the purity of the text—may be reunited with reverence to Washington's model.

These examples illustrate the common theme throughout the initial decades of reading and writing Washington through commemoration that find the relevancy of the Farewell in drawing a contrast between it and the needs of the present. Speakers, in short, readily acknowledged a separation between the hopes of the text and the events of political life. In contradiction to this theme popular in the mid-twentieth century, contemporary practice finds a repetitive turn to confirm the actions of the present as in conjunction with the ideals of Washington and, indeed, the founding generation.

Continuity with Washington: Relevance of the Farewell

Contrary to the reflection in the previous section that Washington might question the actions of the present, recent decades of reading the Farewell Address in the Senate reflect a strong trend toward affirming either the importance of the present as a continuation of the past or the problems faced in the present as having strong relevance to the ideals of Washington. Indeed, an oft-repeated sentiment found throughout the Farewell Address notebook is summarized in Walter Huddleston's (D-KY) 1978 claim that "the wisdom" of the text "is just as certain today as when originally delivered." Craig Thomas's (R-WY) 1995 recital, fast on the heels of the Republican Party's successful midterm elections in 1994, found in Washington's words approval for the new majority: "In a time when the American people have sent us to this place with a mandate for a smaller government more responsible to the need of its citizens—we are in this speech reminded of ideals and principles that lead us down the path of democracy." Thomas, who somehow managed to commemorate a text centrally concerned with avoiding political disunion and party loyalty, nonetheless saw the new Republican majority as vindication of Washington's ideals. Such willful misunderstanding signaled a new phase of the text's effects wherein political occurrences in the present are read anew through the Farewell Address, given a new legitimacy, and tied to the original formation of government.

Etching continuity with Washington is especially difficult in times of political controversy, yet senators have shown a keen adeptness in finding enduring relevancy in uncertain moments. In the early fallout of Watergate in 1973 as well as the aftermath of the Clinton impeachment trial of 1999, Senators Charles Mathias (R-MD) and George Voinovich (R-OH) cited Washington's ideals of law and order in making the present matter to the past. Though Mathias's assessment of the Farewell Address was "clearly dated," his recitation of the address prompted the thought that the American ideal that "government of law" and "accepted rules" still matters, observations no doubt influenced by President Richard Nixon's recent resignation. Judgment of a president, though difficult, is affirmed through a reading of the Farewell. Similarly, Voinovich rationalized the recent impeachment trial of President Clinton by noting that Washington's emphasis on oaths of office remained relevant in 1999: "The oaths of judicial system he [Washington] refers to were the basis of the recent United States Senate Trial on the Articles of Impeachment against President Clinton." Support for Clinton's trial by the Senate may seem to be a stretch for readers of the 1796 text but not the only theme affirmed in contemporary practice. "I suspect [Washington] would be shocked at the role that the United States plays today in maintaining world peace—that the nation he helped found is the most powerful in the world," Voinovich added. Political spectacle and vitriol forgotten, Washington's vision is still embodied in the trials of a president, albeit through a new focus on *which* ideals remain central to the reading.

Recent readings of the address have also shown a consistent turn toward acknowledging the relevance of Washington without indulging specific elements of the text of Washington's ideals. Writing in 1997, Bill Frist (R-TN) saw the importance of the Farewell Address in Washington's vision of "restraint, balance, justice, self-imposed term-limits," which he believed was relevant in the present day: "As I read aloud, the words, I was moved by the expressed spirit of liberty which has flourished over the past 200 years," Frist added. Following the events of September 11, 2001, Jon Corzine's (D-NJ) 2002 reading of the address culminated in the expressed belief that, "[l]ike Washington and his fellow citizens," Americans would have to work toward their freedom. The nation "must remember," Corzine wrote, interpreting the message in light of the recent tragedy, "that our freedom isn't free." "America is a great and free nation because of leaders like Washington and his words are still inspiring," Saxby Chambliss (R-GA) wrote one year later, alluding to nothing specific.[26] When events are elaborated upon, such as when Senator John Breaux (D-LA) wrote in 2004, the application to political issues and situations remains vague, often clouding the intended advice and warning of the Farewell Address to affirm the present: "I think Washington would be proud of America today as he was in 1796 A.D." Was Washington "proud" in 1796 or offering a prescriptive warning? As the Senate's record of readings indicates, the predominant view of the Farewell Address has been increasingly one of approval, regardless of how judiciously selective one must be to find in it confirmation of the contemporary political culture.

From artifact of admonition to an articulation of American pride, Washington's Farewell Address has been made especially malleable through over a century of recitation in the U.S. Senate. While themes of congruity and clash that define the temporal relationship between the political culture of the Senate and Washington's political testament are important, the final observation of this analysis is the most important to crafting a judgment on the Senate's ceremonial repetition of the text. In both recent decades and before, the theme of continuity with the Farewell Address has taken a new form of expression for reciters and writers: a focus on the personal.

The Farewell Address as Individual Experience

Washington's text has spurred reflections of both association and dissociation in decades of recitation. However, no theme resonates more strongly in recent reflections on the Farewell Address than the personal affirmation of the individual speaker. The personal focus of the reading has not always been a sense of selfish interest. "It was a great honor to have been asked to read these historic words," wrote Elbert Thomas (R-UT) in 1944. "I appreciate deeply the honor the Senate has thus done me." A similar tone of grateful thanks pervades entries written in the 1950s, though such content was later replaced with a more purposeful inward turn of written reflection. Frank Church (D-IN) noted that he would "cherish and remember this occasion" when he was given the "privilege to deliver Washington's historic address, in honor of his birthday, to the Senate of the United States."

For others, however, the honor was personal in a sense beyond one's association to the Senate. "Today has been a truly significant one for me!" wrote Jennings Randolph in 1962. Being "the second West Virginian" to have read the text was important for Randolph, whose entire entry is dedicated to the presence of his son and staff in the galleries as he read the text. Randolph's focus on state identity marks the start of a strange episode of ritual observance: Washington's text—affirming the bonds of national unity—is remembered through the lens of attachment to one's state identity.[27] Senators Bill Frist (R-TN, 1997), Saxby Chambliss (R-GA, 2003), Richard Burr (R-NC, 2005), Bob Corker, (R-TN, 2007), Mark Pryor (D-AR, 2008), Mike Johanns (R-NE, 2009), and Roland Burris (D-IL, 2010) each underscored the honor of speaking the address in the context of how many previous state representatives had preceded them. "I understand that I am the first senator from Arkansas to read this address as part of this Senate tradition," wrote Pryor (D-AR) in 2008, further noting, "That surprises me since there have been so many strong senators from my state over the years—Robinson, McClellan, Fulbright, Bumpers, Donald Pryor, and Lincoln—to name just a few. Knowing I am the first makes this honor all the more special to me."[28] "It has been 60 years since an Ohioan Robert Taft read Washington's Farewell Address," George Voinovich (R-OH) began his entry in 1999. "I am carrying on a Tennessee tradition," wrote Bob Corker (R-TN), making a rare allusion to an 1862 reading that predated Hoar's implementation of the ritual, penning, "It was Tennessee Senator Andrew Johnson who first introduced the petition in the Senate as a morale boosting gesture during the Civil War" and further listing home-state readers prior to 2007. From the brief remarks of thankfulness and reverence for procedure, these contemporary compliments to one's position relative to individual state histories add a new shape to the recollection process beyond an institutional or political community.

The individual, not the traditional reverence or the institution, occupies written reflections in more ways than one. Senators Carol Moseley-Braun (D-IL) and Daniel Akaka (D-HI), writing in 1994 and 1996, respectively, each paid tribute to their status as the first African American and the first "senator of Native Hawaiian and Chinese descent" to have read the address. This sentiment is echoed in similar expressions. "As the third Illinoisian to read Washington's Farewell Address before this chamber and [also] a great grandson of a slave, I am deeply honored to share this historic message with my colleagues," wrote Roland Burris (D-IL) in 2010, further noting the importance of the tradition as a way to "reflect upon the things that all Americans hold dear—liberty, equality, justice, and patriotism." Personal honor and reflection on one's role in the commemoration are expressed, finally, in Jake Garn's (R-UT) 1975 contribution to the journal, here quoted in full:

> I have been greatly honored to be asked to present to the Senate George Washington's Farewell Address. I am especially pleased due to the fact that I am a direct descendant of George Washington's youngest Brother[,] Charles Washington. My paternal grandmother[']s maiden name was Martha Virginia Washington and my great grandfather[']s, Charles Augustine Washington.
>
> He was a great, great, great, great grandson of George's youngest full brother. Because of the relationship to the Washington family it was a great thrill to present president Washington's Farewell Address.

Few entries achieve the level of base absurdity that defines Senator Garn's entry, though his exclusive focus on his role in the ceremony underscores a key interpretive application of the text: reading the Farewell Address has moved from a collective ritual of observance to a mode of personal reflection, self-discovery, and bland affirmation.

Were Garn's entry the exception and not the rule, one might find value in such individual ruminations. However, along with the turn toward the individual experience of reading has also emerged a parallel phenomenon of the ritual: the vague attribution of its "timeless" quality. In 1986, Senator Jay Rockefeller (D-WV) heard himself "giving truths as meaningful today as then." Senator John Warner's (R-VA) second recital, in 1989, revealed "principles" that are "as true today as then." Indeed, the extensional claim of the "timeless" quality of Washington's words directed the reflections of senators in 1990, 1991, 1993, 1996, 1997, and 1999. By 2004, Senator John Breaux (D-LA) thought "Washington would be proud of America today as he was in 1796 A.D.," mistaking, perhaps, the functional purpose of the Farewell as one of beaming approval rather than deliberate warning. "Washington would be astounded," Senator Mark Pryor (D-AK) reflected in 2006, by the way the United States was poised for "greatness in ways" the first president would find "hard to imagine." Even when a disjunction exists between past words and current deeds, the end result, contemporary senators find, is near blanket approval of contemporary actions. Earlier reflections found opportunity to both praise Washington and question the application of his principles. By contrast, more contemporary readers increasingly turn praise to the Senate—or themselves—and downplay the distance between past word and current deed.

The missed opportunity for reflexively interpreting Washington's Farewell Address is by far the most dominant theme emerging from the past two decades of this ritual in the Senate. Obvious misunderstandings and disjunctions between Washington's prescriptions and the Senate's behavior are no longer witnessed through a sense of continuity or halting difference but instead are glossed over with vague and often inward-looking praise of Washington the person, the Revolutionary age, or the broad-reaching principles of the founding generation. In this regard, the most astounding result of the Senate's effect on the Farewell Address is an elevation of the text to such regard that ideas both broad and precise are used to create an apparent relevance to whatever constitutes the institutional business, even if it means praising platitudes of political unity or finding a cut against the grain in managing public debt. One cannot imagine a time or circumstance in which senators reading this text would see the Farewell Address as irrelevant or, more important, see a disconnect between Washington's words and the current political culture. As the Farewell Address remains a "timeless" fixture in the Senate's discursive space, the extensional rhetorical energy attributed to the text reflects less certainty in following its tenets, not more—more concern with individual fulfillment and bland platitudes, not collective commitment to its political virtues. The price of lasting effect, it seems, resides in the diminished attention to abiding practice.

Since the introduction of the Senate notebook, in 1900, the functionality of writing in conjunction with the reading of Washington's Farewell Address has shifted from a matter of record to a matter of contrasting ideals, from a matter of complementary ideals to a matter of personal pride and state association with the political ritual. In the conclusion, I attempt to synthesize these observations and trends in the writing within the broader context of transcendental rhetoric and an institutional philosophy of discourse. Last, I speculate how proclaimed value and appreciation might provide greater opportunities for and limitations on understanding rhetorical effect.

Summary

"For all our citizens who are served by our Senate, I am incredibly honored to have been able to read George Washington's Farewell Address to the People of the United States. So much that President Washington said in his address is still relevant today. Our nation is incredibly fortunate to have had Washington's leadership in founding the country. I hope that all of us who serve in the Senate—especially myself—will work hard to do justice to his spirit. [signed] Sen. Jeanne Shaheen (NH), Feb. 27, 2012."[29] Methods to account for rhetorical effect are multitudinous. This study supports the contention that effect is something that happens to a text and that the extensional discourse engaging and reimagining the words of another remains the conventional evidence of such work. For communities that revere an iconic text and seek constitutive identity from it, the study of how they effect the work runs parallel to the emergence of a group's larger philosophy. In this case, the Senate's effect of the Farewell Address mirrors the larger institutional philosophy that is part of the institutional body.

The extensional constitutive rhetoric of the Senate's institutional palimpsest has shifted from themes of continuity and rupture with Washington's intentions to an inward focus on individual experience and on the broad applicability of Washington's counsel and the Senate's action. Perhaps the most abiding effect of the Farewell Address resides in its seemingly necessary place in the Senate's culture: senators feel the need to read their time and experience against or in conjunction with Washington's words. Yet, this habit—available to earlier readers throughout the first half of the twentieth century—has become a mainstay only in recent decades. For texts with particularly rich ideals, such as the design of the Farewell, revolving on an axis of the future of American citizenship, therein lies the opportunity to probe the relevant ideals of a time as read through similar practice and application. Such application, moreover, provides critics with a tangible form of assessing effect: Washington's Farewell Address has shifted attitudes in the sense that contemporary readers operate under a constraint (however fleeting) to abide by his counsel, even if only on a superficial level of patriotic generalizations.

According to the historian Richard Baker, the Senate is an institution in which "[c]hange comes slowly."[30] Indeed, given that the House of Representatives sustained a similar reading of the Farewell Address through the 1970s, when the practice was discontinued because "nobody showed up," the Senate maintains its unique role as the sole government institution purposefully and proudly embracing Washington's 1796 text.[31] A slowness to change, however, does not mean intransigence in the face of change. Through this essay I have suggested that the unique appropriation and form of Washington's Farewell Address through different textual forms gives us a glimpse into an institutional philosophy of rhetoric. The Senate's rhetorical use of the Farewell Address cannot help but change the existing form and shape of the document, emphasizing a private and increasingly personal attachment to the text. The Senate's notebook holds the *potential* to become what Ricoeur calls sites of appropriation from readers and thus constitutes an event through interpretation.[32]

The Farewell is read aloud to all but *understood* and *remembered* and *rationalized* to the present through internal reflection. Herein lies our glimpse of the institutional philosophy of discourse in the United States Senate and the eager task of applying an effect to this "timeless" discourse. Reading the 1796 text distances the interactive and interpretive process from a collective or public view in favor of private reflection, similar to the internal turn of rhetorical theory under George Campbell. According to Thomas Miller, this shift in rhetoric and moral philosophy moved "from the sociological to the psychological, and rhetoric became more concerned with the workings of the individual consciousness."[33] Such a turn in commemorative form, as is apparent from the historical and institutional transitions in remembering Washington's Farewell Address, coincides with several observers of the Senate who have noticed. For example, Ross Baker has noted that, on the basis of institutional size and protocol alone, the Senate remains distinctive from other government bodies (such as the House of Representatives) in that its procedures "magnify the role of the individual senator."[34] Wirls and Wirls, in kind, define the contemporary Senate culture as one that "encourage[s] the exploitation of individual and minority interests (quite unlike the House,)" leading to the "irony" of the Senate's dominant practice in view of its intended design: "the enshrined ability to use the institution for purely individual (as opposed to collective) purposes," leading to legislative gridlock and intransigence.[35] As future transitions in institutional identity emerge, the connection between Senate protocol and uses of discourse should be explored more fully and elaborated in more detail. Treatments of iconic texts—such as the Farewell Address—may be useful barometers for measuring the institutional *ethos* of appropriating and effecting a text in the interest of furthering an institutional identity.

George Washington's opinion of the Senate can be gleaned from the oft-repeated fable whereby he and Thomas Jefferson engaged in conversation on the merits of the country's new deliberative body: "Jefferson asks George Washington why he consented to the idea of a Senate. 'Why did you pour that coffee into your saucer?' asks Washington. 'To cool it,' replies Jefferson. 'Even so,' replies Washington, 'we pour legislation into the Senatorial body to cool it.'"[36] For students of rhetorical studies or U.S. political culture who may or may not know about the Senate's yearly reading of Washington's Farewell Address or remember its continued practice, a look inside the commemorative form of discourse can reveal an institution transcending national ideals in its own distinctive way. As with legislation, the Senate's transcendence of speech and meaning speaks to a longer process of using proclaimed reverence to display the effect of the Farewell. Such an interior, self-congratulating focus, however, begs more questions on the essential importance of the rhetorical form of the deliberative body's commemoration. When personal reflection of the Farewell Address turns inward and, by consequence, moves the discursive construction of effect toward the institutional and personal self, the Senate takes on the public voice of Washington while clandestinely participating in its effect. Such commemorative form, we should hope, extends and enriches the legacy of the Farewell Address and takes measures not to cool it.

Notes

1. United States Senate, Office of the Secretary, "Farewell Address Notebook," http://senate.gov/artandhistory/history/minute/Washingtons_Farewell_Address.htm (accessed April 10, 2010). All additional entries found here unless noted otherwise.

2. Attendance at the ceremony has steadily declined over more than one hundred years. In 1900, the *Washington Post* noted that Senator Joseph Foraker's recital drew "an unusually large attendance of Senators" ("Brief Session of Senate," *Washington Post,* February 23, 1900, 4); the *New York Times* reported in 1910 that Senator Chauncey Depew's reading drew "a throng" of visitors in the gallery but that "few Senators were present" ("The Holiday in Washington," *New York Times,* February 23, 1910, 5). Writers as far back as Joyce Kilmer, writing for the *New York Times* in 1917, have pondered why the Washington commemoration doesn't elicit "the slightest fervor" for citizens of the day ("Thoughts on Washington's Birthday," *New York Times,* February 18, 1917, SM3). In 1933 the House of Representatives fought for its inclusion in the day's proceedings ("Washington Farewell Address Read to House over Protests," *New York Times,* February 23, 1933, 27); a 1954 edition of the *New York Times* noted that the reading of the address would take on a "more contemporary aspect in the light of current debates on Capitol Hill" ("Congress to Hear 'Farewell' Again: Words of Washington Take on Contemporary Aspect in Current Controversies," *New York Times,* February 22, 1954, 20). By 1965 there were "few lawmakers on hand" for the occasion ("Capitol Marks Holiday," *New York Times,* February 23, 1965, 35). In 1980 the House of Representatives discontinued the tradition for practical purposes: "Nobody ever showed up," a political aide noted ("Washington Farewell Address Gets Apathetic Adieu in House," *New York Times,* February 17, 1980, 18 (all accessed through ProQuest Historical Newspapers, http://www.proquest.com). Bill Linden noted how responsibility for the reading had "become a burden for freshmen Senators" while "[r]ows of unoccupied desks" and sparse crowds "had no effect on the fleet execution of the oration." See Bill Linden, "George Just Doesn't Draw the Crowds," *Roll Call,* February 21, 1985, 4. By 1988 the selected senator "gave the traditional reading of . . . [the] farewell address to a nearly empty Senate chamber" ("Washington's Words Echo through Senate" *New York Times,* February 16, 1988, A-11).

3. The Senate's website states the following on the length of the ritual's proceedings: "In 1985, Florida Senator Paula Hawkins tore through the text in a record-setting 39 minutes, while in 1962, West Virginia Senator Jennings Randolph, savoring each word, consumed 68 minutes." See "Washington's Farewell Address," United States Senate webpage, http://www.senate.gov/artandhistory/history/minute/Washingtons_Farewell_Address.htm (accessed April 10, 2010).

4. On the artistry of Washington's "complex style," see Michael J. Hostetler, "Washington's Farewell Address: Distance as Bane and Blessing," *Rhetoric and Public Affairs* 5 (2002): 396.

5. To my knowledge, four respected scholars from various fields have made the false assertion that the ritual has been discontinued. Michael Kammen noted, "the long-standing tradition of reading the entire Farewell Address out loud in the U.S. Senate on Washington's birthday quietly vanished." Barry Schwartz wrote, "Every year we are reminded that the United States House and Senate no longer assemble for the annual reading of Washington's Farewell Address." Finally, the rhetorical scholars Stephen Lucas and Susan Zaeske suggested that the Farewell Address "continued to be read in Congress each February 22 *until the 1970s.*" As of this writing (2013), the ritual has been ongoing for well over one hundred years. See Michael Kammen, "Some Patterns and Meanings of Memory Distortion in American History," in *Memory Distortion: How Minds, Brains, and Societies Reconstruct the Past,* ed. Daniel L. Schacter (Cambridge, Mass.: Harvard University Press, 1997), 335; Barry Schwartz, *George Washington: The Making of an American*

Symbol (New York: Free Press, 1987), 198; Stephen Lucas and Susan Zaeske, "George Washington," in *U.S. Presidents as Orators: A Bio-critical Sourcebook,* ed. Halford Ryan (Westport, Conn.: Greenwood Press, 1995), 11, emphasis added.

6. See Kiewe and Houck, "Introduction" in this volume.

7. "effect, n." OED Online, December 2012, Oxford University Press, http://www.oed.com.lib-ezproxy.tamu.edu:2048/view/Entry/59664?rskey=ueHq7g&result=1 (accessed December 27, 2012); "effect, v." OED Online, December 2012, Oxford University Press, http://www.oed.com.lib-ezproxy.tamu.edu:2048/view/Entry/59665?rskey=ueHq7g&result=2 (accessed December 27, 2012).

8. Herbert A. Wichelns, "The Literary Criticism of Oratory," in *Methods of Rhetorical Criticism: A Twentieth Century Perspective,* 2nd ed., ed. Bernard L. Brock and Robert L. Scott (Detroit, Mich.: Wayne State University Press, 1980), 67.

9. James Jasinski, *The Sourcebook on Rhetoric: Key Concepts in Contemporary Rhetorical Studies* (Thousand Oaks, Calif.: Sage, 2001), 195.

10. Richard A. Baker, *Traditions of the United States Senate* (Washington, D.C.: Senate Office of Printing and Document Services, 2007), 25–27.

11. Lawrence W. Rosenfield, "The Practical Celebration of Epideictic," *Rhetoric in Transition,* ed. Eugene E. White (University Park: Penn State University Press, 1980), 146.

12. Celeste Michelle Condit, "The Functions of Epideictic: The Boston Massacre Orations as Exemplar," *Communication Quarterly* 33 (1985): 296.

13. "Resolution of the Senate," *Congressional Record*, 56th Cong., 2d sess., January 24th, 1901, 1385.

14. Readings in the late nineteenth century found "most of the senators in their seats with a fairly large audience in the galleries, all giving close and respectful attention"; by the 1940s roughly one-third of the Senate was attending the recital, and by the 1960s and 1970s the occasion was drawing about five members. See "Reading the Address: How Senators Commemorated Washington's Birthday," *Atlanta Constitution,* February 23, 1893, 1; "Birthday Evokes Washington Lore," *New York Times,* February 23, 1940, 3; "Washington's Farewell Address Read in Congress; Stand on Foreign Affairs Evokes Interest," *New York Times,* February 23, 1952, 26; "Farewell Address Doesn't Fare Well," *Hartford Courant,* February 20, 1973, 54.

15. As one example, Kathleen Hall Jamieson has documented how Woodrow Wilson's rhetoric advocating a new American foreign policy interpreted Washington's warning against foreign alliances as a "revised principle" by which the United States could intervene in a European war. One would expect that such an open debate on the meaning of the Farewell Address might prompt a response from lawmakers reciting the text. See Kathleen H. Jamieson, *Eloquence in an Electronic Age: The Transformation of Political Speechmaking* (New York: Oxford University Press, 1988), 104–105.

16. James Boyd White offers a cogent summary of constitutive rhetoric. According to White, "Whenever you speak, you define a character for yourself and for at least one other—your audience—and make a community at latest between the two of you; and you do this in a language that is of necessity provided to you by others and modified in your use of it." See White, *When Words Lose Their Meaning: Constitutions and Reconstitutions of Language, Character, and Community* (Chicago: University of Chicago Press, 1984), xi. The social theorist Anthony Giddens offers further perspective on the role of meaning and the interpretation of texts. He notes, "Every instance of the use of language is a potential modification of that language at the same time as it acts to reproduce it." See Giddens, *Central Problems in Social Theory: Action, Structure and Contradiction in Social Analysis* (Berkeley and Los Angeles: University of California Press, 1979), 220.

17. Jasinski notes four general "effects" garnered from the constitutive extension of language: the constitution and reconstitution of individual identity; the constitution and reconstitution of one's

temporal experience; the constitution and reconstitution of political culture; and the constitution and reconstitution of language itself. See James Jasinksi, "A Constitutive Framework for Rhetorical Historiography: Toward an Understanding of the Discursive (Re)constitution of 'Constitution' in the *Federalist Papers,*" in *Doing Rhetorical History: Concepts and Cases,* ed. Kathleen J. Turner (Tuscaloosa and London: University of Alabama Press, 1998), 72–92, and also Jasinski, *Sourcebook on Rhetoric,* 191–195.

18. Robert P. Hay, "George Washington: American Moses," *America Quarterly* 21 (1969): 781–782.

19. Quoted in Hay, "George Washington," 786.

20. Multiple scholars of the Farewell Address have noted the text's response to immediate events, such as the Whiskey Rebellion, and public debate over the Jay Treaty. For a discussion of Alexander Hamilton's influence in drafting the Farewell Address as a Federalist text, see Felix Gilbert, *To The Farewell Address: Ideas of Early American Foreign Policy* (Princeton: Princeton University Press, 1961), especially 115–136.

21. Lucas and Zaeske, "George Washington," 11.

22. Garry Wills, "Washington's Farewell Address: An Eighteenth-Century 'Fireside Chat,'" *Chicago Historical Society* 10 (1981): 179.

23. Matthew Spalding, "George Washington's Farewell Address," *Wilson Quarterly* 20 (1996): 66.

24. Hostetler, "Washington's Farewell Address," 404.

25. Senator McCain's entry was accessed from the United States Senate Historical Office. E-mail correspondence with Dr. Betty Koed, August 21, 2008.

26. Senator Chambliss's entry was accessed from the United States Senate Historical Office. E-mail correspondence with Dr. Betty Koed, August 21, 2008.

27. Consider, for example, Randolph reading a line such as the following before affirming the importance of his state identity: "To the efficacy and permanency of Your Union, a Government for the whole is indispensable. No Alliances however strict between the parts can be an adequate substitute." See George Washington, "Farewell Address," in *George Washington: Writings,* ed John Rhodehamel (New York: Library of America, 2004), 967.

28. Entries from Senator Chambliss, Senator Corker, Senator Pryor, and Senator Johanns were accessed from the United States Senate Historical Office. E-mail correspondence with Dr. Betty Koed, August 21, 2008.

29. Senator Shaheen's entry was accessed from the United States Senate Historical Office. E-mail correspondence with Dr. Betty Koed, March 1, 2012.

30. Baker, *Traditions of the United States Senate,* 1.

31. "Washington Farewell Address Gets Apathetic Adieu in House," *New York Times,* February 17, 1980, 18.

32. Paul Ricoeur, *Interpretation Theory: Discourse and the Surplus of Meaning* (Fort Worth: Texas Christian University Press, 1976), 42.

33. Thomas P. Miller, *The Formation of College English: Rhetoric and Belles Lettres in the British Cultural Provinces* (Pittsburgh: University of Pittsburgh Press, 1997), 216.

34. Ross Baker, *The House and the Senate* (New York: Norton, 2008), 48.

35. Daniel Wirls and Stephen Wirls, *The Invention of the United States Senate* (Baltimore, Md.: Johns Hopkins University Press, 2004), 213–214.

36. Quoted in Nicol C. Rae and Colton C. Campbell, *The Contentious Senate: Partisanship, Ideology, and the Myth of Cool Judgment* (New York: Rowman and Littlefield, 2001), xi.

Letters to Franklin D. Roosevelt following the First Fireside Chat

The Case for Studying Effects

AMOS KIEWE

On March 16, 1933, B. Kurlander of Los Angeles wrote to President Franklin D. Roosevelt congratulating him "for the new confidence and hope you injected into at least a portion of this multitude, thru your immortal speech of last Sunday evening." Edmond Gray wrote that "after hearing your talk on banking, Sunday March 13, I am sure you have the confidence of the people of these United States." Mrs. Whitson of Houston wrote that the speech "closed a week that had been to us mothers, with young mouths to feed, young minds to educate, young fears to quiet, a sort of long nightmare. Your words wakened us to a new, a brighter day." For these letter writers, Franklin D. Roosevelt's radio address on the banking crisis succeeded in replacing fear with renewed confidence and reassurance that United States' banks were stable and that the nation's economy would quickly recover.

Charles H. Baruch of Philadelphia wrote, "I listened with great attention to your very prolific address to the American People last night. I feel sure that it was one of the finest addresses and one to give the utmost confidence in you since Lincoln's time." Mr. Reynolds of Covington, Kentucky, understood the rhetorical forces operating in the nation's economy, writing that "the back-bone of the Nation was Confidence—the confidence that we had in each other—although many of us think that we are the 'whole cheese' . . . [and] that it is mutual confidence that should hold us together for the general good. . . . With you as our Leader of Action, we will not watchfully slip. We shall progress forward." Confidence in the banks and confidence in the president were cited as the tangible material effects of the radio address. Frank Walker of New York City wrote that "you have such wonderful persuasive power that if you went to the radio on a Sunday night and told your great big family to go out and buy what they could and needed the response would be absolutely great. The way you spoke last Sunday everybody who could would obey."

George H. Minnerly of New York City wrote "truthfully, I have been greatly worried about my financial status, but after hearing your speech tonight, I must say that my mind is absolutely at ease." Stanley Stepel of Cicero, Illinois, wrote that "[a]fter your speech Sunday I think the people of this country have thought things over and will put their hoarded money back in circulation, have trust in banks, and have faith in your Presidency." Miss F. I. Hundley of Brooklyn wrote to the president that she was "one of many thousands of citizens who have carried a burden that has been at the breaking point for some time. Our income, savings, homes, everything taken from us and we were helpless to defend ourselves against the forces that seemed bent on our destruction. But now our heads are up again, and our backs will stiffen, too, because you have given us a new hope—the hope that we can once again find ourselves and also recover the pride in our country."

Hugh R. Robertson of San Antonio wrote that "last night my wife and I heard your reassuring address to, or more aptly your heart to heart talk with, the people of the United States, and we both felt the bracing effect of it, as did thousands of others. It strengthened our faith in you and our confidence in your leadership."[1] The Robertsons covered in their short letter most of the themes and sentiments thousands of others would include in their letters to the new president: they found the radio address on the banking crisis (later dubbed the First Fireside Chat) *reassuring,* they appreciated its *bracing effect,* they felt that the address strengthened their *faith* and *confidence* in the president, and they appreciated the *heart-to-heart* talk between the president and the people. Indeed, the crucial radio address had a tremendous effect on the nation: its immediate consequence was a quick and dramatic end to the banking crisis that had plagued the nation's banks for months and had already crippled the country's financial institutions.

These are but a sample of the thousands of letters citizens wrote to the president following his First Fireside Chat. The two hundred letters gathered for this research are rich with references that illustrate just how the First Fireside Chat resonated with each letter writer.[2] Collectively the letters represent a remarkable array of sentiments that prove how desperate people were and how much they were clinging to leadership that might bring them hope again. The letter writers communicated to the president how quickly his address transformed fear and panic into confidence and trust and how desperation at the loss of savings was replaced with optimism. The sheer act of thousands of citizens writing the president, communicating their overwhelming support for the plan to restore confidence in the banks, was one of the material effects of the address. And though likely several situational constraints brought about these reactions and sentiments, strong enough to have thousands write the president in reaction to his radio address, it is equally important to attribute these letters not just to this particular address but to the overall dire financial situation preceding the panic. Yet, none of these situational variables ought to diminish the value of the First Fireside Chat, as rare as it may be, in having a measure of effect on the nation at a critical point in its history. Each of the letter writers say as much.

John Poulakos writes that letter writing "shares a long history with the rhetorical tradition" and that "the kinship between the two traditions . . . is not only historical. It also extends to topical preferences and the impulse to accord significance to subjects close to the heart." To write a letter, argues Poulakos, "amounts to a declaration" that "tells us that one of rhetoric's functions is to circumscribe a topos and issue an invitation to dwell in it."[3] The act of writing a letter in reaction to a rhetorical act is a significant measure of its effect, a declaration of just how important an individual considered a given message and how absorbed one becomes in seeking to communicate one's sentiments to the source of the message.

In this essay I argue for the importance of accounting for effect in rhetorical criticism. More specifically, using Franklin D. Roosevelt's First Fireside Chat as a case study, I show that to ignore the effects of rhetoric or to ignore effects by featuring probable effects in their place is to miss a more astute insight into the speech. If we ignore effects, Roosevelt's First Fireside Chat can be assessed at best as nothing more than a technical speech on the banking industry, and its role in the nation's economy is drastically reduced. If we fail to tap into the archival resources available that can shed light on how the speech was received and how the audience engaged the speech, the value of the address is diminished, the severity of the crisis is misunderstood, and the relationship between the American people and their president at a crucial moment in history is ignored and misunderstood. The larger implications of ignoring effects are significant as the discipline of rhetoric has opened itself to questions of relevance and importance—questions that at least one prominent scholar has exploited to potentially devastating ends.

A Crisis of Confidence

The stock market crash of October 2008 and the collapse of major financial and insurance institutions such as A.I.G, Lehman Brothers, Wachovia, Fannie Mae, and Freddie Mac, as well as the depletion of credit worldwide, have brought much distress to both government officials and citizens. The economic distress of 2008–2009, though not on the scale of that in 1933, can still illustrate the desperation people felt during Roosevelt's entry into the White House. The operative words to describe the economic and financial crisis in 2008 remain "confidence" and a "lack of confidence," or fear. Despite the complex financial transactions that caused the crisis in the first place, the repeated "currency" for the solution to the financial crisis is rhetoric, specifically the need for calming statements deemed necessary to restore confidence to the financial markets. Indeed, various individuals, from the president to the Treasury secretary and others, sought to restore confidence by addressing the nation, reassuring people of the soundness of financial institutions specifically and the economy more generally.

The last time the United States faced such a financial crisis was in 1933, when banks were on the verge of collapse. It would be, therefore, logical to refer to that crisis, as many in the media did, and to look for analogous solutions and perspectives. In 1933, as in 2008, the operative solution was indeed rhetorical, centered on the need to restore confidence. But confidence, rhetorically considered, is but the material effects of the discourse about confidence. By comparison with the crisis of 2008, the banking crisis of 1932–1933 remains an exemplar of rhetoric whose effects yielded confidence and subsequently restored bank solvency and thereby helped the nation's economy recover.

Only a week after the new president assumed office, the effects of Roosevelt's First Fireside Chat were decisive and immediate. Roosevelt entered the White House amid a potentially devastating economic situation. The Great Depression of 1929 with its unprecedented levels of unemployment, along with the growing banking crisis that climaxed during the final days of the Hoover administration, created both an opportunity and a risk. All eyes were focused on Roosevelt as he sought to save the nation from impending financial doom. The banking crisis, in particular, intensified to such a degree during the winter of 1932–1933 that several state governors closed their states' banks in February. Banks that remained open teetered on the verge of collapse. The hoarding of gold and currency by both individuals and foreign governments, which began in 1931 and later intensified significantly in 1932, brought the withdrawal of assets from U.S. banks. The run on the banks spread quickly and threatened to devastate the nation's financial institutions.[4]

As the banking crisis intensified, Roosevelt and his close advisers crafted the initial steps to be taken once the new president was inaugurated, on March 4. No doubt it was easier for the incoming president than for the tarnished incumbent to offer confidence and implement a recovery plan, and it is equally plausible that had Hoover acted the way Roosevelt did at the beginning of his term, he could have been as successful. Yet, ironically, the plan for ending the banking crisis was developed by officials in the Hoover Treasury, but it was never implemented, as the outgoing president in his last two months in office lacked the political courage and the rhetorical skills for its implementation. The essential commodity necessary for a successful turn of events was confidence, and the currency was rhetoric.[5] This is precisely what Roosevelt, and especially his adviser Raymond Moley, focused on.[6] Throughout the interregnum winter months of 1932–1933, both men understood that the new administration had to convince the nation that things would get better. Public confidence was the key materiality of the entire banking crisis,[7] and, with primarily a rhetorical plan that sought to create confidence in the government, its new leaders, and the nation's financial institutions, the foundation on which several "events" were planned was laid.

Much was riding on the nation's perceptions of the incoming president and his actions. Roosevelt, a keen rhetorician with a remarkable sense of timing, dramatized several highly visible and symbolic actions that culminated in building quick confidence in the new administration and its plan to solve the banking crisis. Roosevelt's first week in office was designed primarily for rhetorical effect, and, to that end, the administration choreographed events that carried a consistent message—that of a very active president who immediately began working on the crisis at hand. The first week also highlighted a confident Roosevelt who knew that his rhetorical acts, taken for their symbolic importance, were necessary to bring the crisis to a quick end. After all, taking time during his first week in office to attend to critical economic issues *and* to his stamp collection was just another way for Roosevelt to project confidence during the first few days in office.

On March 4, Roosevelt's inaugural address centered on confidence in the new administration and its ability to solve the banking crisis. After the speech, Roosevelt's first presidential act was to gather the nation's leading bankers on March 5. On March 6, the president declared a bank holiday, closing all banks in order to stop further financial bleeding. This act was highly controversial, and it was based on the 1917 Trading with the Enemy Act.[8] In fact, Hoover had this strategy on his desk, but, fearing the Act's constitutionality as a remedy for the banking crisis, he lacked the courage to use it. Roosevelt had no qualms about employing it despite the act's dubious connection to the financial crisis at hand. The very act of closing the banks was crucially a symbolic act, since many banks were already closed by state governors. On March 9, Roosevelt called Congress into a special session, impressing the nation with another symbolic feat—having both houses of Congress pass an Emergency Banking Act in one day—unprecedented legislation, the likes of which the nation had never seen.[9] With this act, the plan for reopening sound and solvent banks was put into motion. This plan became the blueprint for the final act of the first week—a speech to the nation over the radio airwaves scheduled for Sunday evening, March 12, at 10 o'clock Eastern Standard Time, explaining the causes of the banking crisis and outlining a plan for recovery.

Though Roosevelt was not the first president to resort to the radio, he was by far the most skilled user of this relatively new medium. Roosevelt had used radio as New York's governor, and he did so to great success. His most important and critical radio address as governor, titled "The Forgotten Man," was already situated in the growing banking crisis and preceded the First Fireside Chat by some ten months. Yet much had changed in Roosevelt's approach to the banking crisis during his transition from governor to president. "The Forgotten Man" speech, though, is important because it set in motion a relationship between Roosevelt and the American people that was sure to affect the response of many to his First Fireside Chat. Indeed, many letter writers would mention "The Forgotten Man" speech when writing to Roosevelt about his First Fireside Chat, thus proving the existence already of a favorable relationship between audience and speaker.

The First Fireside Chat

The radio address on the banking crisis was simple, transparent, and straightforward; its thrust was not in rhetorical allusions, attractive metaphors or a grand style. Rather, the emphasis was placed on getting listeners to accept the plan for a carefully choreographed, semitechnical plan for the reopening of banks and to follow the president's advice to have confidence in him and his plan. The very beginning of the radio address signaled the intimate relationship the president had with his audience: "My friends: I want to speak for a few minutes . . . about banking."[10] No formal salutation or the more traditional "Good evening, my fellow Americans" but a conversation among friends. The acknowledgement that "the overwhelming majority of you who use banks for the making of deposits and the drawing of checks" do not fully understand the complexity of the banking system was a direct and frank appeal: "I want to tell you what has been done in the last few days, and why it was done, and what the next steps are going to be." The speech was persuasive but subtly so. The suasion would be in the simplicity and transparency of the appeal and in the factual picture Roosevelt drew.

Acknowledging the hardship many Americans were experiencing, Roosevelt described how banks operated and how easy it was for banks to lose liquidity despite their solvency once a run on the banks began. Once people understood that when they "deposit money in the bank the bank does not put the money into a safe deposit vault" but invest it to move the "wheels of industry and agriculture," the scourge of insolvency was rationalized and any fear thereof might be significantly eased. Thus, Roosevelt explained that many sound banks ran out of cash though their assets ensured their solvency; they simply lacked the necessary cash reserves to accommodate many depositors withdrawing their money all at once. Outlining the several steps taken to solve the banking crisis, especially the Emergency Banking Act, Roosevelt assured the nation that with the measures taken, he had the tools to implement a sound plan. He described that plan, including the different classes of banks and their gradual reopening. Roosevelt's action-oriented address was designed as a mark of confidence and control over the crisis scene.

Clearly understanding that the radio address was to dramatically close what he began a week earlier in his Inaugural Address, Roosevelt tied together the two addresses and their focus on banishing fear. For those "who have not recovered from their fear" and "may again begin withdrawals" once the banks reopened, Roosevelt assured them that "the banks will take care of all needs except, of course, the hysterical demands of hoarders—and it is my belief that hoarding during the past week has become an exceedingly unfashionable pastime." Notwithstanding his fondness for the medical metaphor, Dr. Roosevelt already expected people to have confidence in the banks—and this very expectation was the wellspring for confidence. The reference to the hysterical few was Roosevelt's way of dissuading people from continued hoarding, framing such practice as contrary to sound judgment and ultimately anti-American.

Roosevelt assured people that they "will again be glad to have their money where it will be safely taken care of and where they can use it conveniently at any time. I can assure you that it is safer to keep your money in the bank than under the mattress." He did not shy away from touching on the most troubling banks—those that could not be reopened. "I do not promise you that every bank will be reopened or that individual losses will not be suffered"; however, "there will be no losses that possibly could be avoided; and there would have been more and greater losses had we continued to drift." All banking categories were covered. In this way, Roosevelt hoped that by his very practical and matter-of-fact account of the banking difficulties he could restore confidence and that the people would heed his advice to redeposit money once the banks reopened on Monday morning.

The final appeal put the solution to the banking crisis squarely into the people's hands: "It is up to you to support and make it work. It is your problem no less than it is mine. Together we cannot fail." Thus ended the radio address on the banking crisis, with no formal disengagement of speaker from audience but just as it began: a frank talk among friends.

The Effects of Rhetoric

As noted in the introduction to this book, a serious challenge to the relevance of rhetorical studies of the presidency in general and of Roosevelt's First Fireside Chat in particular was posed by the political scientist George C. Edwards III. Professor Edwards called for evidence that rhetoric indeed carries effects on real audiences as proof of rhetoric's viability.[11] Not wishing to repeat the points already raised in the introduction to this volume, I will simply restate Edwards's thesis that without such evidence, the study of rhetoric can be summed up as irrelevant.[12] More acute, though, is Edwards's statement that directly touches on this study on Roosevelt's rhetoric.

Using an example that could support his thesis, Edwards point to Franklin D. Roosevelt's First Fireside Chat. He admits that Roosevelt was able to move the nation following the banking crisis but is quick to forward an explanation that keeps his thesis tenable: Roosevelt's ability to move public opinion was the result of his charisma, "especially as manifested in his radio speeches."[13] Edwards's criticism of the relevance of rhetoric is sharpened further when he seeks to refute Doris Kearns Goodwin's contention that Roosevelt's First Fireside Chat had a positive effect on the nation: after hearing the radio address, many individuals, Goodwin writes, deposited large sums of money, and these deposits stabilized the banks. Edwards is dismissive of such evidence for effect, stating that "none of these examples, however, represents the president asking the people to change their minds." This is so, claims Edwards, because people usually do not "offer much resistance to banking." In any event, Edwards concludes, "Roosevelt was moving people in the direction they already wanted to go."[14]

According to Edwards, then, Roosevelt's success in ending the banking crisis had little to do with his radio address, and if such an effect is discernible, it is a result only of the president's charisma. Clearly, charisma, or ethos, is discounted as a variable of effect, presumably for lack of evidence of its role. But Edwards goes further, forwarding the sweeping claim that presidential speeches do not work. Indeed, they may not work all the time, but this one did work. Many citizens showed their readiness to deposit money and gold back in the banks by doing so only hours after Roosevelt spoke to them. Clearly, the address resonated with many citizens, and many took the very action Roosevelt asked of them in his First Fireside Chat.

Indeed, the thousands of letters, as well as economic indices, stand as indicators of material effects. The resonance of the address, discerned from the thousands of letters, can serve as evidence for the sentiments therein, and as such they can tell critics much about the interplay between a speech and its audience. And though it is rare that a single speech can yield such a distinct effect—in this case, a macroeconomic effect—this particular address brought about the immediate change Roosevelt sought. It is also reasonable to state that the First Fireside Chat is not the single rhetorical act that "did" all of the material work here and that the larger economic crisis, the depression, fear and loss of confidence, the loss of bank reserves, and, crucially, the rhetorical efforts of Roosevelt's first week in office also contributed to the overall rhetorical situation that yielded the effects as documented in citizens' letters.

Roosevelt's audience was not predisposed to adhere to his message about the safety of bank accounts, and there was no way the president was assured that when the banks opened the following morning, bank liquidity would quickly be restored. If anything, the nation was so fearful that the financial institutions were unsafe and that workers' hard-earned savings would be lost that citizens had initiated a run on the banks a few weeks earlier. People said as much in the letters many wrote to the president. The evidence for the influence of Roosevelt's First Fireside Chat and its emphasis on the need to restore confidence is in the many letter writers who participated in the rhetorical exchange between the president and the nation. Roosevelt asked a fearful and badly frightened nation to feel confidence in the banking system, and the nation reacted positively. Roosevelt asked the nation to engage in a difficult act—to exchange fear for trust, to replace lack of confidence in the banks with renewed trust in the banking system. Roosevelt specifically asked for very material action—the redepositing of currency and gold that only weeks or days earlier had been withdrawn or hoarded.

Roosevelt's request to the nation was of major consequence to many individuals whose livelihood hung in the balance and who feared losing all their savings. Yet, after hearing his radio plea, the nation accepted his request despite the manifest risks. It is crucial to understand that the crisis was so acute that it could have resulted in the complete collapse of the U.S. economy and that similar development in Europe, especially in Germany and Italy, did not bode well for any nation undergoing a banking crisis. The American people were fully aware of the enormous risks to their savings and to the nation's financial institutions. The First Fireside Chat put a stop to such frightening eventualities, and its effect can be proven in two ways: first, by the use of macroeconomic indices that show just how effective Roosevelt's message was and, second, through microeconomics, by documenting the effects of the speech, in this case through the letters thousands of citizens wrote the president, overwhelmingly accepting his challenge to have confidence in the banking system and his banking legislation.

With his radio address on the banking crisis, Roosevelt played out the last act of the banking crisis, and when the banks reopened eleven hours later, hoarding did not resume and the American people redeposited currency and gold in the banks; with such action, the banks quickly returned to solvency and stability. The results of the rhetorical and policy acts of the first week were quickly discerned as the dollar rebounded and the stock market opened with trading volumes at record highs. Treasury certificates that only days earlier were at risk of not being purchased sold at the value of $800 million—the highest rate since World War I. About "seventy percent of the banks reopened immediately," and nearly "3,000 banks opened later. Only about two thousand banks with serious liquidity problems" had to be reorganized, and of those only a few never reopened.[15]

A quick survey of the resumption of banking operations offers tangible evidence of the confidence people had in Roosevelt's message: by the end of March 1933, the sum of $1.2 billion was redeposited in banks; about half of this volume was in gold and gold certificates. A few weeks later, "some 12,817 banks were fully reopened with deposits of about 31 billion dollars." In the final assessment, 14,440 commercial banks were back in operation by the end of the year, and "only a handful of banks were put in the hands of conservators. The Reconstruction Finance Corporation (RFC) made loans to banks in the total amount of 260 million dollars and purchased obligations totaling 227 million dollars, a relatively insignificant amount of money given the overall dimensions of the banking crisis."[16]

The day after the radio address, the *New York Times*, hardly a fan of Roosevelt, featured the following headline on page one: "Dollar Is Strong as Trading Reopens; Sharp Advance in Terms of Foreign Currencies Puts Shorts into a Panic." The report pointed out that "the United States monetary unit rose sharply above the levels at which it had sold just before the banking holiday."[17] The *Wall Street Journal* praised the new administration for having "superbly risen to the occasion."[18] Roosevelt's adviser James Farley noted years later that it was easy with hindsight to conclude that Roosevelt's success in solving the banking crisis was inevitable, "but it is just as easy to imagine the economic and financial chaos that would have resulted if the people had given way to fear and panic."[19] Indeed, no other president in American history, with the exception of Lincoln, had faced such a daunting entry into office and such a precarious situation. Similar deteriorating economic developments in Europe brought to power dictators such as Hitler and Mussolini, ushering in the course of events that would gradually serve as a backdrop for World War II. In the United States, literally in a matter of days, the crisis was over.

Commenting on Roosevelt's rhetoric, Jonathan Alter writes, "[I]n the days following his 'fear itself' Inaugural and first 'Fireside Chat,' the same citizens who had lined up the month before to withdraw their last savings from the banks (and stuff it under the mattress or tape it to their chests) lined up to redeposit patriotically. This astounding act of ebullient leadership marked the 'defining moment' of modern American politics, when Roosevelt saved both capitalism and democracy within a few weeks."[20] The banking crisis came to an abrupt end thanks to the actions of the new president, who was seen by many in the nation as its savior. The First Fireside Chat was a masterful stroke, and the American people appreciated their leader's trust in them; as a result, they gave him their complete trust in return. And the Roosevelt biographer H. W. Brands writes that "as the banks reopened during the week after he spoke, millions of Americans took their money out from under those mattresses and returned it to their banks" and that others who did not or could not withdraw their money before the banks closed opted to leave their money in the banks. Finally and most important, out of a circulation of some $7.5 billion, the amount of money returned to the banks stood at about $1 billion by the end of March.[21] These are the indices of material effect.

Arthur Ballantine, Hoover's Under Secretary of the Treasury, who was asked by Roosevelt to stay in his position for a few weeks under the Democratic administration and who drafted the First Fireside Chat, wrote in 1948 that confidence in the banks was restored because the president "commended the new currency as 'sound currency'" and "expressed assurance that the reopened banks would stand up."[22] And confidence was clearly restored. Materially, then, the First Fireside Chat yielded the desired effects, and as such the address was most successful. That the macroeconomic indices correspond nicely with the sentiments of the letter writers allows the critic greater confidence in assessing the impact of the First Fireside Chat as successful.

For the rhetorical critic the value of individual letters is that they add much needed documentation of the significant success of one address and its effects on many individuals. The dramatic turn of economic events was engendered by Roosevelt's effective persuasion and the people's confidence in his plan to reopen the banks. Thousands wished to tell Roosevelt how they felt about his radio address, and they did so by communicating directly with the president.[23] That thousands saw fit to write and report sentiments not present in the speech demonstrates its agentic quality. The letters collectively argue that the radio address's effects were real, immediate, and decidedly consequential. In short, the letters prove that rhetoric can have very real effects.

Richard A. Cherwitz and John Theobald-Osborne offer a three-dimensional conception of political effects in place of a one-dimensional study that brings the critic to examine a single speech and reflect on the direct or immediate effect of a speech, seeking to assess the audience's attitudes and decision making. A second dimension of effect adds to the first dimension "more subtle types of effect," those that are "at least one step removed from public discussion." Here, rhetoric's effects are indirect and covert and may shift the rhetoric's focus to prioritizing one aspect and downplaying another. The third dimension accounts for the previous two and seeks to understand how rhetoric empowers the public to focus on a specific issue, act accordingly, or move in a different direction. Here, the critic can account for the less obvious effects as well as counterfactual developments.[24]

If we take this three-dimensional model as a flexible orientation, we see that most of the letters were written only hours and even minutes after Roosevelt delivered his radio address and thus speak to the first dimension Cherwitz and Theobald-Osborne developed. The letter writers share one thing in common: they were all eager to put into writing their feelings and sentiments after hearing the speech as well as their overwhelming support of the president, his speech, and the plan it contained. The letter writers vary in their focus and in the message they sent: some limited their letters to congratulating Roosevelt on his address; others indicated their support in him; many sought to indicate their willingness to follow the president's call to restore confidence in the banks; still others saw divine inspiration in the president; some wished to tell the president how relieved they were after years of suffering; many others conveyed their appreciation despite their having voted against Roosevelt; some even regretted their Republican leanings; and many simply commented on the strength of the speech and its rhetorical features.

The range of sentiments expressed in the letters to Roosevelt can, therefore, speak also to Cherwitz and Theobald-Osborne's second dimension, in which sentiments not expressed directly in Roosevelt's address are nonetheless apparent in the letters. Many letter writers in particular saw divine inspiration in Roosevelt's actions and thanked God for sending the president to them; they saw him appearing like a Moses and inspiring them. Similarly, many letter writers noted the intimate nature of the president's address, his "visit" to their parlor and his friendly chat in people's living rooms.

The third dimension of rhetoric's effects allows for the long-range assessment of Roosevelt's address on the banking crisis. The very fact that a speech with a crucial focus on immediate effect became the "First" in a series of much-anticipated Fireside Chats throughout Roosevelt's long presidency speaks volume of its lingering effects. What began as a needed speech that addressed an immediate and acute crisis commenced a tradition that tied the president to the nation during the crucial years of economic hardship and, later, the Second World War. Perhaps most obscure but very significant is the fact that the plan that was at the heart of the address carried a stabilizing effect on the banking system in the United States for some seventy-five years, keeping the banking system in the United States on solid grounds until the banking crisis of 2008.

The primary effect, nonetheless, lies in the address's immediate impact. That it generated so many letters and so much immediate support is in itself testimony to the influence of the speech and its speaker. In short, the letters serve as testimony to the effect the speech had on the nation. The letters must also be put in their unique context. The vast majority of the letters were written before the radio address's economic effects could be discerned and before economic indices and press reports could indicate just how the nation had reacted. The radio address moved the nation's economy at a critical moment in the nation's history, and it alone constructed the confidence, inspiration, and trust as key ingredients of economic recovery.

Summary

Unless the speeches are recorded by someone in the audience, the effects of historical speeches have often been unknown or inconclusive. Even contemporary speeches may lack a sense of audience reaction unless someone documented them, statistically, visually, or qualitatively. The constraints the critic faces in assessing the complete rhetorical package are limiting, but they should not foreclose an important critical perspective—that of engaging the audience's reaction to a rhetorical act. The effects of rhetoric are always present and realized by its audience even though they are not always documented, available, or retrievable. However, when a speech's effects are available to the critic, they might well be analyzed, for they are essential for a better understanding of the function of any rhetorical artifact and for the conclusions critics forward about them. What is perhaps a more critical statement to be made here is that the evidence for effects is contingent upon how effects are defined. In the case of Roosevelt's First Fireside Chat, the evidence for effects comes in two forms: the micro-level effects whereby private citizens wrote the president of their sentiments after listening to the speech, and the macro-level effects in which banks' solvency was restored rather quickly and the nation's economy moved away from the brink of collapse. Clearly, Roosevelt's objective was to achieve the macroeconomic effects, but the microeconomics effects yielded something very important beyond the redepositing of money in the banks—an affirmation of a president and his actions at a critical juncture, the need of many to pour out their relief and gratitude, and the restoration of confidence in the nation, its institutions, and its officeholders.

The usefulness of letters to the speaker, as this case study has shown, is but "low-tech" relative to the kind of effects available today. The kinds of research scholars pursue today, including the unearthing of primary documents and the use of presidential libraries, private collections, Web-based archives (including Web-based finding aids), blogs, tweets, recorded interviews, and diaries, were not the fashion of yesteryear.[25] It stands to reason, then, that the constraints cited by Black, Parrish, and others were, in part, a reflection of the time in which questions about effects were asked. Equally plausible is the notion that ignoring effects because of their inaccessibility or questions about their existence was not a major constraint as scholars have maintained but rather a preference in face of a daunting enterprise many chose not to pursue. Yet, no rhetorical act is uttered in a vacuum, and it stands to reason that not only contemporary but also historical rhetorical acts leave some record of their reception and of reaction to them. Most rhetorical works that scholars pursue date from the past two centuries, and these works, for the most part, were commented upon in official records as well as in the popular press, pamphlets, or diaries. The exclusion of effect in rhetorical studies, then, appears more as a paradigm born of a theoretical framing now rendered anachronistic in an age where instant reactions are the order of the day.

The relevance of rhetoric suggests that it may be productive to reconsider the limitations we put on the study of effect and find the path for its inclusion in rhetorical criticism. The study of the letters written to Franklin D. Roosevelt following his First Fireside Chat seeks to address the possibility, viability, and importance of engaging auditors and the effects of a given rhetorical act. The letters not only corroborate economic markers of renewed confidence and banking liquidity but also provide a personal account, as distinct from a quantitative or statistical account, of sentiments and receptiveness that are equally important in assessing the effects of the radio address. The analysis of the effects hardly reveals direct links between citizens' sentiments and specific statements in the First Fireside Chat. If anything, letter writers added allusions not tied directly to the contents of the address. It is quite plausible that the form of the address—a radio chat in people's living rooms—"did" the rhetorical work and yielded the desired effect born of an intimate talk, a discussion-like talk in people's parlors. The letters as manifestations of effect tell us how the speech was received and why the speaker and the speech were able to generate the sought effects. Finally, the First Fireside Chat had also a long-range effect on the nation's economy, and significantly so.

There are, of course, larger implications as well. To claim that the effects of rhetoric are of little value amounts to claiming that rhetoric does not matter since its effects are nonexistent or, worse, irrelevant to human behavior and action. But this claim, born largely out of a misunderstanding of the function of rhetoric, is grossly erroneous, yet instructive. The historical limitation assigned to the study of effects is primarily the result of the constraints scholars imagined in gauging and accurately assessing the effects of a given public address. But such a limitation should not have driven scholars to discount the notion of effect altogether. If such a limitation is realized, scholars ought to point to it. If sources for discerning effects are available, then scholars should account for them. As Michael Leff reminds us, "rhetorical meaning . . . is designed to reach outward to the world beyond the text and to guide the audience's understanding of and behavior within that world."[26]

Scholars of rhetoric and public address ought to refocus their attention on the effect of rhetoric. In so doing, we may minimize the dismissive attitudes that some have assumed regarding the role and function of rhetoric. This development may perhaps necessitate rethinking some of our methods of rhetorical criticism in favor of seeking more evidentiary proof of effects as well as accounting for long-range effects. The strength and merit of rhetorical criticism ought to stand the tests of some measures of evidence. The case of the letters written by private citizens to Roosevelt following his First Fireside Chat is significant for its sheer evidentiary quality. Such a compelling rhetorical package that includes a speech, a clear account of context, and strong evidence of its effects leads the critic to invaluable insights into a rhetorical exchange and which other cases can warrant similar claims. Scholars need to look for similar instances where a complete rhetorical package allows for an assessment about the many functions of rhetoric. Absent a complete rhetorical package, indicators of effects should not result in a dismissal of the rhetorical exchange but qualify it for a more tentative assessment. And where more cautionary assessments are necessary because of a lack of direct evidence about effect, indirect evidence may be of value in affording the critic a measure of confidence in discerning the effect of a given rhetorical act. Rhetoric is action, and as such it always yields effect and thus always matters, but it is our responsibility to present it convincingly.

Notes

1. All letters sent to the president are from the President's Personal File, Franklin D. Roosevelt Presidential Library, Hyde Park, New York.

2. The Franklin D. Roosevelt Presidential Library at Hyde Park has about two thousand letters from citizens written in response to the First Fireside Chat. Historians account for some 400,000 letters written in total.

3. John Poulakos, "'Special Delivery': Rhetoric, Letter Writing, and the Question of Beauty," in *The Ethos of Rhetoric,* ed. Michael J. Hyde (Columbia: University of South Carolina Press, 2004), 92.

4. For a detailed discussion of this speech and its context see Amos Kiewe, *FDR's First Fireside Chat: The Banking Crisis and Public Confidence* (College Station: Texas A&M University Press, 2007), 37–47.

5. See Davis W. Houck, *Rhetoric as Currency: Hoover, Roosevelt and the Great Depression* (College Station: Texas A&M University Press, 2001), 4–7.

6. Houck, *Rhetoric as Currency,* 179.

7. Jonathan Alter, *The Defining Moment: FDR's Hundred Days and the Triumph of Hope* (New York: Simon and Schuster, 2006), 249.

8. The Trading with the Enemy Act of 1917 prohibited trading with enemy states which Roosevelt modified to the prohibition of hoarding gold and silver. See Kiewe, *FDR's First Fireside Chat,* 53.

9. Kiewe, *FDR's First Fireside Chat,* 48–73.

10. Franklin D. Roosevelt, Fireside Chat, Number One, "The Banking Crisis," March 12, 1933, Master Speech File, No. 616a, Franklin D. Roosevelt Library. All subsequent citations of this speech are from this source.

11. George C. Edwards III, "Presidential Rhetoric: What Differences Does It Make?," in *Beyond the Rhetorical Presidency,* ed. Martin J. Medhurst (College Station: Texas A&M University Press, 1996), 200.

12. Edwards, "Presidential Rhetoric," 210.

13. George C. Edwards III, *On Deaf Ears: The Limits of the Bully Pulpit* (New Haven: Yale University Press, 2003), 93.

14. Edwards, *On Deaf Ears,* 99.

15. Kiewe, *FDR's First Fireside Chat,* 7. See also Frank Freidel, *Franklin D. Roosevelt: Launching the New Deal* (Boston: Little, Brown, 1973), 234.

16. Kiewe, *FDR's First Fireside Chat,* 101. In 1947, congressional testimony of RFC operations indicated that of the total of $3.3 billion loaned by the RFC, $3 billion had been repaid and that the net loss to the government was around $125 million. See Arthur A. Ballantine, "When All the Banks Closed," *Harvard Business Review* 26 (1948): 140–141.

17. *New York Times,* March 14, 1933, 1.

18. H. W. Brands, *Traitor to His Class: The Privileged Life and Radical Presidency of Franklin D. Roosevelt* (New York: Doubleday, 2008), 322.

19. Jonathan Alter, *FDR's Hundred Days and the Triumph of Hope* (New York: Simon and Schuster, 2006), 270.

20. Jonathan Alter, "What FDR Teaches Us," *Newsweek*, May 1, 2006, 29.

21. Brands, *Traitor to His Class*, 322.

22. Ballantine, "When All the Banks Closed," 140.

23. Though thousands of letters were sent to the president, only about two thousand are archived at the Franklin D. Roosevelt Presidential Library in Hyde Park, New York.

24. Richard A. Cherwitz and John Theobald-Osborne, "Contemporary Developments in Rhetorical Criticism: A Consideration of the Effects of Rhetoric," in *Speech Communication: Essays to Commemorate the 75th Anniversary of the Speech Communication Association*, ed. Gerald M. Phillips and Julia T. Wood (Carbondale: Southern Illinois University Press, 1990), 52–80.

25. For example, G. R. Boynton points to how audiences of political rhetoric are interacting today with speakers by resorting to Twitter and engaging other audience members by re-tweeting after reading the tweets of others. He concludes that "the audience has become many as they have become speakers." Boynton, "Reframing Audience: Co-motion at #SOTU," paper presented at the annual meeting of the Rhetoric Society of America, Philadelphia, Pa., May 24–27, 2012.

26. Michael Leff and Andrew Sachs, "Words the Most Like Things: Iconicity and the Rhetorical Text," *Western Communication Journal* 54 (1990): 256.

Why We Love to Hate Larry Kramer

Or, the Polemic's Queer Rhetorical Effects

ERIN J. RAND

"With this article I am calling for a MASSIVE DISRUPTION of the Sixth International AIDS Conference that is being held in San Francisco June 20–24."[1] Thus begins Larry Kramer's 1990 essay "A Call to Riot," whose title and explicit language seem to leave no doubt about his desired outcomes: "WE MUST RIOT! I AM CALLING FOR A FUCKING RIOT!" he proclaims. "WE MUST RIOT IN SAN FRANCISCO!"[2] After reiterating yet again his initial request for a "massive disruption," Kramer concludes his article with what reads as a demonstrator's chant: "MASSIVE! DISRUPTION! RIOT! LIFE!"[3]

Kramer is a prominent gay rights and AIDS activist who played a pivotal role in the founding of both the Gay Men's Health Crisis (GMHC) in 1981 and AIDS Coalition to Unleash Power (ACT UP) in 1987. A prolific speechmaker and editorialist, Kramer is also known, somewhat surprisingly, for being an extremely harsh critic of his fellow gay men. His invectives often take on what he sees as the risky sexual behaviors and apathetic organizing within the gay community, arguing that the fight against AIDS should be more militant. Kramer's scathing criticisms are generally loud and emotional and, like "A Call to Riot," typically make liberal use of boldface type, capital letters, and multiple exclamation points. His propensity to be shrill and nearly hysterical in both speech and print, provoking the ire of gay activists and academics alike, has led to his reputation as an angry prophet, a moralist, and a polemicist.

So forceful and pointed are Kramer's appeals in "A Call to Riot" that there seems to be little room for misunderstanding or misinterpreting his intended effects; indeed, numerous precautions were taken at the San Francisco AIDS conference to contain the potential uprising, and many in San Francisco's gay community were angry at him for his provocation. However, when the piece was reprinted four years later in *Reports from the Holocaust,* Kramer's compilation of his speeches, essays, and letters from 1978 to 1993, his commentary about the article suggests that his intentions might not have been as plain as they seemed. In a passage that is as muddy as "A Call to Riot" is clear, Kramer attempts to explain his use of the word "riot": "I hadn't given much thought to just what I meant by 'riot.' Or rather I knew what I meant but what I meant and what others thought I meant and what the word means were construed very differently by many people. . . . I didn't mean violence, though I can see where it's possible to read into my text that, if you are prone to it, by all means."[4] Despite the explicitness of his objectives, Kramer is clearly quite concerned, at least retrospectively, with the potential for unintended meanings and effects of his words. He finds it "sort of funny" that his article was thought to be a call for violence but also expresses his disappointment that the demonstration in San Francisco turned out to be relatively tame.[5] His unease about the effects of his polemics speaks to their tendency to be somewhat uncontrollable or excessive; interestingly, this anxiety is mirrored by those queer academic writers of the early 1990s who were in the vanguard of queer theory's emergence in the academy. In this case, however, queer theorists engage in a continual refutation of Kramer, staking out their own stances in opposition to his, as if their objections to his positions can never be sufficiently expressed and the effects of his words never sufficiently contained.

If the directness and vehemence of Kramer's polemics seem to indicate that there is no space within this form for interruptive or contrary readings, their tendency to create unintended effects would suggest otherwise. Thus, it is not merely because of Kramer's caustic style and personality or the inflammatory nature of his words that his views have come to occupy such a central (if contentious) position among AIDS activists, within the queer community, and in queer theoretical work. Rather, this is also a result of the polemical form in which his invectives so often are delivered. The effects of Kramer's words emerge across a range of different sites (such as academia and activist practices), highlighting the extent to which polemics are apt to be put to unexpected uses and to have effects that exceed the instrumental. Instead of viewing this unpredictability of the polemical form as a limitation to its usefulness, I understand it as the source of the polemic's productive possibilities to create change. That is, the polemicist's inability to control the effects of the polemic is precisely the necessary condition for the enactment of agency; likewise, unexpected instances of agency may be among the polemic's queer rhetorical effects. This is not to say that the substance of a polemic is necessarily or even usually resistant or progressive but that the form itself enables rhetorical acts that do not merely repeat the status quo.

As a rhetorical form that reveals the general economy of undecidability from which agency emerges, then, the polemic, especially as Kramer wields it, is productively excessive and provocatively queer. By casting the polemic as a queer rhetorical form, I do not mean to suggest that it is a form essentially suited to queers, that it marks gendered or sexual difference, or that it promotes resistance or opposition. Instead, I am claiming as queerness the lack of a necessary or predictable relation between an intending agent and the effects of speech or action. I am thus working against the prevailing academic and popular trends to employ "queer" either as an umbrella term for "gay, lesbian, bisexual, and transgender" identities or as a label for sexualities and politics that disrupt the hetero/homo binary. In other words, this is a de-essentialized notion of queerness that disconnects "queer" from any particular referent and instead refigures it as the undecidability from which rhetorical agency is actualized. The often maligned polemic thus accentuates this undecidability, revealing agency itself as a kind of effect that far exceeds the internal dynamics or persuasive capacity of the text.

To consider the relationship between agency and rhetorical form is certainly nothing new; Karlyn Kohrs Campbell, for example, long has been committed to the formal and generic dimensions of rhetorical agency and identifies the "power of form" as one of the elements central to an audience's ability to take up, categorize, and understand any symbolic act. Campbell explains, "Form is the foundation of all communication, but it is also a type of agency that has a power to separate a text from its nominal author and from its originary moment of performance." Form, for Campbell, is a means for moving away from a rhetor-centered notion of agency; she argues, "agency is textual or, put differently, texts have agency," by which she means that "textual agency is linked to audiences and begins with the signals that guide the process of 'uptake' for readers or listeners enabling them to categorize, to understand how a symbolic act is to be framed."[6] While Campbell's initial claim that "agency is textual" is provocative, what poses as a simple restatement—"put differently, texts have agency"—actually says something quite dissimilar. The textuality of agency refers not to the location or possession of agency but to the fact that agency can be exercised only through available and socially recognizable forms of discourse. Thus, agency's "text" is more properly understood in terms of Jacques Derrida's *texte*—the weave of language through which we can have knowledge of the world and actions can come to make sense.[7] Although particular forms of speech and writing enable agency by allowing for specific kinds of uptake, neither texts nor rhetors "have" agency separate from their contextual articulations.

This notion of form begins with Kenneth Burke's statement that "A work has form in so far as one part of it leads a reader to anticipate another part, to be gratified by the sequence."[8] Since form both creates and satisfies a need, Burke contends that "form *is* the appeal."[9] In a similar vein, Lloyd Bitzer suggests that forms arise from recurring rhetorical situations. He argues, "From day to day, year to year, comparable situations occur, prompting comparable responses; hence rhetorical forms are born and a special vocabulary, grammar, and style are established . . . a form of discourse is not only established but comes to have a power of its own—the tradition itself tends to function as a constraint upon any new response in the form."[10] For Bitzer, rhetorical forms are not simply dictated by the particular situation in which a rhetor finds himself but also influence what can be said in that situation and, by implication, how an audience comes to understand or make sense of what is said. My focus on rhetorical form, then, is less concerned with definitively labeling a text according to the features of a particular form and more interested in noticing how that text enables rhetorical agency as a result of being *received as* a certain kind of form. That is, rhetorical forms are recognizable conventions within which discourse can be intelligible, and they both produce and constrain the force and effects of a text.

Following Campbell's lead to showcase the role of form in agency but resisting the temptation to simply relocate agency from the humanistic subject to the text itself, I employ rhetorical form to explain how texts can be recognizable and intelligible to particular audiences in particular situations and how agency can arise as an effect of a text's circulation. Through a formal reading of Kramer's polemics, then, I argue that one of rhetoric's effects can be the agency enabled by a text's formal features. I view rhetorical agency as the ability for words and/or actions to come to make sense and therefore to create effects through their particular formal and stylistic conventions. These conventions are, I contend, specific materializations of institutional power, and, as such, they are both productive (they enable the force of a text) and constraining (they determine the limits of intelligibility). Hence, rhetorical agency resides neither in the rhetor nor in the text but arises from the positioning of discourse in terms of its formal features.

In this essay, I begin by describing and situating Larry Kramer and his performances of verbal and textual invective within the context of AIDS and queer activism of the early 1990s. I then read Kramer's polemics and queer theorists' responses to them in order to advance three interrelated arguments about polemics, agency, and rhetoric's effects. First, I develop an extensive formal theory of polemics that describes the constellation of rhetorical features suggested by Kramer's polemics. Second, I propose that queer theorists' criticisms of Kramer are, in part, a strategic repudiation of the uncontrollable nature of the polemical form and that the institutional agency of the field of queer theory is one of Kramer's polemics' unexpected effects. Third, I contend that the polemic, by highlighting the risks and undecidability of agency, illustrates the queer unpredictability that is the condition of possibility for all rhetorical action. In other words, I argue not only that the polemic has unique rhetorical features but also that these features entail rhetorical effects—in this case, in the realms of both AIDS activism and academic queer theory—that are identifiable but not predicted or determined by the text itself.

Larry Kramer, Angry AIDS Activist

As one of the most outspoken and visible activists and critics in the gay community and as something of a self-elected spokesperson for gay men since the early years of the AIDS crisis, Larry Kramer expressed opinions about the gay community's sexual behavior and activist practices that were often unpopular. While other AIDS activists were attempting to counter the common sentiment that gay men were to blame for the AIDS virus, Kramer adamantly indicted the gay community for what he perceived to be its failure to give up potentially risky sexual practices and to take action on its own behalf. In "1,112 and Counting," for example, he attempts to prod his community into action, asking, "Why isn't every gay man in this city so scared shitless that he is screaming for action? Does every gay man in New York *want* to die?"[11] In case these questions do not move his listeners to the desired response, he follows them with a direct and damning accusation: "Every gay man who is unable to come forward now and fight to save his own life is truly helping to kill the rest of us."[12]

Though Kramer certainly acknowledges the apathy of government and medical institutions in dealing with AIDS and the obstacles that many gay men have faced in receiving proper medical treatment and effective drugs, he is strident in his belief that it is the gay community's responsibility to take on these injustices. For instance, while speaking to a group at the Gay and Lesbian Community Center in New York in 1987, Kramer contends that the response from the gay community to the devastation of its own ranks has been woefully insufficient, and he attempts to goad his audience into doing more: "How long does it take before you get angry and fight back? I sometimes think we have a death wish. I think we must want to die. . . . I have heard of denial, but this is more than denial; it *is* a death wish. I don't want to die. I cannot believe that you *want* to die. But what are we doing, *really*, to save our own lives? . . . What does it take for us to take responsibility for our own lives? Because we are *not*—we are not taking responsibility for our own lives."[13] Kramer laments the divisiveness, in-fighting, and uncooperativeness that his community has displayed up to this point—even in the face of an extended and deadly crisis. Ultimately, in the midst of issuing dire warnings about the consequences of such disorganization, Kramer concludes, "It's our fault, boys and girls. It's our fault."[14] Although Kramer's words suggest negativity and fatalism, not to mention condescension, this speech at the Gay and Lesbian Community Center eventually resulted in the formation of ACT UP, whose activism has been immeasurably significant to the fight against the AIDS epidemic.[15]

Kramer is a fascinating case study in part because he straddles uneasily the roles of activist, journalist, community spokesperson, and rabble-rouser; hence, the tendency for polemics to create unintended effects is amplified by the array of audiences to which Kramer's words are addressed and the variety of soapboxes from which he has disseminated his messages. For instance, he has written a number of novels and plays, including *The Normal Heart* (1985), the best-selling gay novel *Faggots* (1978), and the screenplay for D. H. Lawrence's *Women in Love* (1969). Published often in the op-ed pages of the *New York Times*, Kramer also has been invited to speak at numerous public events since the early 1980s.[16] He appeared on the cover of the *Advocate* in 1992 and was featured on the cover of *Newsweek* in 2001, where his AIDS activism over the years was chronicled in the magazine's special report "AIDS at 20."

While many authors within both the academy and the mainstream press have engaged the logic of Kramer's arguments, their moral or psychological implications, and their repercussions for queer politics, little attention has been paid to the form in which his words are habitually delivered. In some cases, the polemical form of Kramer's messages is justified in terms of exigency; that is, while polemics may not be a preferred method of public address, Kramer's rhetorical choices are explained or excused by the dire situation that he and other HIV-positive gay men faced. At other times,

Kramer's polemics are understood as a matter of his inflammatory personality and style: in order to get at the potentially worthwhile message contained in his scolding speeches, it is presumed, one must disregard the idiosyncratic arrogance, impatience, and fury with which that message is delivered. In other words, the polemical nature of Kramer's speeches and essays has been treated as at least incidental to their content, if not actually as a hindrance to or distraction from it. I want to suggest, in contrast, that the polemic itself, as a rhetorical form, has a peculiar kind of force and that it is integral to the rhetorical effects of Kramer's words.

Theorizing the Polemic

Attempting to understand the polemic as a rhetorical form presents an immediate problem: the most basic and common definitions of "polemic" describe only the content of a text. For instance, polemics are often understood to be nearly synonymous with controversy; as one of the *OED*'s primary definitions explains, a polemic is "a controversial argument or discussion" or an "aggressive controversy." This definition does little to identify what is unique about the polemic as a rhetorical form, and it does not address the way in which the polemic functions within a controversy. After all, while all polemics may be controversial, not all controversies are polemical. Furthermore, the derision with which polemics are generally regarded, whether because they appear to intentionally and flagrantly disregard reason or because they rely on persuasion at the expense of verifiable evidence, cannot be accounted for by a definition that considers polemics only in terms of controversy. Etymologically speaking, "polemic" is an adaptation of the Greek *polemikos,* or "warlike." Although many wars may be controversial, controversy does not adequately define war, since wars begin precisely when more reasoned, thoughtful means of argumentation or persuasion have been exhausted. Wars, like polemics, are neither fine-tuned instruments for working through the issues at hand nor meant to advance nuanced, rational arguments; instead, they are an attempt to reach resolution through forceful or violent means when more civil and peaceful methods have proven unsuccessful.

Ultimately, when "the polemical" is reduced to "the controversial," the features that distinguish polemics from controversies and the elements of polemics that earn them disfavor are erased. Therefore, rather than understanding the polemic *in terms of* the controversial, I consider it instead as a rhetorical move that sometimes occurs *within* a given controversy. Using Kramer's texts as a guide and a resource, I identify four specific rhetorical features that, collectively, are unique to the polemical form: alienating expressions of emotion, noncontingent assertions of truth, presumptions of shared morality, and the constitution of enemies, audiences, and publics. None of these individual features belongs exclusively to the polemic; rather, it is through their concurrence that they give shape to the polemic as a recognizable rhetorical form.

Alienating Expressions of Emotion

One of the most overt and frequently remarked aspects of Kramer's characteristic texts is his intense and undisguised anger. For instance, in the conclusion to a flyer he distributed to all the guests at a dinner honoring President Bill Clinton's Health and Human Services secretary, Kramer writes, "This new president made us promises and has done nothing to implement these promises or to even discuss with us the possibilities of implementing these promises. We have been completely shut out from any discussions which is bad enough until you realize *there aren't even any discussions going on!* Why do people never believe me until it's too late?! We are being intentionally allowed to die!"[17] In addition to the underscoring that Kramer uses to emphasize certain portions of his text, the font grows progressively bigger toward the bottom of the flyer, until the final sentence—in large boldface type with a double underline—leaps off the page with furious vehemence.

The anger that is textually depicted in this flyer mimics Kramer's usual manner of delivering speeches or writing essays: he commonly builds to a crescendo of rage and indignation that is accompanied by shouting or multiple exclamation points. His reputation for delivering shrill invectives has led *The Advocate* to describe him on its cover as "America's angriest AIDS activist" and *Newsweek* to suggest that when he dies it will be "furiously and uncooperatively."[18] Indeed, the salience of anger is often noted as a primary component of polemics in general. Kathryn Thomas Flannery, for instance, considers polemics as a textual performance of rage, while Jonathan Crewe explains the academic denial of polemics in terms of their violence, belligerence, and aggression.[19]

Of course, emotional appeals are used liberally in many different kinds of public address as a means to persuade or motivate an audience. What is unique about the emotion that operates in polemics is that it does not function as an appeal made through *pathos;* instead, the emotion is performed formally through the text's structural elements. That is, Kramer's angry speeches do not attempt to elicit anger from the audience, unite the audience through a shared sense of anger, or move it to action based on emotion; rather, Kramer performs his own anger at what he perceives to be the audience's failure to behave in the way that he desires, and his performance adheres to a consistent formal pattern in which a series of factual statements rapidly swells to a climactic display of fury and frustration. Sometimes these overflowing expressions of anger seem to work against the apparent goals of his texts, since members of the audience may react negatively to his accusations. Kramer acknowledges this possibility but nevertheless refuses to temper his anger: "I talk that way for a reason," he states. "We don't have time to talk pretty. We don't have time to not try to shake things up."[20] The use of emotion in Kramer's polemics, then, does not function rhetorically in a traditional manner: not only does it violate expectations about decorum in public speaking, but also it is just as likely to alienate—rather than satisfy or motivate—the audience.

Noncontingent Assertions of Truth

Though they may be off-putting or even offensive to his audience, Kramer always presents his expressions of emotion as a natural and legitimate reaction to a truth—or to the violation of a truth—which is, for him, self-evident. For instance, he consistently demonstrates his impatience with gay men who are not helping to fight the battle against AIDS. Part of this struggle, he contends in "1,112 and Counting," involves coming out: "I am sick of closeted gays. . . . There is only one thing that's going to save some of us, and this is *numbers* and pressure and our being perceived as united and a threat. . . . Unless we can generate, visibly, numbers, masses, we are going to die."[21] In this passage Kramer does not attempt to address the various reasons for which individuals may be unable to come out or may choose to not do so; nor does he offer evidence that coming out in large numbers is necessarily linked to empowerment or to increased AIDS research and better medical care. Instead, Kramer merely asserts unequivocally that coming out is absolutely necessary to fighting AIDS and that remaining closeted effectively kills oneself and one's community. When he states that "we are going to die," he may, as he is sometimes accused, be hysterical, extremist, or apocalyptic; more important, however, he is forwarding what is, for him, the truth about the situation in which he finds himself.

Thus, Kramer's passionate belief in a particular version of the truth, even when that truth may not be evident to others, is another characteristic of his polemical form. Polemics forgo the expected methodical construction of an argument through the presentation of evidence and logic in favor of a simple declaration or indictment. The tendency to assert a truth that is not dependent on context, consensus, or logical proof appears so contradictory to the contingency of rhetoric that some have described it as "antirhetorical directness."[22] For example, according to Flannery, the antirhetorical directness of second-wave feminists was demonstrated by their willingness to offer their beliefs as unequivocally true. Polemics are antirhetorical, she explains, because "the polemicist writes out of a belief in a cause or a truth rather than in terms of the inevitable provisionality of a rhetorical gesture."[23] Flannery borrows the term "antirhetorical directness" from Kenneth J. E. Graham, who argues that the rhetorical is marked by dialogue and debate, involves arguing on both sides of an issue, and is necessarily social in outlook.[24] The antirhetorical, on the other hand, refuses rhetoric's tentativeness and need for consensus, involves a nonrhetorical way of knowing and being, and makes "a certain kind of claim to truth—a claim animated by an insistent demand for certainty."[25]

Graham thus narrows the realm of rhetoric to include only cooperative, dialogic, and decorous speech. Utterances that are indecorous or antagonistic, such as Kramer's contention that gay men who refuse to come out are hastening the deaths of their own community members, are not oriented toward the social and therefore are not rhetorical. Graham's notion of the "antirhetorical" is useful in identifying one of the peculiar features of polemics, then, but ultimately it disavows the way in which the form does, in fact, function rhetorically. Rather than excluding Kramer's noncontingent proclamations from the realm of rhetoric, I claim them as a specific rhetorical feature of the polemical form. In other words, when Kramer violates the norms of rhetoric that Graham asserts, his tactics cannot simply be dismissed as antirhetorical; rather, these "violations" are one of the features that define the polemic as a unique rhetorical form.

Furthermore, Kramer's declarations of truth do not merely argue on behalf of an already existent perspective within the current controversy, but they forward a truth that is highly personal. For instance, after repeatedly and forcefully proclaiming that "AIDS is intentional genocide," Kramer next pours out his words in a rush of conviction: "AIDS is intentional genocide and I know with all my heart and soul that it is intentional and I am going to say it over and over and over until I die and I may go to my death with all of you thinking I am crazy but I am going to go to my death knowing that I spoke the truth and I spoke it every single day of this plague and I spoke it over and over and over again."[26] Accenting the "intensely personal" is a crucial component of Kramer's discourse, emphasizing his emotional investment in his positions and portraying disagreements as personal affronts.[27]

Because they advocate personal realities, polemics may make intelligible those "partial" versions of the truth that cannot usually be heard in a public sphere based on the assumptions of shared experiences and a common worldview. Polemics thus abstain from expressing a supposedly universal perspective and instead emphatically endorse the particular. The unabashedly particular can be crystallized because polemics do not face the burden of establishing a common ground as a precondition for their logical appeals. Again, it is not just that the specific truth championed by a given polemic challenges the status quo but also that it is invoked through rapid repetition—literally hammered home with a series of bold and escalating assertions—rather than through rational means of argumentation.

Presumptions of Shared Morality

Since Kramer often presents his version of the truth as a foregone conclusion and without offering supporting evidence, his texts tend to take on a discomfortingly moralistic or self-righteous tone. Rather than moving his audience through a series of logical steps to forward his argument, Kramer describes his polemical truth not as a rational choice but as a moral imperative. The audience is therefore not so much persuaded as it is expected or morally obliged to believe. Consider Kramer's speech at the memorial service for his friend and fellow activist Vito Russo, who is perhaps best known for his groundbreaking book *The Celluloid Closet* and who died of AIDS in 1990. Instead of delivering the expected eulogy, Kramer launched his usual critique of the perceived inactivity of the gay community in the fight against HIV and AIDS, this time with Russo's death offered as proof of this apathy. "We killed Vito," Kramer proclaims, "[a]s sure as any virus killed him, we killed him. Everyone in this room killed him. . . . Vito was killed by 25 million gay men and lesbians who for ten long years of this plague have refused to get our act together."[28] Kramer does not deny the homophobia and outright hostility of medical and government institutions in dealing with AIDS; however, he ultimately refuses to allow the blame for the AIDS epidemic to rest on their shoulders. When medical researchers, hospitals, and insurance agencies treat people with AIDS unfairly, Kramer says, "we let them shit all over us. We let them kill us, too. We're very generous."[29]

Regardless of the larger forces that may have played a role in Russo's death, then, Kramer repeatedly returns to his bottom line: Russo died because "we didn't fight hard enough to save him."[30] In other words, the polemic that Kramer delivers in place of a eulogy resembles a sermon or a moral reprimand. Speaking as a moral leader whose stance need not be substantiated, Kramer preaches a moral truth and warns of the consequences if its integrity is not guarded. Advocating personal responsibility in the face of AIDS as a moral issue, Kramer admonishes that it is immoral to stand idly by while members of one's own community are dying. That he chose to deliver this message on an occasion usually reserved for solemn expressions of grief only adds to its polemical force. As Flannery aptly puts it, the polemicist appears to have "exceeded the bounds of good sense and good taste," therefore shifting the context of the memorial service in important ways: having once viewed it as a place only for mourning, friends and family are now morally compelled to view it also as a site of potential action and mobilization.[31]

Hence, polemics express positions that refute dominant ideologies and modes of thinking by rejecting the primacy of reason and invoking explicitly moral claims. In polemics a moral position is not simply advanced through rhetoric; morality actually does rhetorical work. When Kramer tells his audience that its inaction led to Vito Russo's death, then, his goal is not to encourage the audience to embrace a particular moral stance. Rather, his argument for the necessity of mobilization and activism is made explicitly on the basis of and through a presumed morality.

It is precisely this rootedness in morality that motivates some authors' objections to polemics. For instance, Foucault is sharply critical of the polemical form and claims he refuses to engage in it because of what he views as the morality involved in particular modes of knowing: "a whole morality is at stake, the morality that concerns the search for the truth and the relation to the other."[32] While Foucault is wary of polemics because of the ways in which they bring together morality and truth, Kramer seems happy to acknowledge the extent to which he views his own moral position as coterminous with the truth. Kramer does not deny the moral underpinnings of his polemics against the sexual promiscuity of the gay community, encouraging those who accuse him of being a "moralist": "nothing they could say would please me more," he accedes. In fact, he prefers this role to that of an activist: "I've always slightly bristled when I'm described as an 'activist.' It's a word I'm uncomfortable with."[33] Kramer's religious, moralistic tone is not lost on his readers and reviewers, who tend to describe him as "evangelical" or as a "prophet."[34] For Kramer, being an activist is associated with being "radical"; as a moralist, however, he is being "eminently sensible" or merely telling the truth.[35]

Constitution of Enemies, Audiences, and Publics

Thus far I have described the rhetorical features of the polemic only in terms of the author's contributions to the form, but the most intriguing and important characteristic of the polemic is the way in which it constitutes enemies, audiences, and publics. In keeping with his emphasis on truth and morality, Kramer does not present a set of objective facts for his audience to review; on the contrary, at every moment he attempts to dissolve the distance between the audience and the text by implicating the audience as the cause of the problem, the means for a solution, and the community that is affected by both. One way in which he promotes this complicity is through the use of questions that explicitly or implicitly position the audience as already part of a defined group. For instance, when Kramer asks, "Do you, as a member of a community of liberal and caring and thinking people, accept that a plague can be going on and you are doing nothing to stop it?," he both constructs his audience as "liberal, caring, thinking people" and defines the actions that are expected of such a group.[36] The audience does not merely receive or attend to Kramer's words; rather, the text cultivates the partisanship of the audience, and the audience's participation, whether as skeptics or as believers, inflects the polemical form of the text.

Both John Angus Campbell and Flannery note the ways in which polemical texts force their readers out of the role of passive, nonaligned recipients of information and into more active, participatory positions. For example, Campbell describes how Darwin's dialectical rhythm in *On the Origin of Species* makes readers feel as if they are involved in compiling the evidence and building the logical structure that eventually leads to his conclusions. "At each step along the way," Campbell explains, "Darwin tried to turn his readers from spectators into partisans."[37] Similarly, Flannery contends that polemic adjectivally names a particular kind of orientation or attitude of the reader toward the text. That is, the polemic dissolves the illusion of a reader's dispassionate, objective stance: "Polemic forces an awareness of one's relationship to a text, forces a recognition of how one is positioned by a text, and thus is openly partisan."[38] In short, polemics function to modify not only individual identities but also reader/text relationships in such a way that the allegiances of the reader or audience are shaped by the text itself.

The effects of the polemic are not limited, however, to individuals' relationships to the text. As a number of rhetorical scholars have noted, texts not only address particular "actual" audiences but also constitute imagined groups of people ideologically as those who are addressed or ignored by the text, or even as those who must be secretly complicitous with the text.[39] Hence, Kramer's polemics address—and, through this address, constitute—certain imagined audiences among their readers or listeners. Because polemics virtually always function in opposition to another persona, point of view, or ideology, the construction of the audience takes place in conjunction with the construction of an *enemy* (after all, it is difficult to imagine a polemic that does not rail "against" someone or something). This feature of the polemic is one that Foucault finds especially problematic. In contrast to the partnership that is developed within a dialogue, he contends, the polemicist refuses to question her or his own position or rights, and "the person he [*sic*] confronts is not a partner in the search for the truth, but an adversary, an enemy who is wrong, who is harmful and whose very existence constitutes a threat."[40]

The constitution of an audience and an enemy in Kramer's texts is further complicated by his propensity for scolding, chastising, and otherwise indicting the very group of people on whose behalf he is ostensibly speaking. That is, Kramer condemns what he sees as gay men's irresponsible promiscuity, but in so doing he provokes and offends the very constituency—other gay men—whose support he is supposedly soliciting. He reprimands them: "I am sick of guys who moan that giving up careless sex until this blows over is worse than death. How can they value life so little and cocks and asses so much? . . . I am sick of guys who think that all being gay means is sex in the first place. I am sick of guys who can only think with their cocks."[41] Kramer even goes so far as to tell his audience, "I condemn all of you for your hypocrisy and your silence. . . . Yes, I hate all of you for what you don't do and see."[42]

What is fascinating about polemics, then, is that the enemy and the audience are not just related but closely aligned, perhaps barely distinguishable, factions of the same groups. Foucault is right in noting that the one addressed by a polemic is constituted as an enemy, but he does not acknowledge that in polemical discourse this enemy is also likely to be, as he puts it, "a partner in the search for the truth." Flannery notes that the proximity of the enemy, as it is figured within the polemic, is one of the features unique to this form and what gives the polemic its characteristic "heat":

> What readers may notice as the relative emotional intensity of polemic . . . can be tied not simply to the degree of heat fueled by a commitment to a cause but also the relative proximity of opposition. It is one thing to complain about some distant enemy, and another when one shares much in common with the opponent, when the opponent perhaps has been (or may yet be) an ally. The heat seems to come, in other words, in part from the falling away of a friend—or the potential falling away of a friend—as much as the egregious behavior of an alien and unfamiliar Other.[43]

While the polemicist may share a great deal in common with this immediate or "proximate" enemy, her opposition still takes place in the context of a larger battle. As Flannery points out, second-wave feminists' polemics often were directed against other women in the movement, but ultimately these polemics also figured a more distant enemy—patriarchy or male chauvinism—against which both groups must be aligned. In other words, polemics construct both a proximate enemy (those against whom the polemic is explicitly directed) and a distant enemy (the larger cultural issues that underlie the immediate opposition).

Significantly, the proximate enemy of the polemic is also, at least to some extent, its intended audience. The audience that is constituted by the polemic can never, therefore, be a homogenous group but is marked by internal contradictions and perhaps outright hostility. In Kramer's polemics against the sexual practices of the gay male community, then, his criticisms of activists and gay men might be understood to constitute them as not only the proximate opponent but also as his primary audience; the distant enemy, on the other hand, is the larger homophobic culture. Kramer is able, therefore, to chastise gay men for what he views as their irresponsible promiscuity, while simultaneously explaining that promiscuity as a result of the sanctions against recognized monogamous same-sex relationships. The anger that is often aroused in those who disagree with Kramer's perspective—those who refuse to cede gay men's right to sexual freedom—appears as a consequence of the internecine "heat" to which Flannery refers. Ultimately, Flannery contends that the purpose of the polemic is not to resolve potential conflicts but actually to exploit them. "[P]olemic hinges on identifying areas of contestation," she explains, but not in order to "smooth over those contested areas or to make them go away." Instead, polemic "seeks to resist closure in order to activate agency among the proximate audience."[44] Thus, even though Kramer's polemics may appear to endorse views that are damaging to the queer community, they may nevertheless "activate agency" in those whom they address, enabling not only agreement but also vehement opposition.

Flannery's description of polemics offers a provocative reading of their tendency to lash out at would-be allies as a potentially productive function, but her argument is rooted in a notion of agency that locates the ability to act within individuals, rather than in the institutional forces that make the effects of certain actions intelligible. That is, Flannery understands the agency that arises from polemics to reside in those who hear or read them; the "contested areas" that the polemic highlights provide a space or a motivation for the audience to act. Hence, Flannery's notion of agency fails to account for the ways in which polemics might be used against the grain or be taken up by other audiences and for other purposes.

The rhetorical agency arising from polemics, as well as their construction of audiences and publics, must be conceptualized not through a humanistic understanding of the agency of individuals but through the force of institutions, where form appears as a particular manifestation of institutional power. That is, the conventions of the polemic, as a recognizable rhetorical form, enable the force and effects of discourse. For example, John H. Smith reads Hegel's Jena essays, which were written relatively early in his career, prior to the *Phenomenology of Spirit,* as explicitly polemical. Smith suggests that Hegel adopts a rhetorical, polemical stance in order to enter into the "dialectic of *Kritik,*" or to develop a position from which to make his argument. The goal of Hegel's polemics, then, was to "establish an *audience* that will adopt his assumptions."[45] It is the establishment of an assenting audience through polemic, not the ability of any individual to act as a result of the polemic, that is important to Hegel. While the polemic certainly functions here to "activate agency," as Flannery puts it, this is not an agency that is tied to Hegel himself, to Hegel's texts, or to any particular audience member; rather, it is an institutional agency with the production and distribution of particular kinds of ideas as one of its effects. To put this differently, Hegel's texts constitute a public within which his ideas can circulate.

Also attending to the polemic's activation of institutional agency through the constitution of audiences or publics, Arditi and Valentine argue that polemics produce communities without necessarily reconciling contested issues. They contend that not only are the issues at stake and the identities of those involved shaped by polemics, but also "the very configuration of the field where their engagement is enacted" is effected.[46] That is, polemics produce the public space that enables democratic struggles and political disputes. Accordingly, the agency that arises from a polemic is not the agency of a particular collection of audience members but that provided by a public space in which it becomes possible to speak in the name of or make claims on behalf of particular socially recognized groups.

The possibility for public deliberation, for Arditi and Valentine, is understood through a spatial metaphor; polemics, that is, produce not publics but public space. In order to account for the ways in which texts or ideas may travel not just spatially but also temporally, their notion of public space must be supplemented by the kind of publicity that Michael Warner forwards, in which publics are constituted specifically through the circulation of texts.[47] As Warner explains, texts "can be picked up at different times and in different places by otherwise unrelated people," and we must therefore "imagine a public as an entity that embraces all the users of that text, whoever they might be."[48] By attending to the sometimes asynchronous temporality of Kramer's polemics, then, we can begin to glimpse some of their unforeseen consequences for the proliferation and institutionalization of queer theory. These effects emerge at moments that are temporally distant from the delivery or publication of the polemic texts themselves, posing a distinct challenge to the usual manners of assessing rhetoric's effects. The publics that polemics produce, then, incorporate the unpredictability of the future uses to which the polemic might be put and accentuate the extent to which the polemic's author cannot control the circulation or effects of the text.

The Polemic's Queer Rhetorical Effects

Although the polemic might be identified as a rhetorical form by the concurrence of features that I have described thus far, the rhetorical effects of polemics are never fully determined by these features. Of course, one cannot regulate or predict the circulation of any text, regardless of form, but the characteristics of polemics make them especially prone to being put to unforeseen uses. Perhaps the most unlikely effect of Kramer's polemics has been the productive disciplinary function they have served for the field of queer theory. In spite of Kramer's pivotal role in the mobilization of AIDS activism, when his positions have been engaged in queer scholarship, it is generally in order to repudiate them and to distance the authors from Kramer's ostensibly conservative politics. Frequently present in early queer theory as a favorite rival, Larry

Kramer is a figure, it seems, that queer theorists love to hate. Because of the volume of queer theoretical work devoted to discussions and refutations of Kramer's politics, the institutionalization of academic queer theory exhibits a strange reliance not only on the existence of Kramer but also on the polemic form in which he proclaims his opinions. Thus, as Kramer's polemics provided ample fodder for queer theorists' critical perspectives, they inadvertently enabled not just the agency of individual authors but also a kind of institutional agency as the field of queer theory grew.

For example, Douglas Crimp, perhaps Kramer's most consistent academic antagonist, wrote a number of essays during the 1980s and 1990s in response to and criticism of Kramer's positions, and he compiled many of them in his 2002 book, *Melancholia and Moralism: Essays on AIDS and Queer Politics*.[49] In Crimp's 1987 essay "How to Have Promiscuity in an Epidemic," for instance, he takes on the "ignorance of and contempt for the gay movement," as well as the advocacy for monogamy that is demonstrated by Kramer's play *The Normal Heart*.[50] Fifteen years later, in "Sex and Sensibility" Crimp again engages with Kramer's "moralistic attacks . . . on gay men's sexual desires, behaviors, and public sexual spaces."[51] Writers like Kramer, Crimp contends, "virtually invite a restigmatization of AIDS" by condemning gay men for spreading the AIDS virus without attempting to understand why they might have unsafe sex."[52]

Unlike Crimp, Lee Edelman does not position himself explicitly against Kramer's views; however, his careful analysis of various sites of discourse about HIV transmission reveals the same discomfort with Kramer's perspectives. Edelman compares Kramer's statements at Vito Russo's memorial, in which he castigated members of the gay community for "killing each other" by failing to organize, with Patrick Buchanan's argument that homosexuals (and others with AIDS) "have killed themselves because they could not or would not control their suicidal appetites."[53] Given Buchanan's extreme homophobia and his notorious proclamations that AIDS is "nature's retribution" for sexual deviance, the linkage of his remarks with Kramer's is surely an unexpected uptake of *both* texts.[54] Edelman suggests that while Kramer and Buchanan undoubtedly had different motivations for their comments, the similarity of their polemics "*certainly* bespeaks a political investment in a shared ideology of the subject."[55] In other words, though Edelman does not criticize Kramer at the level of his overt positions, he suggests that the ideology of the subject that Kramer endorses is ultimately problematic for progressive gay and lesbian politics.[56]

In contrast to Kramer's writings and speeches, which are directed toward popular audiences and are delivered through mainstream newspapers and magazines or in public venues, both Crimp's and Edelman's essays appear primarily in academic journals, conferences, and books. Hence, the controversies of AIDS activism and queer politics are resituated, textualized, and critically engaged within the realm of academic queer theory. Importantly, it is only through Crimp's or Edelman's own essays that their debates with Kramer might be said to take place; if the arguments described in their writing reflect an actual conversation that occurred elsewhere, it is not available to those reading the essays, and a refutation of their positions is not developed in Kramer's work. That is, Kramer's position appears for queer theorists only as represented by other queer theorists; Kramer himself is not published in the same journals or books, and he does not similarly critique his academic opponents. Furthermore, there is a temporal gap between the publication of Kramer's editorials or the delivery of his speeches and the academic criticism that is generated in response. In some cases, this delay is more than a decade long, as in the recirculation of Crimp's critiques of Kramer in his 2002 book. The stakes of this "conversation" between Kramer and certain queer theorists, then, are clearly not equal for both parties: Crimp's and Edelman's critiques do not reach Kramer's primary audiences and Kramer does not engage (or even directly acknowledge) them, but his polemics are the subject of fervent examination and debate by queer theorists.

This is a matter not merely of Kramer being cited in a range of discursive contexts or of queer theorists disagreeing with views but of the polemic's queer rhetorical effects: the uptake of Kramer's work enables a certain kind of institutional agency and serves disciplinary functions for the field of queer theory. The frequent refutations of Kramer's work by early queer theorists perform a definitional and territorial gesture whereby queer theory's unique theoretical and political identity is staked out in the world of academia. Furthermore, because Kramer's polemics are delivered in a form that flouts conventions of reason and logical argumentation, they are useful to queer theorists as a foil to the highly complex, rational, and theoretically based language of queer theory. They also establish the field's import for the material lives of queers, serving as a foothold for queer scholarship by providing the necessary link to politics and urgent contemporary issues. In other words, the debates with Kramer help facilitate queer theory's claim to political interventions and effects, while the emphatic condemnation of his polemical, moralistic form underscores queer theory's merit as an academic pursuit.[57] As queer theorists reject Kramer's positions, then, their academic criticisms of him are canonized in this new field; thus, the institutionalization of queer theory is indebted to the existence of Kramer's polemics. This is an effect catalyzed by the polemical form of Kramer's work that most certainly exceeds and contradicts Kramer's own intentions. Ironically, it seems to contradict queer theorists' intentions as well: by taking Kramer up as their opponent, they tend to repeat and recirculate to ever larger audiences the very views that they find harmful and dangerous to queers. Nonetheless, the vehemence with which queer theorists tend to repudiate Kramer's polemics (therefore installing them at the very heart of the field) bespeaks the importance of this definitional gesture, whereby the deferral of the queerness of polemics enables the agency of queer theory as an academic discipline.

As this example of the unexpected uptake and effects of Kramer's polemics illustrates, even as his texts are formally consistent and gratifying, they have a disconcerting tendency to spin out of his control, and their potential to create other effects is never fully contained. In fact, it is the extent to which the polemic's effects are unpredictable and excessive—as evidenced by Kramer's clarification of his intentions in "A Call to Riot" and other works and by queer theorists' anxiety about distinguishing their own views from Kramer's—that makes this form so productive in terms of the rhetorical agency it enables. The excessive nature of polemics prohibits a predictable connection between the delivery of the polemic and the dispersal of the polemic's effects. Although this gap between the act and effects is especially evident in polemics, it is not unique to this form; rather, polemics draw attention to the undecidability that functions as the economy out of which all agency arises. As a form that makes this undecidability especially available to exploration and exploitation, the polemic is therefore productively queer; that is, because it is excessive and promotes a heightened attention to the possibility for failure, it enables action toward unforeseen ends and underscores the riskiness of all action.

Unhinging queerness from a specific sexual or political referent in this manner does not desexualize or depoliticize the implications of the queerness of agency. As Edelman argues in his discussion of homosexuality's relationship to language and writing, homosexuality not only is available to signification but also comes to "signify the instability of the signifying function per se, the arbitrary and tenuous nature of the relationship between any signifier and signified."[58] It is not merely that homosexuality is the binary opposite of heterosexuality, then, but that homosexuality also marks "the potential permeability of every sexual signifier—and by extension, of every signifier as such—by an 'alien' signification."[59] Thus, Edelman notes that sexuality is always already embedded in language; more important, he contends that it is homosexuality in particular that both enables and perpetually destabilizes language's signifying function.[60]

Similarly, I understand queerness as both the resource through which rhetorical agency is possible and the excess and unpredictability that shape the dispersion of effects of a rhetorical act. Any instance of rhetorical agency arises from a catachrestic but provisional gesture that defers temporarily the possibility of acting or speaking otherwise and that inaugurates the illusion of the intending subject: as queer theorists stake out a particular definition and political project for "queer" through their opposition to Kramer, it is precisely that which is the most queer—the excessive and unpredictable character of Kramer's polemics—that is deferred.[61] Thus, I label the undecidability of polemics as queer neither capriciously nor arbitrarily; rather, I make this assignation precisely because of the relevance of the queer to the exercise of rhetorical agency in this situation.

By divorcing queerness from specific categories of identity or brands of politics, I am featuring the polemical form as a means for emphasizing the riskiness of acting, for highlighting the potential for the failure of the sovereignty of intentionality, and as an actualization of the queerness of rhetorical agency. The polemic, then, is no more likely to be progressive, radical, or resistant in its content or in its effects than any other form. On the contrary, redeeming the polemic's productivity as a rhetorical form—regardless of content—takes seriously the centrality of risk and unpredictability to agency. That is, it admits that polemics are likely to be employed across a range of political perspectives and toward a variety of ends (whether admirable or distasteful) and that, while a text's formal features help determine its effects, these effects are never *determined*. After all, rhetorical agency persists only insofar as the meaning and effects of one's rhetorical acts are not settled in advance. Thus, the effects of any given polemic are never fully governed by its substance or intention, and the possibility for radical transformation exists alongside the possibility for retrenchment.

When queer theorists like Crimp and Edelman engage with Kramer's arguments, then, they are exploiting the undecidability of the polemic's effects. Their agency as academic writers emerges from the gap between the polemic and its effects, and their uptake of Kramer's texts participates in the dispersion of those texts' effects in the realm of academia. This is not to say, of course, that queer theorists' agency is solely dependent upon Kramer's polemics or that this is the only or most significant effect of his texts; rather, it is to note that Kramer's polemics are, unexpectedly, one of the factors that enable queer academic writing. But the agency that emerges out of queer theory's uptake of Kramer's polemics is a highly contingent and unpredictable sort of agency, constituted through and always entailing risk as its founding condition. The anxiety that Kramer expresses about the effects of his work is therefore reflected in queer theory's compulsion to repudiate his views. Hence, as queer theorists continually try to position themselves against Kramer's polemics, Kramer is figured as precisely that queerness whose exclusion founds the rhetorical agency of queer theory. To put this differently, the excessive and undecidable nature of Kramer's polemics are both necessary and threatening to queer theory; they must be deferred as vigorously as they are continuously reincorporated. The riskiness and undecidability entailed in polemics thus serve as the very conditions of possibility for queer theory's radical interventions; that is, they enable agency that does not simply function to repeat the status quo and are therefore the resource for resistance, invention, and freedom.

Larry Kramer's polemics appear here, then, not only as a site from which to rethink the relationship between form and rhetorical agency but also as a performance of the unpredictability of rhetoric's effects—a queerness that I propose is the condition of possibility for any rhetorical act.

Notes

1. An earlier version of this essay has appeared in the *Quarterly Journal of Speech* 94 (2008): 297–319, as well in Erin J. Rand, *Reclaiming Queer: Activist and Academic Rhetorics of Resistance* (Tuscaloosa: University of Alabama Press, 2014). Larry Kramer, "A Call to Riot," *Reports from the Holocaust: The Story of an AIDS Activist* (New York: St. Martin's Press, 1994), 314. Unless otherwise noted, all citations of Kramer refer to the reprinted texts that appear in this volume.

2. Kramer, "A Call to Riot," 317–318.

3. Kramer, "A Call to Riot," 318.

4. Kramer, *Reports*, 319.

5. Kramer, *Reports*, 319–321.

6. Karlyn Kohrs Campbell, "Agency: Promiscuous and Protean," *Communication and Critical/Cultural Studies* 2 (2005): 7.

7. Derrida's statement "il n'y a pas de hors-texte" is usually translated as "there is nothing outside the text," leading to the false conclusion that he reduces everything to language and dismisses materiality. A more appropriate rendering of this sentence, however, refers to the impossibility of reaching beyond the signifier to a stable signified; that is, there is no reality that is independent from language. Jacques Derrida, *Of Grammatology,* trans. Gayatri Chakravorty Spivak (Baltimore: Johns Hopkins University Press, 1976), 158.

8. Kenneth Burke, "Lexicon Rhetoricae," in *Counter-Statement,* ed. Kenneth Burke (Berkeley: University of California Press, 1931), 124.

9. Burke, "Lexicon," 138.

10. Lloyd F. Bitzer, "The Rhetorical Situation," *Philosophy and Rhetoric* 1 (1968): 13.

11. Kramer, "1,112 and Counting," 35.

12. Kramer, "1,112 and Counting," 45.

13. Kramer, "The Beginning of ACTing UP," 128.

14. Kramer, "The Beginning of ACTing UP," 136.

15. Kramer is known for helping to found both GMHC and ACT UP, but his role in each organization has been controversial. He split with GMHC over a difference of opinion regarding the group's focus, and his claims to being an important founding figure of ACT UP have been hotly disputed by activists and critics alike. For instance, ACT UP's "Capsule History," provided on ACT UP/ New York's website, does not mention Kramer in relation to the founding of the group, but it does include Maxine Wolfe's essay, "Make It Work for You: Academia and Political Organizing in Lesbian and Gay Communities," in which she denies Kramer's claims to ACT UP, and several other criticisms of Kramer. See http://www.actupny.org/documents/academia.html; "Kramer Media Folly," http://www.actupny.org/reports/Kramer-Folly.html (accessed August 14, 2103).

16. Kramer has not ceased to be active and influential in the gay community. On November 7, 2004, he gave a lengthy speech titled "The Tragedy of Today's Gays" at Cooper Union in New York City. Although it began with Kramer's concern about the results of the recent 2004 presidential election, the bulk of this speech—like Kramer's earlier speeches—dealt with the lack of responsibility and organization within the gay community. For a reprint of the speech, see Larry Kramer, "The Tragedy of Today's Gays: An Address to the Gay Community," address given at Cooper Union in New York City, New York, November 7, 2004, http://www.towleroad.com/2004/11/ larry_kramer_sp.html.

17. Kramer, "Donna Do-Nothing Works for Bill the Welsher," 413.

18. David France, "The Angry Prophet Is Dying," *Newsweek,* June 11, 2001, 43.

19. Kathryn Thomas Flannery, "The Passion of Conviction: Reclaiming Polemic for a Reading of Second-Wave Feminism," *Rhetoric Review* 20 (2001): 113–129; Jonathan Crewe, "Can Polemic Be Ethical? A Response to Michel Foucault," in *Polemic: Critical or Uncritical,* ed. Jane Gallop (New York: Routledge, 2004), 135–152. Though anger is the primary emotion generally associated with polemics, Crewe also makes a case for acknowledging the ways in which polemics might be entertaining or comedic. This does not necessarily indicate that the polemic itself is funny or that the speaker intends to be amusing; rather, it emphasizes the tendency for polemics to have unpredictable effects.

20. Victor Zonana, "Kramer vs. the World," *The Advocate,* December 1, 1992, 48.

21. Kramer, "1,112 and Counting," 45.

22. Flannery, "The Passion of Conviction," 116–117; Kenneth J. E. Graham, *The Performance of Conviction: Plainness and Rhetoric in the Early English Renaissance* (Ithaca: Cornell University Press, 1994), 14.

23. Flannery, "The Passion of Conviction," 117.

24. Graham, *The Performance of Conviction,* 15–16.

25. Graham, *The Performance of Conviction,* 14.

26. Kramer, "Some Thoughts about Evil," 448.

27. In an essay about Charles Darwin's *On the Origin of Species*, John Angus Campbell contends that the "intensely personal" quality of Darwin's work creates a bond between the author and his readers and presents a reality that is "not only objective, but personal." John Angus Campbell, "The Polemical Mr. Darwin," *Quarterly Journal of Speech* 61 (1975): 385.

28. Kramer, "We Killed Vito," 369.

29. Kramer, "We Killed Vito," 371.

30. Kramer, "We Killed Vito," 372.

31. Flannery, "The Passion of Conviction," 116.

32. Michel Foucault, "Polemics, Politics, and Problematizations: An Interview with Michel Foucault" in *The Foucault Reader,* ed. Paul Rabinow (New York: Pantheon Books, 1984), 381.

33. Kramer, "Introduction," xxxiii.

34. Simon Watney, foreword to Larry Kramer, *Reports from the Holocaust: The Story of an AIDS Activist* (New York: St. Martin's Press, 1994), xviii; France, "Angry Prophet," 43. See also Zonana, "Kramer vs. the World," 40–48; Gary Barton, "Why I Love Larry," *The Advocate*, March 1, 2005, 9. As James Darsey contends, much of the rhetoric of American movements for social reform is indebted to the prophetic books of the Old Testament, and the prophetic tradition is a form that is commonly utilized (though not often acknowledged) in radical discourse. James Darsey, *The Prophetic Tradition and Radical Rhetoric in America* (New York: New York University Press, 1997).

35. Kramer, "Introduction," xxxiii.

36. Kramer, "Some Thoughts about Evil," 450.

37. Campbell, "The Polemical Mr. Darwin," 387.

38. Flannery, "The Passion of Conviction," 120.

39. Edwin Black, "The Second Persona," *Quarterly Journal of Speech* 56 (1970): 109–119; Philip Wander, "The Third Persona: An Ideological Turn in Rhetorical Theory," *Central States Speech Journal* 35 (1984): 197–216; Charles E. Morris III, "Pink Herring and the Fourth Persona: J. Edgar Hoover's Sex Crime Panic," *Quarterly Journal of Speech* 88 (2002): 228–244.

40. Foucault, "Polemics," 382.

41. Kramer, "1,112 and Counting," 46.

42. Kramer, "Some Thoughts about Evil," 450.

43. Flannery, "The Passion of Conviction," 122.

44. Flannery, "The Passion of Conviction," 127.

45. John H. Smith, "Rhetorical Polemics and the *Dialectics of Kritik* in Hegel's Jena Essays," *Philosophy and Rhetoric* 18 (1985): 35.

46. Benjamin Arditi and Jeremy Valentine, *Polemicization: The Contingency of the Commonplace* (New York: New York University Press, 1999), 137.

47. Michael Warner, "Publics and Counterpublics," *Public Culture* 14 (2002): 51.

48. Warner, "Publics and Counterpublics," 51.

49. Crimp responds not only to Kramer in these texts but also to other gay conservative writers and journalists (often referred to as "gaycons"), such as Andrew Sullivan and Michelangelo Signorile. (Also including Randy Shilts, Gabriel Rotello, and Bruce Bawer, the "gaycons" held conservative views that differed dramatically from the radical activist practices that attempted to resignify the "queer" label and expose the heteronormative underpinnings of the social order. The "gaycons" were generally quite clear in their reservations about precisely this kind of radical queer

activism and in their indictments of the practices of the queer community. For more on gay conservatives in the 1990s, see Paul Robinson, *Queer Wars: The New Gay Right and Its Critics* [Chicago: University of Chicago Press, 2005].) Other queer theorists also participated in extended disagreements with conservative gay authors such as Sullivan and Rotello. For example, Michael Warner's *The Trouble with Normal* (1999) takes as its primary point of departure (as well as the inspiration for its title) Sullivan's *Virtually Normal.* Warner, along with many other queer theorists, heavily criticized Sullivan's views on the politics of homosexuality, gay marriage, and gays in the military.

50. Douglas Crimp, "How to Have Promiscuity in an Epidemic," in *Melancholia and Moralism: Essays on AIDS and Queer Politics* (Cambridge, Mass.: MIT Press, 2002), 56–57.

51. Crimp, "Sex and Sensibility, or Sense and Sexuality," in *Melancholia and Moralism: Essays on AIDS and Queer Politics* (Cambridge, Mass.: MIT Press, 2002), 286.

52. Crimp, "Sex and Sensibility," 287.

53. Lee Edelman, *Homographesis: Essays in Gay Literary and Cultural Theory* (New York: Routledge, 1994), 107.

54. See, for example, Robert Scheer, "AIDS Stigma Hampering a Solution," *Los Angeles Times,* November 28, 1986; Susan Yoachum, "Buchanan Calls AIDS 'Retribution': Gays Angered by His Bid to Win Bible Belt Votes," *San Francisco Chronicle,* February 28, 1992.

55. Edelman, *Homographesis,* 107.

56. By addressing queer theorists' criticisms of Kramer, I do not mean to suggest that there is a coherent position that might be attributed to the field or authors of queer theory. Indeed, the designation of a body of work known as "queer theory" has occurred only retrospectively and is itself a politically motivated move. Furthermore, even the queer theorists whom I have mentioned here did not share a single perspective: one of Edelman's essays that contains a criticism of Kramer is later critiqued by Crimp, who takes issue with Edelman's treatment of ACT UP's "Silence = Death" symbol. See Douglas Crimp, "Mourning and Militancy," in *Melancholia and Moralism: Essays on AIDS and Queer Politics* (Cambridge, Mass.: MIT Press, 2002), 129–149.

57. A similar relationship exists between second-wave feminist polemics and academic feminism. As Flannery explains, the polemics of second-wave feminists are often cast as "angry and confrontational" in an effort "to distance current feminist practice in the academy from the 'excess' of such volatility in order to ground it in (and derive intellectual legitimacy from) more conventional forms of knowledge production. In short, the aim would be to ensure that women's academic work appear more rational." In other words, current feminist academics have an ambivalent relationship to second-wave feminist polemics: on one hand, those polemics are necessary to establish the *historical* and *political* legitimacy of feminism; on the other hand, those same texts must be repudiated to the extent that they threaten the *academic* legitimacy of feminism as an institutionalized scholarly field. As Flannery points out, this ambivalence demonstrates the extent to which second-wave feminist polemics retain their potential to be disruptive and unsettling; even as the polemics are necessary to the field, their effects can never be fully contained or predicted. Flannery, "The Passion of Conviction," 120.

58. Edelman, *Homographesis,* 6.

59. Edelman, *Homographesis,* 7.

60. For other treatments of the ways that language reveals and reproduces norms of sexuality, see Judith Butler, *Gender Trouble: Feminism and the Subversion of Identity* (New York: Routledge, 1990); Michel Foucault, *The History of Sexuality,* Vol. I: *An Introduction,* trans. Robert Hurley (New York: Vintage Books, 1978); Gayle Rubin, "Thinking Sex: Notes for a Radical Theory of the Politics of Sexuality," in *Pleasure and Danger: Exploring Female Sexuality,* ed. Carole S. Vance (London: Pandora Press, 1992), 267–319; Eve Kosofsky Sedgwick, *Epistemology*

of the Closet (Berkeley: University of California Press, 1990); Monique Wittig, *The Straight Mind and Other Essays* (Boston: Beacon Press, 1992).

61. As Gayatri Spivak puts it in *The Post-Colonial Critic,* being able to act requires that "the subject is always centered as a subject." She later noted that agency arises from a metonymic process of displacement, an essentializing move whereby one emerges as an agent only insofar as a part of oneself stands in for the whole. See Gayatri Chakravorty Spivak, *The Post-Colonial Critic: Interviews, Strategies, Dialogues,* ed. Sarah Harasym (New York: Routledge,1990), 104; Gayatri Chakravorty Spivak, "Agency," lecture given at University of Iowa, Iowa City, October 4, 2004.

Part III

Extending the Boundaries of Rhetoric's Effects

Online Documentaries and Offline Impact

Participatory Culture and the Digital Future of Rhetorical Effects

ANNE T. DEMO

The problem of measuring effects challenges diverse disciplines. Although this volume was prompted by the complicated history of how to approach effects in rhetorical studies, the question of how to assess impact—and the potential for digital platforms to prove it—preoccupies academics, journalists, marketers, filmmakers, and activists alike.[1] Developments in digital and auditing technologies over the past decade have led to sweeping transformations in documentary filmmaking as funding became increasingly tied to outreach. According to the cultural anthropologist and documentary filmmaker Meg McLagan, "the conceptual and practical architecture that comprise what we call 'documentary' has begun to unravel, and in its place have emerged a proliferation of new platforms and interfaces that have reshaped the form, along with its potential to produce political effects."[2] The growing emphasis on outreach and online interactivity designed to generate measurable offline impact is evident in the shift from theatrically released long-form documentaries with supporting website (for example, *An Inconvenient Truth*) to short-form documentaries distributed online as part of a digital campaign seeking to build participatory communities through social media platforms such as YouTube, Instagram, Tumblr, Twitter, and Facebook (for example, *KONY 2012* and *The Dream Is Now*).[3] Aspects of this transformation in documentary advocacy—particularly concerning how projects are conceived and circulated—will inform the future of rhetorical practice and criticism as similar changes are occurring in journalism and politics. This essay explores the opportunities and constraints of using online participatory culture and digital interactivity as evidence of rhetorical effect and considers how emphasizing circulation and reception refigures rhetorical agency and the boundaries of what we study.

Studies of circulation and reception constitute what James Jasinski and Jennifer Mercieca describe as "extremely promising directions" in research on constitutive effects. In each case, the approach is highly contextualized and emphasizes constitutive rather than instrumental effects.[4] Influenced by the work of Michael Warner, studies of circulation trace the ways discourse (including images) are referenced, imitated, or appropriated across mediums and in different locations and times so as to illuminate how that process constitutes a public or counterpublic. Reception-based research within rhetoric of science scholarship compares how different specialized audiences responded to a scientific phrase or concept by reframing it.[5] Each area has been challenged, however, to further account for the agency of audiences. Lester Olson, for example, argues that Warner's theory may "underestimate" the "degree of rhetorical agency" available to audiences.[6] According to Paul, Charney, and Kendall, within the rhetoric of science, the interest in reception has gone even further, prompting calls for a shift away from the "textual analysis of historically important texts and developing genres" to approaches that track the "communal acceptance" of scientific claims by analyzing direct peer responses posted to online forums. These scholars write that "These new forms of exchange make certain kinds of academic debate accessible for analysis. We hope scholars will soon begin analyzing these commentaries as new and important sources of insight into the responses of readers."[7] Attentiveness to the role of collective intelligence in shaping knowledge and the complexity of audience agency motivates not only the emerging focus on circulation and reception in rhetorical studies but also new media scholarship on participatory cultures. At its most basic level, a participatory culture depends on user interactivity to form communities and foster collective intelligence. Nurtured via accessible digital platforms, participatory cultures encourage users to produce and circulate their own content, reshape (to varying degrees) the content of conventional media producers, and (in so doing) create community networks.

In the narrow context of the effects debate within rhetorical studies, the shift to participatory culture and online interactivity may seem a radical turn. Within media studies and political science, however, the relative agency of audiences is being reconceptualized on the basis of transmedia projects and campaigns that seek to convert conventional broadcast media into interactive domains through platforms such as Twitter and Facebook. Such approaches reflect what Kiewe and Houck describe in the Introduction as a conception of agency based on a "circulation model," which assumes that rhetorical effect encompasses the production of a subsequent chain of audiences, not simply a spike or fall in the opinion of one particular audience.[8] Although media studies scholarship has, at this point, a more developed vocabulary for assessing how interactivity both facilitates and complicates conventional assessments of effect, political scientists such as G. R. Boynton are beginning to examine how audiences employ social media platforms as a form of "co-motion" to major speech events such as the State of the Union.[9] The interactivity encompassed by "co-motion" is limited to exchanges that occur as the speech is given or in its immediate aftermath, such as amplifying particular speech quotes through retweets or the use of hashtags to self-identify with a particular community.[10] As this essay suggests, however, the potential extends well beyond the immediate reaction to the online debates and connections triggered by a text, which further produce meaningful offline coalitions.

This essay explores this potential by examining the role of a YouTube channel devoted to a prolonged community debate over a controversial immigration enforcement ordinance in Prince William County (PWC), Virginia. At issue was the July 2007 passage of an ordinance by the Board of Supervisors that required county law enforcement to check immigration status if there was probable cause to believe that an individual had violated federal immigration law. In response, filmmakers Eric Byler and Annabell Park created the *9500 Liberty* YouTube channel and uploaded the first of what would be a six-month chronicle with more than one hundred videos documenting how PWC residents responded to the passage and subsequent revision of the ordinance. Described as the "first interactive documentary," the project garnered national news coverage after the third video uploaded went viral, earning a spot on the top twenty YouTube downloads for the week.[11] While documentary filmmakers have increasingly turned to social media as a way of cultivating an audience prior to a film's completion, *9500 Liberty* was unique in that the filmmakers posted footage to their YouTube channel as events unfolded and quickly became influential forces in the ongoing debate.[12] Although the YouTube footage was eventually edited into a feature length documentary that aired nationally on MTV in September 2010, the focus of this essay is on the participatory culture facilitated by the *9500 Liberty* YouTube channel.

The ensuing analysis engages two lines of argument to advance the claim that markers of participatory culture provide meaningful evidence of rhetorical effect. The first and most radical argument is that social media platforms like YouTube create the possibility of generating measurable rhetorical effects during the production process. As the dynamics of civic life evolve and increasingly rely on social media and transmedia storytelling, the "finished text" may be displaced as the focal point of analysis within the study of rhetorical effects. Second, my analysis answers calls in rhetorical studies to explore how "online activism" impacts "offline organizing."[13] Ultimately, the *9500 Liberty* case raises important questions about the presumed neutrality of circulation in the study of rhetorical effects and privileging texts over platforms or interfaces. To make the case I have outlined requires, first, a more developed overview of participatory culture and, second, a fuller account of the political context that prompted the filmmakers' use of YouTube and their subsequent shift from observers to participants as the participatory culture surrounding the project developed.

Participatory Culture: Agency and Effects

The term *participatory culture* is most associated with new media but has been also used to describe affiliates of the Amateur Press Association founded in 1876, fan culture as early as the 1930s, and contemporary intercollegiate debate.[14] These diverse cultural sites share a commitment to encouraging citizen/consumer engagement in the production of content and/or the deliberation of ideas so as to facilitate bottom-up knowledge formation. In each case, the potential for impact hinges on the agency of the audience in its various forms—amateur, fan, consumer, participant, user, or citizen. Contemporary sites where participatory culture thrives span commercial and civic contexts, from video game design to participatory journalism and grassroots activism. The New Media theorist Henry Jenkins contrasts participatory culture with "older notions of passive media spectatorship" and argues that instead of "talking about media producers and consumers as occupying separate roles, we might now see them as participants who interact with each other."[15] Within the commercial landscape, for example, video game design has led the way in fostering a participatory culture, with designers creating online forums where fans generate game content, even releasing design tools and game engines to encourage user-led innovations.[16] At base, cultivating a participatory culture requires a platform that is easily accessible, facilitates community, and circulates user-generated content often absent from or oppositional to dominant media. Thus, participatory culture shares with effects-oriented research an interest in agency. A key difference, however, is that participatory culture emphasizes the potential interplay between audiences and rhetors *during* the invention process not only after a text circulates in its finished form.

The rationale for examining participatory culture as a marker of rhetorical effects is based on a parallel shift in documentary advocacy. Documentary filmmakers have increasingly adopted what David Whiteman describes as a "coalition model" that assesses impact on the basis of the "entire filmmaking process," which encompasses the participation of targeted community stakeholders in the creation of the film.[17] Whereas the conventional model of impact was based on "a *finished* film's effects on *individual* citizens within the *dominant* discourse," the coalition model established by Whiteman broadened the assessment of impact in three ways. First, the coalition model approaches films as "part of a larger process that incorporates both production and distribution (not simply as a 'product' for consumption)."[18] The attention to production in the coalition model opens up the potential for considering how individuals and groups involved in filming are changed by and seek to enact change as a result of the process. To be clear, viewers still play an important role as change agents. The coalition model simply broadens the frame to consider the "potential effects on the producers and other participants involved in the production, on activist groups that might be associated with the film, and on decision makers and other elites that might be aware of the film, in addition to the typical focus on citizen-viewers."[19] Finally, the coalition model looks beyond dominant discourse to explore how a particular film impacts alternative and local communities.

The coalition model thus shares with participatory culture a shift in focus from product to process, from creative control to collective intelligence, and a preference for distribution via alternative platforms that target counterpublics.[20] More specifically, both the coalition model and participatory culture seek input that decenters the authority of a singular creative vision and foster what Jenkins (drawing on

Pierre Levy) describes as knowledge communities or an online collective that "emerges around the sharing and evaluation of knowledge."[21] A key difference is that the coalition model emphasizes the agency of particular stakeholders, specifically, producers, activists, and decision makers.

In comparison, participatory culture emerged as a concept in scholarship on fan culture, so the agency of everyday users is celebrated even as the power of media producers is acknowledged. As the media critic José van Dijck argues, "Notions of 'participatory culture' tend to accentuate the emancipation of the engaged citizen, who unleashes her need for self-expression and creativity onto the digital spaces created expressly for this purpose."[22] However, the individuals who make up fan communities are, as Jenkins notes, neither "totally autonomous" from nor "totally vulnerable" to media producers and the culture industries.[23] Despite the potential for empowerment afforded by Web 2.0 applications, important caveats persist. As Jenkins notes, (1) "not all participants are created equal"; (2) corporations "still exert greater power than any individual consumer or even aggregate of consumers"; and (3) "some consumers have greater abilities to participate in this emerging culture than others."[24] Platforms such as YouTube face additional critiques regarding the lack of ethnically diverse content and the culture of incivility that hinders deliberation.[25] The case study examined for this essay confirms concerns associated with YouTube comments as a mode of deliberative exchange but also documents the meaningful offline civic participation prompted by the interactive stage of the *9500 Liberty* project.

9500 Liberty: Online Documentary as Real-Time Encyclopedia

9500 Liberty was one of twenty documentaries about illegal immigration in the United States produced between 2000 and 2010 that featured an immigrants' rights perspective.[26] Of those, only seven others aired nationally—on HBO, the Sundance Channel, or the Public Broadcasting series *POV*. Reviews of the finished film were positive—earning 3.5/4 stars from Roger Ebert and the *Boston Globe,* as well as 4/5 stars from the *Arizona Republic*. The similarity between the PWC ordinance and the controversial 2010 Arizona law SB 1070 contributed to the political impact of the finished film, which was broadcast in 100,000 million homes on MTV2, MTV U, and MTV Tr3s (with Spanish subtitles).[27] Despite the finished documentary's success in terms of critical acclaim and broadcast reach, the project's greatest impact was the participatory culture engendered during the interactive stage of filming. Martin Nohe, a member of the Prince William County Board of Supervisors who voted on the measure, characterized the *9500 Liberty* YouTube channel as pivotal in the debate about the measure:

> The interactive stage of the *9500 Liberty* project led to a significant shift in the debate over illegal immigration in Prince William County. Specifically, the use of social media had never previously been widely used in a policy debate in the

County. While blogs had made some impact by providing an opportunity for community discussion, the use of visual media in a very accessible format allowed a discourse that had become very emotional in nature to be re-framed as one that was much more outcome focused.[28]

Nick Miroff, the *Washington Post* staff reporter responsible for covering immigration in Northern Virginia, had a similar assessment: "The site was an important visual for people who had been reading about what was going on but for the first time could really see it unfolding."[29]

Indeed, the project documents the prolonged debate over the ordinance from the time it was announced in July 2007 until the Board of Supervisors voted to "soften" the ordinance in April 2008 by "directing police officers to question criminal suspects about their immigration status only after they have been arrested."[30] The one hundred video uploads posted on the YouTube channel between October 2007 and April 2008 ranged in length from two to nine minutes in length and functioned, according to Miroff, as "an encyclopedia of what was happening here."[31]

Although Park and Byler began the project with the goal of making a feature-length documentary, the polarizing community dynamics that defined the debate pushed the filmmakers to upload the footage as it was shot. In an interview with the *Washington Post,* Byler acknowledged that the typical process was to "shoot, then edit, then enter film festivals," but with that timeline "people would see this film for the first time next summer. That's a long time to wait. If the movie is meant to create dialogue, why release it after things may have already shifted?"[32] The decision to begin posting video clips onto a YouTube channel dedicated to the project was made early on in filming. After attending a meeting for supporters of the immigration enforcement measure, Park realized that the primary mode of news about the debate (print journalism) disregarded key facets of the meetings such the racial composition and demeanor of participants. In an interview with CNN about their YouTube channel, Park remarked, "What we saw there, it is very hard for newspaper reporters to report . . . but with one pan of our camera, people got so much visual information about what the group was like, and so then we decided there was a need for us to do this."[33] Although created as a resource for learning about the issues without having to actually go, in Byler's words, "to a place where there is bound to be conflict," the site quickly transformed into an outlet that allowed people to "participate safely from home."[34] And participate they did. The most popular upload ("Stop Your Racism 2") was viewed over 100,000 times in under a year, and "Stop Your Racism to Hispanics—Liberty Wall #1" had over 100,000 by 2010.[35] Both clips feature a confrontation between an agitated elderly white man and a group of young Latinos standing with the filmmaker Annabell Park near the Liberty Wall. "Stop Your Racism to Hispanics—Liberty Wall #1," the third clip posted on the *9500 Liberty* YouTube channel, went viral and eventually became the films' opening teaser. The upload not only received more than five thousand comments and extensive local media coverage but also prompted a video response uploaded by Arizona immigrants' rights activists and three follow-up video installments from the filmmakers.[36] Since the channel was created on October 7, 2007, the videos featured on the *9500 Liberty* channel have had a total of 897,940 views, and the top five videos have received more than 8,700 comments.

The participatory nature of the project evolved as the interactive stage of filming gained momentum. The filmmakers posted clips as events unfolded, encouraged comments, and often responded to feedback. The first two videos featured an explicit request for feedback in the information summaries that appear below the upload date and view tally: "Part of our ongoing, interactive documentary series: *9500 Liberty, the Battle over Immigration.* We invite viewers to make comments about the videos and leave suggestions for the filmmakers."[37] Because the third upload ("Stop Your Racism to Hispanics—Liberty Wall #1") was among the two most popular videos (in terms of both views and comments), the interactivity between the filmmakers and viewers was established from nearly the beginning of the project. The opening page of the YouTube channel also emphasizes the interactivity of the project during production: "During the first year of production, we often responded to viewer feedback, including requests for more coverage on certain story lines, contextual clarifications, and even on-site production."[38] Between October 2007 and April 2008, the *9500 Liberty* YouTube channel featured numerous contextual clarifications and uploads based on requests for additional footage.

Two months into filming, Byler and Park's level of involvement in the debate changed. Instead of interviewing others about the conflict, Byler was asked to testify at a U.S. Commission on Civil Rights hearing convened in December 2007 to determine whether the immigration ordinance violated the civil rights of PWC residents. The invitation for the filmmakers to testify at the hearing was noteworthy because testimony was restricted, excluding both concerned citizens who favored the ordinance and community leaders who opposed it.[39] Byler was asked to give a five-minute statement in which he discussed the failures in the democratic process that had prompted the filmmakers to post footage on YouTube. In his testimony, Byler acknowledged the difficulty of shifting from observer to participant, stating, "I have respect for everyone that is involved, and I actually feel sorry that I have to, you know, give my view on this," but nonetheless he singled out the "local affiliate" of FAIR, Help Save Manassas (HSM), as creating a climate where "people were afraid to be interviewed and felt helpless to do anything about what was happening to their community."[40] Two days after Byler's testimony, he and Park were featured in the Outlook and Opinions section of the Sunday *Washington Post.* Both of them published commentaries in which they reflected on their experience documenting the clash over immigration in PWC, along with video essays that were linked to the *Washington Post* Outlook and Opinions website. The filmmakers' new positionality and burgeoning visibility shifted the dynamics of reception for the project. As a result of her experience with *9500 Liberty,* Park went onto to found the Coffee Party, a democracy movement that is a "non-partisan, fact-based, solutions-oriented network determined to have an impact in our nation's deliberative process."[41]

To be sure, the case of *9500 Liberty* is an atypical YouTube success. Nonetheless, the project suggests the potential for considering interactivity during production as a marker of rhetorical effect. Scholarship on YouTube generally falls within two camps regarding issues of effect and agency. One view (associated with Jenkins) emphasizes the civic potential of YouTube and the agency that Web 2.0 applications afford users, whereas the other delineates the economic and cultural limitations of the platform.[42] As a study of rhetorical effect, the ensuing analysis confirms problems with key facets of YouTube but focuses on the deliberative potential of participatory platforms by focusing on two issues. First, I make the case for examining effects engendered in the composition or production process by tracing the faith community's potential to meaningful intervene in the debate. Despite widespread acceptance of theoretical discussions on the fragmentation of texts and the proliferation of transmedia storytelling, studies of effect rarely address the production process as a context generative of meaningful impact. Second, I explore the role of platforms in circulation by examining the potential for digital offshoots to develop from sites such as YouTube. In the case of *9500 Liberty,* the online participatory culture that migrated to a platform run by local activists resulted in meaningful offline coalitions. The findings that follow thus extend the extant scholarship that assesses YouTube's deliberative potential only on the basis of exchanges occurring on that site and suggest the need for more critical attention to the dynamics of production, distribution, and circulation as sources of rhetorical effect.

Effect in Production: A Faith Community Gains Force

The PWC ordinance mandating that law enforcement officers verify the residency status of anyone in custody suspected of being in the country illegally prompted immediate reactions from the national and local faith communities. Within a month of the ordinance's passage, the National Coalition of Latino Clergy and Christian Leaders organized a protest rally and threatened a federal lawsuit and local boycott.[43] Prince William County supervisor John T. Stirrup Jr. characterized the threat as an example of "litigious society" in a *Washington Post* article about the protest and coalition actions: "A lot of people sue a lot of people. I think the board is pretty steadfast on its position. . . . We're not going to allow the threat of a lawsuit by any individual or any group to intimidate us on matters of public policy."[44] At the local level, an interfaith organization, Unity in the Community (UIC), issued a statement coordinated with the actions of the National Coalition of Latino Clergy and Christian Leaders. The statement requested that the County Board of Supervisors reconsider the resolution and suspend its implementation on the basis of the county's human rights record and the relatively minor economic costs associated with unenforced immigration. As Byler notes, the PWC faith community was "one of the first to stand up and oppose the new law."[45] Its opposition to the law triggered "a deluge of really angry, frightful replies, intimating replies" that, according to Byler, concerned the congregations and forced the clergy to initially accept "the role of silent and intimidated objectors."[46] In this volatile context, the *9500 Liberty* YouTube channel shielded local clergy and their congregations while also ultimately providing a safe venue for their critiques. Instead of engaging the debate in general terms, clergy had grounds to directly challenge the religious underpinnings of the arguments of Help Save Manassas in support of the ordinance.

The turning point was a video explicitly requested by HSM president Greg Letiecq. One month into the controversy and two months prior to going live with the *9500 Liberty* YouTube channel, Letiecq granted Byler and Parks an interview in which he contextualized the ordinance passed by the Board of Supervisors in relation to a scriptural reference to Romans:

> "All of you must be willing to obey completely those who rule over you. There are no authorities except the ones God has chosen. Those who now rule have been chosen by God. So when you oppose the authorities, you are opposing those whom God has appointed. Those who do that will be judged." God instituted this government. This is part of his plan. Those leaders aren't just there for a win, they're there because God has a purpose here. So when you are going against them . . . when you are trying to go against the laws and policies that are part of God's plan, you are actually fighting against God.[47]

Letiecq twice requested that this excerpt from the interview be posted on the *9500 Liberty* YouTube channel and linked the video to his blog (bvnl.net) on the day that Byler uploaded it.[48] Letiecq's post with the linked video described the filmmakers' decision to upload the interview as evidence that *9500 Liberty* was "changing course" and "being more fair to the anti-illegal side."[49] Letiecq's treatment of the Gospel provided, however, the necessary opening for the clergy to challenge the claims of Help Save Manassas directly. In the month that followed, three clergy members who previously had declined to be interviewed agreed to do video replies to Letiecq's video, "Illegals, God, and Gospel."[50] The same religious leaders invited the filmmakers to record an interfaith community forum on the division created by debates over the ordinance.[51] In January 2008, more than fifty leaders from twenty-five Prince William congregations drafted a letter to the PWC Board of Supervisors offering their "time, energy, and ideas, so that the current discussion might move toward greater understanding and respect within our community."[52] Reverend Jeff Carter of the Manassas Church Brethren characterized the letter in a *Washington Post* article as "an offer for some help in mediating and moderating this dialogue."[53] Corey Stewart, chairman of the PWC Board of County Supervisors, called the group "illegitimate and misguided" and advised the clergy to "do what they do best: serve their congregants and attend to their denominations and not get involved in partisan politics."[54] Despite Stewart's efforts to discredit the clergy's efforts, the video evidence that Letiecq (a key ally of Stewart) understood the HSM mission in providential terms not only justified the clergy's involvement but also raised issues about both Letiecq's leadership and Stewart's judgment. The preceding chronology related to the faith community's evolving status within the debate reveals two aspects of participatory culture relevant to the study of rhetorical effects.

First, participatory cultures function by emphasizing communal input over creative control, encouraging "the formation of alternative spheres of discourse," and mentoring/modeling "collaborative problem-solving."[55] In this context, the conventional building blocks for assessing effects (a single rhetor with a discrete and finished text in the public sphere) are displaced by something beyond what Whiteman envisions with his coalition model. Whereas Whiteman positions activists and community groups as "catalysts in the distribution process," the YouTube stage of the *9500 Liberty* project offers community members agency in the production process and in the circulated aspects of the debate that the mainstream press covered sporadically, such as the local faith community's opposition to the immigration enforcement ordinance. Although the encyclopedic quality of the *9500 Liberty* YouTube channel has the feel of a communal Wikipedia for the controversy, the clergy videos and interfaith activism featured on the site also explicitly model a form of collaborative problem solving associated with participatory cultures.

Second, the interactivity associated with participatory platforms expands the agency of users, but only to the degree in which those in creative control are willing to allow. In this case, Byler and Park would not have uploaded the Letiecq interview without his repeated requests to have the interview featured on the *9500 Liberty* site. Such interplay is rarely made public and is uncharacteristic of even advocacy documentary, which limits feedback to the collaborating activists and organizations. Byler and Park maintained a degree of creative control, however, by contextualizing Letiecq in relation to other community members who supported the ordinance. Byler characterized their editing as an attempt to provide Letiecq "cover."[56] The six-and-a-half-minute video opens at the 2007 Board of Supervisors meeting in which two county supervisors, John Stirrup and Corey Stewart, introduced the ordinance. During the meeting, as shown in the video, Stirrup drew explicit attention to constituent support that associated the ordinance with doing God's work: "It is truly overwhelming . . . and incredibly encouraging to have friends and total strangers tell you that they are praying for you and your success and that they are asking for God's help in your guidance."[57] The video cuts to Letiecq reading the Bible, then to footage of a PWC resident at a Citizen's Time Forum who echoed Letiecq, closing her statement with "without law, the Gospel has no meaning."[58] The video then closes with Letiecq's exegesis of the relationship between Gospel and law. The reply videos from clergy respond only to Letiecq, and all acknowledge a reluctance to correct his exegesis but nonetheless suggest that a broader look at Paul's writings is necessary, with one minister describing Letiecq's position as "flawed theology" and potentially "idolatrous."[59]

Because Letiecq's video not only prompted replies from clergy but also diminished his stature among those who supported the ordinance, he promptly removed the link from his blog. The evidence of defensive repositioning by Letiecq suggests that subtle markers of effect can be tracked online through the interplay of links, reply videos, comment threads, and offline actions.

Participatory Platforms and Effect: Virginia's "Virtual French Resistance"

The coarse and often immature norms of engagement found in online comment threads provide grounds for skepticism regarding the democratic potential of participatory platforms. One commonly cited limit of YouTube in particular is the ad hominem attacks that appear in comments responding to video uploads.[60] Thus, while proponents of participatory platforms often cite comment totals as evidence of effects, a cursory analysis of comment content suggests that exchanges on YouTube often lack the norms of engagement necessary for meaningful civic exchange. For example, Aaron Hess's analysis of responses to YouTube uploads from the Office of National Drug Control Policy (ONDCP) concluded that "the medium of YouTube may be too playful of an environment for an engagement with in-depth political controversy."[61] Indeed, the most popular video uploads from the *9500 Liberty* YouTube channel provoked comments that not only exemplified the flame wars described by Hess but also featured threats of physical violence to Latinos and to Parks and Byler in particular.[62] Unlike ONDCP, which quickly disabled the comment function, Byler and Park considered the comments an instrumental "safe space" for residents of PWC to debate the ordinance despite online warnings that "They'll dance on air from their necks."[63] To be clear, the differences between the case examined by Hess and the *9500 Liberty* channel were significant. Most important, the focus of the *9500 Liberty* YouTube channel was local and real time. ONDCP sought only to expand the agency's distribution of final-cut commercials, whereas Byler and Park created the YouTube channel with the intent of fostering online dialogue that would translate to "bricks and motor" organizing in PWC.[64]

Prior to the *9500 Liberty* YouTube channel, the only local online forum that addressed the issue was a blog, Black Velvet Bruce Lee (BVBL), created by Help Save Manassas founder Greg Letiecq, who was a key proponent of the ordinance. Comments against the ordinance were, however, routinely censored on Letiecq's site.[65] The *9500 Liberty* YouTube channel offered residents who opposed the ordinance a forum for not only voicing their concerns but also seeing that others had similar problems with the policy and climate in PWC.[66] According to Byler, "When you live in a climate of fear without a safe space for debate, you either convince yourself you can live with it or believe everyone else is for it so decide not to speak out."[67] Once residents realized that others shared their views, the *9500 Liberty* site became the conduit for what Byler described as a "virtual French resistance."[68] PWC residents Elena Schlossberg and Alanna Almeda created AntiBVBL.net, a blog dedicated to countering Letiecq, after connecting through Byler and Park. Schlossberg credits the *9500 Liberty* YouTube channel with cultivating an offline coalition to fight the ordinance: "Eric and Annabel were critical" not only in the "contacts that were made" but also in "representing the voice of people, who for whatever reason, couldn't speak out."[69] In a context characterized by hate crimes and face-to-face ad hominem attacks at Board of Supervisor meetings, the online rants from commenters with pseudonyms such as "maximumrace" and "liftskirtandinsert" were a nuisance but easily dismissed as the offline coalition developed.[70]

Cognizant of the limits posed by the comment function on YouTube, Byler and Park developed a number of strategies for encouraging productive exchanges during the time span of the controversy. The *9500 Liberty* YouTube channel had few overt restrictions—all comments were limited to five hundred characters and could not include URLs.[71] Byler and Park did censor threats of direct violence and comments with "dehumanizing" language.[72] In an attempt to "get above the fray" typically associated with YouTube comment threads, Byler and Park created a YouTube channel dedicated to their interactive documentary in early October 2007. The first uploads, focused on PWC Board of Supervisors chairman Corey Stewart, called attention to the site as a local hub for PWC residents.[73] The third upload (Liberty Wall #1), which featured the hostile exchange between an agitated elderly white resident and a group of Latino youth, went viral and raised the site's visibility locally as a result of national media coverage about the channel's popularity. Although the uploads that went viral helped build visibility, Byler acknowledges that those videos "got caught in hate-based online communities."[74] It was videos with views in the "500 or less range" where "people who actually lived in the community had their conversations with each other. They didn't bother to trying to get a word in edgewise [on a viral video] that was caught in one of those jet streams."[75] In this context, conventional markers of impact such as online hits actually deflect attention from videos that produced the most meaningful online exchanges and offline effects.

The ad hominem attacks that typify online threads also circulated on the *9500 Liberty* YouTube channel. According to Byler, "Even with the great number of people who were looking for a place to express the counter-perspective, there was still a tremendous amount of traffic that was anti-immigrant or in favor of the resolution."[76] As a result, Byler and Park would sometime directly engage commenters online through either the *9500 Liberty* tag or Byler's pseudonym, Checkers35.[77] Comments that prompted direct responses included requests for alternative viewpoints and comments specific to PWC events. For example, comments in response to an April 2008 upload, "Stewart Distances Himself from Letiecq," featured a direct reply to a request for alternative viewpoints:

> Doctorate: MobergNixon, you have an excellent point. Perhaps 9500 should interview those folks (myself included).

9500 Liberty: Hey Doctorate, thanks as always for contributing to the discussion here. This is Eric. We'd be happy to interview you or Moberg.

Other direct responses sought to foster critical reflection, such as the exchange prompted by a video of an Anti-BVBL party at a PWC restaurant that had experienced a dramatic loss in business as a result of the ordinance:

hccowbow: A party for illegals nice. My party for pimps and crack whores went well too. We cant wait to provide what everyone needs who cares if it isnt legal. . . .

9500 Liberty: Who in the video looks illegal to you? I could probably guess, but I thought I'd give you a chance to explain. (EB)

1reddawn: Hi, I attended the party and it was a lot of fun. I am AGAINST ILLEGAL immigration and it was NOT about that or I would NOT have been there. . . .

4974972: I am a Republican. I attended the party. I had a great time. I met many people, heard many speeches from both party representatives. You can never "spot an illegal" but you can spot people different than you. . . .

Such exchanges illustrate both the immaturity that can characterize YouTube and the limited potential for teachable moments in online comment threads. The exchange is also typical of the comments found on videos with fewer views, which Byler described as spaces where a virtual town hall for PWC residents were most apt to develop. Indeed, a survey of comments across the videos clearly reveals that the site was a hub for frequent commenters such as lanoistwins, auntieM16, and 1reddawn, who often posted PWC-specific comments to the video uploads.

Challenges from Byler's pseudonym were most prevalent in video uploads that featured either overt racial slurs or particularly personalized attacks. For example, a video of AntiBVBL.net cofounder Elena Schlossberg's April 2008 speech before a meeting of the Prince William Board of County Supervisors prompted more than two hundred posts, including a number of anti-Semitic comments. In that context, Checkers35 posted: "You know you're in good company with brainwashed Anti-Immigrant Lobby drones create profiles on YouTube just to attack you. All the upstanding citizens in Prince William County have been attacked by the same goons. Keep up the fight Elena. We're with you!" Byler stated that he "created personas to weigh in, I knew that I had a heavy hand and I was still struggling as with my role as a journalist and my role as a citizen. Checkers35 would knock some heads if people were getting out of hand.[78] Byler's persona also kept immigrants' rights supporters in check with comments like this one: "Checkers35: darkangel, i have no problem with you schooling MobergNixon, but to be fair, not all Republicans are whipping up the anti-immigrant frenzy. Just the assholes."[79] If the interactivity of the *9500 Liberty* YouTube channel was assessed only at the level of online exchanges in comment threads, then its impact would no doubt be limited. However, the interactivity of the *9500 Liberty* YouTube channel functioned through at least two other levels: linked videos and offline organizing.

The creation of AntiBVBL.net in February 2008 was not a direct outgrowth of the *9500 Liberty* YouTube channel, but the relationship between the film's directors and the creators of AntiBVBL.net was instrumental in fostering a visible opposition to the HSM campaign and Letiecq's influential blog.[80] In the first three month after creating AntiBVBL.net, Almeda and Schlossberg linked to seventeen videos from the *9500 Liberty* YouTube channel, which prompted more than a thousand comments at AntiBVBL.net. The norms of engagement on the AntiBVBL.net differed from those on the *9500 Liberty* YouTube channel in that the AntiBVBL.net comments reflected a clear familiarity with the nuances of PWC and few of the hate-based comments found on the *9500 Liberty* channel. For example, the same video discussing the economic impact of the PWC resolution with Dr. Stephen S. Fuller, director of regional analysis at George Mason University, prompted seventy comments on AntiBVBL.net and 708 comments on the YouTube channel, including more than twenty comments from Checkers35 engaging commenters living outside PWC, including a citizen from the United Kingdom:

> Checkers35: You obviously have not been to Prince William County. Immigration has helped this county tremendously, and it would still be doing so if we had not created a hate and hysteria storm that chased away many of the people we had depended on to fuel our local economy. . . .
>
> OldManInTheRedCap: Well, good luck to you, and all PWC citizens, including the illegal ones. Yahoo! shows many foreclosed homes in PWC. Had those homeowners stayed PWC would have a better tax base. And I agree with you, our government is at fault for upholding the law.[81]

Such exchanges reflect the potential of Web 2.0 platforms for a civil debate; however, the geographic diversity of YouTube viewers actually worked against meaningful exchanges among PWC residents. Such examples underscore the fact that distribution and circulation are not neutral processes and may become increasingly determinative as media and politics become increasingly narrowcast digitally. Differences in the platforms and interface protocols used by YouTube and the AntiBVBL.net blog were often as significant in reception as the text uploaded to both sites.

In comparison to the *9500 Liberty* YouTube channel, the AntiBVBL.net blog was focused on PWC issues and populated by residents. Byler periodically posted (as Eric Byler or 9500 Liberty) on the AntiBVBL.net blog in threads featuring videos from the YouTube channel. He would also refer to offline exchanges during public events like the PWC Citizen's Time meetings in his comments posted to AntiBVBL.net and never used a pseudonym on that site. For example, the video with Dr. Fuller was also linked on AntiBVBL.net and prompted a lively exchange including posts from Byler.

Referring to a point raised by Letiecq during a recent Citizen's Time meeting, Byler followed up with Fuller and posted his reply on the AntiBVBL.net thread about the video.[82] The *9500 Liberty* YouTube channel comment thread on the same video did not feature the follow-up information from Byler but did include three comments from Checkers35 (Byler's alias) confronting the nativism and prejudice often underlying debates over illegal immigration; in one such comment he said, "When you people whine and moan about globalism and multiculturalism, you not only betray your own prejudice and moral shortcomings, you also betray the true purpose of this trumped up anti-immigrant hysteria."[83] The difference in response to the Fuller video reveals both the limits of YouTube as the sole site for fostering a participatory culture and the platform's potential for cultivating meaningful online offshoots. The migration of content and commenters from the *9500 Liberty* YouTube channel to the AntiBVBL .net blog was a necessary step in expanding an offline coalition to counter Letiecq and those who supported the ordinance. Conventional approaches to studying effects that fail to account for such collateral developments in the production process are insufficient in a digital context.

In addition to concerns about the incivility of exchanges on sites like YouTube, the potential for online participation to replace offline activism is increasingly raised. Hess even goes so far as to argue that approaching YouTube as "a place to speak one's mind and engage in productive dialogue about salient issues" entails making a "dangerous" assumption because it "in turn affects citizens' belief about the process of democracy and may trade off with traditional forms of resistance, such as letter writing, petitions, or protests."[84] In the case of the *9500 Liberty* YouTube channel, online activity was a catalyst for offline community building that extended beyond the controversy over due process in the enforcement ordinance. The economic impact of the contentious debate over the ordinance was devastating. In just nine months, local businesses that catered to Hispanic immigrants went from being on pace for record profits to facing losses that put them in jeopardy of closure.[85] In early April, a week prior to the County Board of Supervisors' decision to modify the ordinance, Byler and Park joined with AntiBVBL.net to organize the first "Save PWC Economy" party. The two-minute video invitation, which featured Byler and Park interviewing Manuel Arbaiza, owner of Portal Restaurant in PWC, was uploaded to both the *9500 Liberty* YouTube channel and AntiBVBL.net. Although the party was featured in the final cut of the documentary, the more meaningful impact was creating momentum for offline organizing. Indeed, the day after the party, AntiBVBL.net posted a specific call to action: "Now is the time to make our collective voices heard, some people expressed to me their feelings that our county was hijacked by a very vocal minority. We understand there are community issues that must be dealt with, but there is a right way and a wrong way. . . . Let's talk about specific ways we believe we can move forward."[86]

In the two months that followed, *9500 Liberty* and AntiBVBL.net joined with another local interfaith group, Unity in the Community, to sponsor three additional Save PWC Economy gatherings at local restaurants. The YouTube stage of the *9500 Liberty* project demonstrates the necessity of a coalition model for evaluating effect in a digital context. A focus on the finished documentary would have missed the localized micro-developments such as the Save PWC Economy parties engendered through the online interactivity on the YouTube channel and the AntiBVBL.net sites. Although the rising visibility of the *9500 Liberty* project and the AntiBVBL.net site could have been traced in the mainstream press (thus conforming to more conventional markers of effect), the local partnerships that developed across party lines required a model that can differentiate between the nuances of interactivity and visibility.

Summary

Despite the increasingly sophisticated tracking infrastructure for collecting data with every click of our mouse and every smartphone download, the assessment of rhetorical effect in the digital context remains an interpretive art. In the case of the *9500 Liberty* YouTube channel, conventional metrics of popularity such as the "most views" or "most comments" were actually better measures for videos that sparked controversy in online political enclaves, what Byler described as a "hate-based jet stream."[87] While popularity certainly contributes to national visibility, Byler and Park used the interactive format to foster dialogue *locally* as the debate evolved in real time. Assessed from the perspective of impact on PWC, the best measure of the project's rhetorical effect was not popularity but localized interactivity through comment threads, video replies, online offshoots such as AntiBVBL .net, linked videos, and offline activism such as the Save PWC Economy parties. As Burgess and Green note, "One of the most striking features of YouTubers' community-oriented activities is that they take place within an architecture that is not primarily designed for collaborative or collective participation."[88] Byler and Park, however, found ways to circumvent the platform's constraints on community building such as framing the channel page as a local hub for PWC, making explicit requests for viewer feedback, engaging comment threads using either the screen name 9500 Liberty or Byler's pseudonym, and commenting on and collaborating with the creators of on the online offshoot, AntiBVBL.net.

Because of the global audience for YouTube, popularity was also an insufficient measure for evaluating the *9500 Liberty* channel as an alternative news source for the debate. Rather, recognition from institutions conventionally associated with conferring legitimacy such as the state (the U.S. Commission on Civil Rights) and the mainstream press (the *Washington Post*) positioned the *9500 Liberty* YouTube footage as authoritative and comprehensive. The access to diverse stakeholders within the controversy and the ability to share extended footage from public proceedings that local news media outlets couldn't cover led the *Washington Post* reporter Nick Miroff to characterize the site as an "encyclopedia" of the debate "archived and freely available in all its raw intensity."[89] Similarly, Martin Nohe, a member of the PWC Board of

Supervisors, also emphasized the accessibility of the platform and the visual format as contributing factors to the interactive documentary's local impact. Even the then-director of the Virginia chapter of the Minuteman Civil Defense Corp, which opposes illegal immigration, characterized the videos as "fair" and acknowledged, "They're really trying to do a service."[90] At the local level, metrics of credibility, not popularity, may serve as a better gauge for assessing effect within a digital context.

In additional to complicating the equivalence between online popularity and rhetorical effect, this essay also demonstrates that interactivity during the production of *9500 Liberty* had a greater impact on PWC than the finished documentary, which aired nationally, but a year after the ordinance had been revised. Such findings echo Whiteman's position that documentary film and video require a model for assessing impact that considers the coalitions that develop throughout filming. This essay extends Whiteman's analysis, however, by identifying how participatory platforms used during production create alternative spheres of discourse that not only hold decision makers and activists accountable but also activate citizens, the stakeholders minimized in Whiteman's coalition model. To be sure, the informal coalition between the founders of AntiBVBL.net and the filmmakers developed through both offline and online exchanges. The value of their online interactivity across AntiBVBL.net and the *9500 Liberty* YouTube channel was to cultivate a space where PWC citizens silenced by seemingly pervasive support for the enforcement ordinance could learn about facets of the debate not covered in the mainstream press and express counterarguments without fear of reprisal. The citizens engaged through these online venues also participated offline in events such as the Save PWC Economy parties and thus provide some evidence of how online communities can be mobilized offline.

The process of documentary film production is quite different from that of speech writing. Nonetheless, the historic turn toward interactivity in the 2011 State of the Union Address and the decision by PBS to crowdsource the 2012 speech suggest that the markers of participatory culture are becoming increasingly relevant to the study of public address generally and rhetorical effects specifically.[91] As a result, the need for approaches that assess the impact of interactivity as a text moves from invention to distribution and circulation has never been more pressing. The *9500 Liberty* case and the turn toward interactivity across a range of contexts raise a number of foundational questions related to rhetorical effects. How are we to conceptualize agency if invention, distribution, and circulation are approached from the perspective of users, participants, and collaborators instead of audiences? Will rhetorical studies be pushed to recognize, as documentary scholars and filmmakers have, that impact is no longer anchored to a "single inviolate text" and that our objects of inquiry are "structurally presumed to have different forms of life, to exist in different modalities, extended across multiple platforms and networks"?[92] When texts do circulate, in what ways is circulation accelerated, blocked, or aggregated by the digital platforms and interface designs of sites such as YouTube, Twitter, and Facebook? With the rise of big data and calculative technology, the impact of rhetorical studies may increasingly depend on our ability to provide a compelling humanistic framework to account for these and other questions that will define the digital future of rhetorical effects.

Notes

1. See for example, David Perlmutter, *Photojournalism and Foreign Policy: Icons of Outrage in International Crisis* (Westport, Conn.: Praeger, 1998); Kari Andén-Papadopalous, "The Abu Ghraib Torture Photographs: News Frames, Visual Culture, and the Power of Images," *Journalism* 9 (2005): 24; Larry Bartels, "Messages Received: The Political Impact of Media Exposure," *American Political Science Review* 87 (1993): 267; Clay Shirky, "The Political Power of Social Media: Technology, the Public Sphere, and Political Change," *Foreign Affairs* 90 (2011): 2.

2. Meg McLagan, "Imagining Impact: Documentary Film and the Production of Political Effects," in *Sensible Politics: The Visual Culture of Nongovernmental Activism,* ed. Meg McLagan and Yates McKee (New York: Zone, 2012), 306.

3. On this point see, Meg McLagan, "Imagining Impact," 305–319; and Beth Karlin and John Johnson, "Measuring Impact: The Importance of Evaluation for Documentary Film Campaigns," *M/C Journal* 14 (December 2011), July 16, 2013, http://journal.media-culture.org.au/index.php/mcjournal/article/view/444 (accessed on Feb. 14, 2014).

4. The attention to constitutive effects in visual rhetoric and rhetoric of science scholarship is also addressed in James Jasinski and Jennifer R. Mercieca, "The Constitutive Approach to Effect and the Alien and Sedition Acts," in *Rhetoric and Public Address in the Twenty-First Century: A Handbook,* ed. Shawn J. Parry-Giles and J. Michael Hogan (New York: Blackwell Press, 2010), 313–341.

5. Danette Paul, Davida Charney, and Aimee Kendall, "Moving beyond the Moment: Reception Studies in the Rhetoric of Science," *Journal of Business and Technical Communication* 15 (2001): 372–399; Randy Allen Harris, "Reception Studies in Rhetoric of Science," *Technical Communication Quarterly* 14 (2005): 249–255.

6. Lester Olson, "Pictorial Representations of British America Resisting Rape: Rhetorical Re-Circulation of a Print Series Portraying the Boston Port Bill of 1774," *Rhetoric and Public Affairs* 12 (2009): 7, 27.

7. Paul, Charney, and Kendall, "Moving beyond the Momen; Harris, "Reception Studies in Rhetoric of Science."

8. Amos Kiewe and Davis W. Houck, Introduction to this volume.

9. Henry Jenkins, Sam Ford, and Joshua Green, *Spreadable Media: Creating Value and Meaning in a Networked Culture* (New York: New York University Press, 2013).

10. G. R. Boynton Glenn W. Richardson, "Reframing Audience; Co-motion at #SOTU," http://www.boyntons.us/website/new-media/analyses/state-union-2010–11–12/sotu-RSA-120424.html (accessed August 17, 2013).

11. "Immigration Battle," Fox News, November 4, 2007, http://www.youtube.com/watch?v=6pNFaPTYwBc (accessed on February 14, 2014). Although the filmmakers and news coverage surrounding *9500 Liberty* classified the project as an interactive documentary, the emerging literature on the subject is quickly evolving. For example, see the June 2012 special issue of *Studies in Documentary Film* on i-docs; see also Kate Nash, "Modes of Interactivity: Analyzing the Webdoc," *Media, Culture and Society* 34 (2012): 195–210.

12. On the emerging relationship between documentary films and participatory culture, see Chuck Tryon, "Digital Distribution, Participatory Culture, and the Transmedia Documentary," *Jump Cut: A Review of Contemporary Media* 53 (2011), http://www.ejumpcut.org/archive/jc53.2011/TroynWebDoc/ (accessed on February 14, 2014).

13. Aaron Hess, "Resistance Up in Smoke: Analyzing the Limitations of Deliberation on YouTube," *Critical Studies in Media Communication* 26 (2009): 430.

14. On participatory culture and the Amateur Press Association, see Henry Jenkins, "From Participatory Culture to Participatory Democracy (Part Two)," March 6, 2007, http://www.henryjenkins.org/2007/03/from_participatatory_culture_t_1.html (accessed February 15, 2012). On participatory culture in fandom, see Henry Jenkins, "Quentin Tarantino's Star Wars?: Digital Cinema, Media Convergence, and Participatory Culture," http://web.mit.edu/cms/People/henry3/starwars.html (accessed February 15, 2012). On participatory culture in intercollegiate debate, see G. Thomas Goodnight and Gordon Mitchell, "Forensics as Scholarship: Testing Zarefsky's Bold Hypothesis in a Digital Age," *Argumentation and Advocacy* 45 (2008): 80–97.

15. Henry Jenkins, *Convergence Culture: Where Old and New Media Collide* (New York: New York University Press, 2006), 3.

16. Jenkins, *Convergence Culture*, 164–169.

17. David, Whiteman, "Out of the Theaters and into the Streets: A Coalition Model of the Political Impact of Documentary Film and Video." *Political Communication* 21 (2004): 51–69.

18. Whiteman, "Out of the Theaters," 51.

19. Whiteman, "Out of the Theaters," 54.

20. Henry Jenkins, Ravi Purushotma, Katie Clinton, Margaret Weigel, and Alice Robinson, *Confronting the Challenges of Participatory Culture: Media Education for the 21st Century* (Chicago: MacArthur Foundation, 2006), 7–9.

21. Jenkins, *Convergence Culture*, 328.

22. José van Dijck, "Users Like You? Theorizing Agency in User-Generated Content," *Media, Culture and Society* 31 (2009): 54.

23. Henry Jenkins, *Fans, Bloggers and Gamers: Exploring Participatory Culture* (New York: New York University Press, 2006), 136.

24. Jenkins, *Convergence Culture*, 3.

25. See Jean Burgess and Joshua Green, *YouTube: Online Video and Participatory Culture* (Cambridge: Polity, 2009), 124–125; Christina Smith and Kelly McDonald, "The Mundane to the Memorial: Circulating and Deliberating the War in Iraq through Vernacular Soldier-Produced Videos," *Critical Studies in Media Communication* 28 (2011): 292–313; Aaron Hess, "Democracy through the Polarized Lens of the Camcorder: Argumentation and Vernacular Spectacle on YouTube in the 2008 Election," *Argumentation and Advocacy* 47 (2010): 106–122; Mitchell McKinney and Leslie Rill, "Not Your Parents' Presidential Debate: Examining the Effects of the CNN/YouTube Debates on Young Citizens' Civic Engagement," *Communication Studies* 60 (2009): 392–406; Hess, "Resistance Up in Smoke," 411–434.

26. On immigrants' rights documentaries produced between 2000 and 2010, see Anne T. Demo, "Decriminalizing Illegal Immigration: Immigrants' Rights through the Documentary Lens," in *Border Rhetorics: Citizenship and Identity on the U.S.-Mexico Frontier*, ed. D. Robert DeChaine (Tuscaloosa: University of Alabama Press, 2013).

27. "9500 Liberty: MTV Networks to Bring 'LIBERTY' to 100 Million Homes," http://9500liberty.com/blog/mtv-networks-to-bring-9500-liberty-to-100-million-homes/ (accessed February 14, 2012).

28. Martin Nohe, e-mail correspondence with author, July 11, 2011.

29. "9500 Liberty: Interactive Documentary Scene from Feature Film," *9500 Liberty* YouTube channel, May 17, 2010, http://www.youtube.com/user/9500Liberty#p/a/u/1/wFxPAoZznpo (accessed February 15, 2012).

30. Kristen Mack, "Pr. William Softens Policy on Immigration Status Checks," *Washington Post*, April 30, 2008, http://www.washingtonpost.com/wp-dyn/content/article/2008/04/29/AR2008042902990 .html (accessed August 17, 2013).

31. Mack, "Pr. William Softens Policy on Immigration Status Checks."

32. Nick Miroff, "Raw Look at Immigration Crucible," *Washington Post,* November 3, 2007, http://www.washingtonpost.com/wp-dyn/content/article/2007/11/02/AR2007110202158.html (accessed August 17, 2013).

33. Jeanne Meserve and Mike M. Ahlers, "Filmmakers Take Immigration Debate to YouTube," CNN, May 1, 2008, http://www.cnn.com/2008/SHOWBIZ/05/01/immigration.lens/index.html (accessed August 17, 2013).

34. "9500 Liberty Going Big," *9500 Liberty* YouTube channel, November 4, 2007, http://www.youtube.com/watch?v=6pNFaPTYwBc (accessed on February 14, 2014).

35. "Stop Your Racism to Hispanics—Liberty Wall," *9500 Liberty* YouTube channel, Comments Forum, October 12, 2007, http://www.youtube.com/watch?v=k_Dw1ioGPGY (accessed August 17, 2013); "Stop Your Racism 2: Korean Americans Model Immigrants?," 9500 *Liberty YouTube* channel, Comments Forum, November 4, 2007, http://www.youtube.com/watch?v=29WTKbpYhag (accessed August 17, 2013).

36. "Stop Your Racism to Hispanics—Liberty Wall"; "Stop Your Racism 2: Korean Americans Model Immigrants?"

37. "Chairman Stewart: Fighting Illegal Immigration," *9500 Liberty* YouTube channel, Comments Forum, October 11, 2007, http://www.youtube.com/watch?v=of8XDSKrNzs (accessed on February 14, 2014).

38. "*9500 Liberty:* YouTube Channel Profile," *9500 Liberty* YouTube channel. http://www.youtube.com/user/9500Liberty (accessed February 15, 2012 (accessed February 15, 2012).

39. Kristen Mack, "Conservatives Clash at Briefing on Pr. William Crackdown," *Washington Post,* December 15, 2007, http://www.washingtonpost.com/wp-dyn/content/article/2007/12/14/AR2007121401580.html (accessed August 17, 2013).

40. United Stated Commission on Civil Rights, *Briefing before Immigration Subcommittee of the Virginia Advisory Committee to the U.S. Commission on Civil Rights.* Federal Register vol. 72 no. 223. December 14, 2007, 144.

41. "About Us," The Coffee Party USA, February 23, 2010, http://www.coffeepartyusa.com/about-us (accessed February 14, 2012).

42. On the economic and diversity challenges associated with YouTube, see Jean Burgess and Joshua Green, *YouTube: Online Video and Participatory Culture* (Cambridge: Polity, 2009).

43. Jonathan Mummolo, "Latino Group Vows to Sue if Resolution Isn't Tempered," *Washington Post,* August 19, 2007, http://www.washingtonpost.com/wp-dyn/content/article/2007/08/18/AR2007081801012.html (accessed August 17, 2013). In addition to the National Coalition of Latino Clergy and Christian Leaders, the local chapter of Mexicanos Sin Fronteras promoted a week-long boycott of PWC business and a one-day work stoppage to underscore the importance of the immigrant community to the PWC economy. "Stop Prince William County's Anti-Immigration Resolution," Mexicanos Sin Fronteras, http://www.mexicanossinfronteras.org/PDF/flyer_boycott_march_pwc_english.pdf (accessed February 15, 2012).

44. Mummolo, "Latino Group Vows."

45. Eric Byler, phone interview, January 4, 2012.

46. Eric Byler, phone interview, January 4, 2012.

47. "Illegals, God and Gospel in Manassas/PWC," *9500 Liberty* YouTube channel, October 31, 2007, http://www.youtube.com/watch?v=tpAWEMOgAJw&feature=relmfu (accessed February 15, 2012).

48. "Illegals, God and Gospel in Manassas/PWC."

49. The following background text accompanies this upload: Letiecq interview was recorded in late August 2007. Letiecq requested that this footage be included on 9500 Liberty, and posted this video on his blog as an example of *9500 Liberty* changing course and being more fair to the

anti-illegal side. http://www.bvbl.net/index.php/2007/10/31/9500liberty-changes-course/#more-1739. "Illegals, God and Gospel in Manassas/PWC." In a phone interview, Byler noted that Letiecq had made the request to Byler and then again to Park but removed the link once the video was received critically. Eric Byler, phone interview, January 4, 2012.

50. Eric Byler, phone interview, January 4, 2012.

51. "Religious Leaders' Call to Healing Religion#4," *9500 Liberty* YouTube channel, November 7, 2007, http://www.youtube.com/watch?v=_aE3zcBIpsk (accessed February 15, 2012).

52. Unity in the Community, "Citizen Reaction to the Proposed Implementation of County Resolution No. 07–609 on Immigration," August 17, 2007, http://www.unityitc.org/Announcements/07–609Prt.htm (accessed February 15, 2012).

53. Kristen Mack, "Pr. William Religious Leaders Say Crackdown Is Divisive," *Washington Post,* February 3, 2008, http://www.washingtonpost.com/wp-dyn/content/article/2008/02/02/AR2008020201999.html (accessed August 17, 2013).

54. Mack, "Pr. William Religious Leaders Say Crackdown Is Divisive."

55. Jenkins et al., *Confronting the Challenges of Participatory Culture,* 7–9.

56. Eric Byler, phone interview, January 4, 2012.

57. "Illegals, God and Gospel in Manassas/PWC."

58. "Illegals, God and Gospel in Manassas/PWC."

59. "Reply to: Illegals, God, and Gospel," *9500 Liberty* YouTube channel, November 1, 2007, http://www.youtube.com/9500liberty#p/search/2/_NwUwSfwqLU (accessed February 15, 2012).

60. Although not an issue for the *9500 Liberty* project, another major obstacle associated with platforms like YouTube is the removal of content due to copyright protection. On this point, see Burgess and Green, *YouTube: Online Video and Participatory Culture.*

61. Hess, "Resistance Up in Smoke," 427.

62. "9500 Liberty: Interactive Documentary Scene from Feature Film," *9500 Liberty* YouTube channel, May 17, 2010, http://www.youtube.com/user/9500Liberty#p/a/u/1/wFxPAoZznpo (accessed February 15, 2012).

63. "9500 Liberty: Interactive Documentary Scene from Feature Film."

64. Eric Byler, phone interview, January 4, 2012.

65. Kristen Mack, "Provocative Blog Spawns Its Anti-Blog in Pr. William," *Washington Post,* April 4, 2008, http://www.washingtonpost.com/wp-dyn/content/article/2008/04/03/AR2008040301883.html (accessed August 17, 2013).

66. Letiecq addresses the decision to censor his blog due to costs associated with running the blog: "if you want ensure these bits and bytes are preserved for posterity, and disagree with my decisions, you are free to purchase your own hard drives, power them on your own dime, house them in a computer you buy, and maintain it with your own spare time." The first blog post of AntiBVBL.net (now archived on Moonhowlings: A Place for Civil Debate) links directly to Letiecq's post and offers to "pick up the tab" associated with the numerous dissenting comments. "A Quick Admin Note," Black Velvet Bruce Lee, February 22, 2008, http://www.bvbl.net/index.php/2008/02/22/pwc-committee-of-100-talks-blogs/#comment-55385 (accessed February 15, 2012), and "Picking Up the Tab," Moonhowlings: A Place for Civil Debate, February 22, 2008, http://www.moonhowlings.net/index.php/2008/02/ (accessed August 17, 2013).

67. Eric Byler, phone interview, January 4, 2012.

68. Eric Byler, phone interview, January 4, 2012.

69. Eric Byler, phone interview, January 4, 2012.

70. "Born in the USA; Looks 'Illegal'—Liberty Wall#3," *9500 Liberty* YouTube channel, Comments Forum, http://www.youtube.com/all_comments?v=SmdoicaZKyE (accessed February 14, 2012).

71. "Warnings," *9500 Liberty* YouTube channel Profile, http://www.youtube.com/user/9500Liberty (accessed February 15, 2012).

72. Eric Byler, phone interview, January 4, 2012.

73. Eric Byler, phone interview, January 4, 2012.

74. Eric Byler, phone interview, January 4, 2012.

75. Eric Byler, phone interview, January 4, 2012.

76. Eric Byler, phone interview, January 4, 2012.

77. Eric Byler, phone interview, January 4, 2012.

78. Eric Byler, phone interview, January 4, 2012.

79. "October 16 Flashback w/Subtitles," *9500 Liberty* YouTube channel, Comments Forum, http://www.youtube.com/all_comments?v=Ep-kflxuv3M (accessed February 14, 2012).

80. Mack, "Provocative Blog Spawns Its Anti-Blog in Pr. William."

81. "Immigration, Economics, Intolerance," *9500 Liberty* YouTube channel, Comments Forum, http://www.youtube.com/all_comments?v=20iwJ-_BipU (accessed February 14, 2012).

82. "Dr. Fuller on Real Estate Market," Moonhowlings: A Place for Civil Debate, April 26, 2008, http://www.moonhowlings.net/index.php/2008/04/26/dr-fueller-on-real-estate-market/comment -page-1/#comments (accessed August 17, 2013).

83. "Immigration Myths with Dr. Stephen S. Fuller, PhD," *9500 Liberty* YouTube channel, Comments Forum, http://www.youtube.com/all_comments?v=7EN4QFbclR8 (accessed February 14, 2012).

84. Hess, "Resistance Up in Smoke," 427–428.

85. "9500 Liberty: Aftermath of Immigration Resolution in Prince William," March 28, 2008, http://www.youtube.com/user/9500Liberty#p/search/7/YAvyi1Rutrs (accessed August 17, 2013).

86. "Great Party," Moonhowlings: A Place for Civil Debate, April 5, 2008, http://www.moonhowlings.net/index.php/2008/04/05/what-a-great-party/#comments (accessed August 17, 2013).

87. Eric Byler, phone interview, January 4, 2012.

88. Jean Burgess and Joshua Green, "Agency and Controversy in the YouTube Community," in *Proceedings: IR 9.0: Rethinking Communities, Rethinking Place* (Copenhagen: IT University of Copenhagen, Denmark, 2008), 4.

89. Nick Miroff, "Raw Look at Immigration Crucible," *Washington Post,* November 3, 2007, http://www.washingtonpost.com/wp-dyn/content/article/2007/11/02/AR2007110202158.html (accessed August 17, 2013); "9500 Liberty: Interactive Documentary Scene from Feature Film," *9500 Liberty* YouTube Channel, May 17, 2010, http://www.youtube.com/user/9500Liberty#p/a/u/1/wFxPAoZznpo (accessed February 15, 2012).

90. Quoted in Miroff, "Raw Look at Immigration Crucible."

91. Mallary Jean Tenore, "NewsHour Crowdsources Translations of President Obama's State of the Union," Poynter Institute, January 25, 2012, http://www.poynter.org/latest-news/top-stories/160702/president-obama-state-of-the-union-translated-pbs-newshour/ (accessed August 17, 2013).

92. McLagan, "Imagining Impact," 306.

On the Dance of Rhetoric

Ethnography, Embodiment, and Effect

AARON HESS

As seen throughout this volume, the nature of effect can be understood in a variety of ways. One troubling aspect of any discussion of effect is that it necessarily conjures *cause* as its preceding element. Yet, to establish rhetorical cause and effect is remarkably difficult, especially since the number of factors that go into the construction of a message, presumably constituting "cause," is remarkably difficult to ascertain. Similarly, establishing a connection between one specific cause and the effect of persuasion or identification is equally difficult, as discussed in the Introduction to this book. The ability to recognize specific causes and specific effects is hampered by time and memory, both of which arguably interfere with the recognition of the "true" cause or effect, if such a thing exists. This essay offers an exploratory approach to interpreting cause and effect. Like many, I am hesitant to witness messages constructed in laboratories, preferring instead those messages constructed in their contexts and witnessed firsthand. Ethnography provides an insightful approach to understanding this problem of effects that potentially overcomes many of the epistemological concerns regarding effects (and cause, for that matter). Direct witnessing of messages and immediate inquiry into audiences allow the critic to comprehend the complex relationship among time, space, and speaking. This is especially true in the case of vernacular rhetoric,[1] which is under investigation here. Gerard Hauser calls this form of rhetoric a "performance of jazz—free-form ensemble call and response."[2] In this free form of exchange, speaker and audience, advocate and opponent, and cause and effect become intertwined in ways that are difficult to recognize from a textual perspective. The interplay of discourse and appreciation of effect becomes wrapped up in the space and time of speech, requiring cognizance and presence from the critic. As Gerard Hauser puts it, "Local storefronts, gatherings in neighborhood shops, uses made of local parks and plazas, neighborhood and church festivals, and the like are beseechments to an attitude."[3] Rhetorical inquiry into these places and the effect of the discourses found therein requires an attention to the active production of discourse.

As such, in this essay, I offer a way of witnessing the contextual nature of rhetorical message construction through a participatory approach. In this manner, I analyze and evaluate the causes and effects of a message through ethnography and the direct performance of rhetoric. This level of engagement teases out notions of cause and effect as varied and complex and tied up in the agency of both speaker and audience. Vernacular rhetoric and advocacy, as Hauser puts it, "moved beyond the podium to the streets where the micro-practices of moment-by-moment interactions contribute not only to the organic character of the culture but become a significant source of rhetorically salient meaning and influence."[4] Ethnography offers the means to such an endeavor, especially through participant observation and interview methods. Interviews of speakers and audiences in the context of speaking can illustrate the thread that links message preparation, delivery, and reception, all of which are wrapped up in the microconstructions of rhetorical culture. Moreover, the active participation in message construction affords rhetorical scholars a reflexive opportunity of personal engagement. Effects, then, can be recognized and analyzed both through the interaction with speaker and audience and through self-reflexive means during an ethnographic project.

Vernacular Rhetoric and its Effects

While several essays in this volume discuss the notion of effects as drawn from larger discourses, my approach appears through vernacular and critical rhetoric. Many elements of critical rhetoric inform this project, but three features are worth mentioning here. First, Raymie McKerrow's offering of critical rhetoric foregrounds the performative elements of rhetoric, seeing praxis as a primary drive of the rhetorical critic.[5] Similarly, critical-rhetorical ethnography engages at the level of praxis, meaning that the process of rhetoric is inherent to the project. Second, Michael C. McGee argues that scholars of critical rhetoric are active in the invention of discourses suitable for critical examination, pulling the fragments of discourses together to form a text.[6] Placing critics squarely within invention invites participation in rhetoric, at both the macro and the micro levels. This movement of placing critics within the location of speaking mirrors similar approaches in critical discourse analysis.[7] Finally, and central to the debate about the function and position of discourse, arguments regarding the materialist function of rhetoric situate critical-rhetorical ethnography as affecting social reality. Dana Cloud believes that "to argue for the materiality of discourse is part and parcel of the poststructuralist shift toward discourse theory."[8] She reminds us that rhetoricians must examine the material functions of discourse and reject arguments that label everything as discursive: "To say that hunger and war are rhetorical is to state the obvious; to state that rhetoric is *all* they are is to leave critique behind."[9] In Ronald Greene's follow up on "another" materialist rhetoric, he pushes rhetoricians to examine the governing institutions and their function upon the populace: "When a materialist rhetoric recognizes the interaction between rhetorical forms and institutional forms it resists being limited to a rhetorical politics of subjectivity."[10] These three elements of critical rhetoric, taken together, mesh within critical-rhetorical ethnographers and invite examination of the effects and locations *as they affect* local populations.

Simultaneously, the vernacular turn in critical rhetoric invites a discussion of the "where" and "who" of rhetoric. Rhetorical acts have been reconceived away from the pulpit and moved to the congregation. Kent Ono and John Sloop criticize the limited purview of rhetoric, arguing that the focus on powerful texts has dismissed a crucial part of everyday politics. "[I]f we limit our attention to such documents (of power) . . . then we are missing out on, and writing 'out of history,' important texts that gird and influence local cultures first and then affect, through the sheer number of local communities, cultures at large."[11] Alternatively, they offer vernacular for analysis discourse, or "discourse that resonates within and from historically oppressed communities,"[12] and, later, outlaw discourses.[13] The pair echo Dana Cloud's concern for a materialist judgment of rhetoric, arguing that "the study of rhetoric implies the study of discourse and judgment on the level of everyday life; it implies, in short, a materialist conception of judgment."[14] Elsewhere, they refine this notion of rhetoric, critiquing the retrospective approach to rhetorical criticism[15] and saying that rhetorical critics should investigate the development of local logics as they compete in discourses of power. In other words, rhetoric should be understood through its process, not merely by its textual product. Gerard Hauser also conceptualizes a vernacular turn in rhetoric, locating the formation of public opinion in the coffee shops and street conversations among the populace.[16] To examine such rhetoric, Hauser offers an examination of effects: "these questions are inquiries into how actual members of actual publics respond to appeals, how they themselves actually engage in discourse that allows us to infer their opinion, and the rhetorical conditions that color their interactions."[17] Within such an empirical and materialist turn in rhetoric, new methods are necessary to reposition the critic *among* the exigencies of public life. As I outline later, an ethnographic approach to rhetoric can attend to these discourses and their effects.[18]

This attitude toward rhetoric parallels concerns about what effect may occur by rhetoric. While others in this volume discuss the progression of inquiries into effect in much more detail, I offer some salient points to the present discussion. First, looking back to Herbert Wicheln's proclamation of a criticism of oratory, we find that he situates the critic as "concerned with effect" and that rhetorical criticism "regards a speech as a communication to a specific audience, and holds its business to be the analysis and appreciation of the orator's method of imparting his ideas to his [*sic*] hearers."[19] Certainly, this passage is discussed in great length in this volume. For me, the specificity of the moment is important. Wichelns offers *kairos* as an essential part of the rhetorical situation to be understood by critics. Much later, Carole Blair offers an approach to rhetorical criticism regarding those "having been there" moments. She appreciates the power of public memorials as affecting audiences directly and in material ways.[20] Indeed, as I offer later, an ethnographic approach to rhetoric also attends to the moment of speech and an appreciation for its immediate effect.

Second, Wayne Thompson discusses public address as to be "directly observed by the research worker."[21] Later in the essay, he elaborates upon the type of training necessary to complete such a study of "contemporary public address," including "training in research methods."[22] Pressing for disciplinary reform, he continues: "And the point at which public address becomes unique, as distinguished from history and other subject matter areas, is its aliveness. Speech is a living subject, communication become dynamic. It is the spoken word, not the written page. It is a means of social change, not the social change itself."[23]

In this passage, Thompson entrusts rhetoric and public address as a process-oriented discipline, studying "language *as it is heard,* speech structure in relation to its effect *at the time of delivery,* the ethical power of the speaker *as he* [*sic*] *stands before the audience.*"[24] To this, I add that rhetoric can be understood through the direct performance of it. Thompson also argues that the purpose of such a research project would be to study "the selection of procedures and the evolution of techniques."[25] While I recognize that Thompson and Wichelns are speaking of public address, I follow Raymie McKerrow in arguing that "the reversal of 'public address' to 'discourse which addresses publics' places the critic in the role of 'inventor.'"[26] To gauge its effect, scholars should practice, perform, and invent rhetoric within the spaces of public discussion and deliberation. Ethnographic practices, especially participant observation, situate the critic in direct connection to both the audience and speaker. Recognizing that close readings of texts or biographical methods have limitations that recognize contemporary public advocacy, recent innovations in rhetorical methods have forged novel methodological partnerships between qualitative and ethnographic methods, among others.[27] The rhetorical ethnographer can take up the position of either or both by enacting arguments while in the field. In so doing, the critic can evaluate rhetorical effects, including the invention of arguments, the use of artistic appeals, and the reception from audience members. Here, the critic can examine everything from nonverbal reactions to counterarguments from audience members by following up via observations, informal conversations, or formal interviews. In other words, situating the critic inside the moment of *stasis* and controversy provides vital insights into the production of argument. I now turn to the particular moment of controversy and argumentation under consideration: DanceSafe and the so-called war on drugs.

The Dance of Rhetoric

It's Saturday night in the city. Tucked away in a hidden corner of the industrial district, youth congregate at a local rave. This fast-paced, all-night dance party features three addictive substances: drugs, music, and youth. The decision to take or not take drugs is fought in the minds of youngsters, just as DJs battle each other on stage, spinning trance-inducing electronic music with deep beats. The glassed and glossed faces of many of those at the event answer that question in the affirmative. This does not come as a surprise; raves are well-known destinations for chemical indulgence, and the drug Ecstasy is the preferred substance for its empathic, energetic, and euphoric effects. The music and drug dance with each other with boundless highs and sensual lows. A booth stands in the corner with ravers parsing through a large, clear bowl of candy. Colored lights adorn the table, along with information about drugs, free fruit and water, and pamphlets on how to end the "war on drugs." Adorned with badges featuring names above a small silhouette of a raver against what looks like a yellow street sign, volunteers dance along, stopping only to happily chat about intoxicants, the latest DJ, and the political consequences of mandatory minimum sentences with passersby: an odd place for drug education, it would seem. As the teenagers approach, one asks simply, "What is this?" The volunteer behind the table explains that the table's sponsor is DanceSafe, an advocacy group dedicated to providing drug information without judgment and to ending the war on drugs.

One could wonder about the rhetorical situation of this organization and its membership. What would it be like to attempt persuasion with an audience intoxicated on rebellious youth and Ecstasy? How would a rhetorical scholar learn of such persuasion? Recognize its effects? This chemically induced context offers a suitable case study and exploratory discussion of participatory rhetorical methodology. Positioned within the complex and controversial world of drug use and misuse, DanceSafe offers a compelling form of advocacy to a tough audience, teenage and twenty-something drug users within the culture of raving. Rave culture is an intriguing location for rhetorical inquiry. Understood for its inherent countercultural attitude of resistance, the scene contains "deeply fought rhetorical/ideological battles around communalism and commercialism, performance and product, and sharing and spectacle."[28] Brian Ott and Bill Herman's discussion of rave culture provides insight into a place where the spectacle of dance brushes against the politics of commodification coupled with the use of drugs. Between these struggles is a health concern. The drug of choice, Ecstasy, is widely consumed by ravers. While not every raver uses drugs, rave culture cannot be separated from drugs. The experience of the drug, including feelings of deep connection, euphoria, and empathy, accents the communal atmosphere of the rave and the electronic music of the god-like DJ. However, as the sun comes up and the music fades, ravers are faced with a number of health concerns, including depression and neurotoxicity, as a consequence of their indulgence. As a result, members of rave culture organized to address this concern and created DanceSafe. Established well over a decade ago, DanceSafe is a health advocacy organization that attends to drug use in the rave scene through a harm reduction approach. Its mission is to mitigate the harms of drug use while supporting the culture of raving as a whole, a complex and nearly contradictory approach that couples health information with a strong sense of ethos. Given the corporeal effects of the drug and the embodied health advocacy provided in the heart of a drug-using culture, DanceSafe's exigence offers a difficult yet fitting location for understanding rhetoric's effects. To study the group, I engaged in critical-rhetorical ethnography, which provides a participatory approach to studying rhetoric's effects.[29] This project operates as a case study which, I hope, articulates a promising direction for rhetorical scholarship interested in the first-hand recognition of and reflection upon effects.

DanceSafe, Harm Reduction, and Rhetoric in the "War on Drugs"

Rhetoric has been acutely aware of controversy,[30] and rhetorical scholarship aims to unpack how individuals come together to deliberate or advocate in a moment of *stasis*. Fundamental to such rhetorical exchanges is the context in which they occur and how it relates to the notion of effects.[31] DanceSafe, as an advocacy group, exists in a historical context of the U.S. war on drugs, a widely held position of abstinence-only programs and education. Standing in opposition to abstinence-only approaches, DanceSafe is dedicated to ending the war on drugs. And, the volunteer group does not stand alone. As I will indicate, the United States is at a critical juncture; organizations and individuals are questioning the hardline policy of the war on drugs, and the populace in some states is voting in favor of crucial reforms of laws pertaining to marijuana. This context provides insight into the overall concerns of *stasis*, which inform the advocacy of the group. Within it, I investigate how DanceSafe situates itself symbolically and through its advocacy of a harm reduction message.

Harm Reduction in the War on Drugs

Well documented for its shortcomings and outright failures, the war on drugs continues to be waged on drug users across the globe.[32] Both popular[33] and scholarly[34] accounts have recognized that widely used scare tactics and propaganda have failed to achieve their goals. In the United States, the war on drugs has largely been understood through a model of zero-tolerance policies and abstinence-only rhetoric. With drug use symbolically constructed as a criminal act rather than a health concern, the policies and guidance of the federal Office of National Drug Control Policy (ONDCP) continue to incarcerate thousands of nonviolent offenders. While many have protested,[35] the central policies of the ONDCP have remained entrenched in abstinence-only and zero-tolerance policies. One of the primary mechanisms of the ONDCP is to produce messages in the form of commercials, educational poster campaigns in schools, and online resources targeted at curious youth.[36] The theme of such campaigns is usually peer pressure; often, the campaigns utilize fear tactics as a primary means of persuasion. Drug users, in such messages, are constructed as dupes who foolishly "fell" for peer pressure. The consequences of drug use are catastrophic, leading to such things as social ostracism, emotional and physical pain, and death. While the ONDCP continues to argue that its campaign is successful, many observers have challenged their claims as dubious at best.[37]

To challenge the ONDCP and antidrug policies of the federal government, a number of organizations and volunteer groups have come together, largely under the banner of harm reduction. At the most fundamental level, harm reduction exists as an alternative to the "zero-tolerance" or "abstinence-only" approaches common to American federal drug policy. Alan Marlatt describes harm reduction as "founded on a set of pragmatic principles and compassionate strategies designed to minimize the harmful consequences of personal drug use and associated high-risk behaviors."[38] As a social movement, harm reduction is considered to be a grassroots alternative to "both the moral model (as exemplified by the ongoing 'war on drugs') and the medical model (addiction defined as disease)."[39] Given the failed policies of the war on drugs and of prohibitionist models, harm-reduction efforts began as proactive alternatives that focus on the notion of drug abuse as a public-health problem, not a criminal one. Notably, however, harm-reduction advocates do not reject the idea of abstinence as the safest alternative to drug use but argue rather that abstinence-*only* programs often fail to meet their difficult, if not impossible, goal.

In the United States, harm reduction has not been warmly received. At odds with the federal abstinence-based programs, harm-reduction efforts, such as methadone prescription or syringe exchange, are met with considerable opposition. While in the early twentieth century prescribed opiates and drug maintenance programs existed, their tenure was short lived. Under pressure from conservative voices in the Nixon administration and reinforced by the Reagan administration, the war on drugs began, with drug addicts positioned as public enemy number one.[40] Ernest Drucker and Allan Clear analyze the chilly rhetorical climate surrounding harm-reduction programs, arguing that the "climate of intimidation has limited the national growth and expansion of needle exchange leaving large numbers of injectors unreached and ignored, as virtually any support or social service for drug users, including drug treatment, is considered undesirable and fringe."[41] Under the Reagan and the first Bush administrations, drug use was construed as creating a moral panic, and this construction assisted in guiding public attitudes and subsequent policies.[42] As a social movement, harm reduction has been categorized by the federal drug czars and national drug control strategists as a cover for legalization movements. As Gary Fisher argues, "The United States has taken a hard line against nearly all harm-reduction strategies, seeing them as methods used by legalization proponents to achieve that goal."[43] In short, the discursive climate created in the war on drugs makes harm-reduction advocacy a difficult task.

As a social movement, harm reduction attracts a diverse set of interests and individuals. The primary objectives of harm-reduction programs follow the three principles outlined by Alan Marlatt: "first, working with individuals to reduce harmful behaviors . . . ; second, modifying the environment to enhance safety and reduce risk . . . ; and third, changing policies, laws, and regulations so as to reduce harm to both individuals and the larger society."[44] However, the diverse proponents of harm reduction have different ideas about the means and ends of such programs.

While criticisms from federal officials misrepresent the movement by labeling it a cover for decriminalization or legalization, they are not far off in stating that some advocates do seek goals such as these. As Gary Fisher puts it, "While it is quite likely that individuals and groups who support very liberal legalization policies also support harm-reduction groups, that does not lead to a conclusion that harm-reduction groups are attempting to legalize drugs."[45] Definitional issues complicate the nature of harm reduction, often causing confusion over the boundaries and causes of the movement. Interestingly enough, DanceSafe intersects with a variety of other movements, offering pamphlets for the Marijuana Policy Project and Students for Sensible Drug Policy, both of which seek the goal of decriminalization.

Central to my inquiry into harm reduction and DanceSafe is the belief that drug use/misuse is a social problem that is rhetorically produced. As a rhetorical problem, it is vital to recognize the competing rhetorical goals of the ONDCP and harm-reduction organizations such as DanceSafe. Additionally, investigators studying the rhetorical construction of drug use cannot dismiss the material[46] and real-world negative health risks of drug use but should also recognize that the meanings associated with alcohol and other drugs use are essentially contested concepts in American society.[47] The meanings attached to drug *use* carry over to *users,* making important claims about the nature of drug-user identity. For example, Erich Goode argues that the American drug panic of the 1980s can be understood through both objective and socially constructed measures.[48] On the one hand, frequency of discussion by politicians, levels of awareness in public polling, and media coverage indicate that drug abuse was a top concern of the American public. Yet, data show that overall use of drugs in society was down considerably during the same time period, indicating that the social problem of drug abuse was largely socially constructed. On the other hand, Goode finds that indicators of heavy or dangerous use as well as the negative consequences of use, such as violence or theft, were higher in that time period, indicating that the problem can be understood as objective.[49] In sum, rhetorical approaches to understanding the effects and reception of drug control education, such as DanceSafe's drug advocacy, should recognize both the symbolic and the material power of drug use as a social issue. Methodologically, my active participation within DanceSafe's campaign assists in recognizing this duality.

DanceSafe

DanceSafe is a harm-reduction organization founded in 1999 by Emanuel Sferios, then a thirty-year-old former social worker. He formed the project out of fear that youths might use drugs that they thought to be Ecstasy but that actually contained potentially lethal substances. At its inception, the organization was funded by a collection of dot-commers who had formerly attended raves and were dissatisfied by the scare tactics of the war on drugs.[50] The group is dedicated to "educating their mostly teenage and twenty-something audience about drugs and their dangers in a more effective style than the antidrug rhetoric preached in schools and commercials."[51] The philosophy of the organization declares two primary principles: harm reduction and popular education. First, "in its barest sense, harm reduction is a pragmatic approach to dealing with societal drug use. It begins with the observation that despite all our efforts as a society to stop the use of illicit drugs, people are using them anyway, and it seems unlikely this situation is going to change soon. This necessitates a practical response to reduce the harm that is taking place right now. And this response is called, appropriately enough, harm reduction."[52]

To enact the principles of harm reduction and as its second principle, DanceSafe calls upon popular education models from Paulo Freire: "As opposed to more traditional educational models that see the teacher as a large container full of knowledge and the students as empty containers that need filling, popular education sees learning as a creative process that transforms everyone, teachers and students alike."[53] To achieve its goal of increasing "the ability of our peers to positively influence their own health and safety," DanceSafe tables and booths at raves provide an array of services.[54] First, DanceSafe volunteers offer information about the contents and history of drugs. The information provided comes in the form of colorful cards, specifically made to look like the advertising flyers given out for future events. On the back of each card, information is listed in descriptive categories: "What is the drug?," "How is it used?," "What are the effects?," and "Be careful." The final category does not direct behavior regarding the drug; rather, it indicates the possible side effects of use, including the outcome of mixing it with other drugs, negative side effects, and legal status. DanceSafe offers information pertaining to common illegal drugs such as ecstasy, marijuana, and magic mushrooms but also provides information about legal intoxicants such as alcohol, tobacco, and nitrous oxide. Other information found at DanceSafe tables relates to hearing protection, sexually transmitted diseases, and legal issues related to drug use and the rave scene. DanceSafe also provides pamphlets that describe local rehabilitation centers for treatment of addiction. Second, DanceSafe provides free fruit, candy, water, and condoms for ravers. Food and water are offered to assist ravers who may be unaware of their sugar and hydration levels, a common problem at raves. Finally, and most controversial, some DanceSafe chapters offer onsite pill testing for ravers. In these cases, ravers may bring pills to DanceSafe booths, where a portion of the pill is scraped off and tested with chemical compounds that indicate, by color change and the presence of smoke, the presence of MDMA or other substances. After the test is complete, DanceSafe members inform the raver about the contents of the pill but do not indicate what to do with it, leaving the element of choice in the hands of ravers. The controversy of pill testing bleeds into a larger ethical question of harm reduction.[55]

Method: Critical-Rhetorical Ethnography

To investigate the reception and effects of DanceSafe's campaign, I utilize two methodological lines, ethnography and rhetorical analysis, in what I call critical-rhetorical ethnography.[56] First, the ethnographic side of my research guided my participation in the volunteer group. Using the method of participant observation, I became a complete member of the organization.[57] For nearly two years, I worked with DanceSafe, assisting in organizational planning, attending nearly every event, and recruiting new members into the group. I used participant observation and advocacy to learn how to enact DanceSafe's campaign while also reflecting upon the argumentation strategies being used by the group and its reception by drug users in the rave scene. Throughout my tenure with the organization, I kept detailed fieldnotes, which are a vital source of data for rhetorical ethnographers and are developed over the course of a project. As accounts of the scene, fieldnotes provide the most direct connection between the researcher and his or her advocacy. Fieldnotes should record the field of argumentation, asking fundamental and theoretically progressing questions ranging from "What is going on here?" to "How do advocates of this organization construct persuasive messages for this particular audience?"

I also performed two rounds of interviews, which I conceptualized as "guided empathic conversations." The interviews were *guided* in that I used a semistructured approach to each encounter that helped me ask pertinent questions about the campaign but also provided a flexible interview moment. Following Fontana and Frey, I conducted the interviews with a spirit of *empathy,* through which the "interviewer becomes an advocate and partner in the study, hoping to be able to use the results to advocate social policies and ameliorate the conditions of the interviewee."[58] Finally, my interviews were treated as *conversations* to mirror natural dialogue.[59] In the first round, I interviewed the current DanceSafe membership to inquire about the types of message strategies and general political ideals of the group as it conducts its advocacy. In the second round, I interviewed thirteen ravers while in the scene to ask about how the campaign was received. The individuals selected for interviews were those with whom I had built a rapport through previous interactions. The sampling method was one of convenience, rather than random selection, primarily because of the complex nature of the scene. As mentioned, raves are counterculture spaces, and random selection survey research would be incompatible with the attitude found there. Questions in these interviews included types of experiences with DanceSafe, reflections on its central message, comparisons to federal antidrug campaigns, and reasons for drug use.

Second, the rhetorical side of my research offers theoretical principles that structure the overall purpose and development of fieldwork. Qualitative inquiry asks fundamental questions about how individuals interact within particular contexts; however, the question of advocacy is one of rhetoric. As such, I use the long-standing concepts of *kairos, invention,* and *phronesis* as guiding rhetorical principles and interpret them for critical-rhetorical ethnography at the moment of advocacy and argumentation. Traditionally, *kairos* can be understood as the timeliness and appropriateness of speech and situational context.[60] This dual rhetorical concept provides the rhetorical ethnographer with the means for examining the moment of advocacy.[61] The notion of *kairos* attends to the situated character of rhetoric, as discourse that exists in time and space, with a particular group of people with their own *doxa*. As rhetorical ethnographers exist in the field of argumentation, they develop a local and contextual knowledge through the constant interaction with participants. Thus, to participate in the advocacy of an organization, rhetorical ethnographers must have a thorough knowledge of what types of discourses will be effective in the moment at hand.

Similarly, invention guides the rhetorical ethnographer to create arguments within the context of speaking, paying close attention to each *kairotic* moment. Michael McGee argues that within critical rhetoric, critics invent discourses and texts that are suitable for criticism.[62] Drawing from this conception, invention in rhetorical ethnography engages both in reflection upon extant discourses within the *kairotic* moment and in the production of new arguments toward the overall goal of the organization's advocacy. Murphy speaks of invention being inherent to understanding counterpublic discourse and asserts that it is both a constitutive and an oppositional act.[63] In this way, invention both forms the identity of counterpublic or vernacular communities and strategically positions them within larger public fields of argumentation. Finally, rhetorical ethnography embraces the concept of *phronesis* as prudence or practical wisdom. Robert Hariman believes that the performance of *phronesis,* as an Aristotelian ideal, occurs in "everyday political consciousness."[64] He believes that a thorough revitalization of the virtue "recovers the body as a trope for political communication . . . the body active in political life as a body serving as a field of figuration."[65] The political body, in this sense, references an ontological and political positioning of *phronesis*. Yet, Hariman also underscores the "everydayness" of phronetic judgment.[66] Similarly, Long asserts that the location is not just about place but also about the function of *phronesis* as being "thoroughly embedded in the world of finite contingency."[67] It is in this world of uncertainty, variability, and possibility that the rhetorical ethnographer can utilize the virtue of *phronesis* as a driving ideal of vernacular advocacy.

Overall, this methodology provided a dual perspective into the production of discourse and advocacy within a particular rhetorical moment. While other research into drug users entails a strong qualitative element[68] or textual focus,[69] my approach adds firsthand, participatory experiences to understanding health advocacy and its effect. Separately, ethnography and rhetoric cannot account for the complex advocacy performed by DanceSafe. Ethnography could provide interpretive insights into the culture and performances found at raves, but it would miss the nature of advocacy and argument offered by the volunteer group. Rhetoric, especially coming from a post hoc textual perspective, would miss the situated character of the rave, which is difficult to comprehend without being there, especially as a site for advocacy. To assess the campaign, I asked local youth who had witnessed the campaign about their reactions to and their interpretations of it. While this project existed in a larger project, with other items on the interview guide, the central question dealt with active advocacy and message adaptation with a difficult-to-reach target audience: young drug users. As a gauge of effects, my perspective allowed firsthand reactions to a campaign from an active target audience. Davis W. Houck and Mihaela Nocasian call for the historical and rhetorical examination of "living texts";[70] I have, in parallel fashion, sought to find a text that is still very much active and alive and that offers a view into the ongoing development of rhetoric. The two rounds of interviewing provided a "before and after" picture of the campaign, asking volunteers how they crafted their messages and ravers how they received it. Being a part of the planning process and actively performing the campaign insightfully allowed me to display the complex process of message construction and production. Consequently, I was able to chart specific choices about the campaign made in preparation for raves and its success with the audience.[71] Cause, for me, includes the variety of choices made before messages were produced; effect is the in situ reception of an active campaign. Campaign volunteers adapted messages and learned just as I did, offering insight into the process of rhetoric. Finally, as an active participant in the scene, I developed a unique perspective into the group's training, development, and maintenance of a message campaign. The result of having such a vantage will be elaborated upon.

Analysis: Charting DanceSafe's Effect

Ethnography offers a specific and contextualized understanding of effect at the moment of advocacy. The challenge of effect occurs in both time and space. As time passes since the creation of specific messages, audiences and speakers may change their personal impressions of the message, forgetting key details or supplanting them with new ones. The spaces of speaking are nuanced, with a multitude of factors affecting the reception of a message. Sounds, sights, and smells all affect how individuals react to messages and are difficult to recollect via post hoc surveys or textual approaches. Ethnography, however, offers an approach that can account for the deficiencies created in time and space. The snap judgments made by audience members can be recorded via interview and direct observation. Of course, the "true" nature of effect is ultimately lost, but much can be gained through participatory approaches. The questions asked of ravers as they received DanceSafe's messages provide specific accounts of how advocacy was performed to this audience. Moreover, the critic's engagement in message creation and dissemination through participant observation provides an accounting for cause and effect that is exceptionally difficult to ascertain via other methods. Nonverbal feedback, emotional and affective considerations, and other embodied elements are directly realized by the critic. Conversations and interviews alike provide vital insights into the successes and failures of the campaign.

While the interviews covered a number of issues, under scrutiny in this essay are inquiries into the rhetorical choices made by volunteers and the persuasive effect of the campaign. The questions included the following: Describe your experiences with DanceSafe. How many times have you noticed DanceSafe's presence at raves? Have you received information from DanceSafe? What do you think DanceSafe provides for ravers? How would you characterize DanceSafe's central message? What does DanceSafe want you as a raver to walk away with? How is this message presented? How, if at all, have you used the information presented by DanceSafe? Overall, do you find that DanceSafe provides a service to the rave scene? How do you use that service, if at all? What could DanceSafe do more effectively to better serve ravers? These questions were asked of thirteen different ravers in the scene who had approached the DanceSafe table seeking information. In most cases, the individuals that I contacted for interviews were those with whom I had built a rapport. Interviews lasted between fifteen and forty-five minutes, were conducted within the rave scene, and were fully audio-recorded and transcribed. IRB approval was obtained before research began.

Responses to the interview questions led to a number of conclusions regarding DanceSafe's rhetorical activism. First, DanceSafe was received by a preponderance of ravers as a positive type of nonjudgmental drug education with a central idea of *responsible choices regarding drugs,* consistent with the desired message discussed by volunteers. The mission of the organization stipulates that members cannot pass judgment upon drug users while providing accurate information about drugs, and this message was well received by ravers. Second, ravers interpreted DanceSafe's message largely through a sense of ethos. Ravers remarked that DanceSafe was a comfortable and safe place to discuss drug use, largely because of the character of the volunteers and their attitudes toward the ravers as an audience. Finally, DanceSafe was recognized as having a long-standing presence and as a source of wisdom within the rave scene. This sense of localized judgment, which I articulate with the notion of *phronesis,* was recognized by ravers as having a powerful effect on their reception of the overall campaign. While individual members of the organization would fade in and out, the appearance of DanceSafe booths were understood as long-standing features of the scene.

DanceSafe's Message of Responsible Drug Use and Truth

Working within the harm-reduction philosophy, DanceSafe crafts a message that is about *choice* and *knowledge.* Individuals should be able to make informed choices about drug use, rather than be fed exaggerations and scare tactics as is usually provided from federal antidrug agencies. When curious drug users approach the table to inquire about DanceSafe, volunteers frequently indicate that DanceSafe is an educational organization about informed decision making. In one exchange, a volunteer described DanceSafe's philosophy as "pro-choice" with regard to the decisions made by the youth in the scene. Members continuously sought ways to educate youth about their choices about drugs, sexual activity, and civil liberties. Coupled with a nonjudgmental stance, the central message is designed to invite ravers to talk about health and their choice in drug habit. In response, ravers positioned DanceSafe as choice and "truth," contrasted with official coercion and lies. One raver reflected on this attitude toward drugs, summing up the campaign as saying "that we can't tell you what to do, even if it's illegal. Obviously people are going to do it anyway, and rather have them be safe than not be safe." Understood as rhetorical effect, this recognition of purpose indicates that DanceSafe was, at the very least, effective in its self-portrayal as a drug education and health advocacy group.

In my interviews, ravers, in response to a question about the central message of the campaign, reported that they largely understood DanceSafe in this way. DanceSafe is designed to provide honest, accurate information to its target audience. Ravers interpreted the central message as supporting these two complementary goals: provision of honest information and respect for personal responsibility. First, DanceSafe's mission of providing honest, accurate information was confirmed in my interviews via the perceptions of ravers. Interviewees indicated that DanceSafe offers an array of positive and negative facts about drugs, coupled with an ethos of honesty and trust. Such an ethos was discursively deployed in opposition to governmental or parental authorities, which I discuss in the following section. One raver remarked that "People have a lot of wrong information and they don't know what they're talking about and don't know what they're taking. And so it's really good that there are people out there who are actually informing kids because they're going to be doing it anyway. So it makes it a lot safer for the people who are at least smart enough to try and figure it out. But, I mean I think it's great."

In another case, a young raver indicated that the information was without bias because of its presentation style: "You're not telling me to not do drugs. You're just telling information about it." This type of honesty was supported by DanceSafe's use of a two-sided message about drug use, one that included positive and negative effects about using drugs. Another raver elaborated, quite eloquently, about the nature of the message's appeal and structure: "I, for example, use your cards as one of the many references because I have found, in my opinion, an unbiased source. They seem to have looked at the different sides of the spectrum and come to a particular conclusion that is logical, scientific, and isn't out there to scare anybody away from doing a specific drug. Yet the positive effects of it and the negative effects of it. I appreciate that a great deal."

This summary indicates that the rhetorical message offered by DanceSafe's campaign was interpreted in nuanced ways by its audience. It was received and weighed, as many health-related messages are. One respondent spoke of comparing and contrasting the message with other information available, especially with regard to ethos and logos. The use of scientific logic and methods were important to this raver, which could be found in governmental sources as well. Yet, for him, the message was effective because of its ethos and its two-sided approach, providing information on both positive and negative effects of drugs. This is inherently a discussion of ethos, which, as I discuss in the following section, is laboriously constructed by the campaign to connect with rave culture. Because of that connection, the campaign is able to utilize scientific appeals that bolster its credibility as being objective—as representing "truth"—while subjectively connecting with the individual raver. In speaking of the information disseminated, one raver affirmed the objective nature of the materials: "But I had them [DanceSafe flyers] for a long time wind up on my wall with the picture on one because I grabbed two of every one and the information below because my friends would come over and they'd be like, 'Blah blah blah this and that.' And I'd be like, 'Really, go refer to that. It will tell you the truth.'"

The second aspect of the central message of the campaign is its focus on personal responsibility. Indeed, DanceSafe not only provides information about drugs but also challenges ravers to take personal responsibility for their actions and for those of the people around them. In this case, the campaign's central message carries weight in a seemingly contradictory manner. Effectively, it becomes: "Do drugs safely," which connects to larger concerns about the ethics of harm reduction as a paradigm.[72] Ravers, in discussing this theme, provided interesting analyses of the purpose of DanceSafe. Most directly, ravers commented about how drug use requires personal responsibility, understood in a number of ways. One raver explained that drug use intersects with other elements of responsibility: "The fucked-up thing about the rave scene is like, like I'm all for all-ages parties so all people of all ages can come and party, but these little thirteen-year-old kids dress up like sluts and they have no responsibility and like I don't know. It also gives the scene a bad name when these little kids come and eat a bunch of pills and OD. And I don't know it's just a whole cycle. That's why I think you guys [DanceSafe] are great."

In this example, DanceSafe's message is well received as one that encourages ravers to take responsibility for a number of actions. Looking beyond personal decisions, ravers reflected on the social nature of responsibility. One raver paraphrased John F. Kennedy, saying, "It's not what your rave scene can do for you, it's what you can do for your rave scene." She expressed concern that ravers often neglect themselves and the scene they enjoy and saw DanceSafe's message as reminding them to be accountable for their actions. In other cases, the accounts of personal responsibility were more specific to drug use. One raver remarked, after being asked about DanceSafe's role in drug culture, "And it has built this kind of responsibility for all those people who are coming in, trying to teach them what really was going on and the things to look out for and how not to be stupid." In this case, the raver noted how DanceSafe's message of responsibility is directed both at the individual and at the social scene, an issue I explore in more depth later. Ultimately, the nature of responsibility was intertwined with being informed by DanceSafe. Another raver, drawing from a source that perhaps more aptly fits the scene, paraphrased the 1980s cartoon *G. I. Joe:* "It is so true, knowledge is half the battle."

Ethos Construction and Reception

An essential element of the DanceSafe campaign is the construction of ethos. Gerard Hauser believes that "local ethos grows from adhering to the rules of propriety its vernacular requires."[73] Raver culture is one of distrust and resistance; to be successful in disseminating its message, DanceSafe must find ways to connect to the character of ravers.[74] The DanceSafe president, Lisa, explained that ravers attend parties for drugs, music, and community and that ravers engage in participatory rebellion against mainstream culture. The act of attending a rave is charged, marked with being both social and ostracized. This principle of identification as social outcasts provides ravers with a rallying cry of, as Lisa puts it, "just because I want to be different." Yet, as a population, ravers are fleeting, maturing out of their drug use and rave attendance very quickly. This means that DanceSafe is presented with a new audience of ravers at each rave, many of whom have never experienced a rave and are being initiated into—born into, as ravers put it—the scene. To respond to this morphing audience, DanceSafe utilizes a sense of ethos built on invitation.[75] Engaging in a nonjudgmental approach, the health campaign volunteers invite conversation about drugs from anyone while in any state of mind, including intoxication. This construction of ethos was completed in two ways. First, DanceSafe maintains a positive cultural presence in the scene. Second, DanceSafe situates itself against other, commonly understood health promotion or education agencies, especially perceived governmental programs such as D.A.R.E.

As a positive presence in the scene, DanceSafe is understood by ravers as providing a foundation for knowledge about drugs. One raver discussed DanceSafe, saying, "I see it's a very positive thing; I think it's good particularly that you're handing out the different cards with the different facts on drugs." Another raver, when asked about whether she sees DanceSafe's presence as offering something positive, responded in the affirmative: "Yes, it does it really does. Everyone talks about your booth, and they love your booth. The fact that you guys are actually caring." This positive presence translates directly into the Aristotelian notion of ethos as goodwill. Ravers received and understood the campaign directly through ethos, interpreting the intent of the volunteers as expressing goodwill toward the culture and individuals within it. Given the environment, this element of the campaign was powerful. As discussed, ravers can and should be understood as rebellious and often resistant to authority. DanceSafe approaches this subculture with the educational and philosophical aim of moderation, which is in stark contrast to the celebration of youth and indulgence. However, in this profound moment of contradiction, ravers report that DanceSafe accomplishes its goal of connection. In the words of another youth, "It's great that you guys are concerned with the well-being of the scene and the well-being of these random people that you've never met and don't really have any connection to."

The other construction of ethos found in the campaign is much more in line with the rebelliousness of the raver crowd. Youth who attend raves do so to escape, and drug use is understood as a way to forget the ills of life. One young pair of ravers, when asked about why they attend raves and use drugs, revealed that they seek an escape:

> Interviewee 2: Yeah, because like in today's society we have so many different stresses. We have school, family, friends, relationships, jobs, everything.

Interviewee 1: Yet even for like teenagers, I mean, young kids, adults, these days there is so much stress.

Interviewee 2: . . . and I mean, drugs are a kind of like, kind of like a release from that.

Not only do these pressures affect their decisions to use; they motivate the subculture to act out in resistance. Brian Ott and Bill Herman contend that raves feature a "flattening of hierarchy," which problematizes the notion of ethos as expertise.[76] In other words, ravers come to dance and to escape from the rigidity of everyday life, especially in its hierarchical and authoritative form. How, in this space, does a group like DanceSafe construct a sense of health promotion ethos that embodies authority via expertise while simultaneously rejecting it? To do this, DanceSafe constructs its ethos as a type of rhetorical foil. It operates *against* traditional notions of authority by placing itself in contrast, in effect, fitting in with the larger counterculture theme of resistance. As noted, youth escape from and in some cases reject the types of authority that appear in daily life. Parents, teachers, and police only offer the tribulations that are cause for escape, and so DanceSafe rejects them in much the same way. Volunteers position DanceSafe as "not your parents' drug education" and indicate that programs like the governmentally supported D.A.R.E. are the opposite of the booths at the rave. During one of my observations, the rave was broken up by local police authorities, and DanceSafe members quickly distributed wallet-size cards that explained the concept of illegal search and seizure. In my initial interviews with DanceSafe volunteers and leadership, my interviewees indicated that DanceSafe was like cool "baby-sitters" who allow the kids to do more than Mom and Dad permit or "sober friends" who look out for you when you've overindulged. During my observations, I found DanceSafe, as well as myself, constructing the health organization as "We're not the police, and we're certainly not your parents!"

Beyond performing in this way, ravers reported that the effect of this construction was noticeable and powerful. When asked about the central message of DanceSafe, ravers commonly responded with statements that reflected a "not-your-parents" attitude. One said, "They are giving them [ravers] a viewpoint that's not from their 'parents' so to speak" and added that DanceSafe avoids the "D.A.R.E. education stigma," which she called "bullshit." Another raver told me that DanceSafe is "looking out for these kids when their parents aren't here." This powerful construction allowed DanceSafe access to a vulnerable population to disseminate its campaign message. One of the volunteers indicated that he tries to be as nonjudgmental as possible, that passing judgment would be negative to the campaign. He explained that the preferred approach is to be "just a very calm acceptance, nonjudgmental. Giving out information, and that's it." This character of DanceSafe was well received. One raver recognized that DanceSafe was different from parental or governmental sources of information and that the calming approach was effective: "if it was more hostile like, 'don't do drugs' less people would come by and pick them up." Overall, DanceSafe was effective in constructing a character that was both inviting and oppositional to perceived traditional sources of drug campaigns.

Phronesis and Participant Advocacy

The final aspect of understanding the effect of DanceSafe's rhetoric is through my own personal experiences in the campaign. Rhetorical ethnography positions the rhetorical critic not only within the moment of advocacy but also as an active participant. In turn, the researcher reflects upon his or her own development and performances of the advocacy. Certainly, the researcher learns of the inventive practices of the campaign or protest, as I did with DanceSafe. Looking beyond invention, however, rhetorical ethnography calls upon the notion of *phronesis* as the practical judgment built through experience. *Phronesis* provides an additional tool for reflecting upon the complex idea of effect, especially since it opens personal understandings of cause and effect. I examined *phronesis* not merely as a virtue that other volunteers embodied but as something that *I* needed to embody. Consequently, through the active performance of the message, I experienced a learning curve in the organization and had to learn how to present myself and my personal history as a part of advocacy.

Understood as an effect of rhetoric, *phronesis* begs the researcher to engage in reflexivity[77] and to learn from mistakes and risks taken in the scene.[78] Carrie Birmingham positions *phronesis* as a pedagogical model of self-reflection. In her case, "the conceptualization of reflection as *phronesis* adds clarity to the nature of the relationship between reflection and actions—that is, actions are derived from reflection, and reflection is built through the practice of reflective actions."[79] Christopher Long also believes that an ontological positioning of *phronesis* in much the way that I have here "points to the possibility of developing a critically self-reflective model of ontological knowledge firmly embedded in the finite world."[80] And finally, Frederik Thuesen positions *phronesis* as an embodied virtue: "As moral virtue is defined as 'states of character,' *phronesis* therefore takes embodied dispositions for reflecting—and especially feeling and acting—appropriately."[81] Each of these underscores the socio-relational qualities of *phronesis:* that it is a virtue, experienced between people, that invites reflection on the outcome of those interactions. In this sense, the virtue carries its traditional Aristotelian understanding of practical wisdom but is augmented with recent theorizing in social sciences and interpretive/ethnographic scholarship.[82] Drawn from the qualitative tradition in communication, the notion of reflexivity inherently understands that the researcher is the instrument in any study. In rhetorical ethnography, the measuring of rhetoric's effects is built through systematic reflection upon the process of learning by the researcher in the field of argumentation. To build such an inventory, the rhetorical ethnographer should ask questions about personal effectiveness and growth. At times, *phronesis* is recognized through trial and error, through success and failure. To report upon it is to lay bare the privileged position of the researcher. To understand

DanceSafe's rhetoric through *phronesis,* I have organized my learning as a volunteer into two levels: failures and epiphanies.

Any type of advocacy requires learning. As a fresh recruit in the scene, I quickly realized my limitations and failures in helping advocate on behalf of DanceSafe. In each moment of learning, I was able to realize many of the necessary components of the campaign and to reflect on how they contribute to DanceSafe's overall success. In my first rave, I watched in bewilderment as a raver seemed to be stuck in one place, not talking with anyone and hardly moving. At that same rave, a young woman approached DanceSafe and asked, "I just took two hits of ecstasy and two pills of Vicodin. What's going to happen to me?" During that same rave, I mistakenly called the psychedelic drug 2CB a liquid, when it's actually a pill or powder. In still another rave, I had a prolonged conversation with a raver who was considering taking Ecstasy but was also taking antidepressant medication, and I was unsure about the consequences. Each of these examples taught me that I had much to learn about the *facts* of drug use before I would be able to interact appropriately with youth. As a requisite part of the advocacy, DanceSafe members are responsible for knowing contraindications related to mixing medication and other drugs and that the immobile young raver was likely stuck in a "k-hole" from recreationally ingesting ketamine. Moreover, such knowledge is *always* contextualized and unpredictably called upon and becomes a part of the overall message. Otherwise, it would be like protesting a war but being unfamiliar with the political backdrop of the conflict. As *phronesis,* knowledge of drug use took the form of wisdom, with its requisite flexibility and discernment regarding use. These base failures presented moments of learning, which later became essential components of my performance. As simple as it sounds, I had to *know* before I could advocate. Translating this lesson into measuring effects, DanceSafe was responsible as a broker of knowledge in the rave scene. The effect of its campaign was to inject scientific knowledge into the free-for-all of rave culture. Later, in my interviews, this finding was confirmed as one raver reported in an interview: "I, for example, use your cards as one of the many references because I have found, in my opinion, an unbiased source. They seem to have looked at the different sides of the spectrum and come to a particular conclusion that is logical, scientific, and isn't out there to scare anybody away from doing a specific drug." As such, DanceSafe is responsible for drug knowledge, built from science and, as I quickly learned, filtered through *doxa.* The flyers and their information were not just presented through the culture of the rave; they were bolstered with its wisdom.

While failures provide the opportunity for much-needed reflections upon learning, I experienced a number of epiphanies regarding my advocacy within DanceSafe. These moments were guided by interactions with particular ravers. They are specific and cannot be understood without having been there in the moment of rhetorical production.[83] As ethnographic experiences, they provide an assessment of effects that is nearly impossible to recreate from merely a textual purview or from a social scientific inquiry. One of the first epiphanies occurred early in my observations. A young woman approached the booth and asked all of the volunteers, "Since you all do this, does that mean that you are sober? Do you or will you ever do drugs again?" This question was repeated in one form or another in later observations. It highlights a complication in the performance of advocacy. On the one hand, if DanceSafe members reply that they are sober or that they have given up drugs, they may threaten their ethos. Ravers could perceive volunteers as merely replications of parents, police, or drug counselors who "don't really get it." On the other hand, if volunteers reply that they engage in drug use, that may violate the message of "drug use has consequences." In my observations, I found that volunteers most often chose the latter path, believing that 'fessing up to ravers about past and present drug use was an important type of connection. It provided an opportunity to share the effects of the campaign on their own choices and to situate the scientific knowledge within personal choice. One element of DanceSafe is the testing of Ecstasy pills. One volunteer remarked during a similar exchange that he wouldn't ingest Ecstasy without knowing what's in it from testing. These personal admissions laid bare the type of intuition about how to *discuss* ethos with an audience. It shows how rhetoric's effect is mediated by personal character and can potentially be complicated by the slightest whiff of performative contradiction.

Another epiphany occurred with a young male raver named Coyote. In usual fashion, he approached the DanceSafe booth asking questions about what the group does. After explaining the advocacy of harm reduction, I had a longer conversation with him about drug use and raves. He explained that he has been attending raves for only about five months and that he felt that people at the raves were his "family." He noted that he used drugs but planned on quitting because he didn't want to get "caught up" in drug use. Even though he planned on quitting, he signaled that he would continue attending events. We spent time discussing what drugs mean to ravers (he claimed that they foster connection), but also recognizing that connections can be made without them. Toward the end of our conversation, he thanked me for taking the time to chat and asked for my signature on a colorful sheet of paper. The word PLUR was centered on the page, surrounded by a rainbow of color and signatures from others he had met. He explained that he asks for these signatures from those he considers to be a part of his family. This moment taught me about the importance of listening as a part of advocacy as well as how the sharing of stories can be as important as any argument offered about the pleasures and pitfalls of drug use.

This moment underscores the notion of connection within advocacy. While the epiphanies I have described are largely about ethos through personal decisions, this interaction shows how ethos is established and deployed through listening and sharing. Coyote's story of family and finding connections in the rave scene hints at the importance of DanceSafe's providing a sense of goodwill through communal advocacy. Ravers approach the table, share stories, and disappear back into the music and the glowing lights. Yet, in that moment of sharing, ravers long for a sense of honest interaction and community in the rave. The drug ecstasy, as an empathogen, strengthens that experience as profound connections are made through bursts of serotonin. Certainly, the authenticity of those interactions is questionable, but the *longing* for them is not. As an organization, DanceSafe offers a space to tell stories and *to be heard*. To be an effective advocate within this campaign is to offer a place for sharing experiences regarding drugs, instead of the spewing of arguments about negative side effects. This is a form of intuition about this particular audience—that their judgments and experiences about alcohol and drug use are narratively built.[84] Looking back to interviews with volunteers, I believe that this act of goodwill fits into the strategy of nonjudgment. It forms, in part, the "cause" of DanceSafe's message and can be traced to Coyote's moment of sharing. It reflects a notion of ethos akin to Foss and Griffin's invitational rhetoric.[85] Rhetoric, in this sense, is embodied and shared; the campaign is apprehended socially, through interpersonal connection, as much as it is through fliers, pamphlets, and posters.

Discussion: Participating in the Effect of Rhetoric

This project, an inquiry into the effects of DanceSafe's rhetoric, reveals a number of discoveries. First, DanceSafe strives to connect with youth with a difficult message of responsible drug use. Certainly, the message has its contradictions, performative, internal, or otherwise. However, at its core, the message is nonjudgmental, which connects to the *doxa* of this crowd. Ravers are a rebellious bunch, seeking to escape from parental or local authorities. They come to a rave to meet people and to dance, not to be educated. Yet, DanceSafe offers a space to share stories and to listen. Rhetorically, it invites discussion of drug use, both its pleasures and its pains. Overall, DanceSafe's message is effective because it invites participation, sharing, and honesty.

Second, to connect to youth, DanceSafe discursively establishes its ethos as a trusted organization that enacts goodwill toward its audience. This understanding of effects is an Aristotelian one but is, in my case, determined through interviews that inquire directly into the reception of the campaign. Ravers told me that DanceSafe effectively established rapport and that its volunteers were perceived as differing from parental or traditional drug education sources. They also indicated that, while not parents, DanceSafe volunteers expressed their caring for drug users in ways that family members would. This was purposeful, as I understood through my interviews with volunteers. As a part of their advocacy, DanceSafe members strove to make connections with ravers. Finally, I personally learned about the process of advocacy by performing it. Through critical-rhetorical ethnography, I witnessed and recorded the effect of rhetoric as I experienced it. Using the guiding concept of *phronesis,* I reflected on the recruitment, training, and learning process of becoming a volunteer. This approach provided insight into the effective strategies of vernacular advocacy, through both successes and failures of persuasive attempts.

Through this case study, I have provided some methodological insight into the study of rhetoric's effects. Thinking back to Wayne Thompson's early call for research workers to directly observe rhetoric, I suggest that my ethnographic approach to vernacular advocacy operates as a successful approach to witnessing and participating in rhetoric. Contrasted with textual purviews, this embodied method provides firsthand accounts of how rhetoric is produced. I was privy to organizational planning, recruitment of new volunteers, and the performance of advocacy. This insider perspective provided a thorough inspection of how a vernacular organization performs. Through my interviews with rhetors and audience, I was able to apprehend the entirety of the rhetorical transaction. In my initial interviews with volunteers, I was given strategies and stories of their time in the rave scene. Reflecting on their interactions with campaign, ravers reported back the successful elements of DanceSafe's approach. Finally, as a participant in the group, I directly learned to embrace DanceSafe's nonjudgmental approach to drug education and health campaigns. Taken together, these methodological elements provide a start-to-finish view of rhetoric. From a qualitative perspective, I engaged in a form of triangulation, drawing from multiple sources (including myself) to understand DanceSafe's message. From a rhetorical perspective, I inquired into the reception of messages and learned of the practical judgment of being a volunteer. Thompson calls for adequate researcher training in observation and reporting techniques. Rhetorical ethnography provides such a perspective and pushes further through its participatory aim. Moreover, the virtue of *phronesis* provides rhetorical scholars with a guide to understanding how agency is formed at the point of advocacy and shared between audience and speaker alike. As audiences receive and respond to messages from speakers, they have an impact upon future advocacies. In other words, the development and refinement of messages with multiple audiences over time, the building of *phronesis,* illustrates how the agency of a speaker is molded toward successful persuasion. In return, phronetic speakers are able to recognize the impact of their messages through the process of discernment.

Looking further, ethnography offers something to the discussion of rhetoric that has been missed in the history of the discipline. Early rhetorical training was engaged and embodied in the practice of rhetoric, beginning with Isocrates. Since Wicheln's call for criticism of oratory, the textual or biographical purview has been a mainstay of rhetorical approaches. As displayed in my analysis in this essay, using participatory and ethnographic methods can account for conceptions of rhetorical concepts that are difficult to comprehend otherwise. The ethos of DanceSafe was actively evaluated through immediate reactions to the campaign. But to understand the value of ethos, I had to be a part of the culture and witness its performance. In cases where ravers could and would question the advocacy group's ethos, asking about personal use and motivations, I was able to follow up with audience members or volunteers to discover how estimations of ethos changed or were defended. In other cases, I had to explain the ethos of the organization to those who inquired into the group. Here, I learned firsthand how to construct and invent ethos for DanceSafe. Outside this controversy, rhetorical ethnographers could examine the nature of effects, including political campaigns, public address, and protest activities. Participant observation, in the guise of rhetorical ethnography, is best suited to produce arguments; however, the observational level of the method provides immediate reactions to public discourse.

In answering Gerard Hauser's plea for an ethnographic rhetoric,[86] my case study here outlines an approach that can revitalize the study of rhetoric's effects. The difficult *epistemological* questions of effect can be answered through an *ontological* repositioning of the rhetorical critic. Rather than searching for texts upon texts that answer the question of effect, the rhetorical ethnographer positions him- or herself within the field of argumentation and advocacy. In so doing, the embodied knowledge of the ethnographer, coupled with the inventive requirements of the critic, provides insights into both cause and effect that are otherwise missed. Considerations of character and ethos as they are actively performed surface in ways—nonverbal, affective, or corporeal—that cannot be otherwise understood. Ethnography does not claim to provide a one-to-one connection between rhetorical cause and effect, nor do I claim to do so here. Rather, the rhetorical ethnographer examines a multitude of factors that impact message construction, development, and reception. Rhetoric is not performed in a laboratory; its public nature requires the necessary tools to engage the public. Ethnography offers such tools. Moreover, rhetorical ethnography engages in phronetic judgment, drawing from its roots in rhetorical theory. This element, accented with the performative elements of participant observation, provides the critic of vernacular rhetoric with firsthand knowledge of message delivery. Mere observation of messages offered by advocates in the field misses on the affective and embodied nature of performing those messages. *Phronesis,* as a virtue, adds intuition and wisdom to the critical reflexivity inherent in ethnography. It provides a measure of effect that is nearly impossible to replicate via any other method.

That said, rhetorical ethnography has its limits, especially regarding effects. Many insights can be gathered from the approach, but reliance on the personal experience and reflections of the ethnographer can be questioned. Tracing a specific line between what was planned behind the scenes and what happened at the rave is difficult. Many factors intervene, yet an after-the-fact reflection of the campaign would miss many of the details that go into the rhetorical encounter. Ethnography can capture those split-second reactions, many of which are nonverbal or affective. Additionally, my particular approach does not adhere to rigorous sampling techniques and does not locate a fully representative sample of audience members. While these limits exist, this study does provide insights into how many ravers received the campaign. While I do not claim to generalize from these results to the overall population of ravers, the insights of this study offer potentially transferable results, as many ethnographic works do, to other similar sites or campaigns. This campaign sought to meet young drug users "where they're at," in contrast to other approaches in the war on drugs. Recognizing the strategies inherent to this advocacy could prove valuable to those engaged in health advocacy or drug education.

Through this essay, I have provided an overview of a participatory approach to studying rhetoric, using my time with DanceSafe as a guide. Indeed, this approach requires polishing. As it stands, it follows the line of critical rhetoric and vernacular discourses; however, the methodological assumptions could be expanded to more traditional approaches to rhetoric. Certainly, as I have stated in this study, the measuring of ethos is not a radical departure in the field of rhetoric. However, the direct participation in message campaigns is. New considerations, ethical or otherwise, can fill out the approach. The study of public address, as Wayne Thompson describes, could be a reflection upon discourse rather than participation in it. Interviews with speakers and audience members, as I have provided here, can provide insight into the difficult questions about the effects of rhetoric. For now, for those interested in campaigns and public advocacy, critical-rhetorical ethnography can offer rhetorical critics the means to witness and participate in the rhetorical effects of such messages.

Notes

1. Gerard A. Hauser, *Vernacular Voices: The Rhetoric of Publics and Public Spheres* (Columbia: University of South Carolina Press, 1999).

2. Gerard Hauser, "Attending the Vernacular: A Plea for an Ethnographic Rhetoric," in *The Rhetorical Emergence of Culture,* ed. Christian Meyer and Felix Girke (Oxford and New York: Berghahn, 2011), 166.

3. Hauser, "Attending the Vernacular," 168.

4. Hauser, "Attending the Vernacular," 159.

5. Raymie McKerrow, "Critical Rhetoric: Theory and Praxis," *Communication Monographs* 56 (1989): 91.

6. Michael Calvin McGee, "Text, Context, and the Fragmentation of Contemporary Culture," *Western Journal of Communication* 54 (1990): 274–289.

7. Barbara Johnstone and Christopher Eisenhart, *Rhetoric in Detail: Discourse Analysis of Rhetorical Talk and Text* (Philadelphia: John Benjamins, 2008). See also the special issue of *Critical Discourse Studies* that details ethnographic accounts of critical discourse analyses: Michał Krzyżanowski, "Ethnography and Critical Discourse Analysis: Towards a Problem-Oriented Research Dialogue," *Critical Discourse Studies* 8 (2011): 231–238.

8. Dana L. Cloud, "The Materiality of Discourse as Oxymoron: A Challenge to Critical Rhetoric," *Western Journal of Communication* 58 (1994): 142.

9. Cloud, "The Materiality of Discourse," 159.

10. Ronald Walter Greene, "Another Materialist Rhetoric," *Critical Studies in Mass Communication* 15 (1998): 27.

11. Kent A. Ono and John M. Sloop, "The Critique of Vernacular Discourse," *Communication Monographs* 62 (1995): 19.

12. Ono and Sloop, "The Critique of Vernacular Discourse," 20.

13. John M. Sloop and Kent A. Ono, "Out-law Discourse: The Critical Politics of Material Judgment," *Philosophy and Rhetoric* 30 (1997): 51–69.

14. Sloop and Ono, "Out-law Discourse," 54.

15. Kent A. Ono and John M. Sloop, "Critical Rhetorics of Controversy," *Western Journal of Communication* 63 (1999): 526–538.

16. Hauser, *Vernacular Voices.*

17. Hauser, *Vernacular Voices,* 12.

18. This method is discussed in more detail in Aaron Hess, "Critical-Rhetorical Ethnography: Rethinking the Place and Process of Rhetoric," *Communication Studies* 62 (2011): 127–152. In this essay, I focus on the elements of the method that provide a view into the effects of the method.

19. Herbert A. Wichelns, "The Literary Criticism of Oratory," in *Readings in Rhetorical Criticism,* ed. Carl R. Burgchardt (State College, Pa.: Strata, 1995), 22.

20. Carole Blair, "Reflections on Criticism and Bodies: Parables from Public Places," *Western Journal of Communication* 65 (2001): 271–294.

21. Wayne N. Thompson "Contemporary Public Address as a Research Area," *Quarterly Journal of Speech* 33 (1947): 274.

22. Thompson, "Contemporary Public Address," 277.

23. Thompson, "Contemporary Public Address," 277–278.

24. Thompson, "Contemporary Public Address," 278. Emphasis in original essay.

25. Thompson, "Contemporary Public Address," 280.

26. McKerrow, "Critical Rhetoric," 101.

27. Dwight Conquergood offers a pointed critique about "arm-chair" methods, in contrast to the possibilities opened in ethnographic conditions. See Dwight Conquergood, "Rethinking Ethnography: Towards a Critical Cultural Politics," *Communication Monographs* 58 (1991): 180, and Dwight Conquergood, "Ethnography, Rhetoric, and Performance," *Quarterly Journal of Speech* 78 (1992): 80–123. A number of recent works make parallel claims and search for ways to open up the methodological possibilities of rhetoric: Johnstone and Eisenhart, *Rhetoric in Detail;* Michael K. Middleton, Samantha Senda-Cook, and Danielle Endres, "Articulating Rhetorical Field Methods: Challenges and Tensions," *Western Journal of Communication* 75 (2011): 386–406; Hess, "Critical-Rhetorical Ethnography"; Art Herbig and Aaron Hess, "Convergent Critical Rhetoric at the 'Rally to Restore Sanity': Exploring the Intersection of Rhetoric, Ethnography, and Documentary Production," *Communication Studies* 63 (2012): 269–289; Karen Tracy, James P. McDaniel and Bruce E. Gronbeck, *The Prettier Doll: Rhetoric, Discourse, and Ordinary Democracy* (Tuscaloosa: University of Alabama Press, 2007); Don Waisanen, "Bordering Populism in Immigration Activism: Outlaw—Civic Discourse in a (Counter) Public," *Communication Monographs* 79 (2012): 232–255.

28. Brian L. Ott and Bill D. Herman, "Mixed Messages: Resistance and Reappropriation in Rave Culture," *Western Journal of Communication* 67 (2003): 250. This essay provides a historical backdrop to the use of drugs in the rave scene and a keen analysis of the development of rave culture over time.

29. Hess, "Critical-Rhetorical Ethnography."

30. Ono and Sloop, "Critical Rhetorics of Controversy."

31. McGee, "Text, Context, and Fragmentation"; Davis W. Houck and Mihaela Nocasian, "FDR's First Inaugural Address: Text, Context, and Reception," *Rhetoric and Public Affairs* 5 (2002): 649–678.

32. Gary L. Fisher, *Rethinking Our War on Drugs: Candid Talk about Controversial Issues* (Westport, Conn.: Praeger, 2006); Julian Buchanan and Lee Young, "The War on Drugs—a War on Drug Users?," *Drugs: Education, Prevention, and Policy* 7 (2000): 409–422.

33. Jim Bildner and Madeline Drexler, "The Wrong Way to Fight the War on Drugs," *Boston Globe*, June 27, 2006, http://www.boston.com (accessed May 22, 2008); Taylor W. Buley, "Drug Policy Should Focus on Helping Addicts, not Jailing them," *Baltimore Sun*, June 28, 2006, http://articles.baltimoresun.com/2006-06-28/news/0606280023_1_drug-treatment-war-on-drugs-drug-policy (accessed February 10, 2012); Kari Lydersen, "Drug-Terror Connection Disputed; DEA Defends

Traveling Exhibit as Critics Draw Parallels to Prohibition Era," *Washington Post*, August 12, 2006, http://www.lexis-nexis.com/ (accessed February 10, 2012).

34. Dirk C. Eldredge, *Ending the War on Drugs: A Solution for America* (New York: Bridge Works, 1998); William N. Elwood, *Rhetoric in the War on Drugs* (Westport, Conn.: Praeger, 1994).

35. Cheryl L. White "Beyond Professional Harm Reduction: The Empowerment of Multiply-Marginalized Illicit Drug Users to Engage in a Politics of Solidarity towards Ending the War on Illicit Drug Users," *Drug and Alcohol Review* 20 (2001): 449–458.

36. Aaron Hess, "Resistance Up in Smoke: Analyzing the Limitations of Deliberation on YouTube," *Critical Studies in Media Communication* 26 (2009): 411–434.

37. Office of National Drug Control Policy, "National Drug Control Strategy," February 2007, http://www.whitehousedrugpolicy.gov/publications/policy/ndcs07/ndcs07.pdf (accessed April 13, 2007); Marsha Rosenbaum, "Kids, Drugs, and Drug Education: A Harm Reduction Approach," (San Francisco: National Council on Crime and Delinquency, 1996); Fisher, *Rethinking Our War on Drugs.*

38. G. Alan Marlatt, "Highlights of Harm Reduction: A Personal Report for the First National Harm Reduction Conference in the United States," in *Harm Reduction: Pragmatic Strategies for Managing High-risk Behaviors,* ed. G. Alan Marlatt (New York: Guilford Press, 1998), 1.

39. Marlatt, "Highlights of Harm Reduction," 1.

40. Buchanan and Young, "The War on Drugs."

41. Ernest Drucker and Allan Clear, "Harm Reduction in the Home of the War on Drugs: Methadone and Needle Exchange in the USA," *Drug and Alcohol Review* 18 (1999): 111.

42. James E. Hawdon, "The Role of Presidential Rhetoric in the Creation of a Moral Panic: Reagan, Bush, and the War on Drugs," *Deviant Behavior* 22 (2001): 419–445.

43. Fisher, *Rethinking Our War on Drugs,* 68.

44. G. Alan Marlatt, ed., *Harm Reduction: Pragmatic Strategies for Managing High-Risk Behaviors* (New York: Guilford Press, 1998), xvi–xvii.

45. Fisher, *Rethinking Our War on Drugs,* 57.

46. Cloud, "The Materiality of Discourse."

47. Joseph Gusfield, *The Culture of Public Problems: Drinking, Driving, and the Symbolic Order* (Chicago: University of Chicago Press, 1981).

48. Erich Goode, "The American Drug Panic of the 1980s: Social Construction or Objective Threat?" *Violence, Aggression and Terrorism* 3 (1998): 327–348.

49. Goode, "The American Drug Panic."

50. Elise Ackerman, "Just Say 'Is It OK?' Non-profit DanceSafe Promotes 'Harm Reduction' Approach to Drugs," *San Jose Mercury News*, August 4, 2000, http://www.lexis-nexis.com/.

51. Mark Martin, "The Ecstasy and the Agony: Group Tries to Reduce Risk by Testing Pills," *San Francisco Chronicle,* July 21, 2000, http://www.sfgate.com/cgi-bin/article.cgi?f=/c/a/2000/07/21/MN88496.DTL&ao=all (accessed February 10, 2012).

52. DanceSafe, "Philosophy and Vision," http://www.dancesafe.org/about-dancesafe/philospohy-and-vision (accessed August 13, 2013).

53. Paulo Freire, *Pedagogy of the Oppressed,* trans. Myra Bergman Ramos (New York: Continuum, 2000); DanceSafe, "Philosophy and Vision."

54. DanceSafe, "Philosophy and Vision."

55. Nurit Guttman, "Ethical Dilemmas in Health Campaigns," *Health Communication* 9 (1997): 155–190.

56. Hess, "Critical-Rhetorical Ethnography."

57. Patricia A. Adler and Peter Adler, "Membership Roles in Field Research" (Thousand Oaks, Calif.: Sage, 1987).

58. Andrea Fontana and James H. Frey, "The Interview: From Neutral Stance to Political Involvement," in *The SAGE Handbook of Qualitative Research,* ed. Norman K. Denzin and Yvonna S. Lincoln (Thousand Oaks, Calif.: Sage, 2005), 696.

59. Steinar Kvale, *InterViews: An Introduction to Qualitative Research Interviewing* (Thousand Oaks: Sage, 1996).

60. John Poulakos, "Toward a Sophistic Definition of Rhetoric," *Philosophy and Rhetoric* 16 (1983): 35–48; James L. Kinneavy and Catherine R. Eskin, "Kairos in Aristotle's Rhetoric," *Written Communication* 17 (2000): 433.

61. Carolyn R. Miller, "Foreword," In *Rhetoric and Kairos: Essays in History, Theory, and Praxis,* ed. Phillip Sipiora and James S. Baumlin (Albany: State University of New York Press, 2002), xi-xiii.

62. McGee, "Text, Context, and Fragmentation."

63. Troy Murphy, "Rhetorical Invention and the Transformation of 'We Shall Overcome,'" *Qualitative Research Reports in Communication* 4 (2003); 1–8.

64. Robert Hariman, "Prudence/Performance," *Rhetoric Society Quarterly* 21 (1991): 34.

65. Hariman, "Prudence/Performance," 34–35.

66. Hariman, "Prudence/Performance," 27.

67. Christopher P. Long, "The Ontological Reappopriation of Phronesis," *Continental Philosophy Review* 35 (2002): 48.

68. Brian C. Kelly, "Conceptions of Risk in the Lives of Club Drug-Using Youth," *Substance Use and Abuse* 40 (2005): 1443–1459; Kira B. Levy, Kevin E. O'Grady, Eric D. Wish, and Amelia M. Arria, "An In-Depth Qualitative Examination of the Ecstasy Experience: Results of a Focus Group with Ecstasy-Using College Students," *Substance Use and Misuse* 40 (2005): 1427–1441.

69. Dejong and Wallack, "A Critical Perspective"; Elwood, *Rhetoric in the War on Drugs.*

70. Houck and Nocasian, "FDR's First Inaugural," 674.

71. Arguably, any ethnographic work is inherently participatory, which means that an ethnographer would struggle to separate him- or herself from the message construction of a campaign. Merely meeting with volunteers, for example, and asking questions about message strategies has an impact on future messages. Through the reflection, volunteers may make adjustments or realize something new about how they produce the campaign.

72. Guttman, "Ethical Dilemmas," 164.

73. Hauser, "Attending the Vernacular," 168.

74. Ott and Herman, "Mixed Messages," 261.

75. Sonja K. Foss and Cindy L. Griffin, "Beyond Persuasion: A Proposal for an Invitational Rhetoric," *Communication Monographs* 62 (1995): 2–18.

76. Ott and Herman, "Mixed Messages," 254.

77. Carrie Birmingham, "*Phronesis:* A Model for Pedagogical Reflection," *Journal of Teacher Education* 55 (2004): 313–324.

78. Karen A. Stewart, Aaron Hess, Sarah J. Tracy, and Harold L. Goodall, "Risky Research: Investigating the 'Perils' of Ethnography," in *Qualitative Inquiry and Social Justice,* ed. Norman K. Denzin and Michael D. Giardina (Walnut Creek, Calif.: Left Coast Press, 2009), 198–216.

79. Birmingham, "*Phronesis,*" 317.

80. Christopher P. Long, "The Ontological Reappropriation of *Phronēsis,*" *Continental Philosophy Review* 35 (2002): 36.

81. Frederik Thuesen, "Navigating between Dialogue and Confrontation: *Phronesis* and Emotions in Interviewing Elites on Ethnic Discrimination," *Qualitative Inquiry* 17 (2011): 617.

82. For a thorough discussion of *phronesis* in the social sciences, see also Bent Flyvbjerg, *Making Social Science Matter: Why Social Inquiry Fails and How It Can Succeed Again* (Cambridge: Cambridge University Press, 2001).

83. Blair, "Reflections on Criticism," 274.

84. This is reflected in other health communication literature regarding alcohol use and college-age populations where narrative sharing and listening are effective approaches to getting students to think through their decision to drink. See Marianne LeGreco, Aaron Hess, Linda C. Lederman, Tara Schuwerk, and Angela LaValley, "An Innovative Dialogue about College Drinking: Developing an Immediate Response Technology Model for Health Promotion," *Communication Education* 59 (2010): 389–404; Lisa Menegatos, Linda C. Lederman, and Aaron Hess, "Friends Don't Let Jane Hook Up Drunk: A Qualitative Analysis of Participation in a College Drinking Simulation," *Communication Education* 59 (2010): 374–388; Linda C. Lederman and Lea P. Stewart, *Changing the Culture of College Drinking: A Socially Situated Health Communication Campaign* (Cresskill, N.J.: Hampton Press, 2005).

85. Foss and Griffin, "Beyond Persuasion."

86. Hauser, "Attending the Vernacular," 169.

Rhetorical Cycles

Music, Rhetorical Effect, and Tradition

GREG DORCHAK

In a July 28, 2010, *New York Times* op-ed piece, the columnist David Brooks posed this question: "What would happen if one hemisphere of the world suddenly became sterile?" Instead of pondering sterility, I read this column with my mind wrapped around the question of rhetoric and effects. If critics fault rhetorical theorists for failing to provide any evidence of rhetoric's effects, we might alter Brooks's thought experiment to serve our own rhetorical needs. What would happen if we stopped acting rhetorically? Taking this experiment to its logical conclusion, we could see that those who devalue rhetoric's ability to produce obvious effects might be predisposed to do so because one of the most prevalent effects of rhetoric is rhetoric itself. While this seems tautological, the argument shows that rhetoric's effects span a larger scope than material evidence alone could allow.

While not sharing the current popularity enjoyed by visual rhetoric within rhetorical theory, scholars of both rhetoric and musicology have long recognized the rhetorical capacities of music. Music's rhetorical properties can be seen both within specific performances and at a broader social level. Robert Root, for example, shows how the appeals of ethos, pathos, and logos emerge by examining the relationship among the musician, the audience, and the song's subject.[1] At the social level, Edward Armstrong compares the rhetoric of violence found within the lyrics of rap and country music.[2] Scholars recognize the rhetorical nature of both lyrical and nonlyrical music.[3] Musicians generally operate rhetorically within a specific musical genre; each musical genre composed of a particular audience, an acceptable set of rhetorical practices, and a particular musical style. Some rhetorical scholars have examined how musicians rhetorically operate within musical genres, thereby both constituting communities and reinforcing community standards.[4] Kent Ono and John Sloop, in criticizing rhetorical theorists' aversion to vernacular discourses, cite music's rhetorical ability to constitute community as an area ripe for rhetorical analysis—music both lyrical and nonlyrical.[5]

Musicians as well as scholars have also long acknowledged the relationship between music and rhetorical theory. Musical composers of both vocal music and instrumental music from as early as the sixteenth century relied upon rhetorical theory to explore music's rhetorical possibilities.[6] Jette Barnholdt Hansen illustrates that musicians operated rhetorically in two distinct spheres.[7] On one hand, composers drew from rhetorical topoi recognized by audiences; on the other, performers relied upon the rhetorical canon of invention while improvising and interpreting the composers' score.

The rhetorical capacity of music illustrates the possibility of seeing rhetoric itself as a rhetorical effect. Virtuoso musicians, for example, have a special communal role in their rhetorical ability to innovate style. In traditional music communities, identity is tied to this communal aesthetic taste. In acting rhetorically, virtuosos change the understanding of communal identity and affect the actions of future musical rhetors. The relationship between the virtuoso and community reveals the importance of rhetorical effects, as well as the possibility of what counts as an effect of rhetoric.

This essay explores the implications of viewing rhetoric as an effect of rhetoric by focusing on musical rhetoric within traditional communities. Community itself is an oft-used term, but one typically taken at face value without much consideration for the term's meaning. I begin this essay by defining what I mean by community, especially as it relates to tradition and a platform for rhetorical action. I then discuss the concept of the musical virtuoso and explore how these musicians act rhetorically within communities. Next, I explain how these virtuosi, by operating rhetorically within a community, alter tradition, causing evolution. Finally, I explore these theoretical concepts at the applied level by investigating how a specific musical community has been affected by the rhetoric of musicians within that community.

Community

Tradition and community stand at the fore of how rhetorical effects manifest themselves in shared aesthetic taste. For Gadamer, individuals make judgments only in relation to their fore-structure of understanding, formed by the individual's everyday institutions.[8] Because we conceive of these institutions as evolving, we see the fore-structure influencing individual's judgments dynamically. When the institution changes, so does the individual's everyday understanding. It is possible to see how rhetorical acts change the possibilities for understanding. Musically, the virtuoso, in introducing new ideas into the community, makes claims upon the community's fore-structure of understanding music. For Hyde this process of drawing from the everyday is also how rhetoric works enthymatically: the musician draws upon the everyday practices of a community as a premise of reasoning.[9] The ability to understand these everyday practices to the point of manipulation demonstrates the hermeneutic capacity of the virtuoso. Virtuosos interpret the community's everyday understanding of music, drawing from that understanding to make new rhetorical assertions.

For Arendt, aesthetic taste constitutes community, and since, subsequently, taste constitutes and maintains community, we begin to see the political dimension of aesthetics.[10] This possibility might be seen skeptically because of the subtlety of aesthetic acts—but violations of communal aesthetics can reveal the political dimension more immediately.[11] The function of aesthetic taste's ability to constitute community can be observed when noting the rhetorical cycle of rhetoric producing effects. Community identity is both maintained and cultivated through this rhetorical cycle. Therefore, the notion of rhetorical effects is essential to discussions of the constitutive nature of community. For Charland, a community's rhetorical acts contribute to the narrative of common identity.[12] Arendt sees this constitution as inherently aesthetic.[13] In constituting the community, aesthetic acts make claims upon other communal subjects, affecting individuals' understanding of the possibilities of aesthetic taste. Focused on the effects of rhetoric, these claims invite more claims, contributing to the community's constitution. These rhetorical effects are the source of communal evolution.

Drawing from Gadamer, a community provides the fore-structure of understanding that informs an individual's sense of taste. The nature of this community is important when one points to the political nature of music as a proclamation of values. The folklorist Burt Feintuch makes the distinction between "networks" and "communities" especially relevant for the concept of traditional music.[14] From this perspective, community requires more than occasional events and involves relationships that exist beyond a single set of commonalities. Here, Feintuch specifically refers to the distinction between communities and "revival" traditions that create networks of people who gather to re-enact traditional dances or music but who, apart from this involvement, have little other interaction. Communal relationships, on the other hand, require continuity and obligation on multiple fronts. Among these communities, the political nature of aesthetics looms large in informing identity. The heightened multiplicity of relationships existing within these communities creates the mechanisms for heightened dialogue and deliberation between and among individuals regarding multiple topics. Acknowledging its rhetorical capacity, musical rhetoric creates a possibility for deliberation of communal values within an everyday vernacular. Expanding the possible fronts for interaction between individuals also expands the importance of the aesthetic at an everyday, as opposed to occasioned, level.

Virtuosity

Virtuosity refers to a display of tremendous skill in an artistic performance. The term itself is reserved for the most skilled artists, usually musicians. The talent of the virtuoso is recognizable even by those not familiar with the particular field of art. Part of this talent is that the musician understands not only technical skill but also how to produce effects on an audience. The ability to produce effects separates the virtuoso from other artists.

Arendt sees virtuosity as the link between performing arts and politics. Both politicians and virtuosi require a public and a space for appearances. The virtuoso's art vanishes the moment it ends.[15] Without the effects of performance, nothing would exist after a performance to acknowledge it had occurred. In exploring the rhetorical ability of musical virtuosos in shaping community identity, David Palmer describes the violinist Niccolò Paganini's performance as personifying the romantic period's ideals of art and agency."[16] Paganini stands as one of history's preeminent musical virtuosi, and his effects still resonate in the musical world. Palmer shows how the performance of a virtuoso acts as epideictic rhetoric, making claims of a communal ideal and exhibiting the potential of human ability to a community. The effects of this performance emerge as a new communal aesthetic and also shape the community's understanding of an individual's ability—not just musical ability but overall potential for excellence. This performance alters the community's identity.

The virtuoso understands the audience's expectations and performs to elicit a desired effect, thereby moving the audience's mood. Seen with a hermeneutic lens, the musician must first understand the possibilities of an audience's moods in order to then rhetorically move them. In the conscious act of attempting to move the audience's mood, the musician acts rhetorically. The musician has only limited material to work with, and must understand how to manipulate the music to achieve such effects.[17] But this relationship with the audience advances beyond interpreting possible moods. The virtuoso, through performance, constitutes community. This musician acts as a rhetorician by performing communal values, proclaiming what the virtuoso believes to be the aesthetic ideals of the community. After the performance, the rhetorical effects of this constitution linger. The virtuosic musician alters the community's shared aesthetic values. Through innovative articulation, the virtuoso creates new possibilities of understanding for a community and changes its overall sense of taste and, therefore, its identity.

Solo musicians act with the understanding that, through the performance of music, they affect an audience. Musicians also understand that, via performance, they make aesthetic interpretations and judgments. Virtuosos view their own judgments as valid enough to publicly pronounce to a greater community. Leff describes this characteristic of agency when discussing traditional communities.[18] Agents make pronunciations to the community and, by virtue of rhetorical ability, change tradition. Virtuosos understand their ability to change communal style through the articulation of personal style. Their technical ability allows them to maintain complete control over their instruments during performance. This skill becomes important for the concept of virtuosos' agency, because it demonstrates performative intentionality. For Altieri the intentionality of the agents prove their understanding of their own ability to affect a community.[19]

In transcending the community's understanding of artistic ability, the virtuoso pushes communal understanding to the limits an individual is capable of achieving, whether it be art or some other skill.[20] Changing a community's collective understanding of agency demonstrates an effect of virtuosic performance and therefore an effect of rhetoric: the ability to rhetorically produce more influential agents. Young musicians might witness the abilities of a virtuoso and realize that they too could achieve this ability. Musicians learn through studying other musicians within their community. Agency is exhibited in how one musician weaves other musicians' stylistic characteristics into a personal sense of style.[21] The effects of rhetorical virtuosity can be seen in these musical citations. Each citation itself stands as an effect of rhetoric. A rhetorically effective virtuoso influences contemporary musicians who incorporate the virtuoso's sense of style. Virtuosity, by affecting agency, creates further virtuosity as an effect. To this extent, rhetorical action itself is an effect of rhetoric. Musicians inspire new musicians and, in so doing, shape these musicians' beliefs of individual potential as well as their style. As long as a community endures, there is a cycle of influence, as each musician is influenced by and potentially influences others.

The rhetorical effect of virtuosi can manifest itself not only with individuals but can impact a broader social context. If we do not acknowledge the rhetorical effect of these musicians as individuals, we may romanticize the communal evolution of style as a natural process guided by an invisible hand. While community evolution naturally occurs, rhetorical acts are the evolution's guide. One can trace the current state of any particular community's musical aesthetic, note how contemporary musicians have themselves altered it, and trace those musicians' influences back through history. Musically, this development also shows what "ineffective" rhetoric might look like. Not all musicians inspire, and some might fail to leave impressions upon a community. Here, the measure of ineffective rhetoric is seen as a failure to produce further rhetoric.

In acting rhetorically by asserting aesthetic claims, musicians seek judgment from the community. This situates musical performance as a rhetorical hybrid, as termed by Jamieson and Campbell, incorporating elements of the epideictic in identifying the praiseworthy as well as the deliberative in seeking judgment.[22] For Aristotle, the epideictic speech makes claims upon the present in terms of praise or blame.[23] Garver sees the ethical dimension created by epideictic rhetoric as fundamentally intertwining with the deliberative.[24] The stylistic form taken by virtuosic music makes claims upon the community. These claims essentially state, "This performance represents a part of our community identity. You should value it." Palmer, in highlighting Paganini's rhetorical virtuosity, points to music's ideologic commentary.[25] Belief in the ability of this music to comment on ideology requires agreement with Beiner's point that the aesthetic is political.[26] This political nature of the aesthetic highlights the rhetorical capacity of music and the link between musician and community. Key to the epideictic nature of the musician's performance is the constitution of the community. For Palmer, this comes from the musician's ability to create community through performance. The thrust of the constitutive capacity of music comes from the musician asserting claims and values of identity to the community.

Evolution

A trend of thought, informed by romanticism, paints tradition as a static, unchanging ideal; even when this trend of thought acknowledges change, it conceives of change as the inevitable product of an invisible hand. These conceptions of tradition as either static or evolving inevitably through the influence of an invisible hand mischaracterizes the necessity of individual agents to create change. Here, the inherent "authenticity" of tradition clashes with the "inauthentic" innovation of acting agents. This romanticism ignores the true dynamic of traditions, which have always been composed of networks of individual actors. Leff notes this role of individual action when he acknowledges the agent's potential to change tradition.[27] For musical traditions, the virtuoso stands as a prime example of how rhetorical agents make claims upon traditions. Music operates epideictically, as the musician asks the audience to confirm the musician's aesthetic judgment. For Gadamer, the commonalities of social life determine an individual's judgment of aesthetic taste. What makes the virtuoso distinct from other musicians is not the use of rhetoric. All musicians make rhetorical aesthetic claims. The virtuoso, however, demonstrates the skill of understanding how to best affect an audience, the technical ability to enact this understanding, and the rhetorical skill to successfully affect the audience. In making these rhetorical aesthetic claims and in affecting the community's narrative, the virtuoso changes tradition.

These virtuosi's ability to create more virtuosi shows how rhetoricians generate rhetoricians. For Palmer, Paganini's virtuosity created the realization in others of their own potential for agency.[28] The best evidence of Paganini's effect as virtuoso to inspire other virtuosi is the piano player and composer Franz Liszt. Paganini's performances on the violin inspired and informed Liszt of his own virtuosic potential on the piano. Accounts of agency are not complete when predicated solely upon the agent's ability to act. An account must take into consideration the agent's relationship to and understanding of the community that produces agents, as well as the rhetoric that has informed the agent's own understanding of the possibility for action. In this light, tradition is also incomplete without accounts of the capability of agents to rhetorically affect the community. Accounts of tradition must acknowledge mechanisms for change.

Innovation is not necessarily a turn from tradition. Rather, successful innovation is often grounded on tradition. From the standpoint of rhetorical effects, agents make rhetorical aesthetic assertions to the community. Such rhetoric invites judgment and can reconstitute how members of a community understand a communal narrative. Particularly effective musicians understand the limits for innovation, because their communal understanding guides their understanding of the possibility for action. Communal narratives that rhetorically construct an agent's understanding can also be altered by the agent; in so doing, they affect the fore-structure of understanding for others. This dynamic relationship contains the possibility that a community's aesthetic taste may change over time. This constant reevaluation of communal taste demonstrates Gadamer's claim that tradition is not an uncritical assimilation into a community.[29]

The Cape Breton Musical Community

One criticism of rhetoric, presented theoretically, is the inability to demonstrate real-world rhetorical effects. To show how virtuosic rhetoric impacts community and shifts aesthetic taste in a community over time, I provide a case study of one specific musical community to illustrate how a virtuoso changed that community's understanding of taste. Here, I focus on the traditional musical community of Cape Breton Island in Nova Scotia, Canada. This island is renowned for its long-standing traditional music practices. Cape Bretoners anecdotally claim to have a higher per capita ratio of fiddlers per person than anywhere in the world. While this may or may not be true, it demonstrates the island's identity as tied to its music.

The contemporary traditional Cape Breton musical community traces its roots to the beginning of the 1800s, when Highland Scots settled the region. These highlanders transplanted their communities from Scotland, sometimes with whole villages intact, along with their Scottish Gaelic language and their music, replicating in a new land their traditional way of life. This transplantation maintained aural traditions as a principle practice of entertainment. Isolated in rural Nova Scotia, this community cultivated a musical style that evolved differently from the Scottish music that gave birth to it. The island itself remained separated from mainland Nova Scotia until the completion of the Canso Causeway, in 1955. As well as being separated from the mainland, villages in Cape Breton also remained separated from each other as few roads existed on the island and those that did exist were often in poor condition.

Cape Breton traditional music primarily acts as dance music for step dancing and square dancing. During the summer months, community dances occur every night of the week. At these dances, one fiddle drives the dance, with piano as the accompaniment. This differentiates Cape Breton fiddling from other fiddling traditions that might form around a group session with many musicians. In the Cape Breton musical tradition, the individual sense of style that musicians display is a defining characteristic.

Cape Breton remained relatively isolated until the 1920s, when troubled economic conditions forced some of Cape Breton's youth to leave the island to look for work. The Canso Causeway, which, as noted, opened in 1955, linked the island to mainland Nova Scotia, and improved roads on the island allowed for modern transportation, quickly ending the island's isolation. Changes in transportation, along with television, radio, and the development of an adolescent subculture, led to many social changes within Cape Breton tradition in a short period of time.[30] One of these changes involved fiddle playing; while older musicians continued to fiddle, no one inspired the newer generation into taking part in the tradition. The transmission of the music had, until this point, occurred without the need to actively encourage younger residents to take part; however, the social changes on the island created new possibilities for the youth and led a diversity of interests. Eventually, the community realized the importance of youth and developed new methods, such as formal group lessons, to reintegrate young people into the community. This stabilized the overall health of the community. During this time, one constant that ran through Cape Breton fiddle music was the presence of particularly virtuosic musicians who carried the musical style along, each impacting the music in his own way.

Cape Breton Virtuosi

The virtuoso is not unique to European classical music but can be found in most, if not all, musical communities. This community created conditions especially suited to create virtuosic musicians. Both the isolation and the special attention given to the solo musician help to cultivate agency among musicians and demand talent for performance. The collection of fiddler biographies compiled by the Cape Breton musician Troy MacGillivray traces musicians to the turn of the nineteenth century. One trend evident in this collection is that while each generation included many fiddlers, only a handful were actually influential. This anecdotal evidence cites not just the charisma of the individuals but also the nuances of the individual's style as the determinate for virtuosity. Often, children were integrated into the musical style by falling asleep at the virtuosic fiddler's feet during house parties. Here, the virtuosic fiddler influenced the next generation's musician's styles, creating a musical Darwinism. Individual stylistic traits of the virtuosos got passed on, while less virtuosic fiddle styles eventually died out.

The Cape Breton virtuoso illustrates rhetoric's effect. For the current generation of Cape Breton musicians, Winston "Scotty" Fitzgerald represents the definition of community virtuoso. Born in 1914, Fitzgerald began playing the fiddle at a young age. His style sounded different from the gritty "Coal Mines" style popular on the island at the time. Fitzgerald listened to classical music and completed training in music theory, also familiarizing himself with fiddle playing off the island. He was concerned with both intonation and mastery of technique. He constructed complex variations on traditional tunes and played in difficult keys. Through this lens, Fitzgerald interpreted the community's traditional music. He introduced improvisation, and his variations both demonstrated technical ability and created a new appeal. This technical demonstration represented such a drastic change that it altered the overall sound of fiddlers on the island, an effect that can be seen in the musicians today.

Around the time Fitzgerald gained prominence, the local radio station began to broadcast local music. His flair for performance suited this new medium, and he was one of the first local fiddlers to regularly perform on the radio. Prior to the introduction of the radio, Cape Breton's regional isolation meant that unless a fiddler was from your family or lived in your town, you would have only had a few occasions to hear him. Fitzgerald, as a regular feature on the local Saturday night *Celtic Ceilidh* radio show, had a broader effect. Many young fiddlers heard his fiddle on radio broadcasts, and, even if they lived in musical homes with other fiddlers, they wanted to play like him. When television provided a new opportunity, Fitzgerald also made that transition, performing on a local music variety show, the *Cape Breton Barn Dance*, and, later, on John Allen Cameron's variety show. Community performances such as Fitzgerald's represent displays of epideictic rhetoric by developing the musician's unique aesthetic value and addressing it, musically, to the community. Fitzgerald made assertions of the community's aesthetic identity. He demonstrated his own style as representative of the community. Unique to Fitzgerald was a heightened technical ability as well as an innovative capacity that created new aesthetic understanding among other local musicians.

The most common praise of Fitzgerald concerns his technical skill. Traditional music is sometimes regarded as simpler and less complex than classical music. This notion is partly a result of the fact that not all traditional fiddlers need to have knowledge of complex violin techniques, but it is also a result of the informal settings in which traditional music is performed. But that is not to say that the opportunity doesn't exist for traditional musicians to utilize complex techniques. During the eighteenth and nineteenth centuries, a number of composers from Scotland who worked in both the classical and traditional idioms created traditional tunes in difficult keys, such as the flatted keys of E-flat and B-flat. They also arranged variations to commonly known tunes that required shifted hand positions and advanced bow technique. While these tunes existed in tune books available to all, few musicians performed them because of their difficulty. One of the defining characteristics of Fitzgerald's style was that he actively perfected these difficult tunes and subsequently developed a reputation for playing the violin at all levels of complexity. The variety of tunes that he sought out led to a boom in the community's tune repertoire during the 1940s and 1950s as players attempted to seek out the difficult tunes and to reach his level of skill.[31]

Fitzgerald also understood how to set himself apart stylistically from others in the Cape Breton music community, yet still operate within the community's understanding of acceptability. In this ability to navigate through the expected norms while preserving his uniqueness, Fitzgerald demonstrated a practical understanding of how to use technique and innovation to achieve effects with an audience. When performing a tune, Fitzgerald considered the printed notes of a tune as the skeleton.[32] He referred to the ability to use personal taste in interpreting the skeleton as defining a good musician. His own style demonstrated a particular uniqueness. Cape Breton music was always known for its "dirt." Musicians performed by droning the strings and by using personal ornaments intended to make the music sound "gritty." Fitzgerald's own defining characteristic, conversely, interpreted the Cape Breton style with clarity. Again, because he had a sound technical mastery of the instrument, he was always precise in tune, rather than seeking the "dirty" style, thus stripping the music of many ornaments to highlight the clarity of his playing. Between this and his ability to perform the music in new ways, he produced a new overall style in the community, while still operating within the community's boundaries.

Cape Breton Musical Evolution

The constitution of the Cape Breton community created the conditions for Fitzgerald to rhetorically act. Fitzgerald's performances occurred within an already constituted community. Members of this Cape Breton community relate to each other through bonds that exist beyond music. Relationships through family, religion, industry, and other institutions create communal links in addition to shared musical practices. Discussions about music could occur while at church, while at work, or in any other venue. Fitzgerald's own aesthetic taste was formed through this function of the community's everyday aesthetic judgment. Living within a community that constantly critically evaluates its own aesthetics, Fitzgerald developed a dynamic understanding of aesthetics. He also developed an understanding of his own individual agency. Because Fitzgerald understood the performances of his own musical influences as contributing to the community's taste, he developed an understanding of his own possibility to contribute.

Fitzgerald's performances made claims of aesthetic value upon the Cape Breton community. By developing a clean style, he made the claim that there was room for more than just the usual "grit" in the Cape Breton taste. Fitzgerald asserted new values for the community to judge. In doing so, he attempted to push how the community understood its music by offering new possibilities. The overall effect was that Fitzgerald changed how the community understood its own identity. That he could alter the community's identity through aesthetic means shines light on the political role of musicians within communities that are musically constituted. This rhetorical dynamic of the Cape Breton musician creates the possibilities for more conservative musicians to assert the value of an old style, while musicians such as Fitzgerald assert the value of innovation. The rhetorical success of musicians such as Fitzgerald can be seen in their ability to affect the community's sense of taste.

The case of Winston Fitzgerald as a virtuoso not only demonstrates how virtuosos act rhetorically but also provides examples of the effects of rhetoric. As the least tangible of arts, music itself creates no materiality. Any reference to a musical performance after the fact represents an effect of that performance. Musical rhetoric shows both the temporal and the immaterial possibility of rhetorical effects. Fitzgerald's performance provides the perfect example of the temporal potential for rhetorical effects. Specifically, his playing can be heard in the individual styles of younger Cape Breton fiddlers, such as Jerry Holland and Howie MacDonald. Apart from the individual playing styles of these musicians, the general taste of the community has changed thanks to Fitzgerald. His introduction of a smooth playing style led the traditional community to gradually move from the dirtier aesthetic toward favoring both stylistic clarity and technical mastery. These effects represent no materiality in themselves but point to the temporal aesthetic of the community alongside the enactment of the performances of other musicians.

One of the most influential musicians affected by Fitzgerald was Jerry Holland. When growing up, while Fitzgerald was fiddling, Holland would fall asleep at his feet. From a young age, Holland had an understanding of Cape Breton music that was largely defined by the possibilities opened up to him by Fitzgerald. Fitzgerald's influence is especially apparent in the clean, smooth style of Holland's music. Living in Cape Breton, Holland became one of the most prolific Cape Breton composers, and it is now rare to attend a dance or concert without hearing his compositions.

Holland's success in composing Cape Breton tunes relates to Fitzgerald's influence. Cape Breton musicians describe Holland's tunes as "Fitzgerald sounding." In a personal conversation, Troy MacGillivray, a Cape Breton musician, noted that such effects are seen in Holland's style of composition, which matches the style of tune one might hear Fitzgerald perform. Also in a personal conversation, another Cape Breton musician, Kimberley Fraser, described Fitzgerald's tune choices as "pretty and happy." MacGillivray pointed out that, apart from style, Fitzgerald's influence on Holland's compositions can be seen in tune form. This distinction refers to the notion that Cape Breton fiddlers, in needing to play for dances, have repertoires composed mostly of jig and reel dance tunes. The fiddlers also play marches, strathspeys, and airs, which reflect the music's Scottish heritage. Fitzgerald, in seeking to differentiate himself, sought out polkas, hornpipes, clogs, and a variety of other types of tunes not commonly heard on Cape Breton. Holland both composed and performed these "Winston-style" tunes with frequency, and they eventually became Cape Breton mainstays.

Rhetoric produces long-range effects in second- and even third-generation rhetorical communities. For example, both Jerry Holland's performance and compositions musically refer to the performative elements of Winston Fitzgerald's style. Fitzgerald's technique and style passed through Holland and affected a newer generation of musicians, and so on. These younger musicians who might not have personally heard Fitzgerald incorporate stylistic elements initially introduced to the communal aesthetic through him. Here, an initial rhetorical act moved individuals to action and eventually produced more rhetoric and, subsequently, more effect, creating a rhetorical cycle going back to Fitzgerald's original rhetorical acts.

Listening to Cape Breton fiddlers today, it is hard to miss the effects of specific musicians, such as Winston Fitzgerald. The individual acts of Fitzgerald's rhetoric, combined with the individual rhetoric of others he stylistically influenced, altered the overall musical community. While his style introduced new ideas, this newness was tempered by an acceptable aesthetic argument. So, while he made an argument for newness, he did so as someone already anchored in the community's understanding of aesthetic taste. At the same time that he was anchored by this musical backbone, he understood the possibility for action as one allowing for individual style.

The aesthetic taste of community is temporal, and those who influence a community's understanding of taste leave their mark only for a time. Fitzgerald's rhetorical virtuosity influenced the rhetorical virtuosity of other musicians. In this way, the rhetorical effect of Fitzgerald's music spread beyond what he could have achieved by himself. His innovative style informed the understanding of musicians such as Jerry Holland, who passed on stylistic elements traceable to Fitzgerald. His effect also demonstrates that rhetorical effects emerge on two levels: one seen in his effect on individuals, such as Holland, and the second seen in his effect on the community's aesthetic identity as a whole. By innovating new ideas and acting in new ways, Fitzgerald rhetorically altered the community's understanding of possibilities for action. While traces of this mark may last, because the community is open to further virtuosi, these effects may diminish through the effects of other virtuosos.

Implications

Fitzgerald's rhetorical effects show how rhetors alter individuals' understanding of community. In this light, the concept of opening up possibilities for action is itself an effect of rhetoric. Actions aren't possible on a social level until introduced rhetorically and understood at the individual level. The rhetorical effects of Fitzgerald's actions can be seen in the musicians who stylistically took up his introductions. These musicians understood the possibility of incorporating new stylistic elements based on Fitzgerald's rhetorical performance. This concept of understanding new possibilities can easily be seen in oral rhetoric. Speeches seeking judgment on a course of action open up space for new forms of action to take place. This opening of possibilities exists as rhetorical effect as much as concrete actions.

Fitzgerald's effect upon Cape Breton communal taste reinforces the relationship between hermeneutics and rhetoric and shows how taste is itself the effect of rhetoric. Fitzgerald introduced new stylistic elements into the Cape Breton community that, while new to the community, nonetheless aesthetically appealed to it. Over time Fitzgerald's new stylistic elements became part of everyday Cape Breton life. This everyday notion of taste as an effect of rhetoric is made possible by the community's ability to critically reevaluate aesthetic judgments. Rhetoric's effects as manifested in taste point to taste as a dynamic competition of claims that exist on a continuum. Communal taste cannot be explained as homogenized. But it also points to taste as anchored, since a community's understanding of aesthetic possibilities emerges only as an effect of prior rhetoric.

This dynamic component of community taste shows how community identity can be seen as an effect of rhetoric. Palmer has shown how virtuosi are capable of transforming community ideals of agency of performance. Fitzgerald's role as a virtuoso demonstrates this capacity in Cape Breton, but it also shows his rhetorical effect on other rhetors, Fitzgerald altered the community's understanding. The cyclical nature of rhetorical effects points to constant revisions that alter a community's identity as well as the power of rhetoric to create new rhetorics that shift community understanding over time. Fitzgerald influenced Holland, who influenced others, and so on.

The effects of rhetoric are broad and, in many cases, immaterial. The concept of understanding, itself an effect of rhetoric, cannot easily be quantified or codified. Therefore, in many cases, rhetorical effects might be overlooked. Winston Fitzgerald's effects on the Cape Breton musical community demonstrate how aesthetic understanding can be seen through the concept of rhetorical style. It also shows how a rhetorical act creates more rhetorical acts. Winston Fitzgerald's rhetorical acts spurred the rhetoric of future rhetors. The combined effect of this rhetoric was the formation of a new aesthetic taste. Because Fitzgerald's effects occurred gradually, they can elude observation when one views rhetoric at the singular level. However, over time, these changes became clear. Significantly, the combined effects of Fitzgerald on the Cape Breton community demonstrate that to trace the scope of a rhetorical act, one must trace the rhetorical effects of rhetoric.

Emerging briefly from a view of music as rhetoric, this case study carries implications not only for musical rhetoric but for all forms of rhetoric. Whereas the performing musician rhetorically elicits more musical performance from its audience and likewise shapes community ideals, the same can be seen in oral rhetoric, which calls forth further oral rhetoric, and visual rhetoric, which calls forth further visual rhetoric. Rhetors seek judgment, altering the very understanding of the audience. But in this interaction, the rhetor is not alone either in possessing agency or in being able to act. The audience is not a static community that simply receives a message. Individuals within audiences are capable of exercising agency and do so. A rhetor, in seeking judgment, seeks action from others. As these audience members are also agents, they become intertwined in a chain so that their new understanding compels rhetorical action. In rhetorically shaping community, one rhetor represents only a single link in a long chain of rhetoric begetting rhetoric. In this light, rhetoric itself can be seen as an effect of rhetoric.

Notes

1. Robert Root, "A Listener's Guide to the Rhetoric of Popular Music," *Journal of Popular Culture* 20 (1986): 15–26.

2. Edward G. Armstrong, "The Rhetoric of Violence in Rap and Country Music," *Sociological Inquiry* 63 (1993): 64–78.

3. See Robert Francesconi, "Free Jazz and Black Nationalism: A Rhetoric of Musical Style," *Critical Studies in Mass Communication* 3 (1986): 36–49.

4. For examples of rhetorical analysis of musical genres, see Theodore Matula, "Contextualizing Musical Rhetoric: A Critical Reading of the Pixies' 'Rock Music,'" *Communication Studies* 51 (2000): 218–237; Erik K. Watts, "An Exploration of Spectacular Consumption: Gangsta' Rap as Cultural Commodity," *Communication Studies* 48 (1997): 42–58; Mark Meister, "Drama and Tragedy in Contemporary Folk Music: Nanci Griffith's 'It's a Hard Life Wherever You Go,'" *Communication Studies* 47 (1996): 62–71.

5. Kent A. Ono and John M. Sloop, "The Critique of Vernacular Discourse," *Communication Monographs* 62 (1995): 19–46.

6. See, for example, Gerard LeCoat, "Music and the Three Appeals of Classical Rhetoric," *Quarterly Journal of Speech* 62 (1976): 157–166; Gregory Butler, "Music and Rhetoric in Early Seventeenth-Century English Sources," *Musical Quarterly* 66 (1980): 53–64; Hans Lenneberg, "Johann Mattheson on Affect and Rhetoric in Music," *Journal of Music Theory* 2 (1958): 47–84; Brian Vickers, "Figures of Rhetoric/Figures of Music?," *Rhetorica* 2 (1984): 1–44; Don Harrán, "Toward a Rhetorical Code of Early Music Performance," *Journal of Musicology* 15 (1997): 19–42.

7. Jette Barnholdt Hansen, "From Invention to Interpretation: The Prologues of the First Court Operas Where Oral and Written Cultures Meet," *Journal of Musicology* 20 (2003): 556–596.

8. Hans-Georg Gadamer, *Truth and Method* (London: Continuum International, 2004).

9. Michael Hyde, "A Matter of the Heart: Epideictic Rhetoric and Heidegger's Call of Conscience," in *Heidegger and Rhetoric,* ed. Daniel M. Gross and Ansgar Kemmann (Albany: State University of New York Press, 2005), 81–104.

10. Hannah Arendt, *The Human Condition* (Chicago: University of Chicago Press, 1998).

11. One need look no further than the riots caused by the infamous premiere performance of Igor Stravinsky's *Rite of Spring,* which was stopped by the Paris police, to see how violations of communal aesthetics can manifest themselves both politically and immediately.

12. Maurice Charland, "Constitutive Rhetoric: The Case of the Peuple Quebecois," *Quarterly Journal of Speech* 77 (1987): 133–150.

13. Arendt, *The Human Condition.*

14. Burt Feintuch, "Longing for Community," *Western Folklore* 60 (2001): 149–161.

15. Richard Bernstein, *Beyond Objectivism and Relativism: Science, Hermeneutics and Praxis* (Philadelphia: University of Pennsylvania Press, 1983).

16. David Palmer, "Virtuosity as Rhetoric: Agency and Transformation in Paganini's Mastery of the Violin," *Quarterly Journal of Speech* 84 (1998): 341–357.

17. Material, in this case, refers to the inherent limiting form of musical performance. In Western music, a musician is limited to the twelve notes and to the internal logos that each performed piece develops through how the form is manipulated, that is, key signature, time signature, and harmonic progression.

18. Michael Leff, "Tradition and Agency in Humanistic Rhetoric," *Philosophy and Rhetoric* 36 (2003): 135–146.

19. Charles Altieri, *Subjective Agency: A Theory of First-Person Expressivity and Its Social Implications* (Lynchburg, Va.: Blackwell Press, 1994).

20. Palmer, "Virtuosity as Rhetoric."

21. Altieri, *Subjective Agency.*

22. Kathleen H. Jamieson and Karlyn K.Campbell, "Rhetorical Hybrids: Fusions of Generic Elements," *Quarterly Journal of Speech* 68 (1982): 146–157.

23. Aristotle, *On Rhetoric* (New York: Modern Library, 1954).

24. Eugene Garver, *Aristotle's Rhetoric: An Art of Character* (University of Chicago Press, 1994).

25. Palmer, "Virtuosity as Rhetoric."

26. Ronald Beiner and Jennifer Nedelsky, *Judgment, Imagination and Politics: Themes from Kant and Arendt* (Lanham, Md.: Rowman and Littlefield, 2001), 127.

27. Leff, "Tradition and Agency in Humanistic Rhetoric."

28. Palmer, "Virtuosity as Rhetoric."

29. Gadamer, *Truth and Method.*

30. Marie Thompson, "The Fall and Rise of the Cape Breton Fiddler: 1955–1982," unpublished master's thesis, St. Mary University, Halifax, Nova Scotia, 2003.

31. Elizabeth Doherty, "Paradox on the Periphery: Evolution of the Cape Breton Fiddle Tradition c1928–1995," unpublished Ph. D dissertation, University of Limerick, Ireland, 1996.

32. Paul Cranford, *Winston Fitzgerald: A Collection of Fiddle Tunes,* 2nd ed. (Cape Breton Island, Nova Scotia: Cranford Publications, 1997).

Conclusion

Of "Very Few Men" with "Unusual Gifts" and "Acute Sensitivity"—Whither Wichelns, Black, and Zarefsky?

DAVIS W. HOUCK

To begin, an analogy. As a rhetorician, one of my favorite scriptural moments occurs in the thirty-second chapter of the Book of Exodus. Moses has been on Mt. Sinai for forty days and forty nights receiving the Law. The Israelites, gathered at the foot of the mountain, have grown weary of the wait; as a consequence, they coax Aaron into making a gold bull-calf, to which they bow down. Observing this from on high, an angry and jealous Yahweh tells Moses, "I have considered this people, and I see their stubbornness. Now, let me alone to pour out my anger on them and make a great nation spring from you."[1] Moses, sensing that God wasn't making idle/idol threats, decides to do something rather curious: persuade God. Quickly does the famously communication-apprehensive orphan list the reasons God should hold His temper: the Egyptians would have the last laugh; remember Abraham and Isaac and the covenant with the former. Moses even quotes God to the effect that he promised Israel—and what kind of God would renege on a promise? The writer of Exodus does not record whether God made rebuttal arguments or whether God called Moses out on his emotional appeals, to say nothing of the artful inartistic proof. But in verse 14 we read, "So the Lord thought better of the evil with which he had threatened his people." In other words, the diffident Moses persuaded a very upset God to hold his wrath.

The quixotic idea of persuading God is, well, just a bit profane. Moses had his hands full to begin with in leading a sometimes rowdy and wandering crew—and now to persuade an Omnipotent God that he was wrong? God, wrong!? God, being irrational!? God, not reading his own prose!? And, God changing his mind!? What kind of deity changes His mind because of inartistic proofs offered by a high comm-app former sheep farmer?

I feel a bit like said sheep farmer in my present task. While his voice isn't quite Morgan Freeman's, David Zarefsky passes rather convincingly in every other way.

Among several objectives in the present essay, one of the things I'd like to achieve is to persuade Professor Zarefsky, à la Moses, that he might want to rethink a few things he's said in print over the past fifteen years about Herbert A. Wichelns. Specifically, I hope to convince Zarefsky that several of his characterizations of Wichelns's now-famous prescriptions regarding a rhetorical critic's treatment of effect are, dare I say it, wrong. In making this attempt, my aims go well beyond the specifics of Zarefsky's reading of Wichelns. In what follows, I will argue that public-address scholars would do well to return to what Carole Blair calls the "beast" of effect.[2] Rather than treat audiences as hypothetical or easily manipulated or even beside the point, I want to argue that a return to engaging with real members of an audience might help us become better scholars of public rhetoric.

"The Trouble" seemed to begin for Professor Zarefsky at the inaugural meeting of the Texas A&M Presidential Rhetoric Conference, held in 1995. At this important interdisciplinary conference, and without any warning, Professor George C. Edwards III dropped a rather concussive bomb on his rhetoric colleagues: by name and with detailed examples, Edwards proceeded to list the extent to which many of the field's "stars" had claimed effects for rhetoric—without much evidence. One of those stars was David Zarefsky. That conference presentation and the subsequent book chapter has marked Zarefsky's work ever since.[3] Let me document, proceeding chronologically, briefly.

One of his first published reactions to Edwards appears in his 1998 book chapter, "Four Senses of Rhetorical History." Rather than singling out the political science professor by name, Zarefsky urges his rhetoric colleagues to return to their origins—but with a qualification. "When [Herbert] Wichelns wrote that rhetorical criticism was not concerned with permanence or beauty but with effect, he was not urging us to focus on empirical measurements of the effect of a speech." Rather, Zarefsky argues, "he was directing our attention to the fact that rhetoric is situational. Its assessment must be made somehow in the context of that situation."[4]

Perhaps sensing blood in the academic waters, Edwards moved quickly to parlay his conference remarks into a full-blown research project. With *On Deaf Ears,* published in 2003, Edwards moved in for the kill: presidential rhetoric, as best he could tell, didn't much matter at all.[5] The next year, and as editor of *Presidential Studies Quarterly,* Edwards published Zarefsky's rather mild rejoinder. Without mentioning Herbert A. Wichelns by name, Zarefsky first argued that effects were too often narrowly operationalized "as quantitatively measurable changes in indices of people's attitudes or beliefs." Instead of becoming empirical social scientists, Zarefsky encouraged his presidential rhetoric colleagues "to be more precise about what they are claiming and to eschew misleading causal language when it does not fit."[6] In other words, the ghost of 1995 was alive and well.

Two years hence, in a disciplinary conversation on rhetorical criticism published in *Rhetoric Review,* Zarefsky again brought the issue of effects to center stage. Rather than talk in personal ways about his critical praxis, per his colleagues in the colloquium,

Zarefsky apparently had Wichelns, Edwards, and effect on his mind. After dating the subfield of rhetorical criticism to Wichelns's foundational 1925 essay, scholars misunderstood his counsel: Wichelns was not trying to encourage the study of rhetoric's empirical effects on audiences. "His concern, after all, was with criticism, not empirical measurement. Focusing criticism on effects meant that the questions critics were to ask were about the relationship between the text and its possible effects." Zarefsky's qualifier is extremely important: "possible" effects locate the critic's interpretive emphasis away from audiences and toward speakers: "What does the text reveal about the effects its author might have been seeking?"[7]

Three years later and writing a chapter for the *SAGE Handbook of Rhetorical Studies,* Zarefsky once again reminded his colleagues of Wichelns's intent back in 1925: he "was not calling for an empirical demonstration of a speech's effects, nor even suggesting that most single speeches could have recognizable effects." Instead, "Wichelns was suggesting that analysis and criticism of oratory should focus on how, and how well, it is designed to achieve effects."[8] Without singling out the speaker by name, it's clear that the "design" in question leads us right back to making judgments about the speech and its creator.

Zarefsky's most recent iteration of the Edwards/effect/Wichelns imbroglio appears in the 2010 *Handbook of Rhetoric and Public Address.* "Although he sometimes has been misunderstood, Wichelns was not calling for empirical studies to identify or measure the actual effects of an oration." He was instead calling for "critical studies that both explained and evaluated how the oration achieved its effects."[9] With an emphasis on "how," the critic is to answer the question by reference largely to the speaker, the message, and the context. Audience effects are simply assumed.

More than fifteen years later, it's clear that George Edwards really troubled David Zarefsky; the sheer number of times he's repeated his concern by taking up effects vis-à-vis an "accurate" reading of Wichelns suggests as much. That Zarefsky has repeatedly made the study of effect an urgent priority for the fields of rhetorical studies and public address also suggests a concern with a much larger and consequential set of institutional matters. If a political science professor has his barrel trained squarely on an entire field and is squeezing off rounds in a most public way and in very prestigious outlets, frankly, I'm glad to have David Zarefsky on my side. Rhetoricians and public-address scholars ought rightly to thank him for not burying the Edwards affair under the thin cover of disciplinary turf and instead make it a critical priority. Repeatedly. In many and diverse outlets.

But I still think he misreads Herbert A. Wichelns. Let me specify.

In making the case for effect these past many years, Zarefsky has had to walk a tremulous disciplinary tightrope: calling for studies of rhetoric's effects without simultaneously evoking the desiccated corpse of pre–Edwin Black studies of public address. Those studies, Zarefsky himself notes, often produced lousy scholarship because determining causes for rhetoric's effects made for bad social science, imprecise claims, and reductive criticism that typically relied on an elite newspaper or two for the effects in question.[10] The reception of Black's *Rhetorical Criticism: A Study in Method* ostensibly liberated the field from "neo-Aristotelian" criticism, a bastardized critical program based on a caricatured reading of Aristotle's *On Rhetoric* and one wed unnecessarily to effect. Finally, and thanks to Black, we were free from heavy-handed studies of dead white men who, not surprisingly, used ethos, pathos, logos, prepared their speeches in this way or that, had this much or this little speech training, arranged their speeches inductively or deductively and with these sorts of stylistic propensities, and delivered them in this way. I don't think David Zarefsky, or anyone else for that matter, has designs on returning rhetorical studies to the critical formulas of yore. Thus his re-reading of Wichelns through the prism of Edwards.

But that reading fundamentally misses what Herbert A. Wichelns says; perhaps more important, it shades criticism toward speakers and messages and away from audiences and their reactions. If rhetoricians agree on one thing—and in this case I think they do—it's that Wichelns's 1925 book chapter "The Literary Criticism of Oratory" and its re-publication in 1958, 1961, and 1993 stand as "[t]he Magna Carta for rhetorical critics"; the essay essentially created the area of what we know today as rhetorical criticism.[11] While Wichelns borrows from Hoyt H. Hudson's earlier emphasis on rhetoric's concern with how oratory was actually received, the book chapter remains as our critical urtext; as such does Wichelns fulfill, in keeping with our Old Testament parallels, an Abraham-ic function.[12] Famously does Wichelns say that rhetorical criticism is "not concerned with permanence, nor yet with beauty. It is concerned with effect."[13]

Later in the chapter, Wichelns elaborates what he means operationally by effect; in so doing does my disagreement with Zarefsky come into relief. "Finally, *the effect of the discourse on its immediate hearers is not to be ignored, either in the testimony of witnesses, nor in the record of events*."[14] I'm not sure that Wichelns could have been more clear in specifying exactly who he meant by effect—those who actually heard the speech in question, those who were physically present for it, and how it was recorded by journalists, historians, academics, and even private citizens—what, if anything, the discourse did to them, individually and/or collectively, and how it did it. I think Zarefsky is right in one respect: Wichelns does not call explicitly for some sort of quasi-statistical measurement in delineating causes to effects. But, Wichelns does call for rhetorical critics to adjudicate matters of oratorical effect by talking with and observing audiences. That much is very clear.

If there is any lingering doubt as to what Wichelns might have meant, his 1923 *Quarterly Journal of Speech* essay/editorial speaks rather directly. That is, writing as the spokesperson for the National Association of Teachers of Speech's Research Committee, Wichelns lauds "experimental studies" of audiences as a present and future research area, as well as singling out recent research in the "Psychological Theory of Expression," the studies of which empirically examined factors in oratorical persuasion.[15] That rhetoric and effects research was legion from the very outset of the discipline is reflected in the Research Committee's 1915 report. Under the heading of "Research Problems," six of the eight recommendations for future study directly involve studying audience responses to speakers' verbal and non-verbal messages.[16] What's fairly clear in looking back at the early years of the communication discipline is that speech pedagogy and speech criticism did not necessarily occupy separate spheres of specialization. Success in persuading a classroom audience was not inapplicable to rhetorical criticism in which famous and not-so-famous orators tried to do the same thing.

I think Zarefsky might (mis)read Wichelns because of what rhetoricians later did with his counsel, not because of what he actually said back in 1925—and, later, in 1961.[17] After all, Zarefsky reads pretty darn well, so it seems just a bit odd that the critical program he recommends on the basis of Wichelns's essay is at loggerheads with the latter's counsel on audience. Wichelns is clear: talk to audiences; get their feedback; see how the rhetoric did (or didn't) work. Zarefsky encourages us to think about effect from the angle of the probable: how *might* an audience have responded to this message and its appeals given how the speech interacts with its context(s).

As the reader might infer at this point, I do have an agenda—and only part of that agenda has to do with David Zarefsky; he's only the most prominent critic to voice the position that probable effect is good enough. I think in many cases we can do better. Not all, but many. And by doing better, we can also become better critics. How so? By first taking seriously the evidences of an audience's reaction. Many years ago I was approached about doing a book on FDR's first inaugural address. The task was initially quite daunting: how do I write a fifty-thousand-word book about a single, albeit consequential, speech? I could easily bludgeon a reader into oblivion with a nuanced critical reading from draft to draft. In researching the book I traveled to the Roosevelt Presidential Library, in Hyde Park, New York. One of the finding aids revealed that the White House kept a significant number (all?) of reactions—a really important effect, lest we forget—to the first inaugural. But my time was short at the Library, and I really didn't want to open what was sure to be something of a Pandora's box. After all, I had the speech's drafts, I had oral histories, I had newspaper accounts of the inaugural festivities, I had an audio recording, and I had a number of journalist's reactions. And I had a good deal of contextual information that would help me make sense of the many drafts. Did it really matter what the public wrote to their new president? We public address scholars knew/know it was a "great speech"—the third "greatest" in fact.[18] For whatever reason, I decided to open the box. I'm glad I did. Its contents moved me like no other box of archival documents I've ever examined.

Hundreds of letter writers from around the country poured out their hearts to the new president. Young kids wrote on lined notebook paper. Housewives and business executives wrote with fountain pens on thick, custom cotton stationery. And the unemployed and destitute wrote on whatever was at hand. With my laptop I began to take notes—and those notes rather quickly revealed an unmistakable pattern: FDR's speech had inaugurated confidence in the economy; his message was a sign that he'd been sent by God; and, because he'd been sent by God and the economic situation was so grave, his becoming dictator was acceptable. But what to do with these three categories of response? I was the rhetorical critic in charge, after all; FDR's correspondents were just that: folks writing letters.

I went back to the drafts of the address. I read them with a new set of lenses—those who'd actually heard or seen FDR speak on March 4, 1933. Sure enough, I began to see the three sets of responses manifest themselves in the speech drafts. Yes, many in FDR's audience were looking for confidence, for a sacred purpose, for absolute trust in a new leader—but here they were in the drafts and in the final document. Rhetoric was creating these very realities.[19] I came away a bit humbled by the process. Maybe these folks knew some things a trained rhetorical critic didn't. Or maybe a trained rhetorical critic—and Burke's "trained incapacity" comes readily to mind here—was simply looking in the wrong places. And, ironically, that sublime aphorism, perhaps the best remembered in the long history of presidential rhetoric—"the only thing we have to fear is fear itself"—passed largely without comment by Roosevelt's letter writers.

I'm certainly not the only rhetorical critic to get schooled—in the best possible way—by an audience. Amos Kiewe allowed letter writers to guide his understanding of FDR's First Fireside Chat and in so doing illustrated how rhetoric was absolutely essential to creating the very conditions for economic recovery. Too, Kiewe had evidence far beyond letters: he had the day-after bank deposit information—the very empirical measures that Wichelns recommends and Zarefsky seems to reject.[20] Similarly, in her brilliant and award-winning essay on Lincoln and image vernaculars, Cara Finnegan uses readers' letters in *McClure's* magazine to argue for a new way of seeing an image of Lincoln, one bound up with the president's superior moral character and uniquely American anxieties in the second half of the nineteenth century.

Audiences and their reactions to messages are also central to other scholars' work. Kathleen Hall Jamieson has spent considerable time with focus groups and their reactions to political advertisements. Her criticism is informed in every way by their reactions.[21] Similarly, Carole Blair and Neil Michel use their fieldwork in and around important U.S. memorials sites to make claims about how those memorials perform their many functions. Or not. Their work, for example, on the failure of the Astronaut's Memorial in Cape Canaveral is informed by what they witnessed at the site, namely lots of Disney tourists suffering from entertainment ennui.[22] Minus their interactions and observations, the failure would appear to inhere in the object (message) itself. Even a textual diehard like the late Michael Leff, with some nudging from his former student Leah Ceccarelli, came to at least/last acknowledge an interpretive role for audiences.[23] The constitutive turn in rhetorical studies is also premised on what rhetoric does—for the speaker who speaks it. It took my late dissertation adviser and good friend, Dick Gregg, a few trips to the Harrisburg ghetto in 1968 to understand that he shouldn't take being called a "motherfucker" in a classroom setting personally; it wasn't really about him.[24]

Mindful of such important work on audiences, we must ask why rhetorical critics and public address scholars still so often veer from rather direct encounters with audiences. Why are direct engagements with audiences still the exception and not the rule? To answer these questions with anything resembling a comprehensive manner is well beyond the parameters of this essay. Fortunately, several others have preceded me on the subject. Fred Fejes, for example, writing to his media colleagues back in 1984, found it just a bit ironic that the rise of a "critical communication perspective" (contra the tradition of behaviorism) had spawned a backlash against studying real people engaging with real media messages.[25] The then-new research paradigm lumped effects under the twin rubrics of ideology and hegemony, and neither was amenable to analytical operationalization. Audience effects, as such, were irrelevant, beside the point—a quaint scholarly anachronism in the age of domination and interpellation. The shift to ideology, on Fejes's account, functioned to coax researchers into careful and close readings of media messages. Audiences were busy being interpellated by such dense and insidious messages. But Fejes wasn't buying. He closed the essay by throwing down the gauntlet to his "critical" colleagues: the burden was on them to show that "all the meanings uncovered in media content make a difference."[26] To whom? To audiences.

Writing more than ten years later, Carole Blair arrived at a conclusion similar to Fejes's, but the disciplinary variables she isolates are very different. Instead of ideological critique and its new critical sensibilities, Blair located the twin disciplinary turns to symbols and the privileging of rhetorical theory as pivotal registers in the move away from audiences.[27] The emphasis on symbols, a legacy of the adoption of Kenneth Burke's critical project and an alliance with our social science communication colleagues, functions to make symbolic inducement the locus of nearly all critical activity—the practical result of which is a disciplinary fixation with meaning. If only the recalcitrant symbol could be made to disclose its secrets through relentless and careful readings—theoretically inflected and otherwise—the mysteries of the text could be unlocked. Not surprisingly, such a critical project often privileged difficult and dense texts whose meaning lay far beneath its surface (more on this below). At this point we are a long way from the rationale for rhetorical criticism as articulated by Herbert August Wichelns.

But the problem for Blair wasn't that a concern with symbols or theory production was a bad move; rather, she deplored its assumptions: "virtually all rhetoricians in Speech Communication appear to assume, rather than to explore, a clear and direct relationship between the symbolic production of meaning and the activity of that production in the world." More succinctly, Blair concluded that "the meaning of a message cannot be equated with that message's consequences."[28] I take Blair to mean that the meaning of a message as adjudicated symbolically by a critic doesn't always or even necessarily correspond to the work that same message does out in the world. And, in light of evidence of that sort of work, how would we know? Privileging speakers and their symbols certainly shines a bright light on the critic who, in Leff's words, is "hunkered down" with the text.[29] But it certainly makes the study of rhetoric a very solitary, perhaps solipsistic, endeavor.

Both Fejes and Blair attempt to locate critical praxis within our discipline's intellectual history, and both, I think, succeed. I would offer another, though complementary, explanation—albeit far more quotidian. It is simply easier to turn a blind eye to audiences and how messages resonate (or not) with them and instead focus on speakers and messages.[30] And cheaper. Assembling focus groups is costly and time consuming. So, too, is flying across the country to observe and interview strangers. Traveling to presidential libraries to open Hollinger boxes that may (or may not) contain germane responses to presidential speeches is pricey, time consuming—and risky. Probable responses, carefully determined from my desk chair in Tallahassee, Florida, are certainly beguiling. Even more so with a ticking tenure and promotion clock.

Hard have we rhetorical critics, per Blair, gone down the symbolic road. Certainly the field's adoption of Kenneth Burke's project of symbolic inducement was influential in our heading thus. But perhaps even more influential than Burke was Edwin Black's 1962 doctoral dissertation-turned-1965-academic-best-seller, *Rhetorical Criticism: A Study in Method,* a project directed by the Father, Herbert August Wichelns. And in a not-so-subtle reversal of the Original, the son appears to attempt to sacrifice the Father and the ostensibly false god of Effect.[31] Literary critics and criticism are repeatedly valorized by Black, not rhetorical critics and criticism.[32] If we must focus on effect at all, it should be the effect on the critic, not the audience. In brief, Black argues forcefully that rhetorical criticism, as conceptualized by Wichelns and carried out by a generation or two of "neo-Aristotelian" critics, had all but decimated the critic—the virtuoso critic that Black fancied himself to be.[33] "Since neo-Aristotelianism allows no place for the personal revelations of the critic," Black notes, "the neo-Aristotelian critic is less likely than he would otherwise be to compose effusions of embarrassing confessionals in his exegesis of a rhetorical discourse."[34]

Edwin Black was likely not worried about composing embarrassing effusions—autobiographical or otherwise. Rather, and in one of the very rare moments of personal disclosure in the dissertation or book—and carefully mitigated by the third person—Black discloses how he fancies himself in his professional role: "Sometimes—though rarely—the critic himself is a man of such unusual gifts that his self-portraiture becomes an artful work, and his criticism can be read for its own sake." And not for the sake of Aristotelian categories: "Sometimes, too, the critic is a man of such acute sensitivity that his personal revelations in converse with a work of art do shed light on the potentialities of the work." Not the potentialities of *On Rhetoric*. And lest we not yet have the completed picture, Black, in a rare act of trinitarian repetition, concludes, "Except in the hands of a very, very few men, the critical methodology that minimizes the personal responses, peculiar tastes, and singularities of the critic will be superior to the one that does not." That methodology was neo-Aristotelianism, and it had conspired against the rare critical genius of Edwin Black.

I suppose at this point a note about my intentions is in order. I don't intend to demean Professor Black's critical talents; indeed, those talents were "very, very" rare. No, my point has far more to do with the persona to which Black urges rhetorical critics to aspire: namely the genius, the virtuoso, the precociously original. Certainly not a critical sensibility governed by a "methodology that, independently applied by different men to the same object, can yield the same conclusions." Edwin Black is not talking to the mirror; instead, he is urging his rhetorical critic colleagues to aspire to a greatness unencumbered by the vicissitudes of method: "aesthetic re-creation [Black's preferred "method"] is not a search for contexts; it is, if anything, anti-contextual. Its whole animus is the isolation of the work from all extraneous influences and ancillary considerations, that the work may be comprehended in and for itself."[35] To study things like the immediate effect of the address demeans the role of critics by forcing them into a "deferential posture."[36]

By and large, rhetorical critics followed Professor Black's counsel; after all, who doesn't want to be considered great at what he or she does? Why be an Aristotelian automaton with a jones for comptometrics when we can unlock "the recalcitrant mystery of the work" and "disclose the enigmas of an artistic product"?[37] And the consequences—perhaps we might even say effects—of that choice have been profound. First, and most germane to my objectives, Black's retreat to and elevation of the critical "object" has safely sequestered us from audiences; you and I, as rhetorical critics, are the only important audience members. On Black's view, analyzing the audience's response, singly or collectively, would simply be much too democratic in a world of virtuoso rhetorical critics. Why share the interpretive stage when the talent is third rate and a focus on effects displaces the critic from that sacred, if diffident, object? Second, and not unrelated to the preceding, such a critical emphasis privileges the enigmatic text, the masterful text, and the potentially dangerous text. The critic's job becomes to reveal things previously unrecognized and, in the process of making those revelations known, to demonstrate one's critical genius and importance. Black has led the way with his brilliant and singular readings of Lincoln's Gettysburg Address, an anonymous *New York Times* editorial, and Robert Welch's habitual use of the "cancer of communism" metaphor, among other work.

Regarding this last reading, performed in his very influential article, "The Second Persona," Black argues that it's enough for the critic to disclose what the speaker/author would have her listeners/readers become. Not what in fact they became; such an undertaking would take away from the critic's specialized craft. In fact, the critic "does not focus on a relationship between a discourse and an actual auditor. [The critic] focuses instead *on the discourse alone,* and extracts from it the audience it implies."[38] Indeed, the discourse alone. And the critic alone, too. Black then leverages his creative and provocative reading of a metaphor to render a moral judgment against Robert Welch. In so doing, though, have we not just returned to the speaker's character, that well-worn and perhaps quaint neo-Aristotelian category of ethos, albeit latent in a metaphor that needs quite a bit of unpacking? Moreover, what are we to make of a negative moral judgment that hinges on a virtuoso reading of a metaphor, which on Black's account isn't even the "best evidence" available?[39] Not rhetorical work that was done, but work that might be done? Has our critic jumped the proverbial gun? Or is this what critics do in a dangerous and rhetorically opaque world? Over the past forty years, our journals have suggested that yes, one of the critic's preeminent duties is to offer warnings of what might happen—on the basis of the critic's rather exclusive talents reading dense and potentially dangerous texts. That certainly seems like a noble mission, but to ignore real audiences in favor of hypothetical ones seems to unnecessarily burden the critic.

Before Black's critique of neo-Aristotelianism's practitioners, Wayne N. Thompson and some of his colleagues were thinking about audiences and effects back in the 1940s. Always an outspoken advocate for firsthand observations of speeches and the work they appeared to do with an audience,[40] Thompson noted in an essay on a campaign speech by John Dewey that the Executive Committee of the National Association of Teachers of Speech had recently formed the Committee on Contemporary Public Address (CCPA). The Committee's mission was twofold: to observe speeches as they occurred and to preserve those written observations.[41] In this manner, Thompson claimed, could public address scholars in 1945 help their colleagues in 1995. I wonder what ever became of this CCPA (an acronym uncomfortably close to the CPA, the Communist Party of America) and its "observations." Done on a large and sustained scale, this work could certainly have mitigated that age-old question: what if evidences of a speech's reception don't survive?

Fejes, Blair, and Thompson's lobbying on behalf of effects research invites an obvious question: what might it look like? How might rhetoricians and public address scholars do the sort of work upon which Wichelns (and many of his colleagues) founded the field? On the basis of my review of the literature, Blair is right: the concept of effect hasn't been "explored sufficiently to be a very well understood standard."[42] So, too, say Cherwitz and Theobald-Osborne: "There has been insufficient exploration of the concept [audience effect] theoretically or meta-critically; in short, the concept of political effect has not been informed by nor kept pace with sophisticated advances in other aspects of rhetorical and communication theory."[43] But we do have a few studies in addition to the ones mentioned previously. Wayne Minnick, for example, used the testimony of audience members, the testimony of subsequent scholars, and the record of postspeech behaviors in his analysis of the effects of Lyman Beecher's speech on dueling.[44] Cherwitz used what he deemed "language-in-use" to illustrate how Lyndon Johnson's Gulf of Tonkin speech functioned to influence several groups of elites.[45] Mary Stuckey adopted a long-term approach to the instrumental study of presidential rhetoric's effects in her examination of Jimmy Carter's human-rights discourse.[46] In the same anthology James Jasinski and Jennifer R. Mercieca address the constitutive effects of documents created by various state legislatures at the close of the eighteenth century.[47] Devoting an entire section of this important handbook to effects research suggests that it is still—or ought to be?—at the vital center of our discipline.

As rhetorical criticism and public address scholars look to the future, we would be foolish not to take advantage of the immediacy and accessibility to audiences that the Internet and our mobile technologies deliver. Thompson et al.'s dream of a ready archive of speech reports and audience reactions is a daily reality in our 24/7 live-streaming online world. Surely we can leverage the Web to assist our efforts to locate some of the work that rhetoric does in the social-political world. As a field that no longer exclusively studies speeches and speech texts, nonoratorical subjects enable us to reconceptualize effect—from a moment in time to more dynamic moments in time. The rhetorical work of the National Civil Rights Memorial, to offer but one example, is performed daily and variously with its many visitors.[48]

At the close of fourteen essays, just where are we? Have we made any headway in addressing Blair and Cherwitz and Theobald-Osborne's complaint about "insufficient exploration" of effect? We think so. And our contributors, who span a wide range of academic traditions and intellectual interests, do, too. Long gone, we trust, is that old behaviorist canard redolent of the hypodermic-needle model of media-effects research: surely audiences are more sophisticated, and critics, too. But this we also know: rhetoric does work in the world; each of our contributors proves as much. Whether it's talking with teenagers at a local rave, understanding what is sayable as a register of effect, reading letters sent to a president, or seeing traces of a speech days, months, or years later, rhetoric does in fact matter. Similarly, whether rhetoric is conceptualized in the context of virtuoso musicians, aspiring documentary filmmakers, the reminiscences of a senator, or even the theorizing of prominent European intellectuals traumatized by the Holocaust, rhetoric re-makes the world even as it responds to it. While Blair offers us an important explanation for why questions of effect were displaced in the discipline, Rowland reminds us that claims of "resonance," however coy, require something less than galvanic skin response tests—but something more than a set of maybes, too. In brief, we've traveled some distance to see that there are many different ways to conceptualize effect, each of which entails different evidences and often very diverse audiences across many different registers or platforms. The time, in sum, has never been more auspicious for taking audiences seriously.

None other than David Zarefsky acknowledges as much. In his most recent statement about effect, perhaps our [Y]ahweh has indeed changed his mind. A "promising approach" in effects research, he writes, "is reception studies. Rather than make assumptions about effects from the text itself, reception studies are empirical or quasi-empirical reconstructions of how actual audiences understood and reacted to a text."[49] What appears to be something new and "promising," though, turns out to be something rather dated, even if the word "reception" has been smuggled in for that querulous term "effect." But I think Professor Zarefsky is spot on in (re)emphasizing the role of "actual audiences" in rhetorical criticism. We need to share the critical load, if for no other reason than to acknowledge that our expertise extends only so far. Audiences know things, too. Similarly, rhetoric does things to audiences that matter in the most fundamental ways—and we should want to know about those things.[50] And, as Nilsen asks, "who should be more fitted by training to do this" work than rhetorical critics?[51]

Ed Black's 1962 dissertation at Cornell, "Method in Rhetorical Criticism," became, in 1965, *Rhetorical Criticism: A Study in Method.* Six decades on, its influence is profound; it is also still in print. May it always be so. But I'd like to close by providing a counterbalance to Black's weighty influence: also a dissertation-turned-book that few in our field would recognize, let alone have read. Back in the early 1940s, William Harrison Pipes sold his University of Michigan doctoral committee on a rather odd project: to analyze the speeches of eight "Old-Time Negro preachers" in Macon County, Georgia. Pipes wouldn't analyze the many enigmas and silences of the eight not-so-great texts in his Ann Arbor office; rather, he realized, having grown up in the southern and rural black church, that to understand the rhetorical functions of these vernacular sermons he would have to witness them firsthand, since the audiences responded to the ministers' words to create a unique and consequential performance, one that offered an emotional catharsis amid the stifling oppression of the Jim Crow Deep South. And so, with his bulky recording equipment and team of assistants, Pipes selected several rural sites, notably the churches that had electricity. As he recorded each speech, he and his wife also recorded in careful detail how the audiences reacted and how in turn their reaction shaped the preacher's reaction, climaxing in every instance with an emotional crescendo that was almost always lexically untranslatable. His 1945 article published in the *Quarterly Journal of Speech,* "Old-Time Negro Preaching: An Interpretive Study," did not hedge its bets with a claim of probable effect. Pipes, after all, had been there and seen it happen with his own eyes and ears—on eight different occasions. But William Harrison Pipes was no mere objective recorder of effect, deferentially employing critical categories in a mechanical way that diminished his role or stature. No, to the contrary, our field's first black Ph.D. taught his readers just how consequential spoken and vernacular rhetoric was to a small group of largely illiterate southern black sharecroppers. His audience had taught him as much.

His dissertation-turned-book is still in print. May it, too, always be so.[52]

Notes

1. Exodus 32: 9–10, *The Oxford Study Bible,* ed. M. Jack Suggs, Katharine Doob Sakenfeld, and James R. Mueller (New York: Oxford University Press, 1992), 95.

2. Carole Blair, "'We Are All Just Prisoners Here of Our Own Device': Rhetoric in Speech Communication after Wingspread," paper presented at the 1996 Rhetoric Society of America Conference, Tucson, Arizona. This essay was published in much-truncated form in the conference proceedings; see Theresa Enos, Richard McNabb, Carolyn Miller, and Roxanne Mountford, eds., *Making and Unmaking the Prospects for Rhetoric: Selected Papers from the 1996 Rhetoric Society of America Conference* (Mahwah, N.J.: Lawrence Erlbaum, 1997), 29–36.

3. See George C. Edwards III, "Presidential Rhetoric: What Difference Does It Make?," in *Beyond the Rhetorical Presidency,* ed. Martin J. Medhurst (College Station: Texas A&M University Press, 1996), 199–217.

4. David Zarefsky, "Four Senses of Doing Rhetorical History," in *Doing Rhetorical History*, ed. Kathleen J. Turner (Tuscaloosa: University of Alabama Press, 1998), 21.

5. George C. Edwards III, *On Deaf Ears: The Limits of the Bully Pulpit* (New Haven: Yale University Press, 2003).

6. David Zarefsky, "Presidential Rhetoric and the Power of Definition," *Presidential Studies Quarterly* 34 (2004): 607–619.

7. David Zarefsky, "Reflections on Rhetorical Criticism," *Rhetoric Review* 25 (2006): 384.

8. David Zarefsky, "History of Public Discourse Studies," in *The SAGE Handbook of Rhetorical Studies*, ed. Andrea A. Lunsford, Kirt H. Wilson, and Rosa A. Eberly (Thousand Oaks, Calif.: Sage, 2009), 435.

9. David Zarefsky, "Public Address Scholarship in the New Century: Achievements and Challenges," in *The Handbook of Rhetoric and Public Address*, ed. Shawn J. Parry-Giles and J. Michael Hogan (Malden, Mass.: Wiley-Blackwell, 2010), 67.

10. Zarefsky, "Reflection on Rhetorical Criticism," 384.

11. W. Charles Redding, "Extrinsic and Intrinsic Criticism," in *Essays on Rhetorical Criticism*, ed. Thomas R. Nilsen (New York: Random House, 1968), 99. While I never had the pleasure of meeting Herbert Wichelns, he was clearly a personality and a presence. A favorite story about him was relayed in a 2003 essay by fellow Cornell-ian Thomas W. Benson, who notes a very conspicuous three-year publishing lacunae in *Speech Monographs*. During Wichelns's editorship of said journal, from 1930–1932, nary an issue was published. Why? According to his colleagues, editor Wichelns had "simply not found anything of sufficient merit to deserve publication during his [entire] editorial term." Thomas W. Benson, "The Cornell School of Rhetoric: Idiom and Institution," *Communication Quarterly* 51 (2003): 12.

12. Hudson claims that "in rhetoric a study of the audience is fundamental; and the essence of it is adaptation to the end of influencing hearers"; see Hoyt H. Hudson, "The Field of Rhetoric," *Quarterly Journal of Speech* 9 (1923): 180.

13. Herbert A. Wichelns, "The Literary Criticism of Oratory," in *Studies in Rhetoric and Public Speaking in Honor of James Albert Winans*, ed. A. M. Drummond (New York: Century, 1925), 209.

14. Wichelns, "The Literary Criticism of Oratory," my emphasis, 213.

15. Herbert A. Wichelns, "Research," *Quarterly Journal of Speech* 9 (1923): 233, 239.

16. Research Committee, "Report," *Quarterly Journal of Public Speaking* 1 (1915): 30. For an early summary of the experimental work on audiences, see William A. D. Millson, "Experimental Work in Audience Reaction," *Quarterly Journal of Speech* 18 (1932): 13–30.

17. Wichelns published a much-truncated version of his original 1925 essay in a 1961 anthology. Importantly, he did not edit any of the important counsel he offers on effect; in fact, the prose is identical. So, given the opportunity to revise his earlier formulation, he chose not to. See Herbert A. Wichelns, "Some Differences between Literary Criticism and Rhetorical Criticism," in *Historical Studies of Rhetoric and Rhetoricians*, ed. Raymond F. Howes (Ithaca: Cornell University Press, 1961), 217–224. Wichelns's unwillingness to amend the essay is curious in light of Carroll C. Arnold's 1982 eulogy/essay. "The fame of the essay," reports Arnold, "worried Wichelns because readers turned what he had offered as corrective into methodological prescription. And prescription in criticism was something Wichelns very much disliked." Further, rhetorical criticism might have proceeded "more freely and inventively" had he not published the essay. Carroll C. Arnold, "Herbert August Wichelns (1894–1973)," *Southern States Communication Journal* 47 (1982): 127, 128.

18. I'm referring to the Lucas/Medhurst poll that serves as the foundation of their book, *Words of a Century: The Top 100 American Speeches, 1900–1999* (New York: Oxford University Press, 2009).

19. For the published essay in question, see Davis W. Houck and Mihaela Nocasian, "FDR's First Inaugural Address: Text, Context, and Reception," *Rhetoric and Public Affairs* 5 (2002): 649–678.

20. Amos Kiewe, *FDR's First Fireside Chat: Public Confidence and the Banking Crisis* (College Station: Texas A&M University Press, 2007).

21. See, for example, Kathleen Hall Jamieson, *Dirty Politics* (New York: Oxford University Press, 1991).

22. Carole Blair and Neil Michel, "Commemorating in the Theme Park Zone: Reading the Astronauts Memorial," in *At the Intersection: Cultural Studies and Rhetorical Studies*, ed. Thomas Rosteck (New York: Guilford, 1999), 29–83.

23. Michael Leff, "Lincoln at Cooper Union: Neo-classicism Revisited," *Western Journal of Communication* 65 (2001): 323–348.

24. Dick's work in teaching public speaking to black students in Harrisburg culminated in his very influential essay on the ego-function of protest rhetoric; see Richard B. Gregg, "The Ego-Function of the Rhetoric of Protest," *Philosophy and Rhetoric* 4 (1971): 71–91.

25. Fred Fejes, "Critical Mass Communications Research and Media Effects: The Problem of the Disappearing Audience," *Media, Culture and Society* 6 (1984): 219–232.

26. Fejes, "Critical Mass Communications Research and Media Effects," 230.

27. Blair, "'We Are All Just Prisoners Here of our Own Device,'" 14.

28. Blair, "'We Are All Just Prisoners Here of our Own Device,'" 14. In a later essay Blair raises the same question: "How can we be confident that what critics identify as significant features of the rhetoric they study have significant influence? How do critics distinguish between aspects of rhetorical texts or objects that are merely surface features and those that do rhetorical work?" Carole Blair, "Reflections on Criticism and Bodies: Parables from Public Places," *Western Journal of Communication* 65 (2001): 288.

29. Leff, "Lincoln at Cooper Union," 323–348.

30. As early as 1932, William A. D. Millson excoriated his colleagues in the field of Speech for their "arm-chair speculation" and their "lazy method" for interrogating how audiences respond to messages. While I don't subscribe to Millson's rather rigid prescription for exclusively quantitative studies, I share some of his frustrations about our collective unwillingness to engage audiences. William A. D. Millson, "Experimental Work in Audience Reaction," *Quarterly Journal of Speech* 18 (1932): 14, 15. Woolbert similarly castigated rhetoricians fifteen years earlier: "Rhetoric as a science has been too much of the study, if not of the arm-chair; too many of the conclusions of the rhetoricians, lacking strict empirical basis, are merely verbal shufflings." Charles H. Woolbert, "Conviction and Persuasion: Some Considerations of Theory," *Quarterly Journal of Speech* 3 (1917): 249.

31. Said Ehninger, "If . . . Wichelns' landmark essay of 1925 gave neo-Aristotelianism its birth, this book published exactly forty years later . . . may well deal the school its death blow." Douglas Ehninger, "Rhetoric and the Critic," *Western Speech* 29 (1965): 230.

32. Jellicorse notes that "Black's critiques, however, with their emphasis on timelessness, and vivid style and imagery, do not differ from the analysis and criticism which a literary critic would perform upon the same works." John Lee Jellicorse, "New Books in Review: Rhetorical Criticism," *Quarterly Journal of Speech* 51 (1965): 341.

33. Robert L. Scott notes that Black "seems to argue that to appeal to the immediate audience as the decisive measure of rhetorical merit is to abdicate the role of critic." Scott, "New Books in Review: Rhetorical Criticism," *Quarterly Journal of Speech* 51 (1965): 336.

34. Edwin Black, *Rhetorical Criticism: A Study in Method* (Madison: University of Wisconsin Press, 1978), 76.

35. Black, *Rhetorical Criticism*, 43.

36. Black, *Rhetorical Criticism,* 77.

37. Edwin Black, "Method in Rhetorical Criticism," Ph.D. dissertation, Cornell University, 1962, 1. My thanks to Amos Kiewe and Adam Kiewe for securing a microfilm copy of Black's dissertation—and for painstakingly copying it for me, frame by frame.

38. Edwin Black, "The Second Persona," *Quarterly Journal of Speech* 56 (1970): 112. Emphasis added.

39. Black states, "The best evidence in the discourse for this implication [the implied auditor, or second persona] will be the substantive claims that are made, but the most likely evidence available will be in the form of stylistic tokens." Black, "The Second Persona," 112. Why the most likely evidence is not also the best evidence, given the critic's task of complete disclosure and judgment, remains elusive.

40. Wayne N. Thompson, "Contemporary Public Address as a Research Area," *Quarterly Journal of Speech* 33 (1947): 274–83.

41. Wayne N. Thompson, "A Case Study of Dewey's Minneapolis Speech," *Quarterly Journal of Speech* 31 (1945): 419.

42. Blair, "'We Are All Just Prisoners Here of Our Own Device,'" 20.

43. Richard A. Cherwitz and John Theobald-Osborne, "Contemporary Developments in Rhetorical Criticism: A Consideration of the Effects of Rhetoric," in *Speech Communication: Essays to Commemorate the 75th Anniversary of The Speech Communication Association*, ed. Gerald M. Phillips and Julia T. Wood (Carbondale: Southern Illinois University Press, 1990), 58.

44. Wayne C. Minnick, "A Case Study in Persuasive Effect: Lyman Beecher on Duelling," *Speech Monographs* 38 (1971): 262–276.

45. Richard A. Cherwitz, "The Contributory Effect of Rhetorical Discourse: A Study of Language in Use," *Quarterly Journal of Speech* 66 (1980): 33–50.

46. Mary E. Stuckey, "Jimmy Carter, Human Rights, and Instrumental Effects of Presidential Rhetoric," in *The Handbook of Rhetoric and Public Address,* ed. Shawn J. Parry-Giles and J. Michael Hogan (Malden, Mass.: Wiley-Blackwell, 2010), 293–312.

47. James Jasinski and Jennifer R. Mercieca, "Analyzing Constitutive Rhetorics: The Virginia and Kentucky Resolutions and the 'Principles of '98,'" in *The Handbook of Rhetoric and Public Address,* ed. Shawn J. Parry-Giles and J. Michael Hogan (Malden, Mass.: Wiley-Blackwell, 2010), 313–341.

48. Carole Blair and Neil Michel, "Reproducing Civil Rights Tactics: The Rhetorical Performances of the Civil Rights Memorial," *Rhetoric Society Quarterly* 30 (2000): 31–55.

49. Zarefsky, "Public Address Scholarship in the New Century: Achievements and Challenges," 80.

50. Bryant's treatment is most apt: "Rhetoric as distinct from the learnings which it uses is dynamic; it is concerned with movement. It does rather than is. It is method rather than matter. It is chiefly involved with bringing about a condition, rather than discovering or testing a condition." Donald C. Bryant, "Rhetoric: Its Functions and Its Scope," *Quarterly Journal of Speech* 39 (1953): 412.

51. Thomas R. Nilsen, "Criticism and Social Consequences," *Quarterly Journal of Speech* 42 (1956): 178.

52. William H. Pipes, *Say Amen, Brother! Old-Time Negro Preaching: A Study in Frustration* (New York: William Frederick, 1951). The book remains in print through Wayne State University Press. See also William Harrison Pipes, "Old-Time Negro Preaching: An Interpretive Study," *Quarterly Journal of Speech* 31 (1945): 15–21.

Bibliography

"9500 Liberty: Aftermath of Immigration Resolution in Prince William." *9500 Liberty* YouTube Channel, March 28, 2008. http://www.youtube.com/watch?v=YAvyi1Rutrs (accessed August 17, 2013).

"9500 Liberty Going Big." *9500 Liberty* YouTube Channel, November 4, 2007. http://www.youtube.com/watch?v=6pNFaPTYwBc (accessed August 17, 2013).

"9500 Liberty: Interactive Documentary Scene from Feature Film." *9500 Liberty* YouTube Channel, May 17, 2010. http://www.youtube.com/user/9500Liberty#p/a/u/1/wFxPAoZznpo (accessed February 15, 2012).

"9500 Liberty: MTV Networks to Bring 'LIBERTY' to 100 Million Homes." *9500 Liberty* YouTube Channel. http://9500liberty.com/blog/mtv-networks-to-bring-9500-liberty-to-100-million-homes/ (accessed February 14, 2012).

"9500 Liberty: YouTube Channel Profile." *9500 Liberty* YouTube Channel. http://www.youtube.com/user/9500Liberty (accessed February 15, 2012).

"A Quick Admin Note." February 22, 2008. http://www.bvbl.net/index.php/2008/02/22pwc-committee-of-100-talks-blogs/#comment-55385 (accessed February 15, 2012).

"About Us." The Coffee Party USA, February 23, 2010. http://www.coffeepartyusa.com/about-us (accessed February 14, 2012).

Ackerman, Elise. "Just Say 'Is It OK?' Non-profit DanceSafe Promotes 'Harm Reduction' "Approach to Drugs." *San Jose Mercury News,* August 4, 2000. http://www.lexis-nexis.com/ (accessed May 23, 2008).

"Activists Plan Immigrant Rights Campaign." Cross-posted at Morning Coffee. http://morningcoffee.wordpress.com/2006/06/26/activists-plan-immigrant-rights-campaign/ (accessed July 10, 2010).

Adler, Patricia A., and Peter Adler. *Membership Roles in Field Research.* Thousand Oaks, Calif.: Sage, 1987.

Alter, Jonathan. *The Defining Moment: FDR's Hundred Days and the Triumph of Hope.* New York: Simon and Schuster, 2006.

———. "What FDR Teaches Us." *Newsweek*, May 1, 2006, 29.

Altieri, Charles. *Subjective Agency: A Theory of First-Person Expressivity and Its Social Implications.* Lynchburg, Va.: Blackwell Press, 1994.

Andén-Papadopalous, Kari. "The Abu Ghraib Torture Photographs: News Frames, Visual Culture, and the Power of Images." *Journalism* 9 (2005): 5–30.

Anderson, Benedict. *Imagined Communities.* London: Verso, 1991.

Andrews, James R. *The Practice of Rhetorical Criticism.* 2nd ed. New York: Longman, 1990.

Arditi, Benjamin, and Jeremy Valentine. *Polemicization: The Contingency of the Commonplace.* New York: New York University Press, 1999.

Arendt, Hannah. *The Human Condition.* Chicago: University of Chicago Press, 1998.

———. *The Origins of Totalitarianism.* Cleveland: World, 1958.

Aristotle. *On Rhetoric*. New York: Modern Library, 1954.

Armstrong, Edward G. "The Rhetoric of Violence in Rap and Country Music." *Sociological Inquiry* 63 (1993): 64–78.

Arnold, Carroll C. "Herbert August Wichelns (1894–1973)." *Southern States Communication Journal* 47 (1982): 124–130.

———. "Oral Rhetoric, Rhetoric, and Literature." *Philosophy and Rhetoric* 1 (1968): 191–210.

———. "Reflections on the Wingspread Conference." In *The Prospect of Rhetoric: Report of the National Development Project*, edited by Lloyd Bitzer and Edwin Black, 194–199. Englewood Cliffs, N.J.: Prentice Hall, 1971.

Arnold, Carroll C., and Kenneth D. Frandsen. "Conceptions of Rhetoric and Communication." In *Handbook of Rhetorical and Communication Theory*, edited by Carroll C. Arnold and John Waite Bowers, 3–50. Boston: Allyn and Bacon, 1984.

Aruga, Tadashi. "The Declaration of Independence in Japan: Translation and Transplantation, 1854–1997." *Journal of American History* 85 (1999): 1409–1431.

Asen, Robert. *Invoking the Invisible Hand: Social Security and the Privatization Debates*. Lansing: Michigan State University Press, 2009.

Asen, Robert, and Daniel C. Brower. *Counterpublics and the State*. Albany: State University of New York Press, 2001.

Atkinson, Nathan S. "Celluloid Circulation: The Dual Temporality of Nonfiction Film and Its Publics." *Rhetoric and Public Affairs* 15 (2012): 675–684.

Aune, James A. "Public Address and Rhetorical Theory." In *Texts in Context: Critical Dialogues on Significant Episodes in American Political Rhetoric*, edited by Michael C. Leff and Fred J. Kauffeld, 43–51. Davis, Calif.: Hermagoras Press, 1989.

Bailyn, Bernard. "Common Sense." In *Fundamental Testaments of the American Revolution*. Washington, D.C.: Library of Congress, 1973.

———. *Ideological Origins of the American Revolution*. Cambridge, Mass.: Harvard University Press, 1965.

Baird, Craig A. *American Public Address, 1740–1952*. New York: McGraw-Hill, 1956.

Baker, Peter. "Bush May Be Out of Chances for a Lasting Domestic Victory." *Washington Post*, June 29, 2007. Newsbank. http://www.Newsbank.com/ (accessed July 1, 2010).

Baker, Richard A. *Traditions of the United States Senate*. Washington, D.C.: Senate Office of Printing and Document Services, 2007.

Baker, Ross. *The House and the Senate*. New York: Norton, 2008.

Ballantine, Arthur A. "When All the Banks Closed." *Harvard Business Review* 26 (1948): 129–143.

Balz, Dan, and Haynes Johnson. *The Battle for America 2008*. New York: Viking, 2009.

"Banks Reopen Here." *New York Times*, March 14, 1933, 1.

Barnes, Fred. "Things Fall Apart." *Weekly Standard*, July 9, 2007. ProQuest Historical Newspapers. http://search.proquest.com/doview/232997803 (accessed Julry 10, 2010).

Bartels, Larry. "Messages Received: The Political Impact of Media Exposure." *American Political Science Review* 87 (1993): 267–285.

Barton, Gary. "Why I Love Larry." *The Advocate*, March 1, 2005.

Baskerville, Barnett. "Must We All Be Rhetorical Critics?" *Quarterly Journal of Speech* 63 (1977): 107–116.

———. "Responses, Queries, and a Few Caveats." In *The Prospect of Rhetoric: Report of the National Development Project*, edited by Lloyd Bitzer and Edwin Black, 151–165. Englewood Cliffs, N.J.: Prentice Hall, 1971.

———. "Selected Writings on the Criticism of Public Address." *Western Speech* 21 (1957): 110–118.

Beasley, Vanessa. *You, the People: American National Identity in Presidential Rhetoric*. College Station: Texas A&M University Press, 2004.

Becker, Samuel L. "Rhetorical Studies for the Contemporary World." In *The Prospect of Rhetoric: Report of the National Development Project,* edited by Lloyd Bitzer and Edwin Black, 21–43. Englewood Cliffs, N.J.: Prentice Hall, 1971.

Beiner, Ronald, and Jennifer Nedelsky. *Judgment, Imagination and Politics: Themes from Kant and Arendt*. Lanham, Md.: Rowman and Littlefield, 2001.

Benoit, William L., and Mary Jeanette Smythe. "Rhetorical Theory as Message Reception: A Cognitive Response Approach to Rhetorical Theory and Criticism." *Communication Studies* 54 (2003): 96–114.

Benson, Thomas W. "Commentary: Rhetorical Structures and Primate." In *Critical Questions; Invention, Creativity, and the Criticism of Discourse and Media,* edited by William L. Nothstine, Carole Blair, and Gary A. Copeland, 184–188. New York: St. Martin's Press, 1994.

———. "The Cornell School of Rhetoric: Idiom and Institution." *Communication Quarterly* 51 (2003): 1–56.

———. "History, Criticism, and Theory in the Study of American Rhetoric." In *American Rhetoric: Context and Criticism,* edited by Thomas W. Benson, 1–17. Carbondale: Southern Illinois University Press, 1989.

———. "The Senses of Rhetoric: A Topical System for Critics." *Central States Speech Journal* 29 (1978): 237–250.

———. "'To Lend a Hand': Gerald R. Ford, Watergate, and the White House Speechwriters." *Rhetoric and Public Affairs* 1 (1998): 201–225.

Bernstein, Richard. *Beyond Objectivism and Relativism: Science, Hermeneutics and Praxis*. Philadelphia: University of Pennsylvania Press, 1983.

Biesecker, Barbara A. "Towards a Transactional View of Rhetorical and Feminist Theory: Rereading Hélène Cixous's The Laugh of the Medusa." *Southern Communication Journal* 57 (1992): 86–96.

Bildner, Jim, and Madeline Drexler. "The Wrong Way to Fight the War on Drugs." *Boston Globe,* June 27, 2006. http://www.boston.com (accessed May 22, 2008).

"Bill's Defeat Points to Bush's Dwindling Clout." [Editorial.] *Miami Herald,* June 29, 2007. Newsbank. http://www.Newsbank.com/ (accessed July 1, 2010).

Birmingham, Carrie. "*Phronesis:* A Model for Pedagogical Reflection." *Journal of Teacher Education* 55 (2004): 313–324.

"Birthday Evokes Washington Lore." *New York Times,* February 23, 1940, 3.

Bitzer, Lloyd F. "The Rhetorical Situation." *Philosophy and Rhetoric* 1 (1968): 1–14.

Black, Edwin. *Method in Rhetorical Criticism*. Ph.D. dissertation, Cornell University, 1962.

———. "The Mutability of Rhetoric." In *Rhetoric in Transition: Studies in the Nature and Uses of Rhetoric,* edited by Eugene E. White, 71–85. University Park: Pennsylvania State University Press, 1980.

———. *Rhetorical Criticism: A Study in Method*. New York: Macmillan, 1965. Reprinted 1978.

———. *Rhetorical Questions: Studies of Public Discourse*. Chicago: University of Chicago Press, 1992.

———. "The Second Persona." *Quarterly Journal of Speech* 56 (1970): 109–119.

———. "Secrecy and Disclosure as Rhetorical Forms." *Quarterly Journal of Speech* 74 (1988): 133–150.

Black, Edwin, and Lloyd Bitzer. "Foreword." *The Prospect of Rhetoric: Report of the National Development Project,* edited by Lloyd F. Bitzer and Edwin Black, v–viii. Englewood Cliffs, N.J.: Prentice Hall, 1971.

Black, Jason E. "Native Authenticity, Rhetorical Circulation, and Neocolonial Decay: The Case of Chief Seattle's Controversial Speech." *Rhetoric and Public Affairs* 15 (2012): 635–645.

Blackburn, Simon. "Being and Time." *New Republic* 241, no. 5 (2010): 36–39.

Blair, Amy. "Main Street Reading *Main Street*." In *New Directions in American Reception Study,* edited by Philip Goldstein and James I. Machor, 139–158. New York: Oxford University Press, 2008.

Blair, Carole. "Reflections on Criticism and Bodies: Parables from Public Places." *Western Journal of Communication* 65 (2001): 271–294.

———. "Symbolic Action and Discourse: The Convergent/Divergent Views of Kenneth Burke and Michel Foucault." In *Kenneth Burke and Contemporary European Thought: Rhetoric in Transition,* edited by Bernard L. Brock, 119–165. Tuscaloosa: University of Alabama Press, 1995.

———. "'We Are All Just Prisoners Here of Our Own Device': Rhetoric in Speech Communication after Wingspread." In *Making and Unmaking the Prospects for Rhetoric: Selected Papers from the 1996 Rhetoric Society of America Conference,* edited by Theresa Enos, Richard McNabb, Carolyn Miller, and Roxanne Mountford, 29–36. Mahwah, N.J.: Lawrence Erlbaum, 1997.

Blair, Carole, and Neil Michel. "Commemorating in the Theme Park Zone: Reading the Astronauts Memorial." In *At the Intersection: Cultural Studies and Rhetorical Studies,* edited by Thomas Rosteck, 29–83. New York: Guilford, 1999.

———. "Reproducing Civil Rights Tactics: The Rhetorical Performances of the Civil Rights Memorial." *Rhetoric Society Quarterly* 30 (2000): 31–55.

———. "The Rushmore Effect: Ethos and National Collective Identity." In *The Ethos of Rhetoric,* edited by Michael J. Hyde, 156–196. Columbia: University of South Carolina Press, 2004.

Blair, Carole, Julie R. Brown, and Leslie A. Baxter. "Disciplining the Feminine." *Quarterly Journal of Speech* 80 (1994): 383–384.

Blair, Carole, Marsha S. Jeppeson, and Enrico Pucci Jr. "Public Memorializing in Postmodernity: The Vietnam Veterans Memorial as Prototype." *Quarterly Journal of Speech* 77 (1991): 263–288.

Bolduc, Michelle K., and David A. Frank. "Chaïm Perelman and Lucie Olbrechts-Tyteca's 'On Temporality as a Characteristic of Argumentation': Commentary and Translation." *Philosophy and Rhetoric* 43 (2010): 315–336.

Booth, Wayne C. *The Rhetoric of Rhetoric: The Quest for Effective Communication*. Oxford: Blackwell, 2004.

"Borderline Reform." *Boston Globe,* November 30, 2005. http://www.boston.com/news/globe/editorial_opinion/editorials/articles/2005/11/30/borderline_reform/ (accessed August 21, 2011).

"Born in the USA; Looks 'Illegal'—Liberty Wall#3." *9500 Liberty* YouTube channel. Comments Forum. http://www.youtube.com/all_comments?v=SmdoicaZKyE (accessed February 14, 2012).

Bowers, John W. "On the Pragmeme." Presidential Address, Speech Communication Association Convention, November 2, 1984. *Spectra* 21 (January 1985): 2–3.

———. "The Pre-scientific Function of Rhetorical Criticism." In *Essays on Rhetorical Criticism,* edited by Thomas R. Nilsen, 126–145. New York: Random House, 1968. Reprinted in *Contemporary Rhetoric: A Reader Coursebook,* edited by Douglas Ehninger, 163–173. Glenview, Ill.: Scott, Foresman, 1972.

Bowers, John W., and James J. Bradac. "Contemporary Problems in Human Communication Theory." In *Handbook of Rhetorical and Communication Theory,* edited by Carroll C. Arnold and John Waite Bowers, 871–893. Boston: Allyn and Bacon, 1984.

Boyden, Matthew. *A Rough Guide to Opera*. 4th ed. New York: Penguin, 2007.

Boynton, G. R. "Reframing Audience: Co-motion at #SOTU." Paper presented at the annual meeting of the Rhetoric Society of America, Philadelphia, Pa., May 24–27, 2012.

Boynton, G. R., and Glenn W. Richardson. "Reframing Audience: Co-motion at #SOTU." http://www.boyntons.us/website/new-media/analyses/state-union-2010–11–12/sotu-RSA-120424.html (accessed August 17, 2013).

Brands, H. W. *Traitor to His Class: The Privileged Life and Radical Presidency of Franklin D. Roosevelt*. New York: Doubleday, 2008.

Bratich, Jack. "Activating the Multitude." In *New Directions in American Reception Study*, edited by Philip Goldstein and James I. Machor, 33–56. New York: Oxford University Press, 2008.

Brean, Joseph. "Will Freud Finally Slip? Pushed to the Fringes of Academia, Psychoanalysts Are Concerned Their Practice Is Dying." *National Post*, April 21, 2007, A8.

Brennan, Andrew. "Necessary and Sufficient Condition." In *The Stanford Encyclopedia of Philosophy* (Spring 2009 edition), edited by Edward N. Zalta, Uri Nodelman, and Colin Allen, 2. http://plato.stanford.edu/entries/necessary-sufficient (accessed February 9, 2011).

"Brief Session of Senate." *Washington Post*, February 23, 1900, 4.

Brock, Bernard L., and Robert L. Scott, eds. *Methods of Rhetorical Criticism: A Twentieth-Century Perspective*. 2nd ed. Detroit, Mich.: Wayne State University Press, 1980.

Brock, Bernard L., Robert L. Scott, and James W. Chesebro, eds. *Methods of Rhetorical Criticism: A Twentieth-Century Perspective*. 3rd ed. Detroit, Mich.: Wayne State University Press, 1989.

Brockriede, Wayne. "Toward a Contemporary Aristotelian Theory of Rhetoric." *Quarterly Journal of Speech* 52 (1966): 33–40.

———. "Trends in the Study of Rhetoric: Toward a Blending of Criticism and Science." In *The Prospect of Rhetoric: Report of the National Development Project*, edited by Lloyd Bitzer and Edwin Black, 123–139. Englewood Cliffs, N.J.: Prentice Hall, 1971.

Brooks, David. "Combat and Composure." *New York Times*, May 6, 2008, A27.

Browne, Stephen H. "Edmund Burke's Letter for a Noble Lord: A Textual Study in Political Philosophy and Rhetorical Action." *Communication Monographs* 55 (1988): 215–229.

———. "Encountering Angelina Grimké: Violence, Identity, and the Creation of Radical Community." *Quarterly Journal of Speech* 82 (1996): 55–73.

———. "Generic Transformation and Political Action: A Textual Interpretation of Edmund Burke's Letter to William Elliott, Esq." *Communication Quarterly* 38 (1990): 54–63.

Brummett, Barry. "Commentary: Premillenial Apocalyptic." In *Critical Questions: Invention, Creativity and the Criticism of Discourse and Media*, edited by William L. Nothstine, Carole Blair, and Gary A. Copeland, 281–285. New York: St. Martin's Press, 1994.

———. "How to Propose a Discourse: A Reply to Rowland." *Communication Studies* 41 (1990): 129.

———. "Rhetorical Theory as Heuristic and Moral: A Pedagogical Justification." *Communication Education* 33 (1984): 97–107.

Bryant, Donald C. "Opening Remarks to the Conference [Pheasant Run]." In *The Prospect of Rhetoric: Report of the National Development Project*, edited by Lloyd Bitzer and Edwin Black, 189–193. Englewood Cliffs, N.J.: Prentice Hall, 1971.

———. "Rhetoric: Its Function and Its Scope." *Quarterly Journal of Speech* 39 (1953): 401–424.

———. *Rhetorical Dimensions in Criticism*. Baton Rouge: Louisiana State University Press, 1969.

Buchanan, Julian, and Lee Young. "The War on Drugs—a War on Drug Users?" *Drugs: Education, Prevention, and Policy* 7 (2000): 409–422.

Buley, Taylor W. "Drug Policy Should Focus on Helping Addicts, Not Jailing Them." *Baltimore Sun*, June 28, 2006. http://articles.baltimoresun.com/2006–06–28/news/0606280023_1_drug-treatment-war-on-drugs-drug-policy (accessed February 10, 2012).

Burgess, Jean, and Joshua Green. *YouTube: Online Video and Participatory Culture*. Cambridge: Polity, 2009.

———. "Agency and Controversy in the YouTube Community." In *Proceedings: IR 9.0: Rethinking Communities, Rethinking Place*. IT University of Copenhagen, Denmark, 2008, 1–18.

Burke, Kenneth. *A Grammar of Motives*. Berkeley: University of California Press, 1969.

———. "Lexicon Rhetoricae." In *Counter-Statement*, edited by Kenneth Burke, 123–183. Berkeley: University of California Press, 1931.

———. "The Rhetoric of Hitler's Battle." In *The Philosophy of Literary Form: Studies in Symbolic Action*, 3rd ed. Berkeley: University of California Press, 1973, 191–220.

———. "The Rhetoric of Hitler's Battle." In *Landmark Essays on Rhetorical Criticism*, edited by Thomas W. Benson, 33–50. Davis, Calif.: Hermagoras Press, 1993.

Burton, Jeremy. "Dubya's Dubious Message." jspot, May 16, 2006. http://www.jspot.org/diary/210 (accessed August 31, 2010).

"Bush Calls for Changes on Illegal Workers." CNN.com, January 8, 2004. http://www.cnn.com/2004/ALLPOLITICS/01/07/bush.immigration/ (accessed July 1, 2010).

Bush, George W. "Address to the Nation on Immigration Reform." May 15, 2006. *The Public Papers of the Presidents of the United States: George W. Bush, 2001–2009*, vol. 5, book 1, 928. Washington, D.C.: Government Printing Office, 2007.

———. "Remarks on Signing the Department of Homeland Security Appropriations Act, 2006." October 18, 2005. *Weekly Compilation of Presidential Documents* 41, no. 42, 1554–1558. Washington, D.C.: Government Printing Office, 2005.

Butler, Gregory. "Music and Rhetoric in Early Seventeenth-Century English Sources." *Musical Quarterly* 66 (1980): 53–64.

Butler, Judith. *Gender Trouble: Feminism and the Subversion of Identity*. New York: Routledge, 1990.

Byler, Eric. Unpublished phone interview, January 4, 2012.

Campbell, John Angus. "The Polemical Mr. Darwin." *Quarterly Journal of Speech* 61 (1975): 375–390.

Campbell, Karlyn K. "Criticism: Ephemeral and Enduring." *Speech Teacher* 23 (1974): 9–14.

Campbell, Karlyn Kohrs. "Agency: Promiscuous and Protein." *Communication and Critical/Cultural Studies* 2 (2005): 1–19.

———. *Critiques of Contemporary Rhetoric*. Belmont, Calif.: Wadsworth, 1972.

———. "The Rhetoric of Women's Liberation: An Oxymoron." *Quarterly Journal of Speech* 59 (1973): 74–86.

"Capitol Marks Holiday." *New York Times*, February 23, 1965, 35.

Carolyn R. Miller. "Foreword." In *Rhetoric and Kairos: Essays in History, Theory, and Praxis*, edited by Phillip Sipiora and James S. Baumlin, xi–xiii. Albany: State University of New York Press, 2002.

Ceccarelli, Leah. "Polysemy: Multiple Meanings in Rhetorical Criticism." *Quarterly Journal of Speech* 84 (1998): 395–415.

———. "Rhetorical Criticism and the Rhetoric of Science." *Western Journal of Communication* 65 (2001): 314–329.

Chaddock, Gail R. "A GOP Faceoff over Illegal Immigration." *Christian Science Monitor*, March 29, 2006. http://www.csmonitor.com/2006/0329/p01s04-uspo.html?s=hns (accessed August 21, 2011).

"Chairman Stewart. Fighting Illegal Immigration." *9500 Liberty* YouTube channel. Comments Forum, October 11, 2007. http://www.youtube.com/watch?v=of8XDSKrNzs (accessed August 17, 2013).

Charland, Maurice. "Constitutive Rhetoric: The Case of the Peuple Quebecois." *Quarterly Journal of Speech* 77 (1987): 133–150.

Cherwitz, Richard A. "The Contributory Effect of Rhetorical Discourse: A Study of Language in Use." *Quarterly Journal of Speech* 66 (1980): 33–50.

Cherwitz, Richard A., and James W. Hikins. *Communication and Knowledge: Investigations in Rhetorical Epistemology*. Columbia: University of South Carolina Press, 1986.

Cherwitz, Richard A., and John Theobald-Osborne. "Contemporary Developments in Rhetorical Criticism: A Consideration of the Effects of Rhetoric." In *Speech Communication: Essays to Commemorate the 75th Anniversary of the Speech Communication Association*, edited by Gerald M. Phillips and Julia T. Wood, 52–80. Carbondale: Southern Illinois University Press, 1990.

Cisneros, J. David. "Contaminated Communities: The Metaphor of 'Immigrant as Pollutant' in Media Representations of Immigration." *Rhetoric and Public Affairs* 11 (2008): 569–601.

Clark, Robert D. "These Truths We Hold Self-Evident." *Quarterly Journal of Speech* 24 (1948): 445–450.

Clark, Robert D. "Lessons for the Literary Critics." *Western Speech* 21 (1957): 83–89.

Clemmitt, Marcia. "Lies and Politics." *CQResearcher* 21 (February 18, 2011): 147.

Cloud, Dana L. "The Materiality of Discourse as Oxymoron: A Challenge to Critical Rhetoric." *Western Journal of Communication* 58 (1994): 141–163.

"The Coalition against Illegal Immigration." http://uncooperativeblogger.wordpress.com /2006/06/26/activists-plan-immigrant-rights-campaign/ (accessed July 10, 2010).

Cohen, Herman. "The Development of Research in Speech Communication: A Historical Perspective." In *Speech Communication in the 20th Century*, edited by Thomas W. Benson, 282–298. Carbondale: Southern Illinois University Press, 1985.

Cohen, Herman. *The History of Speech Communication: The Emergence of a Discipline, 1914–1945*. Annandale, Va.: Speech Communication Association, 1994.

Cohen, Patricia. "Freud Is Widely Taught at Universities, Except in the Psychology Department." *New York Times*, "Week in Review," November 25, 2008.

Collins, Richard. *Interaction Ritual Chains*. Princeton: Princeton University Press, 2004.

Condit, Celeste M. "Hegemony in a Mass-Mediated Society: Concordance about Reproductive Technologies." *Critical Studies in Mass Communication* 11 (1994): 205–230.

Condit, Celeste M. "The Functions of Epideictic: The Boston Massacre Orations as Exemplar." *Communication Quarterly* 33 (1985): 284–299.

"Congress to Hear 'Farewell' Again: Words of Washington Take on Contemporary Aspect in Current Controversies." *New York Times*, February 22, 1954, 20.

Conquergood, Dwight. "Ethnography, Rhetoric, and Performance." *Quarterly Journal of Speech* 78 (1992): 80–123.

———. "Rethinking Ethnography: Towards a Critical Cultural Politics." *Communication Monographs* 58 (1991): 179–194.

Cooper, Martha. "Rhetorical Criticism and Foucault's Philosophy of Discursive Events." *Central States Speech Journal* 39 (1988): 1–17.

Cranford, Paul. *Winston Fitzgerald: A Collection of Fiddle Tunes*. 2nd ed. Cape Breton Island, Nova Scotia: Cranford Publications, 1997.

Crewe, Jonathan. "Can Polemic Be Ethical? A Response to Michel Foucault." In *Polemic: Critical or Uncritical*, edited by Jane Gallop, 135–152. New York: Routledge, 2004.

Crimp, Douglas. "How to Have Promiscuity in an Epidemic." In Crimp, *Melancholia and Moralism: Essays on AIDS and Queer Politics*, 43–82. Cambridge, Mass.: MIT Press, 2002.

———. "Mourning and Militancy." In Crimp, *Melancholia and Moralism: Essays on AIDS and Queer Politics*, 129–149. Cambridge, Mass.: MIT Press, 2002.

———. "Sex and Sensibility, or Sense and Sexuality." In Crimp, *Melancholia and Moralism: Essays on AIDS and Queer Politics*, 281–301. Cambridge, Mass.: MIT Press, 2002.

Cronkhite, Gary. "On the Focus, Scope, and Coherence of the Study of Human Symbolic Activity." *Quarterly Journal of Speech* 72 (1986): 231–46.

Crosswhite, James. *The Rhetoric of Reason: Writing and the Attractions of Argument*. Madison: University of Wisconsin Press, 1996.

DanceSafe. "Philosophy and Vision." http://www.dancesafe.org/about-dancesafe/philosophy-and-vision (accessed August 13, 2013).

Darsey, James. *The Prophetic Tradition and Radical Rhetoric in America*. New York: New York University Press, 1997.

Delacampagne, Christian. *A History of Philosophy in the Twentieth Century*. Baltimore: Johns Hopkins University Press, 1999.

Delia, Jesse G. "Communication Research: A History." In *Handbook of Communication Science*, edited by Charles R. Berger and Steven H. Chaffee, 20–98. Newbury Park, Calif.: Sage, 1987.

Demo, Anne. "Sovereignty Discourse and Contemporary Immigration Politics." *Quarterly Journal of Speech* 91 (2005): 291–311.

Demo, Anne T. "Decriminalizing Illegal Immigration: Immigrants' Rights through the Documentary Lens." In *Border Rhetorics: Citizenship and Identity on the U.S.-Mexico Frontier*, edited by D. Robert DeChaine, 197–212. Tuscaloosa: University of Alabama Press, 2013.

Derrida, Jacques. *Of Grammatology*. Translated by Gayatri Chakravorty Spivak. Baltimore: Johns Hopkins University Press, 1976.

Dickinson, Greg. "Landscapes of Memory, Landscapes of Consumption: The Rhetoric of Twentieth-Century Urban Consumption." Ph.D. dissertation, University of Southern California, 1995.

Dijck, José van. "Users Like You? Theorizing Agency in User-Generated Content." *Media, Culture and Society* 31 (2009): 41–58.

"Dr. Fuller on Real Estate Market." Moonhowlings: A Place for Civil Debate, April 26, 2008. http://www.moonhowlings.net/index.php/2008/04/26/dr-fueller-on-real-estate-market/comment-page-1/#comments (accessed August 17, 2013).

Doherty, Elizabeth. "Paradox on the Periphery: Evolution of the Cape Breton Fiddle Tradition c1928–1995." Unpublished Ph.D. dissertation, University of Limerick, Ireland, 1996.

Doty, William G. *Mythograph: The Study of Myths and Rituals*. 2nd ed. Tuscaloosa: University of Alabama Press, 2000.

Dow, Bonnie J. "Commentary: Feminist Criticism and the Mary Tyler Moore Show." In *Critical Questions: Invention, Creativity and the Criticism of Discourse and Media*, edited by William L. Nothstine, Carole Blair, and Gary A. Copeland, 97–101. New York: St. Martin's Press, 1994.

Drucker, Ernest, and Allan Clear. "Harm Reduction in the Home of the War on Drugs: Methadone and Needle Exchange in the USA." *Drug and Alcohol Review* 18 (1999): 103–112.

Durbin, Richard J. Speaking on immigration reform, 109th Cong., 2nd sess. *Congressional Record* 152, Issue 35 (March 27, 2006): S2403. Washington, D.C.: Government Printing Office, 2006.

Edbauer, Jenny. "Unframing Models of Public Distribution: From Rhetorical Situation to Rhetorical Ecologies." *Rhetoric Society Quarterly* 35 (2005): 5–24.

Ede, Lisa. "Rhetoric vs. Philosophy: The Role of the Universal Audience in Chaïm Perelman's *The New Rhetoric*." *Central States Speech Journal* 32 (1981): 118–125.

Edelman, Lee. *Homographesis: Essays in Gay Literary and Cultural Theory*. New York: Routledge, 1994.

Edwards, George C., III. "Presidential Rhetoric: What Differences Does It Make?" In *Beyond the Rhetorical Presidency*, edited by Martin J. Medhurst, 199–217. College Station: Texas A&M University Press, 1996.

———. *On Deaf Ears: The Limits of the Bully Pulpit*. New Haven: Yale University Press, 2003.

Ehninger, Douglas. "Introduction." In *Contemporary Rhetoric: A Reader's Coursebook,* edited by Douglas Ehninger, 1–14. Glenview, Ill.: Scott, Foresman, 1972.

———. "Rhetoric and the Critic." *Western Speech* 29 (1965): 227–231.

———. Unpublished, untitled position paper, compiled with others as "Statements by Conference Participants." Pheasant Run Conference, May 10–15, 1970, 3–4.

Ehninger, Douglas, and Gerard A. Hauser. "Communication of Values." In *Handbook of Rhetorical and Communication Theory,* edited by Carroll C. Arnold and John Waite Bowers, 720–748. Boston: Allyn and Bacon, 1984.

Ehninger, Douglas, et al. "Report of the Committee on the Scope of Rhetoric and the Place of Rhetorical Studies in Higher Education." In *The Prospect of Rhetoric: Report of the National Development Project,* edited by Lloyd Bitzer and Edwin Black, 208–219. Englewood Cliffs, N.J.: Prentice Hall, 1971.

Eldredge, Dirk C. *Ending the War on Drugs: A Solution for America.* New York: Bridge Works, 1998.

Elwood, William N. *Rhetoric in the War on Drugs.* Westport, Conn.: Praeger, 1994.

"The Episcopal Church. "Acts of Convention, Resolution 2006-A017." http://www.episcopalarchives.org/cgi-bin/acts/acts_resolution-complete.pl?resolution=2006-A017 (accessed August 31, 2010).

Eubanks, Ralph T., and Virgil L. Baker, "Toward an Axiology of Rhetoric." *Quarterly Journal of Speech* 48 (1962): 157–168.

Exodus 32: 9–10. In *The Oxford Study Bible,* edited by M. Jack Suggs, Katharine Doob Sakenfeld, and James R. Mueller, 95. New York: Oxford University Press, 1992.

"Farewell Address Doesn't Fare Well." *Hartford Courant,* February 20, 1973, 54.

Farrell, Thomas B. "On the Disappearance of the Rhetorical Aura." *Western Journal of Communication* 57 (1993): 147–158.

Feintuch, Burt. "Longing for Community." *Western Folklore,* 60 (2001): 149–161.

Fejes, Fred. "Critical Mass Communications Research and Media Effects: The Problem of the Disappearing Audience." *Media, Culture and Society* 6 (1984): 219–232.

Felder, Don, Don Henley, and Glenn Frey. "Hotel California." Cass County Music/Red Cloud Music, ASCAP, 1976, The Eagles, *Hotel California,* Elektra/Asylum/Nonsuch Records, 1976. Reproduced in The Eagles, *Hell Freezes Over,* Geffen Records, 1994.

Ferguson, Robert A. "The Commonalities of Common Sense." *William and Mary Quarterly* 57 (2000): 465–504.

Ferreira-Buckley, Linda. "Rescuing the Archives from Foucault." *College English* 61 (1999): 574–576.

Ferrell, Robert H. "Immigration and the Red Scare." In *Who Belongs in America? Presidents, Rhetoric, and Immigration,* edited by Vanessa B. Beasley, 134–148. College Station: Texas A&M University Press, 2006.

Fisher, Gary L. *Rethinking Our War on Drugs: Candid Talk about Controversial Issues.* Westport, Conn.: Praeger, 2006.

Flannery, Kathryn Thomas. "The Passion of Conviction: Reclaiming Polemic for a Reading of Second-Wave Feminism." *Rhetoric Review* 20 (2001): 113–129.

Fletcher, Michael A. "President Hints at Bipartisan Shift." *Houston Chronicle,* December 20, 2006. LexisNexis Academic. http://www.lexisnexis.com (accessed August 21, 2011).

Flores, Lisa A. "Constructing Rhetorical Borders: Peons, Illegal Aliens, and Competing Narratives of Immigration." *Critical Studies in Media Communication* 20 (2003): 362–387.

Flyvbjerg, Bent. *Making Social Science Matter: Why Social Inquiry Fails and How It Can Succeed Again.* Cambridge: Cambridge University Press, 2001.

Fogarty, Daneil S. J. *Roots for a New Rhetoric.* New York: Teachers College Bureau of Publications, Columbia University, 1959.

Foley, Megan. "Sound Bites: Rethinking the Circulation of Speech from Fragment to Fetish." *Rhetoric and Public Affairs* 15 (2012): 613–622.

Fontana, Andrea, and James H. Frey. "The Interview: From Neutral Stance to Political Involvement." In *The SAGE Handbook of Qualitative Research,* edited by Norman K. Denzin and Yvonna S. Lincoln, 695–727. Thousand Oaks, Calif.: Sage, 2005.

Foss, Sonja K. *Rhetorical Criticism: Exploration and Practice.* Prospect Heights, Ill.: Waveland, 1989.

Foss, Sonja K., and Cindy L. Griffin. "Beyond Persuasion: A Proposal for an Invitational Rhetoric." *Communication Monographs* 62 (1995): 2–18.

Foss, Sonja K., Karen A. Foss, and Robert Trapp. *Contemporary Perspectives on Rhetoric.* Prospect Heights, Ill.: Waveland, 1985.

Foucault, Michel. *The Archaeology of Knowledge and the Discourse on Language,* translated by A. M. Sheridan Smith. New York: Pantheon, 1972.

———. *The History of Sexuality.* Vol. I: *An Introduction.* Translated by Robert Hurley. New York: Vintage Books, 1978.

———. "Polemics, Politics, and Problematizations: An Interview with Michel Foucault." In *The Foucault Reader,* translated by Lydia Davis, edited by Paul Rabinow, 381–390. New York: Pantheon, 1984.

———. "Politics and the Study of Discourse." In *The Foucault Effect: Studies in Governmentality with Two Lectures by and an Interview with Michel Foucault,* edited by Grahama Burchell, Colin Gordon, and Peter Miller, 53–72. Chicago: University of Chicago Press, 1991.

France, David. "The Angry Prophet Is Dying." *Newsweek,* June 11, 2001, 43–46.

Francesconi, Robert. "Free Jazz and Black Nationalism: A Rhetoric of Musical Style." *Critical Studies in Mass Communication* 3 (1986): 36–49.

Frank, David A. "1958 and the Rhetorical Turn in the Twentieth Century." *Review of Communication* 11 (2011): 239–252.

———. "After the New Rhetoric." *Quarterly Journal of Speech* 89 (2003): 253–61.

———. "The New Rhetoric, Judaism and Post-Enlightenment Thought: The Cultural Origins of Perelmanian Philosophy." *Quarterly Journal of Speech* 83 (1997): 311–331.

———. "A Traumatic Reading of Twentieth-Century Rhetorical Theory: The Belgian Holocaust, Malines, Perelman, and De Man." *Quarterly Journal of Speech* 93 (2007): 308–343.

Frank, David A., and Michelle K. Bolduc. "Chaïm Perelman's 'First Philosophies and Regressive Philosophy': Commentary and Translation." *Philosophy and Rhetoric* 16 (2003): 177–207.

Frank, David A., and Michelle Bolduc. "From *Vita Contemplativa* to *Vita Activa:* Chaïm Perelman and Lucie Olbrechts-Tyteca's Rhetorical Turn." *Advances in the History of Rhetoric* 7 (2004): 65–86.

Frank, David A., and Mark L. McPhail. "Barack Obama's Address to the 2004 Democratic National Convention: Trauma, Compromise, Consilience, and the (Im)possibility of Racial Reconciliation." *Rhetoric and Public Affairs* 8 (2006): 571–594.

Frank, David A., Paul Slovic, and Daniel Vastfjall. "'Statistics Don't Bleed': Rhetorical Psychology, Presence, and Psychic Numbing in Genocide Pedagogy." *Journal of Advanced Composition* (2011): 609–624.

Freidel, Frank. *Franklin D. Roosevelt: Launching the New Deal.* Boston: Little, Brown, 1973.

Freire, Paulo. *Pedagogy of the Oppressed.* Translated by Myra Bergman Ramos. New York: Continuum, 2000.

Frentz, Thomas S., and Janice Hocker Rushing. "Commentary: The Frankenstein Myth in Contemporary Cinema." In *Critical Questions: Invention, Creativity and the Criticism of*

Discourse and Media, edited by William L. Nothstine, Carole Blair, and Gary A. Copeland, 155–160. New York: St. Martin's Press, 1994.

Gadamer, Hans-Georg. *Truth and Method.* London: Continuum International Publishing Group, 2004.

Gaonkar, Dilip Parameshwar. "Rhetoric and Its Double: Reflections on the Rhetorical Turn in the Human Sciences." In *The Rhetorical Turn: Invention and Persuasion in the Conduct of Inquiry,* edited by Herbert W. Simons, 341–366. Chicago: University of Chicago Press, 1990.

Garver, Eugene. *Aristotle's Rhetoric: An Art of Character.* Chicago: University of Chicago Press, 1994.

Geisler, Cheryl. "How Ought We to Understand the Concept of Rhetorical Agency? Report from the ARS." *Rhetoric Society Quarterly* 34 (2004): 9–17.

George, Ann, and Jack Selzer. *Kenneth Burke in the 1930s.* Columbia: University of South Carolina Press, 2007.

Gerstel, Judy. "Freud Goes Up in Smoke." *Toronto Star,* November 14, 2003, C1.

Gibbs, Nancy. "This Is Our Time!" *Time,* November 17, 2008, 28.

Giddens, Anthony. *Central Problems in Social Theory: Action, Structure and Contradiction in Social Analysis.* Berkeley: University of California Press, 1979.

Gilbert, Felix. *To The Farewell Address: Ideas of Early American Foreign Policy.* Princeton: Princeton University Press, 1961.

Glover, Jonathan. *Humanity: A Moral History of the Twentieth Century.* New Haven: Yale University Press, 2000.

Godfrey-Smith, Peter. *Theory and Reality: An Introduction to the Philosophy of Science.* Chicago: University of Chicago Press, 2003.

Goldstein, Philip, and James l. Machor. "Reception Study: Achievements and New Directions." In *New Directions in American Reception Study,* edited by Philip Goldstein and James L. Machor, xi–xxviii. New York: Oxford University Press, 2008.

Goode, Erich. "The American Drug Panic of the 1980s: Social Construction or Objective Threat?" *Violence, Aggression and Terrorism* 3 (1998): 327–348.

Goodnight, G. Thomas, and Gordon Mitchell. "Forensics as Scholarship: Testing Zarefsky's Bold Hypothesis in a Digital Age." *Argumentation and Advocacy* 45 (2008): 80–97.

Goodrich, Peter. *Legal Discourse: Studies in Linguistics, Rhetoric and Legal Analysis.* London: Macmillan, 1987.

Gourevitch, Philip. *We Wish to Inform You That Tomorrow We Will Be Killed with Our Families: Stories from Rwanda.* New York: Farrar, Straus and Giroux, 1998.

Graham, Kenneth J. E. *The Performance of Conviction: Plainness and Rhetoric in the Early English Renaissance.* Ithaca: Cornell University Press, 1994.

"The Grand Failure." *Los Angeles Times* [Home Edition], June 29, 2007. ProQuest Historical Newspapers. http://www.proquest.com/ (accessed July 1, 2010).

Graves, Robert. *The White Goddess.* Rev. ed. New York: Farrar, Straus and Giroux, 1966.

"The Great American Betrayal." Posted on the website of the Coalition against Illegal Immigration, June 23, 2006. http://uncooperativeblogger.wordpress.com (accessed July 10, 2010).

"Great Party." Moonhowlings: A Place for Civil Debate, April 5, 2008. http://www.moonhowlings.net/index.php/2008/04/05/what-a-great-party/#comments (accessed August 17, 2013).

Greene, Ronald W. "Another Materialist Rhetoric." *Critical Studies in Mass Communication* 15 (1998): 21–41.

Gregg, Judd. Speaking on immigration reform, 109th Cong., 2nd sess. *Congressional Record* 152, Issue 35 (March 27, 2006): S2400. Washington, D.C.: Government Printing Office, 2006.

Gregg, Richard B. "The Ego-Function of the Rhetoric of Protest." *Philosophy and Rhetoric* 4 (1971): 71–91.

Griffin, Leland M. "The Rhetoric of Historical Movements." *Quarterly Journal of Speech* 38 (1952): 184–188.

Grunwald, Michael. "How Obama Is Using the Science of Change." *Time*, April 13, 2009, 28.

Gunn, Joshua. "Gimme Some Tongue (On Recovering Speech)." *Quarterly Journal of Speech* 93 (2007): 361–364.

Gusfield, Joseph. *The Culture of Public Problems: Drinking, Driving, and the Symbolic Order.* Chicago: University of Chicago Press, 1981.

Guttman, Nurit. "Ethical Dilemmas in Health Campaigns." *Health Communication* 9 (1997): 155–190.

Hall, J. E. "Washington's Farewell Address." *Port-Folio*, September 1825, 226.

Hansen, Jette Barnholdt. "From Invention to Interpretation: The Prologues of the First Court Operas Where Oral and Written Cultures Meet." *Journal of Musicology* 20 (2003): 556–596.

Hariman, Robert, and John L. Lucaites. *No Caption Needed: Iconic Photographs, Public Culture, and Liberal Democracy.* Chicago: University of Chicago Press, 2007.

Hariman, Robert. "Prudence/Performance." *Rhetoric Society Quarterly* 21 (1991): 26–35.

Harold, Christine, and Kevin Michael DeLuca. "Behold the Corpse: Violent Images and the Case of Emmett Till." *Rhetoric and Public Affairs* 8 (2005): 263–286.

Harrán, Don. "Toward a Rhetorical Code of Early Music Performance." *Journal of Musicology* 15 (1997): 19–42.

Harris, Randy A. "Reception Studies in Rhetoric of Science." *Technical Communication Quarterly* 14 (2005): 249–255.

Hart, Roderick P. "The Functions of Human Communication in the Maintenance of Public Values." In *Handbook of Rhetorical and Communication Theory*, edited by Carroll C. Arnold and John Waite Bowers, 749–791. Boston: Allyn and Bacon, 1984.

Hart, Roderick P. *Modern Rhetorical Criticism.* Glenview, Ill.: Scott, Foresman/Little, Brown, 1990.

Hart, Roderick P. "Theory-Building and Rhetorical Criticism: An Informal Statement of Opinion." *Central States Speech Journal* 27 (1976): 70.

Hart, Roderick P. "Thinking Harder about Presidential Discourse." In *The Prospects of Presidential Rhetoric*, edited by James Arnt Aune and Martin J. Medhurst, 238–248. College Station: Texas A&M University Press, 2008.

Hauser, Gerard A. "Attending the Vernacular: A Plea for an Ethnographic Rhetoric." In *The Rhetorical Emergence of Culture*, edited by Christian Meyer and Felix Girke, 157–172. Oxford and New York: Berghahn, 2011.

Hauser, Gerard A. *Introduction to Rhetorical Theory.* Prospect Heights, Ill.: Waveland, 1986.

Hauser, Gerard A. *Vernacular Voices: The Rhetoric of Publics and Public Spheres.* Columbia: University of South Carolina Press, 1999.

Hawdon, James E. "The Role of Presidential Rhetoric in the Creation of a Moral Panic: Reagan, Bush, and the War on Drugs." *Deviant Behavior* 22 (2001): 419–445.

Hawk, Byron. *A Counter-History of Composition: Toward Methodologies of Complexity.* Pittsburgh: University of Pittsburgh Press, 2007.

Hay, Robert P. "George Washington: American Moses." *America Quarterly* 21 (1969): 780–791.

Heidt, Stephen. "The President as Pastiche: Atomization, Circulation, and Rhetorical Instability." *Rhetoric and Public Affairs* 15 (2012): 623–633.

Heiskanen, Benita. "A Day without Immigrants." *European Journal of American Studies.* Special Issue (December 1, 2009). http://ejas.revues.org/7717 (accessed July 10, 2010).

Henry, David, and Richard J. Jensen. "Social Movement Criticism and the Renaissance of Public Address." *Communication Studies* 42 (1991): 83–93.

Herbig, Art, and Aaron Hess. "Convergent Critical Rhetoric at the 'Rally to Restore Sanity': Exploring the Intersection of Rhetoric, Ethnography, and Documentary Production." *Communication Studies* 63 (2012): 269–289.

Hertzberg, Hendrik. *¡Obámanos!: The Birth of a New Political Era.* New York: Penguin Press, 2009.

Hess, Aaron. "Critical-Rhetorical Ethnography: Rethinking the Place and Process of Rhetoric." *Communication Studies* 62 (2011): 127–152.

Hess, Aaron. "Democracy through the Polarized Lens of the Camcorder: Argumentation and Vernacular Spectacle on YouTube in the 2008 Election." *Argumentation and Advocacy* 47 (2010): 106–122.

Hess, Aaron. "Resistance up in Smoke: Analyzing the Limitations of Deliberation on YouTube." *Critical Studies in Media Communication* 26 (2009): 411–434.

Hill, Forbes. "The Forum: Reply to Professor Campbell." *Quarterly Journal of Speech* 58 (1972): 460.

Hobsbawm, E. J. *The Age of Extremes: A History of the World, 1914–1991.* New York: Vintage Books, 1996.

Hochmuth, Marie. "Burkeian Criticism." *Western Speech* 21 (1957): 89–95.

Hochmuth, Marie. "The Criticism of Rhetoric." In *A History and Criticism of American Public Address,* vol. 3, edited by Marie Hochmuth, 1–23. New York: Russell and Russell, 1955.

Hochmuth, Marie. "I. A. Richards and the 'New Rhetoric.'" *Quarterly Journal of Speech* 44 (1958): 1–16.

Hochmuth, Marie. "Kenneth Burke and the 'New Rhetoric.'" *Quarterly Journal of Speech* 38 (1952): 133–144.

Hochmuth, Marie Nichols. *Rhetoric and Criticism.* Baton Rouge: Louisiana State University Press, 1963.

Hogan, J. Michael, and Glenn Williams. "Republican Charisma and the American Revolution: The Textual Persona of Thomas Paine's *Common Sense.*" *Quarterly Journal of Speech* 86 (2000): 1–18.

"The Holiday in Washington." *New York Times,* February 23, 1910, 5.

Hostetler, Michael J. "Washington's Farewell Address: Distance as Bane and Blessing." *Rhetoric and Public Affairs* 5 (2002): 393–407.

Houck, Davis W. "Textual Recovery, Textual Discovery: Returning to our Past, Imagining Our Future." In *The Handbook of Rhetoric and Public Address,* edited by Shawn Parry-Giles and J. Michael Hogan, 111–132. Walden, Mass.: Blackwell, 2010.

Houck, Davis W. *Rhetoric as Currency: Hoover, Roosevelt and the Great Depression.* College Station: Texas A&M University Press, 2001.

Houck, Davis W., and Mihaela Nocasian. "FDR's First Inaugural Address: Text, Context, and Reception." *Rhetoric and Public Affairs* 5 (2002): 649–678.

Hudson, Hoyt H. "The Field of Rhetoric." *Quarterly Journal of Speech* 9 (1923): 167–180. Reprinted in *Historical Studies of Rhetoric and Rhetoricians,* edited by Raymond F. Howes, 3–15. Ithaca: Cornell University Press, 1961.

Hulse, Carl, and Rachel L. Swarns. "Blame and Uncertainty as Immigration Deal Fails." *New York Times,* April 8, 2006. LexisNexis Academic. http://www.lexisnexis.com (accessed August 21, 2011).

Hume, David. *An Enquiry Concerning Human Understanding.* La Salle, Ill.: Open Court Publishing Co., 1958.

Hyde, Michael. "A Matter of the Heart: Epideictic Rhetoric and Heidegger's Call of Conscience." In *Heidegger and Rhetoric,* edited by Daniel M. Gross and Ansgar Kemmann, 81–104. Albany: State University of New York Press, 2005.

"Illegals, God and Gospel in Manassas/PWC." *9500 Liberty* YouTube channel, October 31, 2007. http://www.youtube.com/watch?v=tpAWEMOgAJw&feature=relmfu (accessed February 15, 2012).

Iltis, Robert S., and Stephen H. Browne. "Tradition and Resurgence in Public Address Studies." In *Speech Communication: Essays to Commemorate the 75th Anniversary of the Speech Communication Association,* edited by Gerald M. Phillips and Julia T. Wood, 81–93. Carbondale: Southern Illinois University Press, 1990.

"Immigration Battle." Fox News, November 4, 2007. http://www.youtube.com/watch?v=6NFaPTYwBc (accessed on February 14, 2014).

"Immigration, Economics, Intolerance." *9500 Liberty* YouTube channel. Comments Forum. http://www.youtube.com/all_comments?v=20iwJ-_BipU (accessed February 14, 2012).

"Immigration Myths with Dr. Stephen S. Fuller, PhD." *9500 Liberty* YouTube channel. Comments Forum (accessed February 14, 2012). http://www.youtube.com/all_comments?v=7EN4QFbclR8 (accessed August 17, 2013).

"Immigration 'Nirvana,' Lost." *Washington Post,* April 8, 2006. http://www.washingtonpost.com/wp-dyn/content/article/2006/04/07/AR2006040701713.html (accessed August 21, 2011).

Inabinet, Brandon. "Democratic Circulation: Jacksonian Lithographs in U.S. Public Discourse." *Rhetoric and Public Affairs* 15 (2012): 659–666.

"In Their Own Words: The Debate Dispute," *New York Times,* September 25, 2008, A23.

Isakson, Johnny. Speaking on Comprehensive Immigration Reform Act of 2006, S. 2611, 109th Cong., 2nd sess. *Congressional Record* 152, Issue 60 (May 16, 2006): S4576. Washington, D.C.: Government Printing Office, 2006.

"It's the President's Turn." [Editorial.] *New York Times,* April 9, 2006. http://www.nytimes.com/2006/04/09/opinion/09sun1.html (accessed August 21, 2011).

Ivie, Robert L. "Productive Criticism Then and Now." *American Communication Journal* 4 (2001). http://acjournal.org/holdings/vol4/iss3/special/ivie.pdf (accessed February 9, 2011).

Jamieson, Kathleen H. *Dirty Politics.* New York: Oxford University Press, 1991.

Jamieson, Kathleen H. *Eloquence in an Electronic Age: The Transformation of Political Speechmaking.* Oxford: Oxford University Press, 1988.

Jamieson, Kathleen H., and Karlyn K. Campbell. "Rhetorical Hybrids: Fusions of Generic Elements." *Quarterly Journal of Speech* 68 (1982): 146–157.

Jasinksi, James. "A Constitutive Framework for Rhetorical Historiography: Toward an Understanding of the Discursive (Re)constitution of 'Constitution' in the *Federalist Papers.*" In *Doing Rhetorical History: Concepts and Cases,* edited by Kathleen J. Turner, 72–92. Tuscaloosa: University of Alabama Press, 1998.

Jasinski, James. *The Sourcebook on Rhetoric: Key Concepts in Contemporary Rhetorical Studies.* Thousand Oaks, Calif.: Sage, 2001.

Jasinski, James, and Jennifer R. Mercieca. "The Constitutive Approach to Effect and the Alien and Sedition Acts." In *Rhetoric and Public Address in the Twenty-First Century: A Handbook,* edited by Shawn J. Parry-Giles and J. Michael Hogan, 313–341. Malden, Mass.: Blackwell Press, 2010.

Jellicorse, John Lee. "New Books in Review: Rhetorical Criticism." *Quarterly Journal of Speech* 51 (1965): 339–342.

Jenkins, Henry. *Convergence Culture: Where Old and New Media Collide.* New York: New York University Press, 2006.

———. *Fans, Bloggers and Gamers: Exploring Participatory Culture.* New York: New York University Press, 2006.

———. "From Participatory Culture to Participatory Democracy (Part Two)." March 6, 2007. http://www.henryjenkins.org/2007/03/from_participatatory_culture_t_1.html (accessed February 15, 2012).

———. "Quentin Tarantino's Star Wars?: Digital Cinema, Media Convergence, and Participatory Culture." http://web.mit.edu/cms/People/henry3/starwars.html (accessed February 15, 2012).

Jenkins, Henry, Sam Ford, and Joshua Green. *Spreadable Media: Creating Value and Meaning in a Networked Culture*. New York: New York University Press, 2013.

Jenkins, Henry, Ravi Purushotma, Katie Clinton, Margaret Weigel, and Alice Robinson. *Confronting The Challenges of Participatory Culture: Media Education for the 21st Century*. Chicago: MacArthur Foundation, 2006.

Johannesen, Richard L. "Editor's Introduction: Some Trends in Contemporary Rhetorical Theory." In *Contemporary Theories of Rhetoric: Selected Readings*, edited by Richard L. Johannesen, 1–16. New York: Harper and Row, 1971.

Johannessen, Richard L., ed. *Contemporary Theories of Rhetoric: Selected Readings*. New York: Harper and Row, 1971.

Johnson, Laura. "(Environmental) Rhetorics of Tempered Apocalypticism in *An Inconvenient Truth*." *Rhetoric Review* 28 (2009): 29–46.

Johnstone, Barbara, and Christopher Eisenhart. *Rhetoric in Detail: Discourse Analysis of Rhetorical Talk and Text*. Philadelphia: John Benjamins, 2008.

Jones, Robert E. "Washington's Farewell and Its Applications." *Forum* (September 1899): 13–29.

Joseph, H. W. B. *An Introduction to Logic*. London: Clarendon Press, 1906.

Jost, Walter. *Rhetorical Investigations: Studies in Ordinary Language Criticism*. University of Virginia Press, 2004.

Judt, Tony. *The Burden of Responsibility: Blum, Camus, Aron, and the French Twentieth Century*. Chicago: University of Chicago Press, 1998.

Judt, Tony. *Past Imperfect: French Intellectuals, 1944–1956*. Berkeley: University of California Press, 1992.

Kammen, Michael. "Some Patterns and Meanings of Memory Distortion in American History." In *Memory Distortion: How Minds, Brains, and Societies Reconstruct the Past*, edited by Daniel L. Schacter, 329–345. Cambridge, Mass.: Harvard University Press, 1997.

Karlin, Beth, and John Johnson. "Measuring Impact: The Importance of Evaluation for "Documentary Film Campaigns." *M/C Journal* 14, no. 6 (December 2011). http://journal.media-culture.org.au/index.php/mcjournal/article/view/444 (accessed February 14, 2014).

Kelly, Brian C. "Conceptions of Risk in the Lives of Club Drug-Using Youth." *Substance Use and Abuse* 40 (2005): 1443–1459.

Kennedy, Edward. Speaking on Comprehensive Immigration Reform Act of 2006, S. 2611, 109th Cong., 2nd sess. *Congressional Record* 152, Issue 60 (May 16, 2006): S4578. Washington, D.C.: Government Printing Office, 2006.

Kennedy, George A. *Classical Rhetoric and Its Christian and Secular Traditions: From Ancient to Modern Times*. Chapel Hill: University of North Carolina Press, 1980.

Kibler, Robert J., and Larry L. Barker. "Recommendations Formally Adopted by the Conference." In *Conceptual Frontiers in Speech Communication: Report of the New Orleans Conference on Research and Instructional Development*, edited by Robert J. Kibler and Larry L. Barker, 16–47. New York: Speech Association of America, 1969.

Kiewe, Amos. *FDR's First Fireside Chat: Public Confidence and the Banking Crisis*. College Station: Texas A&M University Press, 2007.

Kimball, Bruce A. *Orators & Philosophers: A History of the Idea of Liberal Education*. New York: Teachers College Press, Columbia University, 1986.

Kinneavy, James L., and Catherine R. Eskin. "Kairos in Aristotle's Rhetoric." *Written Communication* 17 (2000): 432–444.

Klein, Ezra. "The Unpersuaded: Who Listens to a President?" *The New Yorker* 88 (March 19, 2012). http://www.newyorker.com/reporting/2012/03/19/120319fa_fact_klein/ (accessed October 18, 2012).

Koed, Betty. Unpublished e-mail communications, August 21, 2008, and March 1, 2012.

"Kramer Media Folly." ACT UP/New York. http://www/acti[mu/prg/reports/Kramer-Folly.html (accessed August 14, 2013).

Kramer, Larry. "1,112 and Counting." In Larry Kramer, *Reports from the Holocaust: The Story of an AIDS Activist* (1983), 33–50. New York: St. Martin's Press, 1994.

———. "The Beginning of ACTing UP." In Larry Kramer, *Reports from the Holocaust: The Story of an AIDS Activist* (1987), 127–136. New York: St. Martin's Press, 1994.

———. "A Call to Riot." In Larry Kramer, *Reports from the Holocaust: The Story of an AIDS Activist* (1990), 314–318. New York: St. Martin's Press, 1994.

———. "Donna Do-Nothing Works for Bill the Welsher." In Larry Kramer, *Reports from the Holocaust: The Story of an AIDS Activist* (1993), 413. New York: St. Martin's Press, 1994.

———. "Introduction." In Larry Kramer, *Reports from the Holocaust: The Story of an AIDS Activist*, xxxi–xxxiv. New York: St. Martin's Press, 1994.

———. *Reports from the Holocaust: The Story of an AIDS Activist*. New York: St. Martin's Press, 1994.

———. "Some Thoughts about Evil." In Larry Kramer, *Reports from the Holocaust: The Story of an AIDS Activist* (1993), 433–451. New York: St. Martin's Press, 1994.

———. "The Tragedy of Today's Gays: An Address to the Gay Community." Cooper Union, New York City, November 7, 2004. http://towleroad.com/2004/11/larry_kramer_sp.html (accessed August 14, 2013).

———. "Who Killed Vito." In Larry Kramer, *Reports from the Holocaust: The Story of an AIDS Activist* (1990), 363–372. New York: St. Martin's Press, 1994.

Krzyżanowski, Michał. "Ethnography and Critical Discourse Analysis: Towards a Problem-Oriented Research Dialogue." *Critical Discourse Studies* 8 (2011): 231–238.

Kuypers, Jim A. "Framing Analysis." In *Rhetorical Criticism: Perspectives in Action*, edited by Jim A. Kuypers, 181–203. Lanham, Md.: Lexington Books, 2009, 181–203.

Kvale, Steiner. *InterViews: An Introduction to Qualitative Research Interviewing*. Thousand Oaks, Calif.: Sage, 1996.

LeCoat, Gerard. "Music and the Three Appeals of Classical Rhetoric." *Quarterly Journal of Speech* 62 (1976): 157–166.

Lederman, Linda C., and Lea P. Stewart. *Changing the Culture of College Drinking: A Socially Situated Health Communication Campaign*. Cresskill, N.J.: Hampton Press, 2005.

Leff, Michael. "Dimensions of Temporality in Lincoln's Second Inaugural." *Communication Reports* 1 (1998): 26–31.

———. "Lincoln at Cooper Union: Neo-classical Criticism Revisited." *Western Journal of Communication* 65 (2001): 323–48.

———. "Textual Criticism: The Legacy of G. P. Mohrmann." *Quarterly Journal of Speech* 72 (1986): 377–389.

———. "Things Made by Words: Reflections on Textual Criticism." *Quarterly Journal of Speech* 78 (1992): 223–231.

———. "Tradition and Agency in Humanistic Rhetoric." *Philosophy and Rhetoric* 36 (2003): 135–146.

Leff, Michael, and Andrew Sachs. "Words the Most Like Things: Iconicity and the Rhetorical Text." *Western Journal of Speech Communication* 54 (1990): 252–273.

Leff, Michael C. "Rhetorical Timing in Lincoln's 'House Divided' Speech." The Van Zelst Lecture in Communication, Northwestern University School of Speech, Evanston, Ill., May 1983.

Leff, Michael C., and Margaret Organ Procario. "Rhetorical Theory in Speech Communication." In *Speech Communication in the 20th Century,* edited by Thomas W. Benson, 3–27. Carbondale: Southern Illinois University Press, 1985.

LeGreco, Marianne, Aaron Hess, Linda C. Lederman, Tara Schuwerk, and Angela LaValley. "An Innovative Dialogue about College Drinking: Developing an Immediate Response Technology Model for Health Promotion." *Communication Education* 59 (2010): 389–404.

Lehn, Melody. "Jackie Joins Twitter: The Recirculation of 'Campaign Wife.'" *Rhetoric and Public Affairs* 15 (2012): 667–674.

Leland, John. "The Trouble with Sigmund." *Newsweek,* December 18, 1995, 62.

Lenneberg, Hans. "Johann Mattheson on Affect and Rhetoric in Music." *Journal of Music Theory* 2 (1958): 47–84.

"Letter to Paine." *Connecticut Gazette,* March 3, 1776, 1.

Levy, Kira B., Kevin E. O'Grady, Eric D. Wish, and Amelia M. Arria. "An In-Depth Qualitative Examination of the Ecstasy Experience: Results of a Focus Group with Ecstasy-Using College Students." *Substance Use and Misuse* 40 (2005): 1427–1441.

Library of Congress. "Bill Summary and Status, H.R. 4437 Border Protection, Antiterrorism, and Illegal Immigration Control Act of 2005." http://thomas.loc.gov/cgi-bin/bdquery/z?d109:h.r.04437 (accessed January 1, 2013).

Library of Congress. "Bill Summary and Status, S. 2612 The Comprehensive Immigration Reform Act of 2006." http://thomas.loc.gov/cgi-bin/bdquery/z?d109:SN02611 (accessed January 1, 2013).

Library of Congress. "S.2454 Securing America's Borders Act, All Congressional Actions." http://thomas.loc.gov/cgi-bin/bdquery/z?d109:SN02454:@@@X (accessed January 15, 2013).

Limbaugh, Rush. "Senate 'Compromise' Bill Must Change." Transcript, May 16, 2006. http://www.rushlimbaugh.com/daily/2006/05/16/senate_compromise_bill_must_change_or_this_country_will_change_forever2 (accessed January 31, 2013).

Lincoln, Abraham. "Speech in Independence Hall, Philadelphia, Pennsylvania (Feb. 22, 1861)." Reprinted in *The Collected Works of Abraham Lincoln,* vol. 4, edited by Roy P. Basler, 240. New Brunswick, N.J.: Rutgers University Press, 1953.

Linden, Bill. "George Just Doesn't Draw the Crowds." *Roll Call,* February 21, 1985, 4.

Long, Christopher P. "The Ontological Reappopriation of Phronesis." *Continental Philosophy Review* 35 (2002): 35–60.

Lucaites, John Louis, and Celeste Michelle Condit. "Reconstructing <Equality>: Culturetypal and Countercultural Rhetorics in the Martyred Black Vision." *Communication Monographs* 57 (1990): 5–24.

Lucas, Stephen E., and Medhurst, Martin J. *Words of a Century: The Top 100 American Speeches, 1900–1999.* New York: Oxford University Press, 2009.

Lucas, Stephen, and Susan Zaeske. "George Washington." In *U.S. Presidents as Orators: A Bio-critical Sourcebook,* edited by Halford Ryan, 3–17. Westport, Conn.: Greenwood Press, 1995.

Lucas, Stephen E. "Justifying America: The Declaration of Independence as a Rhetorical Document." In *American Rhetoric: Context and Criticism,* edited by Thomas W. Benson, 67–130. Carbondale: Southern Illinois University Press, 1989.

Lucas, Stephen E. "The Renaissance of American Public Address: Text and Context in Rhetorical Criticism." [Review essay.] *Quarterly Journal of Speech* 74 (1988): 241–260.

Lucas, Stephen E. "The Schism in Rhetorical Scholarship," *Quarterly Journal of Speech* 67 (1981): 1–20.

Lundberg, Christian, and Joshua Gunn. "'Quija Board, Are There Any Communication?' Agency, Ontotheology, and the Death of the Humanist Subject, or, Continuing the ARS Conversation." *Rhetoric Society Quarterly* 35 (2005): 83–105.

Lunsford, Andrea A., Kirt H. Wilson, and Rosa A. Eberly, eds. *The SAGE Handbook of Rhetorical Studies*. Sherman Oaks, Calif.: Sage, 2009.

Lydersen, Kari. "Drug-Terror Connection Disputed; DEA Defends Traveling Exhibit as Critics Draw Parallels to Prohibition Era." *Washington Post*, August 12, 2006. http://www.lexis-nexis.com/ (accessed February 10, 2010).

Lyon, Janet. *Manifestoes: Provocations of the Modern*. Ithaca: Cornell University Press, 1999.

Mack, Kristen. "Conservatives Clash at Briefing on Pr. William Crackdown." *Washington Post*, December 15, 2007. http://www.washingtonpost.com/wp-dyn/content/article/2007/12/14/AR2007121401580.html (accessed August 17, 2013).

Mack, Kristen. "Provocative Blog Spawns Its Anti-Blog in Pr. William." *Washington Post*, April 4, 2008. http://www.washingtonpost.com/wp-dyn/content/article/2008/04/03/AR2008040301883.html (accessed August 17, 2013).

Mack, Kristen. "Pr. William Religious Leaders Say Crackdown Is Divisive." *Washington Post*, February 3, 2008. http://www.washingtonpost.com/wp-dyn/content/article/2008/02/02/AR2008020201999.html (accessed August 17, 2013).

Mack, Kirsten. "Pr. William Softens Policy on Immigration Status Checks." *Washington Post*, April 30, 2008. http://www.washingtonpost.com/wp-dyn/content/article/2008/04/29/AR2008042902990.html (accessed August 17, 2013).

Markowitz, Arthur A. "Washington's Farewell and the Historians: A Critical Review." *Pennsylvania Magazine of History and Biography* 94 (1970): 173–191.

Marlatt, G. Alan. "Highlights of Harm Reduction: A Personal Report for the First National Harm Reduction Conference in the United States." In *Harm Reduction: Pragmatic Strategies for Managing High-Risk Behaviors*, edited by G. Alan Marlatt, 1–29. New York: Guilford Press, 1998.

Marlatt, G. Alan, ed. *Harm Reduction: Pragmatic Strategies for Managing High-Risk Behaviors*. New York: Guilford Press, 1998.

Martin, Mark. "The Ecstasy and the Agony: Group Tries to Reduce Risk by Testing Pills." *San Francisco Chronicle*, July 21, 2000. http://www.sfgate.com/cgi-bin/article.cgi?f=/c/a/2000/07/21/MN88496.DTL&ao=all (accessed February 10, 2012).

Matula, Theodore. "Contextualizing Musical Rhetoric: A Critical Reading of the Pixies' 'Rock Music.'" *Communication Studies* 51 (2000): 218–237.

McCain, John. Speaking on immigration reform, S. 2454, 109th Cong., 2nd sess. *Congressional Record* 152, Issue 38 (March 30, 2006): S2560–S2561. Washington, D.C.: Government Printing Office.

McCormick, Samuel. "Mirrors for the Queen: A Letter from Christine de Pizan on the Eve of Civil War." *Quarterly Journal of Speech* 94 (2008): 273–296.

McCumber, John. *Time in the Ditch: American Philosophy and the McCarthy Era*. Evanston, Ill.: Northwestern University Press, 2001.

McDonald, Marci. "Burying Freud and Praising Him." *U.S. News and World Report*, October 19, 1998, 60.

McFarling, Usha Lee. "If Freud Was So Wrong, Why Is He Still So Irrepressible?," *Ottawa Citizen*, May 16, 2000, A7.

McGee, Michael C. "A Materialist's Conception of Rhetoric." In *Explorations in Rhetoric: Studies in Honor of Douglas Ehninger,* edited by Ray E. McKerrow, 23–48. Glenview, Ill.: Scott, Foresman, 1982.

McGee, Michael C. "The 'Ideograph': A Link between Rhetoric and Ideology." *Quarterly Journal of Speech* 66 (1980): 1–16.

McGee, Michael Calvin. "Text, Context, and the Fragmentation of Contemporary Culture." *Western Journal of Communication* 54 (1990): 274–289.

McKerrow, Raymie E. "Critical Rhetoric: Theory and Praxis." *Communication Monographs* 56 (1989): 91–111.

McKinney, Mitchell, and Leslie Rill. "Not Your Parents' Presidential Debate: Examining the Effects of the CNN/YouTube Debates on Young Citizens' Civic Engagement." *Communication Studies* 60 (2009): 392–406.

McLagan, Meg. "Imagining Impact: Documentary Film and the Production of Political Effects." In *Sensible Politics: The Visual Culture of Nongovernmental Activism,* edited by Meg McLagan and Yates McKee, 305–319. New York: Zone, 2012.

Mechling, Elizabeth W., and Jay Mechling. "The Atom According to Disney." *Quarterly Journal of Speech* 81 (1995): 436–453.

Mechling, Elizabeth W., and Jay Mechling. "Commentary." In *Critical Questions: Invention, Creativity and the Criticism of Discourse and Media,* edited by William L. Nothstine, Carole Blair, and Gary A. Copeland, 118–124. New York: St. Martin's Press, 1994.

Medhurst, Martin J. "The Academic Study of Public Address: A Tradition in Transition." In *Landmark Essays on American Public Address,* edited by Martin J. Medhurst, xi–xiii. Davis, Calif.: Hermagoras, 1993.

Medhurst, Martin J. "Afterword: The Ways of Rhetoric." In *Beyond the Rhetorical Presidency,* edited by Martin J. Medhurst, 218–226. College Station: Texas A&M Press, 1996.

Medhurst, Martin J., and Thomas W. Benson. "Rhetorical Studies in a Media Age." In *Rhetorical Dimensions in Media: A Critical Casebook,* edited by Martin J. Medhurst and Thomas W. Benson, ix–xxiii. Dubuque, Iowa: Kendall/Hunt, 1984.

Meister, Mark. "Drama and Tragedy in Contemporary Folk Music: Nanci Griffith's 'It's a Hard Life Wherever You Go.'" *Communication Studies* 47 (1996): 62–71.

Menegatos, Lisa, Linda C. Lederman, and Aaron Hess. "Friends Don't Let Jane Hook Up Drunk: A Qualitative Analysis of Participation in a College Drinking Simulation." *Communication Education* 59 (2010): 374–388.

Mercieca, Jennifer Rose. "Did the 2008 Election Change Everything?" *Rhetoric and Public Affairs* 15 (2012): 717–735.

Meserve, Jeane, and Mike M. Ahlers. "Filmmakers Take Immigration Debate to YouTube." CNN, May 1, 2008. http://www.cnn.com/2008/SHOWBIZ/05/01/immigration.lens/index.html (accessed August 17, 2013).

Meyer, Michaela D. E. "Utilizing Mythic Criticism in Contemporary Narrative Culture: Examining the 'Present-Absence' of Shadow Archetypes in Spider-Man." *Communication Quarterly* 51 (2003): 527.

Middleton, Michael K., Samantha Senda-Cook, and Danielle Endres. "Articulating Rhetorical Field Methods: Challenges and Tensions." *Western Journal of Communication* 75 (2011): 386–406.

Miller, Carolyn R. "Foreword." In *Rhetoric and Kairos: Essays in History, Theory, and Praxis,* edited by Phillip Sipiora and James S. Baumlin, xi–xiii. Albany: State University of New York Press, 2002.

Miller, Thomas P. *The Formation of College English: Rhetoric and Belles Lettres in the British Cultural Provinces*. Pittsburgh: University of Pittsburgh Press, 1997.

Milligan, Susan. "Immigration Bill Dies in Senate." *Boston Globe,* June 29, 2007. Newsbank. http://www.Newsbank.com/ (accessed July 1, 2010).

Millson, William A. D. "Experimental Work in Audience Reaction." *Quarterly Journal of Speech* 18 (1932): 13–30.

Minnick, Wayne C. "A Case Study in Persuasive Effect: Lyman Beecher on Dueling." *Speech Monographs* 38 (1971): 262–276.

Miroff, Nick. "Raw Look at Immigration Crucible." *Washington Post,* November 3, 2007. http://www.washingtonpost.com/wp-dyn/content/article/2007/11/02/AR2007110202158.html (accessed August 17, 2013).

Montgomery, Dave. "Senate Strongly Supports Bush's Immigration Goals." *Philadelphia Inquirer,* May 17, 2006. Lexis-Nexis Academic. www.lexisnexis.com (accessed January 30, 2013).

Morris, Charles E., III. "Pink Herring and the Fourth Persona: J. Edgar Hoover's Sex Crime Panic." *Quarterly Journal of Speech* 88 (2002): 228–244.

Morris, Charles E. III, and Stephen H. Brown, eds. *Readings on the Rhetoric of Social Protest*. State College, Pa.: Strata, 2001.

Mott, George S. "Formation of Washington's Farewell Address to the American People." *Pennsylvania Magazine of History and Biography* 21 (1897): 392–408.

Mouat, L. H. "An Approach to Rhetorical Criticism." In *The Rhetorical Idiom: Essays in Rhetoric, Oratory, Language, and Drama,* edited by Donald C. Bryant, 161–178. New York: Russell and Russell, 1966.

Mummolo, Jonathan. "Latino Group Vows to Sue if Resolution Isn't Tempered." *Washington Post,* August 19, 2007. http://www.washingtonpost.com/wp-dyn/content/article/2007/08/18/AR2007081801012.html (accessed August 17, 2013).

Murphy, Troy. "Rhetorical Invention and the Transformation of 'We Shall Overcome.'" *Qualitative Research Reports in Communication* 4 (2003): 1–8.

Nakayama, Thomas K., and Robert L. Krizek. "Whiteness: A Strategic Rhetoric." *Quarterly Journal of Speech* 81 (1995): 295–309.

Nash, Kate. "Modes of Interactivity: Analyzing the Webdoc." *Media, Culture and Society* 34 (2012): 195–210.

Natanson, Maurice. "The Limits of Rhetoric." *Quarterly Journal of Speech* 41 (1955): 133–139.

Newport, Frank, et al. *Winning the White House 2008: The Gallup Poll, Public Opinion, and the Presidency.* New York: Checkmark, 2009.

Nichols, Marie Hochmuth. *Rhetoric and Criticism.* Baton Rouge: Louisiana State University Press, 1963.

Nilsen, Thomas R. "Criticism and Social Consequences." *Quarterly Journal of Speech* 42 (1956): 173–178.

The 9/11 Commission Report. New York: Norton, 2004.

Nohe, Martin. Unpublished e-mail correspondence with author, July 11, 2011.

Nothstine, William L. "Commentary: Pseudo-Private and the PTL Ministry Scandal." In *Critical Questions: Invention, Creativity and the Criticism of Discourse and Media,* edited by William L. Nothstine, Carole Blair, and Gary A. Copeland, 15–70. New York: St. Martin's Press, 1994.

Nothstine, William L., Carole Blair, and Gary A. Copeland, "Professionalization and the Eclipse of Critical Invention." In *Critical Questions: Invention, Creativity and the Criticism of Discourse and Media,* edited by William L. Nothstine, Carole Blair, and Gary A. Copeland, 15–70. New York: St. Martin's Press, 1994.

Nothstine, William L., Carole Blair, and Gary A. Copeland, eds. *Critical Questions: Invention, Creativity and the Criticism of Discourse and Media*. New York: St. Martin's Press, 1994.

Novak, Michael. "President of all the People." In *Who Belongs in America? Presidents, Rhetoric, and Immigration*, edited by Vanessa B. Beasley, 19–36. College Station: Texas A&M University Press, 2006.

"Nowhere to Hide: Illegal Immigration." *Economist*, July 9, 2007. ProQuest Historical Newspapers. http://search.proquest.com/docview/223997538 (accessed July 10, 2010).

Nunberg, Geoffrey. *Talking Right: How Conservatives Turned Liberalism into a Tax-Raising, Latte-Drinking, Sushi-Eating, Volvo-Driving, New York Times-Reading, Body-Piercing, Hollywood-Loving, Left-Wing Freak Show*. NewYork: Public Affairs, 2006.

"'Nuts!' Revisited: An Interview with Lt. General Harry W. O. Kinnard." http:www.thedropzone.org/eurogpe/bulge/kinnard.html, no date (downloaded June 10, 2010).

Obama, Barack. "Speech in Philadelphia, May 2, 2011." http://www.npr.org/templates/story/story.php?storyId=88478467 (Accessed August 19, 2013).

"October 16 Flashback w/Subtitles." *9500 Liberty* YouTube channel. Comments Forum. http://www.youtube.com/all_comments?v=Ep-kfIxuv3M (accessed February 14, 2012).

Office of National Drug Control Policy. "National Drug Control Strategy." February 2007. http://www.whitehousedrugpolicy.gov/publications/policy/ndcs07/ndcs07.pdf (accessed April 13, 2007).

Office of the White House Press Secretary. "Fact Sheet: Comprehensive Immigration Reform." May 15, 2006. http://georgewbush-whitehouse.archives.gov/news/releases/2006/05/ 20060515–10.html (accessed August 21, 2011).

Office of the White House Press Secretary. "Fact Sheet: Securing America through Immigration Reform." November 28, 2005. http://georgewbush-whitehouse.archives.gov/news/releases/2005/11/20051128–3.html (accessed August 21, 2011).

Oliner, Samuel P., and Pearl M. Oliner. *The Altruistic Personality: Rescuers of Jews in Nazi Europe*. New York: Free Press, 1988.

"The Olive Branch Petition; in Congress in Philadelphia, October 26, 1774." http://www.constitution.org/primarysources/olive.html (accessed August 17, 2013).

Oliver, Robert T. "Philosophy and/or Persuasion." *Logique el analyse* 6 (1963): 571–580.

Oliver, Robert T., and Marvin G. Bauer. *Re-Establishing the Speech Profession: The First Fifty Years*. New York: Speech Association of the Eastern States, 1959.

Olson, Lester. "Pictorial Representations of British America Resisting Rape: Rhetorical Re-Circulation of a Print Series Portraying the Boston Port Bill of 1774." *Rhetoric and Public Affairs* 12 (2009): 1–36.

Ong, Walter J. *Ramus: Method, and the Decay of Dialogue: From the Art of Discourse to the Art of Reason*. Cambridge, Mass.: Harvard University Press, 1958.

Ono, Kent A., and John M. Sloop. "Critical Rhetorics of Controversy." *Western Journal of Communication* 63 (1999): 526–538.

Ono, Kent A., and John M. Sloop. "The Critique of Vernacular Discourse." *Communication Monographs* 62 (1995): 19–46.

Ono, Kent A., and John M. Sloop. *Shifting Borders: Rhetoric, Immigration, and California's Proposition 187, Mapping Racisms*. Philadelphia: Temple University Press, 2002.

O'Reilly, Bill. "Talking Points Memo." Transcript, May 17, 2006. http://www.foxnews.com/on-air/oreilly/2006/05/17/opposing-bush-border (accessed January 31, 2013).

O'Rourke, Sean P. "Circulation and Noncirculation of Photographic Texts in the Civil Rights Movement: A Case Study of the Rhetoric of Control." *Rhetoric and Public Affairs* 15 (2012): 685–694.

Osborn, Michael. "Archetypal Metaphor in Rhetoric: The Light Dark Family." *Quarterly Journal of Speech* 53 (1967): 115–126.

Osborn, Michael. "The Evolution of the Archetypal Sea in Rhetoric and Poetic." *Quarterly Journal of Speech* 63 (1977): 347–363.

Ott, Brian L., and Bill D. Herman. "Mixed Messages: Resistance and Reappropriation in Rave Culture." *Western Journal of Communication* 67 (2003): 249–270.

Paine, Thomas. *Common Sense.* In *Thomas Paine, Common Sense, and the Turning Point to Independence,* edited by Scott Liell, 165. Philadelphia: Running Press, 2003.

Palmer, David. "Virtuosity as Rhetoric: Agency and Transformation in Paganini's Mastery of the Violin." *Quarterly Journal of Speech* 84 (1998): 341–357.

Parrish, Wayland M. "The Study of Speeches." Reprinted in *Readings in Rhetorical Criticism,* edited by Carl R. Burgchadt, 34–46. State College, Pa.: Strata, 1995.

Parrish, Wayland M., and Marie Hochmuth. *American Speeches.* New York: Longmans, Green, 1954.

Paul, Danette, Davida Charney, and Aimee Kendall. "Moving beyond the Moment: Reception Studies in the Rhetoric of Science." *Journal of Business and Technical Communication* 15 (2001): 372–399.

Pearce, W. Barnett. "Scientific Research Methods in Communication Studies and Their Implications for Theory and Research." In *Speech Communication in the 20th Century,* edited by Thomas W. Benson, 255–281, 433–436. Carbondale: Southern Illinois University Press, 1985.

Pearl, Robert, and Carl Hulse. "Immigration Bill Fails to Survive Senate Vote." *New York Times,* June 28, 2007. http://www.nytimes.com/2007/06/28/washington/28cnd-immig.html?_r=1 (accessed July 1, 2010).

Pencak, William. "The Declaration of Independence: Changing Interpretations and a New Hypothesis." *Pennsylvania History* 57 (1990): 225–235.

Perelman, Chaïm. *Letter to Emily M Schossberger. 29th November 1967.* Chaïm Perelman Papers, File: *Traité de l'argumentation.* Archives, Université Libre de Bruxelles, Bruxelles, Belgium.

Perelman, Chaïm. "Le libre examen, hier et aujourd'hui." *Revue de l'Université de Bruxelles* (1949): 39–50.

Perelman, Chaïm. "Le problème du bon choix." *Revue de l'Institut de Sociologie* 3 (1948): 383–398.

Perelman, Chaïm. "Les deux problèmes de la liberté humaine." In *Library of the Xth International Congress of Philosophy,* edited by H. J. Pos, E. W. Beth, and J. H. A. Hollak, 217–219. Amsterdam: North Holland Publishing, 1948.

Perelman, Chaïm. "Logique 1944–1945." Notebook, in Archives, Université Libre de Bruxelles, Brussels, Belgium.

Perelman, Chaïm. "The New Rhetoric and the Rhetoricians, Remembrances and Comments." *Quarterly Journal of Speech* 70 (1984): 188–196.

Perelman, Chaïm. "The Theoretical Relations of Thought and Action." *Inquiry* 1(1958): 130–136.

Perelman, Chaïm, and Lucie Olbrechts-Tyteca. *The New Rhetoric: A Treatise on Argumentation.* Notre Dame, Ind.: University of Notre Dame Press, 1969.

Perelman, Chaïm, and Lucie Olbrechts-Tyteca. *Traité de l'argumentation: La nouvelle rhétorique.* 1re éd. Logos: Introduction aux Études Philosophiques. Paris: Presses Universitaires de France, 1958.

Perlmutter, David. *Photojournalism and Foreign Policy: Icons of Outrage in International Crisis.* Westport, Conn.: Praeger, 1998.

Pessen, Edward. "George Washington's Farewell Address, the Cold War, and the Timeless National Interest." *Journal of the Early Republic* 7 (1987): 1–25.

"The Petition of Rights, 1628." http://www.constitution.org/eng/petright.htm (accessed August 17, 2013).

Phelps, William W. "Washington's Valedictory." *American Magazine of Civics* 7 (1895): 466–474.

"Picking Up the Tab." Moonhowlings: A Place for Civil Debate, February 22, 2008. http://www.moonhowlings.net/index.php/2008/02/ (accessed August 17, 2013).

Pipes, William H. *Say Amen, Brother! Old-Time Negro Preaching: A Study in Frustration*. New York: William Frederick, 1951.

Pipes, William Harrison. "Old-Time Negro Preaching: An Interpretive Study." *Quarterly Journal of Speech* 31 (1945): 15–21.

Plouffe, David. *The Audacity to Win: The Inside Story and Lessons of Barack Obama's Historic Victory*. New York: Viking, 2009.

Polanyi, Michael. *Personal Knowledge: Towards a Post-Critical Philosophy*. Chicago: University of Chicago Press, 1958.

Pos, H. J. "Speech by Mr. H.J. Pos." In *Library of the Xth International Congress of Philosophy,* edited by H. J. Pos, E. W. Beth, and J. H. A. Hollak, 3–10. Amsterdam: North Holland Publishing, 1948.

Poulakos, John. "'Special Delivery': Rhetoric, Letter Writing, and the Question of Beauty." In *The Ethos of Rhetoric,* edited by Michael J. Hyde, 89–97. Columbia: University of South Carolina Press, 2004.

Poulakos, John. "Toward a Sophistic Definition of Rhetoric." *Philosophy and Rhetoric* 16 (1983): 35–48.

Rae, Nicol C., and Colton C. Campbell. *The Contentious Senate: Partisanship, Ideology, and the Myth of Cool Judgment*. New York: Rowman and Littlefield, 2001.

Rand, Erin J. "An Inflammatory Fag and a Queer Form: Larry Kramer, Polemics, and Rhetorical Agency." *Quarterly Journal of Speech* 94 (2008): 297–319.

Ray, John W. "Perelman's Universal Audience." *Quarterly Journal of Speech* 64 (1978): 361–375.

"Reading the Address: How Senators Commemorated Washington's Birthday." *Atlanta Constitution,* February 23, 1893, 1.

Reagan, Ronald. *Speaking My Mind: Selected Speeches*. New York: Simon and Schuster, 1989.

Redding, Charles W. "Extrinsic and Intrinsic Criticism." *Western Speech* 21 (1957): 96–102.

———. "Extrinsic and Intrinsic Criticism." In *Essays on Rhetorical Criticism,* edited by Thomas R. Nilsen, 99–107. New York: Random House, 1968.

Reilly, Kaitlynn. "Death of a Bill." Catholic News Service, July 2, 2007. http://www.catholic.org/national/national_story.php?id=24577 (accessed September 7, 2010).

"Religious Leaders' Call to Healing Religion#4." *9500 Liberty* YouTube channel, November 7, 2007. http://www.youtube.com/watch?v=_aE3zcBIpsk (accessed February 15, 2012).

"Reply to: Illegals, God, and Gospel." *9500 Liberty* YouTube channel, November 1, 2007. http://www.youtube.com/9500liberty#p/search/2/_NwUwSfwqLU (accessed February 15, 2012).

"Research Report." *Quarterly Journal of Public Speaking* 1 (1915): 24–32.

"Resolution of the Senate." *Congressional Record*, 56th Cong., 2d sess., January 24th, 1901, 1385.

"Rethinking the Revolving Door for Immigration." http://www.brookings.edu/opinions/2007/0423immigration_ruiz.aspx (accessed July 10, 2010).

Ricoeur, Paul. *Interpretation Theory: Discourse and the Surplus of Meaning*. Fort Worth: Texas Christian University Press, 1976.

Robinson, Paul. *Queer Wars: The New Gay Right and Its Critics*. Chicago: University of Chicago Press, 2005.

Roosevelt, Franklin D. Fireside Chat, Number One, "The Banking Crisis." March 12, 1933, Master Speech File, No. 616a, Franklin D. Roosevelt Library, Hyde Park, New York.

Roosevelt, Franklin D. President's Personal File, Franklin D. Roosevelt Presidential Library, Hyde Park, New York.

Root, Robert. "A Listener's Guide to the Rhetoric of Popular Music." *Journal of Popular Culture* 20 (1986): 15–26.

Rosenbaum, Marsha. *Kids, Drugs, and Drug Education: A Harm Reduction Approach.* San Francisco: National Council on Crime and Delinquency, 1996.

Rosenfeld, Sophia. "Tom Paine's Common Sense and Ours." *William and Mary Quarterly* 65 (2008): 633–668.

Rosenfield, Lawrence W. "The Practical Function of Epideictic." In *Rhetoric in Transition: Studies in the Nature and Uses of Rhetoric,* edited by Eugene E. White, 131–155. University Park: Pennsylvania State University Press, 1980.

Rottinghaus, Brandon. *The Provisional Pulpit: Modern Presidential Leadership of Public Opinion.* College Station: Texas A&M University Press, 2010.

Rowland, Robert C. "On Mythic Criticism." *Communication Studies* 41 (1990): 101–116.

Rowland, Robert C. "Purpose, Argument Fields, and Theoretical Justification." *Argumentation* 10 (2008): 235–250.

Rowland, Robert C., and John M. Jones. "One Dream: Barack Obama, Race, and the American Dream." *Rhetoric and Public Affairs* 14 (2011): 125–154.

Rowland, Robert C., and John M. Jones. *Reagan at Westminster: Foreshadowing the End of the Cold War.* College Station: Texas A&M University Press, 2010.

Rowland, Robert C., and John M. Jones. "Recasting the American Dream and American Politics: Barack Obama's Keynote Address to the 2004 Democratic National Convention." *Quarterly Journal of Speech* 93 (2007): 425–448.

Rubin, Gayle. "Thinking Sex: Notes for a Radical Theory of the Politics of Sexuality." In *Pleasure and Danger: Exploring Female Sexuality,* edited by Carole S. Vance, 267–319. London: Pandora Press, 1992.

Rushing, Janice Hocker. "On Saving Mythic Criticism—A Reply to Rowland." *Communication Studies* 41 (1990): 136–149.

Rutenberg, Jim. "President to Push for Line-Item Veto Power." *New York Times,* June 28, 2006. http://www.nytimes.com/2006/06/28/washington/28bush.html (accessed August 21, 2011).

Safranski, Rüdiger. *Martin Heidegger: Between Good and Evil.* Cambridge, Mass.: Harvard University Press, 1998.

Salazar, Ken. Speaking on Comprehensive Immigration Reform Act of 2006, S. 2611, 109th Cong., 2nd sess. *Congressional Record* 152 no. 60 (May 16, 2006): S4577.

Scheer, Robert. "AIDS Stigma Hampering a Solution." *Los Angeles Times,* November 28, 1986. http://articles.latimes.com?1986-11-28/news/mn-15918_1_aids-stigma-hampering (accessed August 14, 2013).

Schwartz, Barry. *George Washington: The Making of an American Symbol.* New York: Free Press, 1987.

Scott, Robert L. "New Books in Review: Rhetorical Criticism." *Quarterly Journal of Speech* 51 (1965): 335–338.

Scott, Robert L. "On Viewing Rhetoric as Epistemic." *Central States Speech Journal* 18 (1967): 9–17.

Scott, Robert L., and Bernard L. Brook. "An Introduction to Rhetorical Criticism." In *Methods of Rhetorical Criticism: A Twentieth-Century Perspective,* edited by Robert L. Scott and Bernard L. Brock, 13–27. New York: Harper and Row, 1972.

Sedgwick, Eve Kosofsky. *Epistemology of the Closet.* Berkeley: University of California Press, 1990.

Sells, Laura. "'Where Do the Mermaids Stand?' Voice and Body in The Little Mermaid." In *From Mouse to Mermaid: The Politics of Film, Gender, and Culture,* edited by Elizabeth Bell, Lynda Haas, and Laura Sells, 175–192. Bloomington: Indiana University Press, 1995.

Shannon, Claude E., and Warren Weaver. *The Mathematical Theory of Communication*. Urbana: University of Illinois Press, 1949.

Shelton, Michael W. *Talk of Power, Power of Talk: The 1994 Health Care Reform Debate and Beyond*. Westport, Conn.: Praeger, 2000.

Shirky, Clay. "The Political Power of Social Media: Technology, the Public Sphere, and Political Change." *Foreign Affairs* 90 (2011): 28–41.

Shome, Raka. "Postcolonial Interventions in the Rhetorical Canon: An 'Other' View." *Communication Theory* 6 (1996): 40–59.

Simons, Herbert W. "Toward a New Rhetoric." *Pennsylvania Speech Annual* 24 (1967): 7–20. Reprinted in *Contemporary Theories of Rhetoric,* edited by Richard Johannessen, 50–62. New York: Harper and Row, 1971.

Sloan, Thomas O., et al., "Report of the Committee on the Advancement and Refinement of Rhetorical Criticism." In *The Prospect of Rhetoric: Report of the National Development Project,* edited by Lloyd F. Bitzer and Edwin Black, 220–227. Englewood Cliffs, N.J.: Prentice Hall, 1971.

Sloop, John M., and Kent A. Ono. "Out-law Discourse: The Critical Politics of Material Judgment." *Philosophy and Rhetoric* 30 (1997): 51–69.

Slovic, Paul, and and David Zionts. "Can International Law Stop Genocide When Our Moral Intuitions Fail Us?" In *Understanding Social Action, Promoting Human Rights,* edited by Ryan Goodman, Derek Jinks, and Andrew K. Woods, 100–134. New York: Oxford University Press, 2012.

Slovic, Paul. "The More Who Die, the Less We Care." In *The Irrational Economist: Making Decisions in a Dangerous World,* edited by Erwann Michel-Kerjan and Paul Slovic, 30–40. New York: PublicAffairs, 2010.

Smith, Arthur L. Unpublished, untitled position paper, compiled with others as "Statements by Conference Participants." Pheasant Run Conference, May 10–15, 1970, 24–25.

Smith, Christina, and Kelly McDonald. "The Mundane to the Memorial: Circulating and Deliberating the War in Iraq through Vernacular Solider-Produced Videos." *Critical Studies in Media Communication* 28 (2011): 292–313.

Smith, John H. "Rhetorical Polemics and the Dialectics of *Kritik* in Hegel's Jena Essays." *Philosophy and Rhetoric* 18 (1985): 31–57.

Solomon, Martha. "Responding to Rowland's Myth or in Defense of Pluralism—A Reply to Rowland." *Communication Studies* 41 (1990): 117–120.

Solomon, Martha. "The Things We Study: Texts and Their Interactions." *Communication Monographs* 60 (1993): 62–68.

Spalding, Matthew. "George Washington's 'Farewell Address." *Wilson Quarterly* 20 (1996): 65–71.

Spalding, Matthew, and Patrick J. Garrity. *A Sacred Union of Citizens: George Washington's Farewell Address and the American Character.* Lanham, Md.: Rowman and Littlefield, 1998.

"The Speech Bush Didn't Give." [Editorial.] *Chicago Tribune,* June 29, 2007. ProQuest Historical Newspapers. http://www.proquest.com/ (accessed July 1, 2010).

Spivak, Gayatri Chakravorty. *The Post-Colonial Critic: Interviews, Strategies, Dialogues,* edited by Sarah Harasym. New York: Routledge, 1990.

Spivak, Gayatri Chakravorty. "Agency." Lecture, University of Iowa, Iowa City, October 4, 2004.

Sproule, J. Michael. "The New Managerial Rhetoric and the Old Criticism." *Quarterly Journal of Speech* 74 (1988): 468–486.

Stelzner, Herman. "War Message, December 8, 1941: An Approach to Language." *Speech Monographs* 33 (1966): 419–437.

Stevenson, Richard W. "Bush, Touring the Border, Puts Emphasis on Enforcement." *New York Times,* November 30, 2005. LexisNexis Academic. http://www.lexisnexis.com (accessed August 21, 2011).

Stewart, Charles J. "Historical Survey: Rhetorical Criticism in Twentieth Century America." In *Explorations in Rhetorical Criticism,* edited by G. P. Mohrmann, Charles J. Stewart, and Donovan J. Ochs, 1–31. University Park: Pennsylvania State University Press, 1973.

Stewart, Karen A., Aaron Hess, Sarah J. Tracy, and Harold L. Goodall. "Risky Research: Investigating the 'Perils' of Ethnography." In *Qualitative Inquiry and Social Justice,* edited by Norman K. Denzin and Michael D. Giardina, 198–216. Walnut Creek, Calif.: Left Coast Press, 2009.

Stoler, Ann Laura. *Along the Archival Grain: Epistemic Anxieties and Colonial Common Sense.* Princeton: Princeton University Press, 2010.

"Stop Prince William County's Anti-Immigration Resolution." Mexicanos Sin Fronteras. http://www.mexicanossinfronteras.org/PDF/flyer_boycott_march_pwc_english.pdf (accessed February 15, 2012).

"Stop Your Racism 2: Korean Americans Model Immigrants?" *9500 Liberty* YouTube channel. Comments Forum, November 4, 2007. http://www.youtube.com/watch?v=29WTKbpYhag (accessed August 17, 2013).

"Stop Your Racism to Hispanics—Liberty Wall." *9500 Liberty* YouTube channel. Comments Forum, October 12, 2007. http://www.youtube.com/watch?v=k_Dw1ioGPGY (accessed August 17, 2013).

Stormer, Nathan. "Articulation: A Working Paper on Rhetoric and *Taxis.*" *Quarterly Journal of Speech* 90 (2004): 257–284.

Stuckey, Mary E. "Jimmy Carter, Human Rights, and Instrumental Effects of Presidential Rhetoric." In *The Handbook of Rhetoric and Public Address,* edited by Shawn J. Parry-Giles and J. Michael Hogan, 293–312. Malden, Mass.: Wiley-Blackwell, 2010.

Stuckey, Mary E. "On Rhetorical Circulation." *Rhetoric and Public Affairs* 15 (2012): 609–612.

Sullivan, Andrew. "Bush's Speech." Daily Dish, May 15, 2006. http://andrewsullivan.theatlantic.com/the_daily_dish/2006/05/bushs_speech.html (accessed August 31, 2010).

Swarns, Rachel L. "House Votes for 698 Miles of Fences on Mexico Border." *New York Times,* December 16, 2005. LexisNexis Academic. http://www.lexisnexis.com. (accessed August 21, 2011).

Taylor, Brian C. "Commentary: Reminiscences of Los Alamos." In *Critical Questions: Invention, Creativity and the Criticism of Discourse and Media,* edited by William L. Nothstine, Carole Blair, and Gary A. Copeland, 417–422. New York: St. Martin's Press, 1994.

Taylor, Bryan C. "*Fat Man and Little Boy:* The Cinematic Representation of Interests in the Nuclear Weapons Organization." *Critical Studies in Mass Communication* 10 (1993): 367–394.

Taylor, Charles. "Review of Cahiers de Royaumont." *Philosophical (La philosophie analytique) Review* 73 (1964): 132–135.

Tenore, Mallary J. "NewsHour Crowdsources Translations of President Obama's State of the Union." Poynter Institute, January 25, 2012. http://www.poynter.org/latest-news/top-stories/160702/president-obama-state-of-the-union-translated-pbs-newshour/ (accessed August 17, 2013).

Terrill, Robert E. "Unity and Duality in Barack Obama's 'A More Perfect Union.'" *Quarterly Journal of Speech* 95 (2009): 365.

Thomas, Douglas. "Burke, Nietzsche, Lacan: Three Perspectives on the Rhetoric of Order." *Quarterly Journal of Speech* 79 (1993): 336–355.

Thompson, Marie. "The Fall and Rise of the Cape Breton Fiddler: 1955–1982." Unpublished master's thesis, St. Mary University, Halifax, Nova Scotia, 2003.

Thompson, Wayne N. "A Case Study of Dewey's Minneapolis Speech." *Quarterly Journal of Speech* 31 (1945): 419–423.

Thompson, Wayne N. "A Conservative View of a Progressive Rhetoric." *Quarterly Journal of Speech* 49 (1963): 1–7.

Thompson, Wayne N. "Contemporary Public Address as a Research Area." *Quarterly Journal of Speech* 33 (1947): 274–283.

Thonssen, Lester, and A. Craig Baird. *Speech Criticism: The Development of Standards for Rhetorical Appraisal*. New York: Ronald Press, 1948.

"Thoughts on Washington's Birthday." *New York Times*, February 18, 1917, SM3.

Thuesen, Frederik. "Navigating between Dialogue and Confrontation: *Phronesis* and Emotions in Interviewing Elites on Ethnic Discrimination." *Qualitative Inquiry* 17 (2011): 613–622.

Tindale, Christopher W. "Ways of Being Reasonable: Perelman and the Philosophers." *Philosophy and Rhetoric* 43 (2010): 337–361.

Toulmin, Stephen E. *Human Understanding: The Collective Use and Evolution of Concepts*. Princeton: Princeton University Press, 1972.

Toulmin, Stephen E. *The Uses of Argument*. Cambridge: Cambridge University Press, 1958.

Tracy, Karen, James P. McDaniel, and Bruce E. Gronbeck. *The Prettier Doll: Rhetoric, Discourse, and Ordinary Democracy*. Tuscaloosa: University of Alabama Press, 2007.

Trasciatti, Mary A. "Hooking the Hyphen: Woodrow Wilson's War Rhetoric and the Italian American Community." In *Who Belongs in America? Presidents, Rhetoric, and Immigration*, edited by Vanessa B. Beasley, 107–133. College Station: Texas A&M University Press, 2006.

Tryon, Chuck. "Digital Distribution, Participatory Culture, and the Transmedia Documentary." *Jump Cut: A Review of Contemporary Media* 53 (2011). http://www.ejumpcut.org/archive/jc53.2011/TryonWebDoc/ (accessed February 14, 2014).

Tulis, Jeffrey K. *The Rhetorical Presidency*. Princeton: Princeton University Press, 1987.

Tyrrell, R. Emmett, Jr. "Our Immigration Imbroglio." *The American Spectator*, December 1, 2005. LexisNexis Academic. http://www.lexisnexis.com (accessed October 25, 2006).

United States Commission on Civil Rights. *Briefing before Immigration Subcommittee of the Virginia Advisory Committee to the U.S. Commission on Civil Rights*, December 14, 2007, 1–258.

United States Senate, Office of the Secretary. "Farewell Address Notebook." http://senate.gov/artandhistory/history/minute/Washingtons_Farewell_Address.htm (accessed April 10, 2010).

Unity in the Community. "Citizen Reaction to the Proposed Implementation of County Resolution No. 07–609 on Immigration." August 17, 2007. http://www.unityitc.org/Announcements/07–609Prt.htm (accessed February 15, 2012).

Usher, Ronald G. "Washington and Entangling Alliances." *North American Review* 24 (1916): 29–39.

Vickers, Brian. "Figures of Rhetoric/Figures of Music?" *Rhetorica* 2 (1984): 1–44.

"Vietnamese Declaration of Independence, 1945." Internet Modern History Sourcebook. http://www.fordham.edu/halsall/mod/1945vietnam.html (accessed August 17, 2013).

Waisanen, Don. "Bordering Populism in Immigration Activism: Outlaw–Civic Discourse in a (Counter) Public." *Communication Monographs* 79 (2012): 232–255.

Wallace, Karl R. *Understanding Discourse: The Speech Act and Rhetorical Action*. Baton Rouge: Louisiana State University Press, 1970.

Walter, Otis. "On Views of Rhetoric, Whether Conservative or Progressive." *Quarterly Journal of Speech* 49 (1963): 367–382.

Wander, Philip. "The Ideological Turn in Modern Criticism." *Central States Speech Journal* 34 (1983): 1–18.

Wander, Philip. "The Third Persona." *Central States Speech Journal* 35 (1984): 197–216.

Wanzer, Darrel A. "Delinking Rhetoric, or Revisiting McGee's Fragmentation Thesis through Decoloniality." *Rhetoric and Public Affairs* 15 (2012): 647–657.

Warner, Michael. "Publics and Counterpublics." *Public Culture* 14 (2002): 49–90.

"Warnings." *9500 Liberty* YouTube channel. Profile. http://www.youtube.com/user/9500Liberty (accessed February 14, 2012).

"Washington Farewell Address Gets Apathetic Adieu in House." *New York Times,* February 17, 1980, 18.

"Washington Farewell Address Read to House over Protests." *New York Times,* February 23, 1933, 27.

Washington, George. "Farewell Address." In *George Washington: Writings,* edited by John Rhodehamel, 962–977. New York: Library of America, 2004.

Washington, George. "Farewell Address." in *Washington's Farewell Address: The View from the 20th Century,* edited by Burton Ira Kaufman, 15–30. Chicago: Quadrangle Books, 1969.

"Washington's Anti-militarism." *Advocate of Peace* (March 1903): 39–40.

"Washington's Doctrine and Arbitration." *Independent,* February 20, 1896, 48.

"Washington's Farewell Address Read in Congress; Stand on Foreign Affairs Evokes Interest." *New York Times,* February 23, 1952, 26.

"Washington's Farewell Address." http://www.senate.gov/artandhistory/history/minute/Washingtons_Farewell_Address.htm (accessed April 10, 2010).

"Washington's Words Echo through Senate." *New York Times,* February 16, 1988, A-11.

Watney, Simon. "Foreword: The Persistence of Memory." In *Reports from the Holocaust: The Story of an AIDS Activist,* edited by Larry Kramer, xv–xxix. New York: St. Martin's Press, 1994.

Watts, Erik K. "An Exploration of Spectacular Consumption: Gangsta' Rap as Cultural Commodity." *Communication Studies* 48 (1997): 42–58.

Webster, Richard. *Why Freud Was Wrong: Sin, Science, and Psychoanalysis.* New York: Basic Books, 1995.

Weisman, Jonathan, and Jim VandeHei. "Immigration Debate Is Shaped by '08 Election." *Washington Post,* March 24, 2006. LexisNexis Academic. http://www.lexisnexis.com (accessed August 21, 2011).

Weisman, Jonathan. "House Votes to Toughen Laws on Immigration." *Washington Post,* December 17, 2005. LexisNexis Academic. http://www.lexisnexis.com (accessed August 21, 2011).

Weisman, Jonathan. "Immigration Bill Dies in Senate—Bipartisan Compromise Fails to Satisfy the Right or the Left." *Washington Post,* June 29, 2007. Newsbank. http://www.Newsbank.com/ (accessed July 1, 2010).

White, Cheryl L. "Beyond Professional Harm Reduction: The Empowerment of Multiply-Marginalized Illicit Drug Users to Engage in a Politics of Solidarity towards Ending the War on Illicit Drug Users." *Drug and Alcohol Review* 20 (2001): 449–458.

White, James B. *When Words Lose Their Meaning: Constitutions and Reconstitutions of Language, Character, and Community.* Chicago: University of Chicago Press, 1984.

Whiteman, David. "Out of the Theaters and into the Streets: A Coalition Model of Political Impact of Documentary Film and Video." *Political Communication* 21 (2004): 51–69.

"Who's Behind the Immigration Rallies," *FrontPage.* http://archive.frontpagemag.com/readArticle.aspx?ARTID=5022 (accessed July 10, 2010).

Wichelns, Herbert A. "Research." *Quarterly Journal of Speech* 9 (1923): 232–240.

Wichelns, Herbert A. "Some Differences between Literary Criticism and Rhetorical Criticism." In *Historical Studies of Rhetoric and Rhetoricians,* edited by Raymond F. Howes, 217–224. Ithaca: Cornell University Press, 1961.

Wichelns, Herbert A. "The Literary Criticism of Oratory." In *Landmark Essays on Rhetorical Criticism,* edited by Thomas W. Benson, 1–32. Davis, Calif.: Hermagoras Press, 1993.

Wichelns, Herbert A. "The Literary Criticism of Oratory." In *Methods of Rhetorical Criticism: A Twentieth Century Perspective,* 2nd ed., edited by Bernard L. Brock and Robert L. Scott, 32–70. Detroit: Wayne State University Press, 1980.

Wichelns, Herbert A. "The Literary Criticism of Oratory." In *Readings in Rhetorical Criticism,* edited by Carl R. Burgchardt, 3–27. State College, Pa.: Strata, 1995.

Wichelns, Herbert A. "The Literary Criticism of Oratory." In *The Rhetorical Idiom: Essays in Rhetoric, Oratory, Language, and Drama,* edited by Donald C. Bryant, 5–42. New York: Russell and Russell, 1966.

Wichelns, Herbert A. "The Literary Criticism of Oratory." In *Studies in Rhetoric and Public Speaking in Honor of James Albert Winans,* edited by A. M. Drummond, 181–216. New York: Century, 1925.

Wichelns, Herbert A. "The Literary Criticism of Oratory." In *Studies in Rhetoric and Public Speaking in Honor of James Albert Winans.* New York: Century, 1925. Reprinted in *Methods of Rhetorical Criticism,* edited by Robert L. Scott and Bernard L. Brock, 27–60. New York: Harper and Row, 1972.

Wilentz, Sean. *The Age of Reagan: A History, 1974–2008.* New York: HarperCollins, 2008.

Willard, Charles A. *Liberalism and the Problem of Knowledge: A New Rhetoric for Modern Democracy, New Practices of Inquiry.* Chicago: University of Chicago Press, 1996.

Wills, Garry. *Lincoln at Gettysburg: The Words That Remade America.* New York: Simon and Schuster, 1992.

———. "Washington's Farewell Address: An Eighteenth-Century 'Fireside Chat.'" *Chicago Historical Society* 10 (1981): 176–179.

Wilson, Kirt H. "Interpreting the Discursive Field of the Montgomery Bus Boycott: Martin Luther King Jr.'s Holt Street Address." *Rhetoric and Public Affairs* 8 (2005): 299–326.

Wilson, Woodrow. "The Author and Signers of the Declaration of Independence." In *Woodrow Wilson: The Essential Political Writings,* edited by Robert J. Pestritto, 99–106. Lanham, Md.: Lexington Books, 2005.

Wirls, Daniel, and Stephen Wirls. *The Invention of the United States Senate.* Baltimore: Johns Hopkins University Press, 2004.

Wittig, Monique. *The Straight Mind and Other Essays.* Boston: Beacon Press, 1992.

Wolfe, Maxine. "Make It Work for You: Academia and Political Organizing in Lesbian and Gay Communities." ACT UP/New York, 1997. http://www.actupny.org/documents/academia.html (accessed August 14, 2013).

Wood, James. "The Good Freud Guide." *Guardian,* August 25, 1990, 3. LexisNexis Academic. http://www.lexisnexis.com (accessed June 10, 2010).

Woolbert, Charles H. "Conviction and Persuasion: Some Considerations of Theory." *Quarterly Journal of Speech* 3 (1917): 249–264.

Wrage, Ernest J. "Public Address: A Study in Social and Intellectual History." Reprinted in *Readings in Rhetorical Criticism,* edited by Carl R. Burgchardt, 28–34. State College, Pa.: Strata, 1995.

Wrage, Ernest J. "Public Address: A Study in Social and Intellectual History." *Quarterly Journal of Speech* 33 (1947): 451–457.

Yoachum, Susan. "Buchanan Calls AIDS 'Retribution': Gays Angered by His Bid to Win Bible Belt Votes." *San Francisco Chronicle,* February 28, 1992, 1.

Zarefsky, David. "Four Senses of Doing Rhetorical History." in *Doing Rhetorical History,* edited by Kathleen J. Turner, 19–32. Tuscaloosa: University of Alabama Press, 1998.

Zarefsky, David. "History of Public Discourse Studies." In *The SAGE Handbook of Rhetorical Studies,* edited by Andrea A. Lunsford, Kirt H. Wilson and Rosa A. Eberly, 433–459. Thousand Oaks, Calif.: Sage, 2009.

Zarefsky, David. "Presidential Rhetoric and the Power of Definition." *Presidential Studies Quarterly* 34 (2004): 607–619.

Zarefsky, David. "Public Address Scholarship in the New Century: Achievements and Challenges." In *The Handbook of Rhetoric and Public Address,* edited by Shawn J. Parry-Giles and J. Michael Hogan, 67–85. Malden, Mass.: Wiley-Blackwell, 2010.

Zarefsky, David. "Reflections on Rhetorical Criticism." *Rhetoric Review* 25 (2006): 384–387.

Zaresfky, David. "The State of the Art in Public Address Scholarship." In *Text in Context: Critical Dialogues on Significant Episodes in American Political Rhetoric,* edited by Michael C. Leff and Fred J. Kaufeld, 13–29. Davis, Calif.: Hermagoras, 1989.

Zolberg, Aristide R. *A Nation by Design: Immigration Policy in the Fashioning of America.* New York: Russell Sage Foundation, 2006.

Zonana, Victor. "Kramer vs. the World." *The Advocate,* December 1, 1992, 40–48.

Zuckman, Jill. "Immigration Issue Becomes Politics' Newest Third Rail." *Chicago Tribune* [Chicago Edition], June 30, 2007. ProQuest Historical Newspapers. http://search.proquest.com/docview/459243905 (accessed on September 5, 2010).

Contributors

CAROLE BLAIR (Ph. D. Penn State University) is a professor in the department of communication studies and fellow of the Institute for the Arts and Humanities at the University of North Carolina, Chapel Hill. Her work on U.S. national commemorative places, historiography, and the rhetoric of inquiry has garnered nearly every major award in the communication discipline, including the Golden Anniversary Monograph Award, the Charles H. Woolbert Research Award, the Paul Boase Prize, and the B. Aubrey Fisher Award. Named a distinguished scholar by the National Communication Association in 2009, Blair is focusing her present scholarship (with William Balthrop and Neil Michel) on American memorial sites in Europe from World War I.

STEPHEN H. BROWNE (Ph. D. University of Wisconsin) is a professor of rhetorical studies at the Pennsylvania State University. His books include *Jefferson's Call for Nationhood: The First Inaugural Address*, *Angelina Grimke: Rhetoric, Identity, and the Radical Imagination*, and *Edmund Burke and the Discourse of Virtue*. Professor Browne specializes in the rhetorical culture of colonial America and the early republic.

ANNE T. DEMO (Ph. D. Penn State University) is an associate professor in the department of communication and rhetorical studies at Syracuse University. Her work explores the relationship among visual rhetoric, identity, and U.S. cultural politics. A past recipient of the National Communication Association's Golden Monograph award, she has had articles published in the *Quarterly Journal of Speech, Critical Studies in Media Communication, Rhetoric and Public Affairs, Environmental History,* and *Women's Studies in Communication*. She is the coeditor of *Rhetoric, Remembrance, and Visual Form: Sighting Memory*.

GREGORY DORCHAK (Penn State University) is a doctoral student in the department of communication at the University of Massachusetts at Amherst as well as Northeastern University Law School. His research focuses on the intersection of hermeneutics and rhetoric.

SARA A. MEHLTRETTER DRURY (Ph. D. Penn State University) is the Byron K. Trippet Assistant Professor of Rhetoric at Wabash College. Her research interests include political rhetoric, religious rhetoric, and the intersections between rhetoric and democratic practices.

DAVID A. FRANK (Ph. D. University of Oregon) is dean of the Robert D. Clark Honors College and a professor of rhetoric at the University of Oregon. He is the author and coauthor of six books and fifty book chapters and journal articles. His most recent book is *Frames of Evil: The Holocaust as Horror in American Film* (with Caroline Joan S. Picart).

ADAM J. GAFFEY (Ph.D, Texas A&M University) is an assistant professor of rhetoric and philosophy at Black Hills State University. His research focuses on rhetorical theory and public address.

PAT J. GEHRKE (Ph. D. Penn State University) is an associate professor in the program in speech communication and rhetoric and in the department of English at the University of South Carolina. His research focuses on communication ethics, the history of communication and rhetoric in America, and theories of public rhetoric. He is the author of more than two dozen articles and essays as well as a recent book, *The Ethics and Politics of Speech: Communication and Rhetoric in the Twentieth Century.*

AARON HESS (Ph. D. Arizona State University) is an assistant professor of communication in the School of Letters and Sciences at Arizona State University, Downtown Phoenix. His primary research focuses on public advocacy, especially regarding health topics and within digital contexts. His previously published articles in outlets such as *Critical Studies in Media Communication, Communication Studies,* the *International Journal of Communication,* and *Media, Culture and Society* have examined the intersection between rhetorical and qualitative methods, the use of social media for deliberation and protest, and September 11 public memory.

DAVIS W. HOUCK (Ph. D. Penn State University) is a professor in the School of Communication at Florida State University. He works in the areas of presidential rhetoric, sport and media, and the American civil rights movement. His most recent work includes anthologies on Fannie Lou Hamer (with Maegan Parker Brooks) and two volumes of collected speeches on the civil rights movement (with David E. Dixon). His book *Rhetoric as Currency: Hoover, Roosevelt and the Great Depression* won the 2002 Marie Hochmuth Nichols prize for best book in the National Communication Association's public address division.

AMOS KIEWE (Ph. D. Ohio University) is a professor of communication and rhetorical studies at Syracuse University. His primary research focuses on presidential rhetoric, rhetorical criticism, and public address. He is the author of several books and articles. His most recent books are *FDR's Body Politics: The Rhetoric of Disability* (with Davis W. Houck); *FDR's First Fireside Chat: Public Confidence and the Banking Crisis;* and *Confronting Anti-Semitism: Seeking an End to the Rhetoric of Hate.*

ERIN J. RAND (Ph.D. University of Iowa) is an assistant professor of communication and rhetorical studies and is affiliated with LGBT studies at Syracuse University. She is author of *Reclaiming Queer: Activist and Academic Rhetorics of Resistance.* Her work has also appeared in the *Quarterly Journal of Speech, Rhetoric and Public Affairs, Communication and Critical/Cultural Studies, Text and Performance Quarterly, Western Journal of Communication,* and *Women's Studies in Communication.*

ROBERT C. (ROBIN) ROWLAND (Ph. D. University of Kansas) is a professor in and director of graduate studies in the department of communication studies at the University of Kansas. Rowland has published several books, including the award-winning *Shared Land/Conflicting Identity: Symbolic Trajectories of Israeli and Palestinian Symbol Use* (with David Frank), as well as more than eighty articles and book chapters. His most recent book is *Reagan at Westminster: Foreshadowing the End of the Cold War* (with John Jones). Rowland has been awarded the Douglas W. Ehninger Distinguished Rhetorical Scholar Award and the Donald H. Ecroyd Award for outstanding teaching in higher education.

Index

www.ingramcontent.com/pod-product-compliance
Lightning Source LLC
LaVergne TN
LVHW050147080826
844660LV00002B/110

* 9 7 8 1 6 1 1 1 7 4 5 5 7 *